Textual Life

BLACK LIVES IN THE DIASPORA: PAST / PRESENT / FUTURE

BLACK LIVES IN THE DIASPORA: PAST / PRESENT / FUTURE

EDITORIAL BOARD

Howard University

Clarence Lusane, Rubin Patterson, Nikki Taylor, Amy Yeboah Quarkume

Columbia University

Farah Jasmine Griffin, Frank Guridy, Josef Sorett

Black Lives in the Diaspora: Past / Present / Future is a book series that focuses on Black lives in a global diasporic context. Published in partnership with Howard University's College of Arts and Sciences and Columbia University's African American and African Diaspora Studies Department, it builds on Columbia University Press's publishing programs in history, sociology, religion, philosophy, and literature as well as African American and African Diaspora studies. The series showcases scholarship and writing that enriches our understanding of Black experiences in the past, present, and future with the goal of reaching beyond the academy to intervene in urgent national and international conversations about the experiences of people of African descent. The series anchors an exchange across two global educational institutions, both located in historical capitals of Black life and culture.

Jarvis McInnis, *Afterlives of the Plantation: Plotting Agrarian Futures in the Global Black South*

Lauren Coyle Rosen and Hannibal Lokumbe, *Hannibal Lokumbe: Spiritual Soundscapes of Music, Life, and Liberation*

Laura E. Helton, *Scattered and Fugitive Things: How Black Collectors Created Archives and Remade History*

Sarah Phillips Casteel, *Black Lives Under Nazism: Making History Visible in Literature and Art*

Aïssatou Mbodj-Pouye, *An Address in Paris: Emplacement, Bureaucracy, and Belonging in Hostels for West African Migrants*

Vivaldi Jean-Marie, *An Ethos of Blackness: Rastafari Cosmology, Culture, and Consciousness*

Imani D. Owens, *Turn the World Upside Down: Empire and Unruly Forms of Black Folk Culture in the U.S. and Caribbean*

Gladys L. Mitchell-Walthour, *The Politics of Survival: Black Women Social Welfare Beneficiaries in Brazil and the United States*

James V. Koch and Omari S. Swinton, *Vital and Valuable: The Relevance of HBCUs to American Life and Education*

For a complete list of books in the series, please see the Columbia University Press website.

TEXTUAL LIFE

Islam, Africa, and the Fate of the Humanities

WENDELL H. MARSH

COLUMBIA UNIVERSITY PRESS *NEW YORK*

Columbia University Press
Publishers Since 1893
New York   Chichester, West Sussex

Copyright © 2025 Wendell H. Marsh
All rights reserved

Library of Congress Cataloging-in-Publication Data
Names: Marsh, Wendell H. author
Title: Textual life : Islam, Africa, and the fate of the humanities / Wendell H. Marsh.
Description: New York : Columbia University Press, [2025] | Series: Black lives in the diaspora : past / present / future | Includes bibliographical references and index
Identifiers: LCCN 2024061908 | ISBN 9780231210706 hardback | ISBN 9780231210713 trade paperback | ISBN 9780231558556 ebook
Subjects: LCSH: Kamara, Muusa, 1864–1945 | Muslim historians—Senegal—Biography | Muslims, Black—Senegal—Historiography | Senegal—History—To 1960—Historiography | France—Colonies—Africa—Intellectual life | Islam and humanism
Classification: LCC DT549.77.K37 M37 2025 | DDC 966.30088/297—dc23/eng/20250520

Cover design: Elliott S. Cairns
Cover image: Arébénor Basséne, *Kumpo (Ghost Game) #1* (2022).
Courtesy of the artist and Selebe Yoon, Dakar.

GPSR Authorized Representative: Easy Access System Europe,
Mustamäe tee 50, 10621 Tallinn, Estonia, gpsr.requests@easproject.com

In service to the shaykh

Contents

Overture: Philology as the Love of Study ix

Introduction: Deaths of Philology 1

ONE Beginnings: The Text, the World, and the Sufi 38

TWO A Degree of Prophecy 61

THREE Islam Noir: Surveillance Ethnography and the Politics of Representation 86

FOUR A Monumental Text in an Orientalist Season 115

FIVE The Pitfalls of National Literature 142

SIX The Secular-Religious Afterlife of Shaykh Musa Kamara 180

Coda: Long Live Philology! Or, Remembering the Future of the Humanities 213

Notes 229
Acknowledgments 271
Index 277

Overture

Philology as the Love of Study

Philology, made plain, is the love of study. The modern coinage from ancient Greek terms captures the two opposing sides of the human mind: the irrational commitment of love, *philia*, and the rational urge to know systematically, *logos*. Philology constituted an ur-discipline in the nineteenth century for two separate domains of knowledge that academia now refers to as the humanities and the social sciences, the first aligning more with *philia* and the second more with *logos*. To be sure, the word conjures images of Old World traditions of learning and obsolete assumptions about the racist division of humanity according to differences in language. However, like many other human pursuits that have been overrepresented as white, European, and male—such as philosophy, history, and even art—philology as the inquiry into the traces of the past transmitted through language and the meaningful composition of language into texts has been a far broader and deeper feature of the human experience than is often granted.

Philology is an underrecognized practice in the tradition of Black thought, a capacious term that embraces intellectual, psychic, and spiritual revolt. It encompasses both elite and popular thinking by racialized groups and individuals since the acceleration, intensification, and concentration of the global slave trade on peoples of African descent and its still-evolving forms of captivity and colonization. Conditioned by racially ideological figures such as the Kantian Negro, incapable of the sublime, and the Hegelian African, without history or politics and lacking development, Black thought has both been preoccupied with and rejected the idea of blackness as being absence or lack. Given that the myth of primordial African orality and the fantasy of Black illiteracy in American slave ideology posited incapacity as the cause of inferiority, philology has had a particular purchase for Black thinkers seeking to undo the psychic injury of racial slavery and colonization and to actualize their humanity. Here the power of the written word and its capacity to hold worlds of meaning have been prized. Phillis Wheatley's study of the classics in their original Greek and Latin, Frederick Douglass's heroic struggle to learn to read through *The Columbian Orator*, and Edward Blyden's controversial orientalist studies are all examples of this practice. Taken together, I call this tradition and practice Black liberation philology.

To define Black liberation philology, a detour through the testimony of Malcolm X is necessary. The life of the great orator, strategist, and martyr of the Black freedom struggle has received a hagiographic treatment in both the autobiography cowritten with Alex Haley and the biopic directed by Spike Lee. In the depths of his moral wilderness, Malcolm appears functionally illiterate. His illegible correspondence compels his younger brother Reginald to instruct him to learn how to write. His transformation begins with his discovery of the life of the mind through the gift of the prison library and the prison debate club. His devoted study, his love of study, enables him to emancipate himself and prepare for his religious discoveries with the help of the Nation of Islam and Elijah Muhammad. One of the most memorable scenes of the film represents this episode as an encounter with a dictionary, the details of which come from Haley's epilogue in which he describes the cowriting process. Malcolm is so taken with this memory of the dictionary while narrating it to Haley that he cannot shake his interest in the infamous aardvark:

> When reading about the period when he had discovered the prison library, Malcolm X's head jerked up. "Boy! I never will forget that old aardvark!" The next evening, he came into the room and told me that he had been to the Museum of Natural History and learned something about the aardvark. "Now, aardvark actually means 'earth hog.' That's a good example of root words, as I was telling you. When you study the science of philology, you learn the laws governing how a consonant can lose its shape, but it keeps its identity from language to language." What astonished me here was that I knew that on that day, Malcolm X's schedule had been crushing, involving both a television and radio appearance and a live speech, yet he had gone to find out something about the aardvark.[1]

OVERTURE

Haley's astonishment results from witnessing Malcolm's love of study. In the last year of his life, when he was tortured by the prospect of his departure from the Nation of Islam and by the taxing demands of the Black freedom movement, of which he would become a central theorist and inspiration, Malcolm took time out of his schedule to go to a museum to look at an aardvark. It was an action that did not reflect a logical and economic use of time and energy. Instead, it was an opportunity to perceive the relation between a word and the world. In this moment, Malcolm saw philology as a discipline that enabled him to work out the relationship of the two. In that way, philology for Malcolm was a necessary detour to arrive at understanding.

It was this understanding of the relationship of language and the world as mediated by texts acquired through study that represented freedom for Malcolm X. Reflecting on the moment of personal transformation while in prison, Malcolm expresses his love of reading as freedom:

> I suppose it was inevitable that as my word-base broadened, I could for the first time pick up a book and read and now begin to understand what the book was saying. Anyone who has read a great deal can imagine the new world that opened. Let me tell you something: from then until I left that prison, in every free moment I had, if I was not reading in the library, I was reading on my bunk. You couldn't have gotten me out of books with a wedge. Between Mr. Muhammad's teachings, my correspondence, my visitors—usually Ella and Reginald—and my reading of books, months passed without my even thinking about being imprisoned. In fact, up to then, I never had been so truly free in my life.[2]

If Malcolm's inexplicable excursion to see an aardvark exemplifies Black liberation philology, his thought helps us define it. In describing his love for and the importance of language, Malcolm introduces his understanding of philology to Haley: "It's a tough science—all about how words can be recognized, no matter where you find them."[3] This understanding of philology is, in fact, Malcolm's theory of diaspora and a potential method for diasporic Black thought. For him, philology uses language—that thing we had the most of, even if nothing else, as deterritorialized peoples—to find all the traces of the past and the transformations of history. We might read his casual statement linguistically as meaning "philology is the study of the changes of sounds in words that nevertheless retain the same semantic content."

[xi]

OVERTURE

But given Malcolm's attention to the situation of African-descended peoples wherever they may be lost or found and his insistence on recognizing the relationships and commonalties of people of color throughout the world—indeed his Black internationalism—this line strikes me as being about the people who carry language with them as much as it is about the language itself. In other words, identity (whether racial, religious, or cultural) and meaning are interchangeable for Malcolm. He uses one to understand the other. A word's identity referred to its lexical meaning, and this conception served as a metaphor. Racial identity, like the ultimate meaning of language as the vehicle of truth, is essential and unified. There are, of course, many objections to such a theory about either language or race, but I would like to point to the basic resonance of Malcolm's theory of diaspora with the model of African retentions and survivals, of Black nationalism and internationalism, that has animated so much rich scholarship on, as well as the politics of, Black experiences in the world. If we take this as a basis of African diaspora studies, as many do, then our task is to study language as transmitted through meaningfully composed texts and use the meanings therein to make sense of our historical position.

Embracing philology in African diaspora studies as the love of study poses the question of whose philology and which method. Long a devoted student of Malcolm, I feel guided to take his lead in answering both questions. The poet Julia Fields subtly and beautifully pointed out long ago that, like so much, Malcolm's aardvark was something to which we have not paid enough attention.[4] What appears to be a detour through thought is a necessary process in what Stuart Hall describes as the recovery of the traces of the past accumulated in the self.[5]

While majoring in English at Morehouse College, I was constantly looking for texts to study that would allow such a detour. There was a rich body of African American, Caribbean, and African literature that we read in a building located between a statue of Martin Luther King Jr. and the mausoleum of his mentor Benjamin E. Mays. I relished what we did with language across the diaspora, conjugating and calquing, bending and breaking the language of slaveholders and colonizers into stunning expressions, captivating stories, and moving songs. But I felt the European languages were still a prison and wanted to know what freedoms other languages learned beyond the prison, the plantation, and the colonial school could provide. These were the kinds of questions that I followed until I ended up at the feet of a shaykh

OVERTURE

in Medina Baye, Senegal, a global hub of the Tijaniyya, a Sufi order of Islam. There were people from all over the world sitting in small circles in a modest space that functioned as both a study and a bedroom. What awed me in that moment was that, without hesitation, the shaykh held several conversations at once in English, French, Wolof, Arabic, and likely others I could not recognize. What is more, bound volumes with Arabic writing and sheets of loose paper engulfed the room, filling every space not occupied by a person. If I wanted to study non-European texts, I had to learn more about the intellectual tradition from which this teacher came.

I soon discovered the hotly contested debates among history majors at Morehouse and Spelman Colleges as to whether jihads in West Africa during the nineteenth century were anticolonial revolutions or just another form of colonization extending the long history of the destruction of Black civilization. That is when I learned about historical personalities of the region, such as Uthman dan Fodio, the founder of the Sokoto Caliphate in what is now Nigeria; Ahmad Lobbo, the founder of the Masina Empire in what is now Mali; and Hajj Umar Tal, the founder of the Tukulor Empire, which included much of what is now Senegal, Mauritania, Guinea, and Mali. Tal stood out to me, as he had led a millenarian movement that transformed the religious, intellectual, and political landscape of much of West Africa. Most importantly, he had been a leading elaborator of the Tijani path that I first learned about with the shaykh. I would spend many years reading texts by and about Hajj Umar Tal.

At some point, I found myself returning most often to *The Life of Hajj Umar* by Shaykh Musa Kamara. At first blush, the text was a straightforward, if classically styled, account of the life of the *wali* (friend of God or saint). But the more I read it, the more questions I had, and the more possible paths of understanding appeared—but more than anything, the less straightforward the work seemed. Kamara, I discovered, was a prolific but little-known author whose life spanned much of the French colonial episode in the Senegambia, stretching from his birth in the same year as Umar's death (1864) to the end of the World War II (1945). In a remote village, he wrote in many genres, including history, hagiography, traditional medicine, and Islamic law. Parallel to my learning about Kamara, Africa's Arabic written heritage had been receiving increased attention around the world. And in Senegal, Kamara was making a comeback, as Islamist political violence in the broader region made his ecumenicalism and positions against jihad newly relevant.

OVERTURE

While these new readings of Kamara were certainly accurate, I grew to feel they missed something vitally important about him. That is, the readings of Kamara did not recognize Kamara as a philologist, a lover of study.

This book is the product of a tour of detours through thought, an inventory of barely legible and sometimes only intuited traces of the past. Through Malcolm, through Tal, through Kamara, and through the body of texts that connect them, I have practiced a kind of philology, a love of study, through imitation, that very old method of learning. It may be thought traditional and outdated, but with all seriousness and audacity, I propose that this philology should be at the heart of the study of the worldwide African diaspora—for the love of study is, after all, preoccupied with the question of what it means to be human.

Orthographies

As a book about textual life in Muslim West Africa, I discuss material originally written in Arabic, French and Pulaar. Each have their own writing system and their own standards for transliteration in Latin script. For Arabic, I have used the conventions used by the International Journal of Middle East Studies (IJMES) in the body of the main text. In the citations, however, I use the Library of Congress conventions to facilitate locating the references in library collections. Unfortunately Shaykh Musa Kamara's works appear in bibliographic databases inconsistently under Muusa Kamara and Mūsá Kamara. I have decided to use Mūsá Kamara for citations, following the convention for Arabic references. For Pulaar, I follow Mamadou Niang's Pulaar-English Dictionary (Hippocrane Books, 1997). All instances of foreign languages are italicized, with the exception of well-known French words like "Islam noir." I have generally translated the titles of Arabic works into English in the main text and included the transliteration of the original Arabic titles in the footnote. The goal here has been to render the foreign familiar whenever possible. An exception to this is the Timbuktu Chronicles, which are well known even among non-specialists. Translations from Arabic and French are my own except when the material is cited from an English language source, on which occasions I use the translation provided.

Textual Life

Introduction

Deaths of Philology

IN MAY OF 1924, the Senegalese Muslim scholar Shaykh Musa Kamara (1864–1945) must have felt an urgency to document the histories and cultures of those then subject to French colonization. After years of consulting Arabic manuscripts and collecting oral testimonies from griots, village chiefs, and others, Kamara could not wait any longer. Eager to have his work translated into French and then published, he sent off an incomplete manuscript of *Flowers from among the Gardens in the History of the Blacks* to Henri Gaden (1867–1939), once the French lieutenant governor of Mauritania and an amateur philologist who had married into a network of important Pulaar-speaking families along the Senegal River.[1] With the work already several hundred pages long, Kamara made sure to include a teaser for a special chapter on the history of Futa Toro that he had not yet finished. He wagered that Gaden, who had been involved in publishing a cohort of indigenous writers, would be interested in a chronicle about the state that was established following an Islamic revolution during the peak of the global slave trade. He was right. Gaden wrote back, enthusiastically asking Kamara to send the rest without delay. Kamara took this as a favorable sign and picked up the pace of his work, writing the rest and sending it off just a few months later. But then Kamara had to wait. He never stopped waiting.

From the perspective of the postcolonial present, the story of a West African Muslim intellectual who wrote a monumental history to give to French administrators seems improbable. Nevertheless, the context of establishing colonial rule was characterized by a great interest in local Arabic written production and in Muslim scholars who encouraged a favorable position toward the French. The agency responsible for managing this interest, the Service des Affaires Musulmanes, combined an orientalist training in languages and the study of canonical works with the practical goals of surveilling a population. Its operations were modeled on the relationships between knowledge and power the French had established in their older colony in Algeria. An entire cohort of native authors emerged in this period, among whom Kamara ranked as the most important. He appeared as a useful interlocutor for the production of colonial knowledge from two contradictory but complementary regards: those of humanist philology and colonial engineering. He developed a prolific correspondence with officials who were interested in him as a source of information about the histories and customs of the greater western Sahel, which stimulated his writing endeavors. It was under these conditions that Kamara undertook the primary research for *The History of the Blacks*. From 1920 to 1926, he traveled throughout the region, recording oral testimony about the past and accounts of various lineages and consulting relevant texts. He focused on the history of his native Futa Toro in the middle Senegal River Valley but situated his work within both a broader regional history and the macrohistory of the world from an Islamic perspective. Looking at his library collection today and the citations within his texts, we can see that Kamara was familiar with many of the developments in historical writing coming out of North African and Levantine printing presses, including works by the Lebanese intellectual of the *Nahḍa* (Arab awakening) Jurji Zaydan (1861–1914) and the Moroccan scholar Ahmad ibn Khalid al-Nasiri (1835–1897), as well as a history textbook used at al-Azhar in Cairo, Egypt, one of the world's oldest universities. Kamara anticipated notoriety and compensation for his lengthy research, as he expected it to be published in a bilingual print edition by the colonial state.

Little did Kamara know that colonial thinking about Africa was changing. The window of opportunity opened by a colonial humanist philology that ventured to read African texts was rapidly closing in response to the unquestionable hegemony of engineering that emerged with the mechanization wrought by World War II. While this colonial humanism entertained a textual attitude—an orientation toward the world through the mediation of meaningfully composed texts—colonial governance in the late colonial period gave way to a practical attitude developed in response to the

INTRODUCTION

dominance of an engineering paradigm of getting things done. A creeping antihumanism would become the new common sense, with few sources of competition to challenge it. Texts could no longer stand in for direct experience of the world; observable facts on the ground superseded, and often invalidated, received ancient wisdom. The colonial philologist was replaced with the bureaucrat-ethnographer, the planner, and the spy. Part and parcel of this shift from the textual attitude to the practical one was a growing racial common sense that associated blackness with illiteracy. Kamara's dream of a bilingual edition and remuneration slipped between the cracks of two regimes of colonial knowledge and power. Despite the singularly contingent opening that made African texts legible in colonial projects, the more dominant practical attitude cohered with the representation of Africa as a continent without writing in global discourses. And Kamara, with his body of almost thirty works, would become an oddity known only by specialists in the study of Muslim Africa.

Had it been only a matter of his place in colonial knowledge production, Kamara's fate of obscurity would have been sealed. Two factors prevented this from being the case. As a respected master of Sufism, a powerful Muslim tradition of contemplation that embraces the role of spiritual intercession, he enjoyed recognition from his contemporaries and has been remembered for his saintliness by his descendants and disciples. This tradition of Kamara has long existed independently of both the colonial archive and the colonial library. The formal reception of Kamara reached a major turning point after independence, when Senegalese intellectuals began to construct a national literature and history while articulating an African humanism. More recently, the militarization of the Sahel and the threat of Islamist political violence have favored a new return to Kamara for his religious messages of quietism, tolerance, and noninvolvement in politics. His religious significance and the historical conditions in which his work has been transmitted inform his meaning beyond the limits of both colonial humanism and colonial engineering.

On one level, this book narrates a reception history of Kamara from the time he composed his major works (1910s to 1940), through periods of colonial attention and disregard, to the projects of nation building and secularization. I argue that shifting political and epistemic conditions inflected by ideas about racial and religious differences have made the reading of Kamara possible but have also limited his interpretation. On a deeper level, this book serves as a parable about the fate of the humanities after colonialism. In following the rise, fall, and return of Kamara, I chart the path of the humanities, understood as the offspring of philology, less as a set of subjects than as an orientation to study. I describe the fate of the humanities as neither a teleology of progress nor of decline, nor do I assert claims of distinct origin or originality. Rather, I want to consider the consequences of philology's one-time complicity with the colonial enterprise so as to chart a potential decolonial future for the humanities. Colonialism was always the crisis of the humanities. Through an encounter with Kamara's works and legacy in conversation with literary and postcolonial theory, I develop the idea of the textual attitude, an orientation to the world disciplined by philological practice, an orientation toward making sense by reading. This mode of reading both confronts the historical fact of colonialism and thinks beyond it. I argue that the textual attitude is a vital human orientation toward knowledge whose time has come again, liberated from its former burden of representation.

Islamic Thought in the Greater Western Sahel

Kamara's birth, life, and death connect him to some of the most important episodes in the modern history of Islam in the greater western Sahel, that area between the Sahara and the African savanna, west of Timbuktu. The time and place of his birth, in particular, hold a symbolic, or perhaps spiritual, significance that will help narrate both Kamara's life as a Muslim scholar and the broader sweep of history in which he and his peers found themselves. He was born around 1864 in the village of Guriki Samba Dioum, in the easternmost part of what was at the time Futa Toro, in the middle Senegal River Valley. Futa Toro was established as an imamate, a state with an imam at its head, in 1776 by the Tooroodo revolution, a multiethnic movement of Muslim scholars, their families, and their students who sought to limit the population's vulnerability to the Atlantic slave trade by enshrining the rule of justice based on Islamic principles. The establishment of this new order constituted the first major episode of the modern history of Islam in the western Sahel. A long, narrow territory of 240 miles of fertile soil through which an important river-based trade flowed, Futa was prone to predation from outside and fragmentation from within.[2] For

INTRODUCTION

some thirty years after the founding of the Futa Toro, the movement's second leader, Almamy Abdul Kader Kan (1726–1806), maintained security, but his attempts to expand the space of Islamic rule would bring his end. *Guriki* means "slanted tree" in Pulaar, Kamara's native language, and this village is remembered as the site of the defeat of the almamy in 1806.[3] One of Kamara's mentors, Shaykh Mamadou Mamadou Kane of Maghama (d. 1890), a scholar, military strategist, and descendant of the almamy, appreciated the significance of Kamara's birth in Guriki when he reportedly declared that "since Shaykh Musa Kamara was born there, the tree shall regain its upright position."[4]

In the wake of the almamy's defeat, Futa Toro's fortunes declined, and the rule of justice was undermined by a competition between traditional elites and the new class of scholars and merchants that rose to power with the revolution. The memory of the movement eventually inspired Hajj Umar Tal (1797–1864), a native of Halwar in central Futa who undertook the pilgrimage to Mecca, to become one of the most important scholars of the Tijaniyya Sufi order and to lead a jihad in the upper Senegal and Niger River Valleys.[5] Between 1852 and 1864, his messianic movement sought to expand the space of Islamic economics against the encroachments of a French mercantile colonization, constituting the second major episode in the modern history of Islam in greater western Sahel. One of the most consequential figures in this broader history, Umar met his end in 1864 in an explosion in the fabled cliffs of Bandiagara in present-day Mali. Born in this same year, Kamara eventually claimed a special connection to Umar, who figured prominently in Kamara's writings over the course of his life. Most notably, Kamara claimed to have received direct instruction from Umar in a dream.

By the time of Kamara's birth, the autonomy of this agriculturally rich region had been compromised by French domination of the river-based trade in cloth and in gum arabic, an all-important raw material for both the globalizing textile industry and the global print revolution. His life span tracks with the expansion of French colonization in the region. While his youth was marked by the instability of organized resistance to what was understood in the region as Christian rule, Kamara came to his intellectual maturity at the dawn of the so-called Pax Gallica in West Africa, the peak of French administration of much of West Africa and the third episode in the narrative of Senegalese modernity.

INTRODUCTION

Before the eighteenth century, being a Muslim resembled being a part of a caste as much as it did being a part of a community of faith. The documented record of Islam in the region dates back to the eleventh century, when Warjabi b. Rabis (d. 1041), a sovereign whose kingdom bordered the Senegal River, testified to his belief in God and the prophecy of Muhammad.[6] Between that time and the age of the Atlantic Revolutions at the end of the eighteenth century, many African sovereigns of the largest political entities did profess Islamic faith—most notably, the rulers of the Mali and Songhai trade empires. However, the dominant pattern in the region was that Muslims were specialists in trade, literacy, and court affairs who operated alongside other, non-Muslim knowledge specialists and craftspeople. Muslims carved out space for themselves in which they offered traditional sovereigns their knowledge and services in administration, trade, education, and religion.[7] In exchange, they were offered quasi autonomy in spaces adjacent to, but clearly separate from, power. Accordingly, Muslims became part of a social fabric whose weft and weave have been described as occupational specialties, or castes, since at least the Mali Empire.[8] They had a prescribed place in society within an overarching caste structure. In other words, Islam constituted one form of life among many others.

Growing inequalities resulting from the Atlantic trade in persons and goods, as well as the desiccation of the southern Sahara and Sahel, contributed to the conditions that would make dramatic change possible.[9] The warrior aristocracies that had ruled over small principalities since the fall of the Songhai Empire oversaw the unequal exchange, which allowed them to accumulate wealth in multiple stores of value.[10] Subject populations throughout the region grew increasingly resentful of their leadership's predation and disrespect of social well-being. Through a diverse set of initiatives during this time of instability, Islam became more central to many West African societies, providing the dominant model for individual behavior, social interactions, and, most importantly, statecraft. Following the failed Shurr Bubba (1673), a conflict that pitted Zwaya lineages of religious specialists against Hassani warrior lineages in what is now Mauritania, and the founding of Bundu by Muslim scholars farther to the south in the upper Senegal River Valley (1698), the prospect of independent Muslim communities became increasingly real.[11] A subsequent sequence of jihads resulted in the formation of several new Islamic political entities.[12] These movements sought to strengthen Islam where it was already in place through processes of reform and renewal. In contrast to the earlier model, in which Islam, understood as one way of life among others, existed apart from power either near or far, the new political entities that emerged in the eighteenth and nineteenth centuries took Islam as the normative source of knowledge and practice. They were Islamic insofar as they created geographic spaces in which principles of Islamic governance were enshrined—most notably, the sanctity of a Muslim's life, the protection of a Muslim's wealth, and the preservation of a Muslim's honor. The newly paradigmatic quality of Islam in these political entities provided a moral minimum for states that had before preyed on their own people. In short, the establishment of Islamic political entities during the age of revolution in Muslim West Africa enshrined the rule of justice where the rule of arbitrary violence had once reigned supreme.

Central to this new order was the Muslim scholar.[13] The primary job of a scholar in the broader tradition has been the exercise of judgment about which actions, behaviors, and social arrangements are obligatory and which are forbidden. In between these absolutes of the imperative and the prohibited are degrees of permission, recommendation, and disapproval. The scholar's judgment is based on knowledge, which implies the knowledge of the sharia, or God's intended form of life for humanity, often overtranslated as "Islamic law."[14] While God's will is perfect, humanity's understanding of it must be interpreted. This interpretation is, however, neither an exercise of free association nor a rigid code; it reflects a highly sophisticated rule-governed system that has proved to be highly adaptable and flexible across history and geography. The most important domains of this knowledge are transmitted knowledge and rational knowledge, which in Arabic form a conveniently rhymed couplet, *naql* and *ʿaql*.

What might be called religious knowledge, the *ʿulūm al-dīn* (the disciplines or sciences of religion), represents the queen of transmitted knowledge, as it refers to revealed knowledge, the Qurʾan and the Sunna (a set of sayings and behaviors) of the Prophet Muhammad. Transmitted knowledge also includes any information that might be transmitted from the past but that is not necessarily religious in the sense of providing direct communication of divine revelation and its associated obligations and norms. Such knowledge, however, might be elaborated on and marshaled for a fuller understanding of properly religious knowledge. It includes disciplines like grammar, biography, poetry, and history. Rational knowledge, such as philosophy, natural science, and medicine, is acknowledged as valid according to its context and coherence. These two domains of transmitted and rational knowledge are accompanied by a third domain of experiential knowledge of divine presence cultivated through the practices and traditions of the discipline of taṣawwuf (Sufism).[15] Such experience of maʿrifa (divine gnosis) could be a source of inspiration for those who have attained the highest levels of closeness to God through their discipline.

Whether guided by transmitted knowledge, reason, or inspiration, the scholar could exercise judgment in changing and diverse contexts. Because of the multiple combinations of disciplines, schools of thought, and circumstances that a scholar might encounter, differences in judgement are inevitable. Thus, to be a scholar has long meant to engage in debate. The space of debate that was preserved as the classical ideal across Muslim contexts was that the sharia, and its custodians among the scholars, constituted a horizontal institution that maintained an independence from political power. However, the pressures and possibilities of modernization in West Africa favored the transformation of these scholars into a class that might capture state power.

Feeding off but distinct from the political entities that were taking shape in the Islamic revolutions described here, the Qadiriyya Sufi order developed as an important connection for the scholars and would become an essential part of West Africa's political, social, and economic dynamics. The Kunta family led by Sidi al-Mukhtar al-Kunti (d. 1811), based in and around Timbuktu, consolidated a vast network of spiritual relationships based in the centuries-old Qadiriyya ṭarīqa (Sufi religious order), transregional trade in tobacco, salt, and many other goods, as well as Islamic jurisprudential and mystical production, to become a veritable power in the region through its wide-ranging presence.[16] It is important to note that until this time, to be a Muslim scholar likely meant to engage in some form of ritual that today would be identified as Sufi practice. That practice, whether individual or collective, would likely have been conveyed through a Qadiri chain of transmission. What was new at the end of the eighteenth century was that ṭarīqa became an institution that crisscrossed and buttressed distinct political entities in the region, cementing the social relations for what was becoming a regional scholarly class in what had been a caste system.[17]

Growing out of a geography in which decentralized authority was the rule, ṭarīqa itself was not necessarily a political entity, but it nevertheless compensated for the absence of sovereigns where they did not exist and complemented the work of sovereigns where they did. To be a Qadiri came to mean that one had a metaphysical framework that put initiates in a spiritual-social hierarchy with other initiates, participating in a political economy of trade, knowledge production, and ritual services and ascribing to them a set of attitudes and practices that both signaled membership and conditioned one's experience in the temporal world. In many ways, the Qadiriyya—specifically, that branch led by the Kunta—balanced the two positions current in the region on the relationship of the Muslim scholar to the sovereign: pious distance from power and the Islamic rule of justice. They maintained a nonpolitical identity at their highest echelons but achieved their goals and fulfilled their commercial interests through agents strategically placed in the courts of the region's rulers. The alignment of commercial interests, political order, and spiritual organization subsequently became the standard in much of the greater Sahel and Sahara.[18]

The way this general historical pattern manifested in the Senegal River Valley of Futa Toro has created a potent memory of the importance of Islam and of Muslim scholars as its authoritative representatives in the people's self-defense against the rapacious aristocratic elites and their alliances with white Christians. The charismatic core of Futa Toro's Islamic revolution is embodied in the personality of Ceerno Sulaymane Baal. An archetypal Qurʾanic teacher who had sought out learning throughout the Senegambia, Baal initiated the events that would culminate in 1776 in an autonomous Futa Toro. According to Kamara, writing in the 1920s, Baal was returning from his studies in present-day Mauritania with an entourage of disciples when they stopped at a riverside village.[19] Baal was shocked to find a man bound in restraints who was reciting the Qurʾan. The man had been kidnapped and sold to the owners of a boat who intended to take him downriver to Saint-Louis, where he would no doubt be shipped to labor in the Americas. Baal told the people on the boat to release the man, saying "this is a Muslim; therefore, he is free." When the appeal to the religious-legal precept that Muslims should not be enslaved failed in the face of the material logics of property, Baal resorted to force. One of his students, Aali Mayram, who was a large and skilled fighter, single-handedly overcame the owners of the boat and liberated the enslaved Muslim. This confrontation would be the first of many battles in which Muslim scholars, their families, and their disciples would rally to protect themselves against the predation of the interethnic alliance of warrior aristocracies on either side of the Senegal River who were profiting from the Atlantic trade. Commenting on this account, Kamara notes that the memory of this initial act is often recalled at traditional wrestling tournaments through the songs sung alongside the dance of competing fighters.[20]

If the liberation of an enslaved Muslim symbolizes the broader struggle of righteous self-defense by Muslim scholars, the memory of Baal's last speech before he dies enshrines the Islamic rule of justice and its custodians, the scholars, as the political establishment. After waging a war that ended the rule of the Deeniyankoobe aristocratic elite, who had been supported by the Hassani Arabs, as both groups were aligned in the entangled Atlantic and Saharan trade systems, Baal gained a substantial following and was poised to take power. An account written a century and a half later by Kamara recounts the stirring speech delivered by Baal before the fateful battle in which he would be killed:

> I do not know if I will die in this battle, if I die name a knowledgeable imam, pious and ascetic, who does not interest himself in this worldly life; and if you find that his possessions are growing, depose him and take his possessions from him; and if he refuses to abdicate, fight him and hunt him so that he will not establish tyranny which his sons will inherit. Replace him with another, among the people of knowledge and action, from any of the clans. Never leave power inside one clan alone, so that it does not become hereditary. Put in power the one who merits it, one who prevents his soldiers from killing children and old men without strength, undressing the women, and most of all killing them.[21]

This speech functions as a sort of unwritten constitution that enshrines the role of Muslim scholars as custodians of the rule of justice at the head of a community. More specifically, this constitution endows the echelon of scholars with the political responsibilities of selecting the worthiest among them based on learning and faith and resisting the un-Islamic transmission of kingship that operates in and through the rule of violence that had come to characterize politics in the region.

After Ceerno Sulayman Baal's death, one of his pupils, Almamy Abdul Kader Kan, assumed leadership of the budding Islamic state of Futa Toro. Under his leadership, the imamate was able to stop the export of enslaved people into the Atlantic economy, thus forcing the trade to move elsewhere in Africa, even as regional regimes of coercive labor persisted.[22] Ultimately, the almamy was not be able to set up the kinds of governing institutions that Futa Toro needed to last for very long after he overextended his military resources in conflicts with neighboring kingdoms. Nevertheless, Kan was successful in building mosques and appointing imams throughout the territory. As individuals, the imams were entrusted with both governance and social well-being, a spectrum of activities within the purview of "religion" that included ritual practice such as congregational prayer but also encompassed commanding the good, forbidding the bad, and adjudicating the just in interpersonal relations. Before this episode of the founding of Futa Toro, Muslim scholars were specialists in learning, literacy, trade, and worship who had a prescribed role in a mostly hereditary caste structure that left most people vulnerable to the arbitrary violence of the warrior aristocracies. But after this episode, Muslim scholars came to occupy the central organizing and mediating social position. Islam was no longer one form of life among others; it was the paradigmatic basis of thought and action.

The following period of Islamic thought in the Senegambia might best be characterized by the encounter between popular messianism and the colonial engineering project. While many Muslim scholars of the Senegal River Valley had led the revolution against warrior aristocracies and their trade interests in the region, a new division emerged among members of this echelon. Establishment figures, often associated with the Qadiriyya, aligned themselves with French commercial interests. For example, Bou el-Mogdad Seck (1829–1880), the first salaried employee of the colonial state, led the interpreter corps and advocated on behalf of Saint-Louisan Muslim civil society.[23] Coming from a Muslim scholarly family, he convinced the administration to establish a Muslim tribunal and to sponsor the pilgrimage to Mecca for allies such as himself. On the other side, Hajj Umar Tal presented an alternative to living under Christian rule.[24] Tal had undertaken the pilgrimage to Mecca, lived in the Arabian Peninsula, and traveled throughout the Levant while professing the litany of the Tijaniyya Sufi order. This Sufi order took several radical positions on the nature of knowledge and on the relative position of their founder in relation to other Sufi guides. Tal's elaboration of Tijani thought, as recorded in his *Book of Lances*,[25] served as the doctrinal basis of a movement, and his organizational role as head of the West African Tijanis provided the infrastructure of mobilization that would eventually erupt in armed struggle, first against followers of ancestral religions in the region in 1852, then against the French, and eventually against the Muslim state of Hamdullahi in Mali. This brought Umar and the Tijanis into conflict with the Muslim establishment of the region, which ultimately organized the successful resistance to Umar's revolutionary state that led to his demise in the cliffs of Bandiagara in 1864.

What is important about this second period in the development of Islamic thought in the Senegambia is that the threat of Umar's popular messianism encouraged a modus vivendi between the region's elite and the fledgling colonial state. Islam would be a civilizing force by way of using Muslim intermediaries and encouraging the development of hybrid colonial-Islamic institutions. Any threats originating from religious exuberance would be neutralized by the otherwise enfranchised elites who were tasked with managing religion. In a pattern that is seen throughout the colonized Muslim world, these figures would eventually be tasked with indirect rule more generally, with roles in managing economic production and policing order.[26] This durable arrangement has come to be known as the Senegalese social contract.[27]

The period of Kamara's most prolific output as a scholar has been described as the period of accommodation.[28] Muslim scholars as a group established different strategies for interacting with the colonial state that cannot be defined simply as resistance or as collaboration. Two such strategies of accommodation were popular among Muslim clerics. The first strategy was to negotiate islands of autonomy. In return for accepting colonial rule, Muslim leaders were assured a degree of noninterference. This strategy is best embodied by Shaykh Amadou Bamba and the organization of disciples, or Mourides, that emerged around him in the groundnut basin, an area distant from the colonial centers of the four communes but with economic activity that had become central for the export trade. The second strategy, which relied on proximity to the colonial administration, was to become involved in the colony's affairs through working as intermediaries. This strategy is best exemplified by Malick Sy's Tivaouane-based Tijaniyya, which located its organizational center within the ligaments of the colony's transportation and communications infrastructure. The first strategy negotiated its autonomy through distance and economic cooperation, while the second achieved its autonomy through proximity and involvement in administration.

INTRODUCTION

The two dominant strategies of the scholarly class, which were pursued either at a distance from or in proximity to the colonial state, reflected the capacity for debate and difference among the leaders of a profoundly Muslim society. But they did so along lines that could be read as representative tendencies among broader social forces. Kamara, as prolific a scholar as he was, did not reflect a broader social position, whether aligned with the establishment or the antiestablishment, and often found himself embroiled in intellectual controversy. Senegalese Arabist Abdoul Malal Diop has collected a precious oral testimony of one such colorful controversy.[29] Since at least the eighteenth century, West African scholars have debated the permissibility of smoking tobacco. It is a debate that continues today. Hajj Umar Tal, for example, famously forbade his disciples from smoking the substance, but a generation later Kamara would challenge anyone who dared question its permissibility. One day in his youth, Kamara is said to have sat in the courtyard of a rival who had argued that smoking was prohibited. He took out his pipe, packed it, and proceeded to smoke it. The rival's student ran inside to inform his teacher, who, upon hearing the news, is said to have refused to exit his home so as to avoid engaging with Kamara in an intellectual duel. Kamara was also known to take an idiosyncratic position on the number of wives one could marry, arguing in a work dedicated solely to the topic that one could marry well above the number of four that many Sunni Muslims take for granted as the maximum number.[30] Kamara himself had fifteen wives and several concubines.

Beyond questions of individual piety or social interactions, Kamara famously weighed in on one of the most politically significant questions a scholar might engage with at the time. He argued that while jihad in the path of God was indeed permitted in the early Muslim community, the absence of prophetic authorization in the present invalidated it as a legitimate practice.[31] This was a significant claim in a region in which some of the most prominent religious leaders had taken up the mantle of jihad since the seventeenth century and had used it as a means of enshrining principles of Islamic governance. Moreover, in contrast with figures such as Hajj Umar Tal, Samory Touré (1828–1900), and Muhammad Ma al-ʿAynayn (1831–1910), who fought the French as enemies of God, Kamara viewed French rule favorably for securing peace and creating the conditions for Islam to flourish as a religious practice and not as a mode of governance. These positions were hotly contested before Kamara was born, they were open questions during his lifetime, and they continue to be interrogated today. Kamara's idiosyncratic positions either contributed to or resulted from his paradoxical status of being respected but unrepresentative.

Accordingly, Kamara's strategy of accommodation was distinct. He jealously maintained his autonomy far from the centers of colonial power, but he also engaged colonial administrators intellectually. What is more, he genuinely viewed the French administration favorably, as it brought security to the region. A Qadiri by affiliation, he argued against the viability of jihad while identifying with the intellectual legacy of the Tijani Hajj Umar Tal. No doubt Kamara was seen as a source of information from the perspective of colonial officials. Indirectly, this information may have functioned to influence the administrators in much the same way intermediaries could capture and influence the power of the state. But the impact of this influence was likely limited. He routinely found himself on the losing end of petitions to the state in competition for land with his son-in-law Abdul Salam Kane (1879–1955), who was a colonial employee; his request for citizenship to relieve his tax burden was refused; and his attempt to have a school built in the village of Ganguel, his home as an adult, failed. At most, Kamara likely saw himself as an interlocutor with specific French scholars who had a genuine interest in African histories, cultures, and languages. As I will explore in the following chapters, the encounters between Kamara and French officials generated singular works with an enduring legacy that should be understood in the context of the organic and unique developments in Islamic thought in West Africa that intervened in a social world marked by the slave trade and colonization.

Islam in the French Engineering Project

By the time Kamara was born in 1864, the Senegal River Valley had been transformed as a part of a large-scale engineering project. For centuries, it had been an important regional center of agricultural production, a breadbasket of sorts, with its two annual harvests. Since the seventeenth century, the valley had become a theater of mercantile competition for enslaved Africans, textiles, and gum arabic among the French, British, Portuguese, and Dutch, making it a thoroughfare of global trade. But by the nineteenth century, after the initiatives of the imamate of Abdul Kader Kan that halted the

INTRODUCTION

export of persons, gum arabic had become the most important export[32]—and reasonably so. Gum arabic is the resin that comes from the acacia tree, one of the primary types of flora that populate the hot and dry Sahel. Used as an emulsifier, gum arabic is critical for the chemical composition of inks and adhesives, materials necessary in the explosion of print culture and textile production, which is so often identified as the material condition for modern societies that were emerging in the nineteenth century. The Senegal River Valley was a leading source of the best gum arabic in the world at that time. To get a sense of the scale of its export, in 1864 it was estimated that 1.6 million kilograms of gum arabic (worth Fr. 4 million at the time) would be exported that year to France from Saint-Louis.[33] In exchange, local consumption favored dark blue textiles from India, spurring the British commitment to growing that industry in the South Asian subcontinent, even though it competed with textile mills in England.[34]

This trade, however, required a complex network of intermediaries that relied on careful negotiation and an understanding of the many different political entities, trade cultures, and languages of the region. It also required respect for African terms of trade and recognition of African political power. As a result, Saint-Louis, the island town situated at the point where the Senegal River flows into the Atlantic Ocean, developed a creole culture composed of Wolof, Pulaar, Mande, Arab, and European elements.

French commercial interests would not be satisfied for long with reliance on their African trade partners. Nor would they come to respect African equality with the maturation of white supremacy as a global political project. The conquest of Algeria farther north and the dawn of France's second colonial empire had put the possibility of a more muscular presence in African territories on the table. Dependence on the patterns of trade set by the Moors north of the river and the various tolls and tributes that different sovereigns along the river demanded to allow trade to pass through their territories led actors such as Maurel & Prom, a Bordeaux-based shipping and trade company, to pursue a policy of so-called free trade[35]—so-called because it was less free than it was policed, with gunboats patrolling the river. As a result, French interests developed the Plan of 1854, which projected the rationalization of the Senegal River by way of building forts, mapping the region, and creating a zone of free trade where gum arabic would flow out and consumer goods would flow in on terms over which French traders had greater control. Having grown frustrated with Auguste

Protet (1808–1862), a French naval admiral who had become governor of Senegal in 1850, the Maurel family worked to replace him with the military engineer Louis Faidherbe (1818–1889). Despite the colonial hagiography of the future war hero and senator, Faidherbe, who became governor in late 1854, was more the construction site foreman than the architect of colonial Senegal. While Senegalese history is often presented as a civilizing mission, Leland Barrows shows that the colony was primarily a commercial venture established at gunpoint. But perhaps it is useful to describe it also as an engineering project. Faidherbe, a graduate of Napoleon's Grande Ecole of Engineering (Polytechnique at Metz), is important in this story not because his historical agency explains the causality of transformation but rather because he symbolizes the broader project to transform the space of the Senegambia into a space of rationalization—that is, to eliminate difference or at least to reduce it to manageable limits, an objective articulated and pursued with the practical attitude of the engineer.[36]

By engineering, I refer to the pursuit of an instrumentalist mastery of the physical and social world. It is as much an attitude as it is an activity, one we might describe as practical. It assumes a set of beliefs about the world: namely, it exists to be acted on and perhaps to be known—if not definitively, then with ever-increasing degrees of certainty. Knowing the world with exactitude allows one to manipulate it for particular ends. The world becomes a means to achieve ends that are calculable and predictable. Such a paradigm was part and parcel of the modern era: Napoleon's project at home was to rationalize the nation, to exhaustively know it with exactitude. In practice, this meant eliminating difference through standardization as much as it meant producing a precise picture of the world as it existed. He did this by and large through a military reorganization of space at home and abroad.[37]

Two precedents in the French colonial experience and critical reconstructions of those precedents furnish us with material with which to think through the dual nature of colonial knowledge. Edward Said famously critiques the ways that the Western study of Islam in its institutional form and its broader representation in colonial discourses was undermined by a certain instrumentalization of knowledge. He draws a straight line between the will to know Muslim societies and the colonial will to exercise power over them. Orientalism constituted everything in between. The definitive case in point that Said uses to make his argument is Napoleon's invasion of Egypt with an actual army and a figurative army of scholars, who were to definitively catalog and tabulate every facet of Egyptian geography, history, and society, even as they translated the dictates of French rule into Islamic idioms.[38] This dual process of rationalization and translation was marked by the creation of the Institute of Egypt and the production of the large-scale *Description of Egypt*, key pillars of Napoleon's project. Even after his departure, Said adds, Napoleon instructed the administration to govern *through the scholars*. Napoleon's foray into Egypt, a space of difference needing translation and representation, was but another instance in the almost timeless representation of the Other, according to Said's theory of orientalism.

In addition to highlighting the relationship between knowledge and power in Napoleon's attempt to conquer Egypt, Said curiously argues that such a venture was characterized by a "textual attitude."[39] Napoleon, he shows, knew Egypt before ever going there through reading books. The grandeur of Alexandria and the dramas of past empire made Egypt a theater for Napoleon's ambitions. Implicitly, Said compares Napoleon to Don Quixote, who upon reading *Amadis of Gaul* imagines himself to be a great knight in search of adventure. In effect, Said argues that it is ridiculous that one would be oriented to the reality of experience through the mediation of texts. The greatest failure of orientalism as the strategic will to knowledge/power would seem to be this reliance on texts to stand in for an understanding of the world instead of direct experience.

As much as my own thinking has been shaped by Said's arguments and the broader field of thinking and writing that his critique ushered in under the name of postcolonialism, I find it ironic that the learned scholar of literature would be so dismissive of a textual attitude. *Orientalism* itself is a monumental tour de force of literary learning. And yet he dismisses a habit of mind that relied on books to know the world. What might account for such an irony? I do not think, even in this stage of his thought, that Said was opposed to textual study. His own work is the proof that he was not. What he argued against was a selective engagement with a part of the world of geostrategic interest through a textual attitude. Moreover, his critique sought to describe the ways in which that limited engagement *stood in for* that part of the world through the work of representation. What was particularly offensive about the textual attitude in Napoleon's conquest was that at a time when Europe was clearly moving beyond the dictates of received wisdom and tradition, it would rely on that approach when dealing with the so-called Orient. That it committed itself to the rationalization of space for its own advantage in North Africa and the Middle East while satisfying itself with mediated half memories and elaborate fantasies transmitted in texts, with tradition, indicated an aporia in colonial thought and action. While the colonial reorganization of space relied on modern engineering, the representation of the colony relied on a traditional mode. In other words, Said's critique of orientalism was equally a secular criticism of the persistence of a religious orientation in worldly affairs.[40]

We should recall that Napoleon's foray into Egypt was largely a failure. The textual attitude was always poorly suited for the practical demands of empire. In the evolution of colonial knowledge, Napoleon's Egyptian adventure is unique, as it was characterized simultaneously by the textual and practical attitudes of its administration.

The beginning of France's second colonial empire with the invasion of Algeria in 1830 marked the emergence not only of a new will to power but also a new will to know that assumed a much more practical attitude. Following the model of Napoleon's military and scientific mission to take over Egypt and to know it as exhaustively as possible, the "civilization" of Algeria would also be undertaken by an army of both soldiers and scholars in what Wael Hallaq has called an engineering project of colonialism.[41] The physical world and the cultures that inhabited it needed to be surveyed, categorized, and rationalized to maximize the extraction of material value and to, in an overly generous reading, spread the Enlightenment values of the French Revolution.[42] This engineering project necessarily relied on the exact and natural sciences to know the world, but it also required a social calculus. Where Napoleon's conquest of Egypt relied on textual and practical attitudes in equal measure, the colonization of Algeria relied much more heavily on the practical attitude of getting things done.

In considering the historical experience of the French in Algeria, it is helpful to look beyond Said's critical intervention. The historian Edmund Burke has made an important distinction between philological orientalism and what has developed as the more practically oriented sociology of Islam. Since Silvestre de Sacy (1758–1838), metropolitan orientalists located in their Parisian institutions represented Islam to the rest of the academy and to French society through the concept of Islamic civilization, situating the study of Islam in the humanist tradition but locating Muslim societies at an intermediate stage of human progress.[43] Inflected by historicism and the formalist study of canonical texts, French orientalism operated at such an essentialist and universalizing level that its inadequacy for producing useful administrative knowledge eventually necessitated a more direct, empirical form of knowledge. The colonial enterprise and its demand for a more practical attitude, in contrast, required a different kind of documentation, which we see in the famous *Exploration scientifique de l'Algerie*.[44] This process of documentation produced useful knowledge that allowed France to govern more efficiently through its own measures. Although the metropolitan and colonial ways of representing Islam and Muslim societies differed, they nevertheless interacted, particularly for sourcing personnel tasked with administering the colonies, especially from the early period until around 1870.

The more dominantly practical attitude that replaced the textual one in Algeria manifested itself in a few key ways that would influence the colonization of the Senegambia and the greater western Sahel. This was particularly important because one of the most significant problems to be engineered away in Algeria was the role that Islam appeared to play in the resistance to French colonization led by Emir Abd al-Qadir (1808–1883). To manage the threats of antagonistic forces, the administration in Algeria invested in the development of the *médrasa*, a Muslim college for the education of indigenous intermediaries, and the Bureaux Arabes, local offices staffed by agents knowledgeable *enough* in the Arabic language and Islam to give advice to the army, based on their largely textual knowledge. These agents may have been *arabisants* (speakers of Arabic), but they were not scholars of orientalism. The colonial government also standardized policies derived from Islamic law by creating handbooks for administrators. Perhaps most importantly, the so-called Algerian school of expertise developed "an understanding which emphasized the power of Islamic structures, and which attached particular importance to the role of the Sufi brotherhoods in providing the organizational infrastructure and the inspirational ideology."[45] Such a discovery had clear implications for the engineering project of colonial indirect rule.

To elaborate on the implications of colonial rule as an engineering project and the relevance of the colonization of Algeria to the colonization of the Senegambia and greater western Sahel, we should return to Faidherbe. As a leading practitioner and theorist of French colonialism who began his career in Algeria, he makes these relationships explicit. "In Algeria and Senegal, the aim is the same: to dominate the country with minimal costs while drawing maximum advantage from commercial activities; also, the difficulties are the same and so the means to overcome these problems."[46] In this quote, we see the principle of efficiency clearly articulated: Get the greatest effect with minimal expenditure. It is, in fact, a calculation. Value equals advantage minus costs. To increase value, one must increase advantage while reducing costs. In this statement, "these problems" largely refers to the unruly subject population that could alternatively be mobilized by inspirational Muslim leaders or be restrained by more "reasonable" ones. Indirect rule through religious leaders, specifically religious organizations, would offer the best bang for the buck in conquering and managing the colony.

"Islam," or some notion of it, was no less a problem for the colonial administration in the Senegambia and the Sahel than it was for that in Algeria and became the object of important calculations and engineering. Would Islam be a civilizing force that facilitated the colonial enterprise, or would it be an obstacle to the rationalization of space? In other words, would Islam as construed by the French reduce the cost of governance while maximizing profits, or would it be a source of risk to be accounted for? This problem can be viewed from two sides: the problem of Muslim politics within the colony and the possibility of a Muslim alternative beyond it.

To better understand why Muslims were thought to facilitate the civilizing process,[47] we should return to philology. Philology was a humanist master science that made sense of difference and existence.[48] It did so in the terms of "Man" and "Civilization." Islam had to be known from the texts that it had produced, its textual monuments. Because these texts were in Arabic, a Semitic language, they came from a civilization that was inferior to that mythical Indo-European civilization that produced the genius of the ancient Greeks, the western Europeans, and the lost Aryan cousins in South Asia. All the same, in Africa, Arabo-Islamic civilization represented an intermediate step between uncivilized Africa and the civilization of Christian Europe. There were practical reasons too. The chancellery and diplomatic functions that Muslims had been performing in West African courts for centuries would be useful for colonial administration.

But we should not assume that enfranchising Muslim intermediaries was simply a result of colonial dictates. Muslim residents of Saint-Louis

INTRODUCTION

had resented the 1830 imposition of French civil law and had organized themselves to have it changed. In 1843, a group of Muslim religious leaders, traders, and craftsmen petitioned for "the rights accorded to the Muslims of Algeria: that is to say, that it be recognized and declared that in any case the Muslims at Saint-Louis cannot be subjected to civil laws contrary to their religious laws, that to this effect there be created a tribunal composed of our religious leaders."[49] The colonial government seemed to capitulate in 1848, when a plan for the tribunal reached an advanced stage, although without it being established. One figure emerged as a key player in the Muslim politics of the colony at this time: Bou el-Mogdad Seck mentioned in the previous section. He eventually convinced the French to support Senegalese pilgrims on Hajj to Mecca, and he was sent on diplomatic missions to Morocco, thus institutionalizing Senegal's connections with North Africa and the broader Muslim world within and through the colony-state, as opposed to the already existing religious and political networks. His case largely relied on the argument that the French needed their own *hajji* (a person who has performed the hajj) that was sensible and could counteract the supposedly irrational appeal of Hajj Umar Tal. In this phase before the military imperialism that defined the second half of the nineteenth century, the Muslim community's refusal to be subjected to French civil law in Senegal and its self-identification with Algerian Muslims conditioned the social engineering to come. Colonial thought was forced to account for, adjust to, and eventually confront this reality in determining how it would manage the colony.

As the French pivoted from holding a trading post to building a colony, the easiest solution to the problem of Muslim politics was to approach Senegal as if it were Algeria. As in Algeria, where Abd al-Qadir waged a compelling resistance to colonization, the people of Senegal had the option of rallying around Umar, a charismatic leader who promised an alternative to living under Christian domination. Governor Faidherbe knew that the colony would have to depend on the Muslim community if it was ever going to achieve military domination of the area, and after studying the Algerian system, he approved the establishment of a Muslim tribunal in Senegal. He had first encountered the "Algerian model" of dealing with Muslim populations during two tours in the violent military campaigns of the 1840s. He now argued that the colony needed to follow the Algerian example, which had placed the tribunal under the aegis of political authority, rather than its

1848 plan, which had placed the tribunal under judicial authority. The Muslim tribunal was just one part of an instrumentalist strategy that nevertheless responded to Muslim political pressure within the colony. The French response to Muslim politics in this early phase of colonization was to favor Muslims in the work of colonial governance over adherents to ancestral forms of worship and to instrumentalize Islam for their political ends.

Because Umar invoked religious grounds for his war against French expansion in the upper Senegal River Valley and eventually called for emigration away from areas of French rule, Faidherbe could not afford to abandon the field of religious arguments and sensibilities.[50] He discouraged Christian missionary activity in schools, supported the establishment of a Muslim tribunal, and argued for integration of the Senegalese colony into the colony of Algeria. This integration would have implied an approach to Islam that included the training of an indigenous civil service to work in Arabic and French, encouraged standardization of the interpretation of Islamic law, and used the writing of *fatāwā* (nonbinding legal opinions) to achieve their goals. But as much as these policies reflected the colony's practical and utilitarian view of Islam, they also expressed the politics of a cohort of Muslim leadership, represented by Seck, that aligned with French interests.

All the same, Umar's messianism remained attractive to the broader African population of the colony. Accordingly, Islam had to be managed as a threat. Umar would become the archetype for colonial knowledge and the development of an operationalizable expertise described later. The representations of him that came to define the colonial view were conditioned by established beliefs about Muslim fanaticism and Islam's enmity with Christian, or secular, Europe. These views were already available but were activated and made useful by the conflict over control of the upper Senegal River Valley. The competition between the expanding colonial space of "free trade" and the space of an Islamic economy advocated by Umar resulted in the battle of Médine, a French fort and a key part of the physical infrastructure in the colonial engineering project.

Following the Umarian attempt to siege Médine in the upper Senegal River Valley, lobbying campaigns garnered more resources from metropolitan France and more authorization for expansion. A text apparently intended to encourage interest and investment in the budding colony of Senegal was the first to offer what would become the colonial view of Umar as outside of modernity, as an obstacle in the civilizing process of

INTRODUCTION

rationalization. Paul Holle and Frédéric Carrère outline the career of Umar, placing particular emphasis on his accumulation of wealth and followers through esoteric practices, especially miracle working and talisman writing. In contrast to many of the traditions circulating within the Umarian movement and its descendants, as American historian Amir Syed has shown, Holle and Carrère insist that from at least 1846, when Umar toured his native country, he had set his sights on ruling Futa Toro, which by the time of their writing had already become dominated by the French.[51] Citing a letter Umar wrote declaring his love for the French, the authors italicize part of the reported speech: "when a Christian has paid the custom." They then comment, "One already sees clearly, at that time, that, under the mask of religious proselytization, he had wanted to create a grand empire in Senegambia."[52] At stake in the contest over dominating the upper Senegal River was the expansion of the space of "free" trade. The threat of a trade barrier based on religion ran afoul of colonial philosophy more generally. The opposition to Umar, then, was not so much about religion per se. What troubled colonial officials was that the religious language used by the man they alternatively called a false prophet and an impostor covered up what they thought to be backward, antieconomic, and disingenuous ideas of political order. Proclaiming their position on the antagonism with Umar, they conclude: "Once he is the master from Cayor to Kaarta, he will close the river to us in one word: he is therefore an enemy to destroy." These representations of Umar as the enemy on religious and economic grounds follow well-worn clichés associated with the *longue durée* of orientalist discourse. From false religion to economic unproductivity, the perceived irrationality of the Umarian movement represented a threat to the engineering project to render the Senegambia a modern, rationalized space.

The colonial view of Umar is admittedly a convenient caricature of French orientalist and colonialist discourse in the most generic sense. But the Muslim discourse against Umar is tantalizingly surprising. For the Muslim regional elite, Umar challenged the theological-political status quo that had defined their place in regional dynamics. As a result, their contemporaneous representations of Umar complemented those of the French but in contradicting ways. Writing in the colonial journal of record, *Le moniteur*, Governor Faidherbe included an Arabic-language letter that was spread as part of the colonial propaganda campaign within the subregion. The letter is entitled "From some of the believing brothers living in the lands of the West," with "the West" referring to the lower Senegal River Valley and Saint-Louis.[53] The letter refers to Umar as "a self-proclaimed prophet" (*al-rajjal al-muttanaba*) and highlights the cost to human life and its toll on social harmony. The primary claim of the letter is that Umar's acts reveal that his only desire is to be a king on earth and to have authority over the Blacks and their wealth. Interestingly, this letter calls into question the nature of Umar's knowledge: "And his interest was indeed attached to this [i.e., to have authority over the Blacks]. And he went around with an arrogant and haughty idea for a number of years in the Levant and in Egypt doing kinds of base occupations for a livelihood. And in this he learned a few things of the sciences of the Christians."[54] The letter accepts as true Umar's central claim of having undertaken the Hajj and obtained esoteric knowledge. However, it introduces an interpretation that undermines those claims, emphasizing his low status and interest in accumulating wealth, as well as questioning the nature of his knowledge. In the western Sahel, *naṣārā* (Christians) was used to refer to Europeans. In the letter, "the sciences of the Christians" refers to a knowledge that is not founded within the space of Islamic epistemology; that is, it is not based on the authorities of the Qurʾan, the Sunna, scholarly consensus, individual reasoning, or even customary beliefs. As a result, the sciences of the Christians have a questionable moral character.

In the middle of the nineteenth century, in a moment of rapid technological change in which the steam engine, more advanced weaponry, and new building techniques were introduced in the western Sahel, the sciences of the Christians signified technical knowledge and an overall rationalization of the river-based trade. The American historian David Robinson has argued that Umar's success was due in large part to his implementation of this technical knowledge. To suggest that Umar's successes were linked to these sciences as opposed to his claim to esoteric insight cast him as a disruptive and dangerous force in the region, one that needed to be isolated, even though he was more up to speed with developments in Islamic thought elsewhere in the world. The letter voiced preference, instead, for Muslim leadership that adhered to sound and sensible knowledge that could manage the interactions and business dealings with the French, leadership like that displayed by Bou el-Mogdad Seck, who made such arguments and very well may have been the author of this letter, as he was a leading Arabic interpreter for the colony. The letter offers a unique interpretation, but it is nevertheless reflective of the ways Muslim leadership in the colony began to hedge against the risks introduced by popular Muslim messianism.

Islam as a problem to be engineered in the colonization of the Senegambia was resolved with Umar's death in 1864. After the defeat at Médine, Umar's forces turned east and pursued a path that would pit them against another Muslim state at Masina. A broad coalition of Muslim and non-Muslim fighters then isolated Umar from his forces in the caves of Bandiagara, and he famously disappeared in an explosion of gunpowder. The resolution was this: Islam would be a civilizing force by using Muslim intermediaries and encouraging the development of hybrid colonial-Islamic institutions.[55] Meanwhile, any threats originating from religious exuberance would be neutralized by the otherwise enfranchised elites who were tasked with managing religion. These figures would eventually be tasked with indirect rule more generally, with roles in managing economic production and policing colonial order. The practical attitude that evolved in the engineering projects in first Egypt, then Algeria, and finally the Senegambia came to define a particular form of knowledge best described as expertise that was most concerned with surveillance and a mode of analysis that distinguished good Muslims from bad ones.[56] Nestled within the discipline of the sociology of Islam and the broader epistemology of scientific imperialism, this expertise, which we will call surveillance ethnography, was intended to manage these intermediaries. Kamara first appears in the colonial archive as subject to this expertise.

The Hermeneutics of Islam in Africa

There exists a modest historiography that uses Kamara's writings as primary sources in an early era of professional African history.[57] Many of these same texts are also the basis of Islamic studies scholarship that examined the specificity of Islam in Senegal.[58] A smaller group of scholars has directed their attention to Kamara as the subject of research proper in article-length treatments.[59] This work has established the chronology of Kamara's life, the motivation of his writing, and his intended audience. Since the 1990s, a large-scale multinational effort directed by Jean Schmitz and Saïd Bousbina has worked on the translation of Kamara's major work, *The History of the Blacks* from Arabic to French.[60] But only the first of four volumes has appeared. An Arabic edition of the work has also appeared, but without a critical apparatus, by a publisher in Kuwait, and appears to be based on an incomplete manuscript witness.[61] Kamara's work has been included in a new wave of publishing since the Sahel became an important front in the Global War on Terror, making his ecumenicalism and quietism a socially relevant reference for scholars such as Thierno Kâ and Mbaye Lo.[62] Abdoul Malal Diop, one of the translators from the multinational project, has published an extensive dissertation on the life and works of Kamara.[63]

This work fits within a broader current in the literature on Islam in Africa. A key feature of this history and anthropology literature has been a critique of the colonial knowledge forms that have long established the way Islam in Africa is theorized.[64] Where the colonial theory of *Islam noir*—the French designation for a Black Islam that was supposed to be more charismatic and syncretic than a so-called Moorish or Arab Islam—emphasized the local specificity of Islam in Africa and its disconnection from the rest of what was becoming known as "the Muslim world,"[65] new theory has emphasized circulation, contact, and connectivity on the planetary scale, as well as commonality with Muslims living elsewhere.[66] Islam noir long disfavored the development of scholarship on Muslim scholarly discourses, Muslim intellectuals, and the nature of knowledge itself, which a generation of work has now completely revised.[67] Scholars are showing that, in fact, Muslims in Africa have been thinkers and not mere ethnographic specimens. As disappointing as it is that this work is still necessary, the move to intellectual history has added depth and texture by interrogating specific discourses, traditions, and individual scholars. The general trend has been to shift emphasis from representation to interpretation.

The hermeneutic turn of this field has been characterized by two tendencies: one of new contextualism and the other of normativity. For the hermeneutics of contextualism, meaning is ultimately a function of historical context. But unlike the older generation of historians who used Arabic texts as sources of data for the reconstruction of various historical contexts, the new generation reverses the order by using context to better understand texts. This approach was pioneered by Paolo Farias.[68] Using overlooked epigraphic evidence on Saharan and Sahelian stelae, Farias showed that the anchors of the West African Arabic chronicle tradition, *Tarikh al-Fattash* and *Tarikh al-Sudan*, which had been used to write the medieval and early modern history of West Africa, were not faithful and accurate transmissions of a deeper past but rather intellectual interventions in the postconquest context of the fall of the Songhai Empire in the sixteenth and seventeenth centuries. This new contextualism is being expanded on by various students and intellectual heirs of Farias.[69] Overall, they seek to demonstrate how texts constitute interventions in their moments of composition; their meanings are ultimately defined by this relationship between text and context.

Turning to the hermeneutics of normativity, this group of authors views a text's meaning as ultimately tied to its religious meanings, which emerge from the relationship between texts (whether scriptural, devotional, or documentary) and Islamic forms of life. In practice, this mode of reading African Arabic texts tends toward discussions of the normativity of Islam in Africa. These scholars contradict the anti-Black stereotypes of African religious expression in general and of African Muslims in particular. They argue that African Muslims are authentic and proper Muslims, learned in their religion. Accordingly, clerics and clericalism become a focus of their attention.[70]

Both the new contextualism and the new normativity scholarship have greatly enriched knowledge of the Arabic-script heritage of West Africa. Readings that alternatively emphasize historical specificity and transhistorical Islamic normativity are necessary for understanding this massive but understudied corpus and its contexts. However, juxtaposing these two kinds of readings of a given text challenges the idea that meaning is singular. Accordingly, I build on both trends of the scholarship by integrating their insights along with other possible interpretive horizons into a literary approach to a field of writing that has been largely absent from literary studies because its languages, forms, and themes largely remain illegible to the organization of modern knowledge.[71]

Beyond the specific field of Islam in Africa, which finds its professional home in African studies as a division of area studies, this book is a work of comparative literature. The originating premise of my training, if not the research project itself, was that there is a generative potential in the encounter of area studies and comparative literature.[72] A mode of deep reading is necessary that can do justice to the diversity of the world's expressive cultures and traditions of thought, that goes beyond the fetishization of exotic difference, the rendering of culture into specimens of scientific study, and ultimately the dehumanization of the Other. A humanities that lives up to its name.

INTRODUCTION

The justifications for this encounter were as pragmatic as they were theoretical when they were first conceived by people such as Gayatri Spivak. After the fall of the Berlin Wall, the infrastructures of area studies—which had built within them interdisciplinarity; linguistic competence in the "less commonly taught languages" of the Global South; a political awareness, even if that awareness often was that of the state; and a seeming endless supply of empirical specificity and particularity that begged to be read—appeared to be on the verge of disappearance, subsumed into the universalizing thrust of the nomothetic theorization of the disciplines into a placeless globality.[73] Meanwhile, in the face of globalization, comparative literature—which had a sophisticated tradition of interpretation and a robust theoretical orientation that celebrated the singularity of the ideograph—began to appear overly parochial in its Eurocentrism and methodologically, if not politically, conservative in light of challenges by cultural and ethnic studies. But while Spivak was making the case for this encounter that she would help institute as the study of comparative literature and society, the events of September 11, 2001 brought a sea change that reendowed area studies with new purpose and an infusion of resources and talents, thus reinvigorating it even as the new horizon of global security needs and the digitization of life left the place of deep language study an open question in the face of data science.[74]

Materially, this transformation of area studies made my work possible. A Black product of (mostly) public education in the American South, I received almost every grant, fellowship, and scholarship offered by the U.S. government dedicated to language study and area expertise: Fulbright to study modern standard Arabic and Egyptian dialect, Critical Language Scholarship to study modern standard and Moroccan Arabic, Foreign Language and Area Studies Fellowship to learn Pulaar.[75] These programs and their instruction and funding were necessary for me to even be considered for enrollment in the transareal doctoral program in which I would train alongside the program in comparative literature, both of which had extensive language requirements. But I landed in an odd place that was critical of—if not repulsed by—the strategic interest of our work. Despite the desired distance from strategic interest, our day-to-day production in the language classroom had to accommodate a range of contradictory concerns from the classicist, the aimlessly curious, the human rights activist, the diplomat, and the special forces operator. So I learned firsthand, and without too much exaggeration or substitution, what C. L. R. James said about Black studies and the contemporary student in that 1969 moment of radical possibility: Sometimes one must hunt with the hounds and run with the foxes.[76] Perhaps my intellectual development—situated as it has been betwixt and between academic disciplines, in and out of institutional spaces, through movement study groups, and on editorial boards of blogs and amateur journals and always furthered by reading—can best be understood with Fred Moten and Stefano Harney as theft and flight.[77] But I still want to call it comparative literature—and for good reason.

What makes this project comparative is that making sense of any of Kamara's texts requires thinking across and through difference. He worked in a space defined by Islamic thought, ancestral African traditions, and Euromodernity—what Kenyan political scientist Ali Mazrui famously described as the triple heritage.[78] One might take the languages associated with each of these as proxies to demonstrate the point. Kamara's intended space of intervention was a real lived space that was linguistically rich, multiple, and entangled. Reading his work has required language study in Arabic, Pulaar, and French, complemented by study and exposure to Wolof. While a growing trend in scholarship on Islam in Africa emphasizes the distinction and mutual exclusivity of Europhone and non-Europhone traditions of learning, I remain unconvinced of this argument beyond its validity as a strategy to support subordinated languages and the African intellectuals who continue to elaborate their worlds in those languages.[79] My studies and experiences leave me in agreement instead with an approach to language that "would disclose the irreducible hybridity of all languages."[80] Neither the monolingualism of the national frame nor the Francophony of the postimperial frame nor the monological classicism of traditional Islamic studies will suffice to recover the texture and life of Kamara and all that to which his story grants access. Beyond linguistic difference, an engagement with the disciplines of history and anthropology as potential objects of knowledge in their own right has allowed me to identify the historical specificity of knowledge forms, thus relativizing the work of colonial bureaucrats alongside that of Kamara. The spirit of comparison, then, promises to animate the reading of Kamara and of African Arabic texts more generally.

In particular, recent work in comparative literature has revisited the so-called language question in the study of African letters and has highlighted the importance of the Senegal case. Tobias Warner seeks to interrogate the very meaning of literature and the literary by tracing textual practices and intellectual debates about language throughout Senegalese modernity in and across Wolof and French.[81] Using a diverse set of materials from the nineteenth and twentieth centuries, he shows that processes of vernacularization should challenge both dominant and oppositional views on questions of authorship and audience, form and function, and the inevitability of literary nativism. Where Senegal provides the arena for the competition and collusion of colonial and African languages for Warner, Annette Lienau draws our attention to the place of Arabic in Senegal as a prestige language of a counterimperial literature. In her groundbreaking study of global Arabophone literature in Senegal, Egypt, and Indonesia, Arabic constitutes an axis of South-South comparison.[82] The result is a postcolonial literary criticism of anticolonial nationalism, the global circulation of pluralist ideas in nonhegemonic forms, and vernacularization that does not center metropolitan referents. I read both of these works as affirming arguments made in the field by R. A. Judy in the 1990s that demonstrated that African Arabic texts, such as those of enslaved Muslims in the Americas, pose a fundamental challenge to the canon formation and legibility that founds modern thought.[83]

In brief, this book contributes to the study of Islam in Africa and its associated written heritage by bringing the interpretive sophistication of comparative literature into the conversation. In so doing, this field of study—which has long been isolated, falling as it does between African studies and Middle Eastern and Islamic studies—can be brought into broader academic discourses beyond a small community of experts. At the same time, the textual forms and broadly religious themes of Kamara's writings challenge the common sense of comparative literature that privileges the novel as the paradigmatic modern literary form and a disenchanted secular as the defining condition of modern life.

Textual Life and Afterlife

The promise of writing produces a paradox of its own possibility. In making an utterance transcend the finitude of a single moment in a single place, writing also embeds infinity in the specificity of the sign. The result is that a text holds both a timelessness demarcated by the word and a reiterating of possible timelines released with every new reading. As much as the text is ahistorical in the way its synchronic use of language and form must freeze time, it nevertheless participates in making history, as a text persists diachronically. So questions about when and where something is read; the conditions that make that reading possible; the horizons that might direct or redirect the reading in the first, second, or third place; and so on are as relevant for textual study as are questions about the conditions of composition, the author's intention, and the intended audience. Accordingly, a consideration of Kamara's textual life and afterlives invites a description of the present in which we have resolved to read Kamara's texts. Disciplined as I am as a reader—that is, an unsystematic poacher of words, phrases, and expressions that help me make sense of the things and worlds beyond words—I offer here conjunctural readings, a selective rendering not of a period isolatable from other periods but of a moment whose composition of elements pulls from antecedents and announces yet-to-be-read future repetitions.[84]

Rather than a comprehensive biography of Kamara or a systematic reception history of his works, I consider this book to be a parable. A tale of texts, the story of Kamara—his life and his work—is also an exemplary account of the durability of the textual attitude as a commitment to reading. As a scholar of global Black studies trained in intellectual history, comparative literature, and postcolonial theory, I pursued something of a hybrid method. I performed close reading for the purposes of both periodization and appreciation of form. I use Kamara's texts—particularly his autobiographical work *The Announcement*, which includes his own recollections, dream reports by others, and excerpts of letters written to him by his Muslim scholarly peers and colonial interlocutors; *Most of the Would-Be Jihadists*, which is a long essay challenging the validity of jihad in a modern context; *The Most Delicious of the Sciences and the Tastiest of the News in the Life of Hajj Umar*, a hagiography of Hajj Umar Tal, the militant Muslim saint whose popular messianic movement transformed the religious, intellectual, political, and economic landscape of the greater western Sahel in the nineteenth century; and *The History of the Blacks*, a monumental history of Muslim West Africa.[85] I also consulted archival documents in the colonial surveillance file, the Kamara collection at the Institut Fondamental d'Afrique Noire in Dakar, and the private family collection in Ganguel, Senegal. Using this library and archive, I examined French and Arabic published works from the late colonial, nationalist, and contemporary periods to ascertain shifting frameworks for understanding. While a recent wave of works has proposed new readings of West African Arabic texts in their historical context and through their religious significance, I approached this body of work as literature. In attending to the shifting historical contexts that have conditioned Kamara's reception, I highlight the political stakes and epistemological commitments that have made the reading of his work possible but that have limited its interpretation. Such an account is essential even if insufficient for the exercise of reading. I have cultivated my own textual attitude by reading Kamara, for whom transmission and commentary were as important as the central text itself. These are enduring values for the future of the humanities.

In chapter 1, "Beginnings: The Text, the World, and the Sufi," I develop a readerly mode of engaging African Arabic texts in general and Shaykh Musa Kamara in particular by insisting on a linear close reading of Kamara's autobiography. Inspired by, without being an application of, Edward Said's approach in *Beginnings: Intention and Method*, I construct a method through the act of reading the text itself.[86] In so doing, I develop the idea of the textual attitude as an orientation to the world through the excess of text, that is, the interpretive abundance afforded by language. Along the way, I pick up much from the text itself and bring it into dialogue with a wide variety of traditions of interpretation. I then deploy this method in close readings of what I call scenes of election in the beginning chapter of Kamara's autobiography, whose core theme is *walāya* (friendship with God or Muslim sainthood). For the first scene, I situate my reading in the context of two literary traditions, one Sufi Muslim and the other African, in a way that blurs the boundaries of the two. For the second scene, which describes his education and in which he shares the peculiar fact that he has perfect memory but has failed to memorize the Qurʾan, I provide context in the broadest sense to show why this detail warrants our attention. Altogether, the three close readings of the introduction and opening pages of Kamara's *Announcement* allow us—you the reader and me—to develop not so much a theoretical framework that we might apply but an orientation that will direct our action over the course of the book. Text is a form of human intention that exceeds communication, understood as the direct relay of information from sender to receiver. Reading Kamara will invite us to do many things with his words and ours.

In chapter 2, "A Degree of Prophecy," I continue to elaborate an understanding of textuality by exploring the relationship between texts and dreams as forms of significance that shaped Kamara's life. Starting with a

INTRODUCTION

peculiar dream report in which Hajj Umar Tal appears to Kamara in a dream, I theorize text as disclosure that augments reality. I then argue that what appears as most salient across Kamara's texts and dreams is his saintly subjectivity, his sense of self as a *walī* (close friend of God, connected through a genealogical chain of being and spiritual hierarchy). Close readings of Kamara's *Life of Hajj Umar* and his own autobiographical *The Announcement* allow me to detail the middle phase of Kamara's life from the mid-1880s, when he began his spiritual journey on the Sufi path, until around 1912, when he first entered the colonial archive. Few historical documents understood in a narrow sense are available for this period, thus highlighting the value of close reading and other horizons of interpretation that privilege what was most meaningful to Kamara.

Departing from the readerly mode of chapters 1 and 2, in chapter 3, "Islam Noir: Surveillance Ethnography and the Politics of Representation," I consider more directly the micro-, regional, and global historical contexts that conditioned the encounter between Kamara as an African Muslim intellectual and colonial power and its forms of knowledge—specifically, the sociology of Islam. I argue that up and down these scales of context, representation—as both a political mechanism of indirect rule inherent in modern governance and a discursive and aesthetic regime—had undergone a process of scientization. Race appears at this point as a regulating concept. This process constituted a paradigm shared in both the metropole and the colony. Politics in this context becomes the politics of representation— the production and reproduction of identities through twinned activities of administrative institutions and research practices in colonial spaces. I thus attend to the content and form of Kamara's entry in both the colonial archives and the colonial library. What emerges is a practically interested regard toward Kamara defined by the surveillance ethnography at the heart of the sociology of Islam. From this perspective, Kamara was viewed as an asset for his ability to procure information useful to the work of governance. His own self-understanding as a Muslim friend of God is absent, and his textually mediated relationship to reality is reduced to information. I conclude by showing how Kamara, in his efforts to represent the political in his historical critique of the practice of jihad, was an outlier in the emerging consensus that privileged the politics of representation.

In chapter 4, "A Monumental Text in an Orientalist Season," I narrate the tragic tale of Kamara's magnum opus, the monumental *History of the Blacks*.

INTRODUCTION

I pose two key questions in this chapter: How did late colonial officials read or fail to read Kamara? And why did Kamara bequeath his intellectual work to a colonial institution despite this disregard? The story of Kamara and his *History of the Blacks*, which begins with energy and enthusiasm before yielding to frustration and disappointment, is also the story of a short-lived opening made by the encounter of colonial humanists seeking to identify a native literature and promote indigenous scholars from the region. Ultimately, this window of opportunity was never fully opened, as colonial philology was an institution of partial translation, undermined as it was by its complicity with and proximity to colonial engineering. The contradictions of colonial humanism eventually rendered philology a technical discipline ancillary to history and religious studies. Nevertheless, a singular body of work emerged that remains an invaluable resource for thinking about the past, present, and future of Senegalese society. I base this argument on Kamara's surveillance file, close readings of his autobiographical *The Announcement* and *The History of the Blacks*, and relevant secondary literature. His capacity to see beyond the immediate physical reality was ignored by colonial interlocutors and was paradoxically at the heart of his decision to transmit his legacy by bequeathing his work to the colonial research institute. I also demonstrate the nonresolution of the contradictory regards of colonial knowledge and power that limited the humanist project with the practical attitude elaborated on in chapter 3. Finally, in marking the end of Kamara's textual life, I anticipate his textual afterlife of ongoing retrievals and returns after independence.

After Senegal won independence from France, nationalist scholars such as Amar Samb strove to establish an authentic African humanism and to define the specificity of Islam in Senegal. In chapter 5, "The Pitfalls of National Literature," I answer the question of how Kamara was read in the context of decolonization. I argue that he reemerges in the 1970s as a key reference. The construction of a national literature out of an Arabo-Islamic written heritage would be a major response to the problem of the negation of African humanity in colonial discourses. Kamara featured prominently for a generation of historians and Islamic studies scholars working from the late 1960s to the 1990s who saw in the colonial-era Muslim intellectual an invaluable resource for making this literature. I focus on the body of work of Samb, Senegal's first French-trained Islamicist, whose academic, popular, and creative works sought to nationalize tradition while situating himself within the development of an African humanism. However, this project was not without its

INTRODUCTION

contradictions and ruptures. The nationalist reading of Kamara has a great deal in common with the late colonial reading of him, in which the practical attitude constituted the most important lens for understanding. Even as Samb sought to refute the negation of African humanity in post-Enlightenment thought, the models of national literature he deployed to read Kamara and others reinforced the subordination of Africa to European measures.

In chapter 6, "The Secular-Religious Afterlife of Shaykh Musa Kamara," I answer these two questions: How do contemporary Senegalese intellectuals read Kamara? And who reads him and why? Since the 2012 insurgency, when militant Islamists seized Timbuktu in neighboring Mali, Kamara has reemerged as a key reference for understanding modern Senegal. This has come about because reference to him does the kind of intellectual and political work at the national scale that the Timbuktu manuscripts have done for the discourse on the African Renaissance at the continental scale. He is remembered today as a scholar and as a Muslim saint, legible to both the rationality of the state and the spirituality of society. I argue that Kamara's present circulation in contemporary discourses is limited to the definitional work he performs in exemplifying Islam as a modern religion that abstains from politics, is ecumenical in orientation, and is learned in practice. In short, Kamara has become a paradigm in defining the "good Muslim." This chapter is based on close readings of the discursive practices reflected in recent translations of and publications about Kamara by contemporary Senegalese intellectuals—most notably, a series of new translations, conference proceedings, and biographic profiles on Kamara published by the Islamic Institute of Dakar. This final substantive chapter concludes the story of Kamara's textual afterlife, bringing us up to the present day. It announces the possible return of a textual attitude with a view to the current opportunities and challenges such an attitude now faces vis-à-vis the political stakes and technological conditions of the present. It is this new context that provides new meanings to Kamara's works and to philology more broadly. This chapter echoes the first and second, as some of Kamara's self-understandings have entered the public discourse in Senegal. It contrasts with the story of the colonial instrumentalization of textual knowledge presented in chapter 3 by focusing on Senegalese initiatives, even as it suggests surprising continuities in the wake of colonial domination.

In the coda, I discuss a conversation I had with students at the Center of Religious Studies at Gaston Berger University in Saint-Louis, Senegal, in

INTRODUCTION

June of 2024. This discussion helped me realize that the conjuncture that defined the ten years or so that have conditioned the appearance of this book has ended. Questions from the students and an ongoing conversation with my host, Abdourahmane Seck, provided me the opportunity to reflect on what this work might mean within the emergent intellectual landscape of contemporary Senegal.

Paradoxically, I propose a return to a form of knowledge that was fundamental to colonial humanism: philology. That discipline has long been associated with the emergence of humanism during the Renaissance. Petrarch's study of classical Latin in the works of Cicero gave access to the living language of the ancients instead of the dead Latin of the church bureaucracy. And Lorenzo Valla's textual criticism of the Donation of Constantine proved the document that supposedly authorized the pope's temporal power and ownership of land was a forgery. As a result, the study of the lives of men of action, *studia humanitas*, came increasingly in view, and philology was its queen discipline. But as philology became so broad and unwieldy, the study of texts and classical languages dissolved into that we today call the modern humanities, a constellation of subjects that constantly struggles to justify itself in an antihumanist present.[87] All the same, philology persisted as a more narrow and technical discipline associated with oriental languages—that is, until 2003, when, on the eve of the Iraq war, state agencies ironically determined that they no longer needed language experts. This decision broke with a standard practice of empire going back to and embodied by Napoleon's invasion of Egypt with an army of scholars. Who needs the study of language and texts for strategic interest when you can come up with a better, more precise picture much more quickly with an informatic approach? With the closure of these government offices and the emergence of human terrain systems thinking,[88] the textual attitude's long-in-the-making irrelevance was complete. In the same year, the famous critic of orientalist philology, Edward Said, called for a return to philology in his final work before his death.[89] What had changed in the decades since the original publication of his *Orientalism* in 1978 was the definite departure of textual scholarship from the work of representing civilizational difference in the structures governing knowledge and power.

Today, knowing the world requires big data, algorithmic reasoning, and artificial intelligence to make sense of the overwhelming crush of

INTRODUCTION

information that we collect on the physical environment and our experiences within it. This is the algorithmic attitude, an antihumanist orientation toward the world through data. It begs this question: What is the value of reading when no single, meaningfully composed text (a form of human intention that exceeds the act of communication) or any number of texts that a person might actually read can reveal an accurate truth about the world? The leading front of scientific innovation, the military-intelligence-diplomatic-business complex, appears to have come to the conclusion that neither the scale nor the speed nor the scope of reading can provide information about facts on the ground, facts whose relevance makes them necessary for human action.

But I want to propose, following an evolution in critical thought associated with Said, that the obsolescence of philology as an imperial project of the state—that of knowing a people through their texts—should not be mourned but celebrated. The irrelevance of the textual attitude has liberated it from the burden of representation; that is, it is now free of the structural condition of being an instrumental knowledge in the work of power. Philology has often been thought of as either a contemporary technical discipline or an antiquated soft science that ordered human difference in racial and religious hierarchies in a time better left in the past. That is, philology was a quintessentially colonial form of knowledge. But if we approach it differently, as a human tradition across time and cultural difference—as indeed the love of study—we might better appreciate what the textual attitude has meant in places as diverse as Malcolm X's prison cell and Kamara's riverside village at the edge of the French colonial empire. Once prized for what it could do and then dismissed as irrelevant, philology now returns as a vitally human orientation toward the world. In this account, considering philology as a particular form of knowledge has been a way to track developments in the organization of knowledge more broadly. Unburdened from the work of representing reality, philology as the love of study and the cultivation of the textual attitude promises a future for the humanities beyond the world slavery and colonization made. Thus, the story of the Senegalese Muslim scholar Shaykh Musa Kamara, who devoted his life to reading and producing monumental texts that were initially celebrated but eventually disregarded before being retrieved by postcolonial intellectuals, provides a parable of the rise, fall, and return—the fate—of the humanities.

ONE

Beginnings

The Text, the World, and the Sufi

In the name of God, the Compassionate, the Merciful.

Oh God, bless our master Muhammad, his family, and his companions, and grant them peace.

Shaykh Musa, may God preserve him in the two realms from every severity and misery, said: This is my *tarjama*. Many of the people of God, The Exalted, have done similarly. Among them are Shaykh ʿAbd al-Wahhab al-Shaʿrani (may God be pleased with him). He made it a book in two volumes named *The Subtleties of the Benefactor and the Morals in the Obligations of Conversation with the Blessing of God the Absolutely Exalted*.[1] And similarly, Shaykh Muhammad al-Khalifa bin Shaykh Sidi Mukhtar al-Kunti, named *Original and Inherited Knowledge Regarding the Marvels of the Two Shaykhs, My Mother and My Father*.[2] A lot of what Shaykh Hajj Umar points out has this same function when he says with clarity in *The Lances*: "The chapter in which they are informed of what God, the Exalted has granted me, etc."[3] Accordingly, those who composed the virtuous exploits (*manāqib*) of their Shaykhs such as Shaykh Ibn ʿAtaʾ Allah in his composition named *The Subtleties of Benefaction in the Marvels of My Shaykh Abi al-Abbas al-Mursi and My Shaykh Abi al-Hassan*, may God be pleased with the both of them, amen.[4]

I say: What a person says about himself approaches the truth, even if the opposite is said. God the Exalted praised John (peace be upon him) when he said: "Peace be Upon him the day he was born, and the day he dies, and the day he is raised alive."[5] And Jesus (peace be upon him) praised himself with the permission of his lord when he said: "Peace be upon me the day I was born, the day I die, and the day I am raised alive!"⁶

I named this *tarjama*: *The Announcement of the Good News to the Fearful and Confused and His Reminder of the Breadth of the Mercy of God, the Generous Bestower.*

It is time to get started.

So, I say: My name is Musa son of Ahmad, known as Hamad Dudu, May God grant his mercy, son of Mahmud, son of Famudi, may God have mercy on all of them. Shaykh Saʿad Buh, may God be pleased with him, gave me the title Shaykh Musa. My mother's name is Maryam Daḍî. Daḍî is the name of her mother. The meaning of "daḍî" in our language Fulani is "safety" [*al-najah*]. I came across something on her lineage, which is as follows: Togalla Jajji, father of Aliyati Togalla, father of ʿAli Hasan Aliyati, father of Sowel ʿAli, father of Sow Somel, father of Golgol Samba. The meaning of "Golgol" is a diminutive of *galgol*, a bird with an excellent voice and long in the neck that the Arabs call *al-ʿandalīb* [nightingale]. She got this name for her excellent voice as she was renowned for it. She was the mother of Kumba Golgol the mother of Daḍî Kumba mother of Maryam Daḍî, my mother, may God grant pardon to us and them and forgive us and them. I do not know anything other than this for her. The mentioned Togalla Jajji is the brother of Yalt Jajji and Sawt Jajji. The informant mentioned the branches of Togalla, Yalt, Sawt until the last thing mentioned. I left it out for concision. According to what has been handed down, the genealogists are liars.⁷

CONCERNED AS I AM with learning from the textual life and afterlife of Shaykh Musa Kamara, I should begin by reading a text. The West African Muslim scholar was above all else a reader. Taking stock of the shifting political and epistemological horizons that have conditioned the way he has been understood would profitably ground itself in a text that he wrote about himself. Such an exercise cannot be limited to a transparent exposition of the contents of a given work as if a text was only a medium through which an intended meaning was deposited to be found and deciphered later—that is, as if a text was only a technology of communication. A reading of Kamara, of any author, of one writing in a so-called traditional mode no less, requires an awareness of the conditions of transmission to be sure. But it also invites a reimagining as well as a reconstruction, both of which must be attuned to present conditions as much as they may look backward or project themselves into the future. In short, Kamara requires commentary—that classical philological activity.

In particular, we, you and I, should begin with a reading of one of Kamara's final works, *The Announcement of the Good News to the Fearful and Confused and His Reminder of the Breadth of the Mercy of God, the Generous Bestower*.[8] Written in 1937, this autohagiographic work offers the closest thing we have to a cumulative self-portrait, a reading of the self, using the conventions that were most meaningful to the author. The text includes memories of his childhood, a record of his intellectual training and travels, reports of dreams indicating his election, laudatory reports about him written by his Muslim peers and colonial interlocutors, and essays on core topics of discussion in his milieu—namely, the nature of the master-disciple relationship and the unreliability of genealogy as a form of social reckoning. Reading it allows us to gather language, ideas, and forms that were relevant and meaningful to Kamara himself and enables new understanding for interested readers. To be clear, Kamara's autobiographical *Announcement* is wholly generic, as its form and themes are conventional. And yet, as I will show in this chapter, Kamara is totally unrepresentative of the tradition of Islamic scholarship in West Africa. I hope this paradox will help us "linger" with the text in lieu of establishing equivalents or simply relaying information.[9]

The primary question that drives this chapter is methodological. Given the increased visibility of West African Arabic and Arabic-script texts in African languages such as the works of Kamara discussed in this book's introduction and their increased use in contemporary scholarship, how might we *appreciate* a text such as *The Announcement*? As an intellectual skill that one might teach, learn, or practice, appreciation has conventionally been understood as the goal of college-level literary studies.[10] It includes the skill of recognizing the value or merit of a text through an examination of its use of the elements and devices of literary form, its themes, and its relation to a canon. My use of the term "value" here is not abstractly figurative. It indicates a process of appraisal that emerges out of a given mode of economic production. As literary theory that situates literature in culture, history, and society has established, appreciation requires a direct engagement with the language of a text, but it is also the product of a vast assemblage of institutions, market forces, and material culture beyond any given text.[11] In other words, the designation of literature *as literature* is an inherently ideological process. It is my premise that the broader class of texts to which Kamara's *Announcement* belongs has not been subject to critical appreciation for historico-ideological reasons. Instead, those texts have been approached with a practical attitude; they have been used to do things. Viewed as sources of data from which useful information might be extracted for some other end or marshaled as proofs of literacy and historicity in antiracist arguments of civilizational value, they have rarely enjoyed attention as texts in their own right in Euro-American academic scholarship. They have yet to be appreciated. A great amount of effort, time, and resources has been dedicated to the collection, preservation, cataloguing, and translation of African Arabic texts. This work has been valuable and makes appreciation possible. But we have yet to appreciate this literature, and I want to do so by affirming the value of reading as an end unto itself.[12] It is especially valuable in the undervalued tradition of Muslim scholarship in West Africa, as it is there that we might appreciate the textual attitude, an orientation to making sense through reading. In so doing, we might recover the kinds of commitments and orientations that have classically animated humanistic inquiry—but with a double difference.

Accordingly, I begin with a close reading of the opening of *The Announcement* to theorize text and textual study. Writing and text are not synonymous.[13] Writing is a technology of communication, a medium through which a text might be transmitted from one moment and place to another.[14] Text is a form of intention that exceeds communication, or the relay of information. This form of intention might appear in any number of media. Instead of trying to eliminate or cut through it, how might we begin to appreciate this excess? I pursue this question with reference to *The Announcement*, keeping two rather straightforward questions in mind: What is a text? And how might we read one? I then describe Kamara's textual life through a close reading of two scenes of saintly election, asking how his textual attitude as an orientation to experience defined his self-understanding.

Close Reading

The text begins, as all things sincere and good should, in the name of God. Such a convention of opening is ubiquitous in Islamic texts and enjoys an abundant tradition of interpretation. One of my personal favorites explains the meaning of the dot that sits under a cup-shaped grapheme (ب) together representing the sound "b" in *bismillah*. It is said to be the point at which a giant beam of light is transmitted from the heavens to the earth at the beginning of creation, a pen that writes existence into being. I like to think of it as a laser beam. Most chapters of the Qur'an begin with this convention, but it is not limited to opening texts, whether scriptural, and therefore divine and immutable, or human, and therefore imperfect and contingent. It is the formula for opening all manner of activity. The *basmala*, the name of this convention, is used for ritual activities such as prayer, as well as for mundane ones such as driving a car.[15] It is, in fact, a statement of intention. This activity is undertaken in or with—depending how one renders the preposition *bi*—the name of God, who is also known by the names the Compassionate and the Merciful. Such a designation is the first distinction one can make between good and evil, light and dark, order and chaos, sense and nonsense, meaning and incoherence. Edward Said famously distinguished beginnings from origins, arguing that the former is secular, whereas the latter is theological.[16] For him, the difference between a secular text and a religious one rests in the intentional production of meaning through its difference from a tradition and not its similarity. *The Announcement*, however, invites us to relativize this distinction, as the text pursues its meaning through its proximity to the sources of, and its location within, tradition. The *basmala* at the beginning of *The Announcement*, then, is the means by which an intention has begun to form.

But to whom is such an intention addressed? A prepositional phrase, "in the name of God," standing alone seems incomplete; it suggests the need for a complement, whether stated explicitly or left unexpressed. The following words give us more to understand: "Oh God, bless our master Muhammad, his family, and his companions, and grant them peace." God, then, is the first to be addressed explicitly in this text. The purpose of this sentence is to call for blessings to be granted to the Prophet Muhammad and those closest to him. From a certain utilitarian or interested perspective, the benefit is not for God, or for Muhammad, or for the Prophet's family, or for his companions; rather, it is for the one making the invocation. From a more humane perspective, the benefit is reciprocal, issuing as it does from an imagined author's sense of responsibility and respect, an obligation to contribute to the permanent flow of grace. The invocation, along with the *basmala*, creates a clear order, a chain of being, that starts with God, or perhaps in God, and bridges over to the rest of creation. The text that is to follow is directed elsewhere, below the upper echelons of the chain of being already invoked, perhaps to the very large audience of the rest of humanity.

Next, there is a statement of authorship and identification. It follows an important pivot that signals a move from the doxological formula of the opening prayer to the direct content of the text at hand: "Shaykh Musa ... said." The verb "said" is the hinge that alerts readers that what follows is the speech of the Shaykh Musa. Speech here is figurative, as the author is not so much saying the text aloud as he is writing it. This trace of orality in written language is by no means unique to this text or this context, but it nevertheless invites us to consider the implications of orality in providing important models and forms for writing. It suggests the possibility of doing things with words, both written and oral.[17] The text that follows is authored by Kamara insofar as it is his verbal performance on the page. But where an oral performance may imply a specific time and place, a moment in a space, the text as a written performance detemporalizes and despatializes speech. The written performance can move through space and time by virtue of the writing. Shaykh Musa is made to accompany the written performance by virtue of this signature that opens the text.

But what kind of performance is it? What is its name? The one "speaking," the author, Shaykh Musa, after a request to be preserved from every severity and misery in this world and the next, plainly names the text as a sort of biographical profile or entry: "This is my *tarjama*," wherein "this" refers to the text before us and "*tarjama*" refers to the generic identity of that text. If we have avoided the problem of translation until now, we can do so no longer, for the translation of the name of the text's genre has more than one possibility, begging the question of what translation is more generally. I have already translated much, making careful selections to convey meaning across barriers of linguistic and historical difference. Instead of moving meaning across an expanse of incomprehension to close the gap of understanding, as *naql*, another Arabic word for the practice, suggests, we might open up this space of difference for generative theory.[18] After all, *tarjama* is both the name for a kind of text, a genre, and a modern Arabic word that signifies "translation." In coupling these two issues of translation and genre, I am pursuing the meaning of context beyond the situating of a text or person within a historical period. For this reason, I want to linger over the question of genre, for what is a text's "con-text"—that which comes *with* a text—if not its genre—that is, its citation of form?

One strategy for translating a term as important as *tarjama* is to refer to expertise on the topic. In some ways, I have already done this by introducing the citation with the gloss of "biographical profile or entry." I might present a modular microsurvey of biographical literature in the tradition of Arabo-Islamic letters, citing, for example, the thoughtful work of Michael Cooperson, who has elucidated the nonidentity of "writing that foregrounds the human subject" in the tradition—which presumes a permanence of an individual's character—and modern biography—which understands a person's life as a product of becoming and agency.[19] I could explain continuities with and departures from this tradition in early twentieth-century West Africa. Or I could describe the broader semantic field to which *tarjama* belongs, situating it with *manāqib*, *tadhkira*, *sīra*, and other such terms. It would even be helpful to frame the genre as subject to a scholarly debate between lumpers and splitters who argue, on the one hand, that taken together, these texts can be coherently thought of as hagiography and, on the other, that they are far too complex in form, content, and context to be taken as a single class.[20] The underlying dispute concerns, in part, the difference between those who view translation as a more or less seamless transference across difference and those who insist on carrying the singularity of a meaning across difference. Difference matters. Such moves would indeed be useful for a work of scholarship, as expertise underwrites the entire enterprise.

But what if translation resembled commentary more than explanation? What if translation required us to stay within the text itself instead of reaching outside it? In other words, what if my effort here to render *tarjama* legible to a broad Anglophone academic audience relied not on a definitive statement about the textual form in general but on an appreciation of a single, specific example of a *tarjama*? In the case of *The Announcement*, this approach to translation would require a slow unraveling of the text that revolves not around authoritative statements of meaning but around situational engagements with the text itself—what is being referred to by the demonstrative pronoun "this" in the phrase "This is my *tarjama*." It would require gathering as much as possible from the text to identify that for which *tarjama* is a name, but this task is as impossible as it is necessary. It is open, unfinished, and ongoing. It insists on the primacy of the text itself as indispensable in responding to the question, reflecting a commitment to the text itself as a text. It refuses to dispense with the text as if it was a document that might be "summed up" in a bottom line.[21] Rather, it approaches the text as an inexhaustible resource that is generative of meaning and that plays a role in mediating and framing the readers' ongoing experience of the world. Indeed, such a strategy of translation would require a textual attitude.

Immediately after describing *The Announcement* as a *tarjama*, Shaykh Musa situates the text within a literature and positions himself as belonging to a specific class of rare individuals. "Many of the people of God, the Exalted, have done similarly"—that is, they have either written a *tarjama* or had one written about them. Among the people of God he mentions are, in order, the prolific early modern Sufi ʿAbd al-Wahhab al-Shaʿrani (d. 1565);[22] a leading figure of the West African branch of the Qadiri Sufi order Sidi Mukhtar al-Kunti (d. 1811); the historically consequential messianic Hajj Umar Tal (d. 1864) of the Tijaniyya order; and the late medieval Cairene Sufi Ibn ʿAtaʾ Allah (d. 1310). Likely readers of *The Announcement* would know that the named authors are among the leading lights of Sufi thought, both globally and in the specifically West African context. As Nile Green, the historian of the Indian Ocean, puts it, Sufism is "a powerful tradition of Muslim knowledge and practice bringing proximity to or mediation with God and believed to have been handed down from the Prophet Muhammad through the saintly successors that followed him."[23] These successors function as intercessors between the aspirant and God and therefore belong to a rare but essential group of human beings. The suggestion, then, is that the author of this text belongs to a very elevated class of Sufis, the *khāṣṣ* (the spiritual elite, in technical terminology). Even without reading the works of these people of God that Shaykh Musa cites, a consideration of their titles elaborates the semantic field to which *tarjama* belongs. The *karamāt* (tokens of nobility or marvels, as well as the narrative representation of those marvels) of al-Kunti and the *manāqib* (exemplary acts, as well as the accounts of those acts) of Ibn ʿAtaʾ Allah both refer to spiritual accomplishments and marvelous feats, as well as to their entextualization in writing. The marvelous here refers to miracle-like happenings associated with the friends of God that attest to divine intervention but fall short of the public declaration of a miracle, which can be made only by prophets.[24] In short, Shaykh Musa thus defines the text's genre by qualifying the statement "This is my *tarjama*" with a reference to other authors and texts of the Sufi tradition that have focused on individual lives of holy men.

The explicit reference to and implicit modeling on other texts makes *The Announcement* dialogical. Where the text itself is a statement (i.e., what "Shaykh Musa said"), the cited texts are the statements with which it enters into dialogue. The model of dialogue is helpful, in that we can understand the text as both a response to previous statements and an anticipation of future ones.[25] Meaning is made from the relationship of the statement to both, and these relationships together make the texts inherently social. It is no longer about the individual identity or the meaning of the statement itself. This is an important insight for reading what might be described as scholastic texts, in which the materiality of manuscript culture necessitated that each carry its archive with it. Texts that historically have been read or not read as being repetitive or derivative take on new horizons of interpretive possibility when approached as being articulative of meaning in a dialogue.[26]

This opening paragraph of the text, then, provides the con-text for reading it.[27] It presents upfront the other texts that *The Announcement* brings *with* it, to take the etymology of "con" literally, for, as noted before, context is not only what is historical but also whatever accompanies a text. In Shahab Ahmed's conceptualization of Islam as the human and historical phenomenon defined by hermeneutical engagements with what he calls the "Pre-Text, Text, and Con-Text" of Revelation, con-text refers to "the entire accumulated lexicon of means and meanings of Islam."[28] To read *The Announcement*, then, is to also read the texts it refers to, if not in its content, at least in its use of a shared form. The four works cited provide the models that Shaykh Musa used in writing *The Announcement*—that indicate its belonging in the genre of *tarjama*. The text cites these explicitly as being models, justifications, even warrants. It also cites them in their very form. Generic convention, after all, is how readers develop expectations that might be satisfied, denied, or changed. This intertextuality is the quality that defines one sense of the term *literature*, a body of texts that refers to itself, either explicitly in content or implicitly in form.[29] Shaykh Musa's context, based on the indications he provides, is not just the historical period of interwar French West Africa but also the environment of the "Sudanic" region, the Arabic and Pulaar languages, the Islamic creed, and the lives of Sufi saints in theme and form. This teaches us that to read in context is to read in genre as much as in a historical moment or place. To be more extreme, to read is to read in genre.

It would seem Shaykh Musa anticipated skeptical readers. After situating his text within the canon of Sufi hagiography, he provides a rationale: "I say: What a person says about himself approaches the truth, even if the opposite is said." Nestled between the declaration of his own perspective and that of an unnamed, passively voiced contrarian, Shaykh Musa here provides a rationale for what might be considered an immodest act of writing about the self. He quickly validates this perspective with a juxtaposition of Qurʾanic scripture. First, he cites in full Maryam 15, which speaks of the major events in Yahya's (John's) life in the third person, and then he cites Maryam 33, when Jesus echoes the earlier verse but instead uses the first person. Without going into the rich tradition of commentary and interpretation of these verses—a resource of meaning implied in *The Announcement* by the citation of the scripture itself and not its elaboration in the text—we can note that when deployed by Shaykh Musa, it highlights an instance when an individual praises the trajectory of their own life.[30] Such a reference effectively authorizes the project of saintly autobiography that this text reflects, thus anticipating any possible objections.

Having identified the form of the text, situated it within dialogue, and cleared the ground for its legitimacy, Shaykh Musa then gives the poetic title of the work: *The Announcement of the Good News to the Fearful and Confused and His Reminder of the Breadth of the Mercy of God, the Generous Bestower*.[31] It consists of two basic parts separated by the connector "and." Each part independently names the text. The first part describes the text as the *tabshīr*. This word is the verbal noun form of *bishara* and *bushrā* and means "good news, glad tidings, or auguries," prophetic signs that indicate something of divine worth. It might be rendered as the spreading of the good news or, more simply, as the announcement, as I have so far done.[32] The first part finishes with a possessive construction that answers the question "Announcement for whom?" It is for the one who is fearful and confused. The second part employs the term *tadhkira* (memoir), which functions both as a common generic name of the literary form we have been discussing and as a functional description of the text's purpose—that is, to be a reminder. The text is to be a reminder for the already named fearful and confused one of the breadth of the mercy of God, the Generous Bestower. Where the first part of the title (the announcement) seems directed outward to a grand public, the second (the memoir) is directed to the interiority of the author. And where the announcement belongs to a reticent, unsure, and perhaps diminished subject, the reminder relieves the tension of fear and confusion introduced in the first half of the title through the promise of divine abundance and certainty. Far from offering a straightforward or self-evident title describing a life, Shaykh Musa, following convention, packs the title of this work with poetry and religious significance.

The author then informs readers that it is time to get started. Only now, in the final paragraph of the introduction, do we get anything that might properly be understood to be biographical in the modern sense—that is, explicit information on the subject of the text in question. All that has come before has required inference and reference. Even the name Shaykh Musa is revealed to be as much the name of a saintly persona and of an authorial voice as it refers to a historical person. The name of the author situated in a genealogical chain identifies the person behind the signature: "So, I say: My name is Musa son of Ahmad, known as Hamad Dudu, May God grant his mercy, son of Mahmud, son of Famudi, may God of have mercy on all of them." Thus, Shaykh Musa's biography begins with his name in a chain of names, a lineage. We first learn the names of the three generations of men that sired the author. The list of fathers is then interrupted and cut short by the naming of a spiritual father: "Shaykh Saʿad Buh, may God be pleased with him, gave me the title Shaykh Musa." Shaykh Saʿad Buh (ca. 1850–1917), leader of a branch of the Qadiri Sufi order in the Senegalo-Mauritanian zone and a well-known religious personality of the colonial period often thought of as one of the key architects of the accommodation between saintly lineages and the colonial state, served as Kamara's spiritual guide for much of his life.[33] That he follows immediately after Kamara's patriline and is associated with the granting of the title of shaykh indicates his importance to the author. The point I am making is that there is an intimate connection among names, genealogy, biography, and saintly status.

But Kamara's line of fathers and the naming of his spiritual guide do not complete the presentation of his genealogy. In fact, patriarchal origins, both carnal and spiritual, only begin this statement of identity. The most extensive portion of his genealogy is taken up with his matriline. The next part of the passage provides a much longer genealogy than was provided for the patriline. Where he could identify his father's ancestors for only two generations, he traces his mother's ancestry to eight, the first three of which are all women before a switch to male ancestors. Beyond the difference in numbers between the patriline and the matriline is a qualitative difference.

There is no commentary on Kamara's patriline, but his matriline receives a *philological* treatment. "My mother's name is Maryam Dadî. Dadî is the name of her mother. The meaning of "dadî" in our language Fulani is "safety" [*al-najah*]." By glossing his maternal grandmother's name, Kamara introduces an awareness of linguistic and even cultural difference into a text that is otherwise a statement about a timeless and placeless normative Islam. "Our language Fulani," written in Arabic, speaks to a reservoir of meaning that the author has access to and ushers into the text but that likely evades would-be readers if they are familiar only with the language of composition. The philological treatment reflects an attempt to translate a proper name.[34] Sometimes this works from language to language. Bonhomme conveniently becomes Goodman, just as Dadi felicitously becomes Najah, which is also a feminine name in Arabic. However, the translation of the proper noun into English here is unhappily awkward. Kamara does the same thing further up his matriline with the oldest female ancestor, Golgol Samba. "The meaning of 'Golgol' is a diminutive of *galgol*, a bird with an excellent voice and long in the neck that the Arabs call *al-ʿandalīb* [nightingale]." This time we get an Arabic gloss of the proper name but with reference to Arabs as the differing group. The contrasts between these two juxtaposed philological moments are interesting for the ways they establish translation as relational in a multilingual context.

The first instance domesticates Pulaar in an Arabic-speaking context, whereas the second marks the Arab as a bearer of difference. For Kamara, domestication or differentiation is plausibly necessary, as the Senegal River Valley and the broader Senegambian and Sahelo-Saharan zones were linguistically diverse, even if Arabic maintained a privileged status as an acrolect because of its liturgical association.[35] While these are indeed translations, they are more the commentaries of the learned philologist than the expert conversions of meaning for distinct linguistic audiences. Shaykh Musa goes on to add that his female ancestor, the first woman in what was a line of men, was so named for the notoriety she had gained for her beautiful voice. The noticeably more extensive and detailed genealogical account of the matriline eclipses that of the patriline. Where the patriline is remembered only for the names of individuals, the matriline is remembered for what the names meant.

What is the significance of Shaykh Musa's inclusion of his genealogy in the introduction to his *tarjama*? How are we to read it, make sense of it? To present himself is to present his name in a chain of names. To be the subject of a *tarjama*, the presence of this chain suggests, one must be socially located in a line of descent among other lines of descent—in this instance, those of Yalt Jajji and Sawt Jajji. One must also be located in a spiritual chain, represented by the Sufi master Saʿad Buh, who had initiated him and named him a shaykh. These lineages are social facts that condition the representations to come. But Shaykh Musa seems ambivalent about these social facts, although he indulges in the philological asides that explain the meaning of the names of his mother's mothers. There is other information that he came across about the more distant branches of his matriline that situates him even more in social terms. An informant had supplied him with this information, but he does not include it for the sake of brevity and because, as it is often said in the tradition, "the genealogists are liars." Presumably Shaykh Musa's informant was a griot, a master of the oral tradition tasked with remembering social order and history. This editorial decision to be selective in his genealogy reflects a genealogical skepticism that Shaykh Musa has come to be known for—most famously, elaborated on in his *Precious Collection*.[36] He returns to this theme in the final chapter of his autobiography, thus forming a compelling parenthesis to frame the entire work. The relationship between the introduction and the last pages, then, is striking not simply because they both invoke a genealogy but also because they both emphasize the importance of doubting it.

Having gathered as much as we can from a close linear reading of the brief four-paragraph introduction to Shaykh Musa's autobiographical *The Announcement*, we are ready to offer some provisional responses to our opening questions: What is a text? And how might we read one? A text has an intention, whether or not we might confidently retrieve it. A text has an address, sometimes multiple addressees. A text is performative; that is, it does things with words. A text might confront the problem of translation modestly as an act of commentary. A text is a text by virtue of its relation to other texts—that is, by its generic identity—and is therefore social. This relationship highlights that a text always comes with a great deal beyond itself and should be read with these con-texts in mind. A text has warrants and reasons. A text is a reminder. A text provides a memory. Certainly, all texts are not all or even necessarily any of these things. But as our appreciation of *this* text—which is somehow both wholly generic and totally unrepresentative—has shown, at least one text does, making every statement in this paragraph true. In other words, texts exceed the communication of information. If we are willing to accept this as true, to accept as valid both the singularity and the excess of textuality, we might ourselves be developing a textual attitude. We might then be ready to read the textual life of Shaykh Musa in ways in which he himself approached it.

Beginnings of a Textual Life

When Kamara was a little boy, before he reached the age of responsibility, he left home to live with a teacher and his wife as if he were their son. One day a beggar visited the home. Standing outside the door, he asked for alms. Kamara's teacher told Kamara to take the man food. Naked, the small boy took the beggar a bowl of millet. When the young Kamara turned around to return to his childly affairs in the house, the beggar followed him in, pulling back the curtain that blocked the view of the home's interior from the outside. The beggar asked, "Who is this boy? Is he your son or your student?" Kamara's teacher replied that the boy was his student. The beggar admonished the teacher not to beat the boy, as was typical for Qurʾanic students receiving their first discipline of life, for the boy was a friend of God. The teacher scoffed at such a suggestion.[37]

This scene of election opens the body of Kamara's autobiography. It follows the brief justification for the potentially immodest act of writing such a text that refers to four towering spiritual figures—two of whom were close to home in both time and space and two of whom were a bit farther afield and represented a broader Sufi legitimacy—and the brief paragraph on Kamara's genealogy. Why did Kamara prioritize such a scene in the textual representation of his life? Placed so close to what is essentially the beginning of the text, immediately after the framing genealogical remarks, it initiates the discussion of the text's central theme of a saint's life with a vivid account of his own election. This is, in effect, the first proof of his argument put forward in the book: that Kamara was indeed a friend of God. This had been known, identified, and foretold by an enigmatic figure who was marginal to social life. The trope of a wandering dervish in tattered rags that is central to the unraveling of a plot is certainly a convention in Sufi literature.[38] This character type emerged from the historical practices of asceticism associated with classical Sufism, which according to one etymology associates the Sufi with $ṣūf$, or the roughly hewn wool that renunciants wore.[39] The social marginality of such a figure belies their position in a hidden spiritual hierarchy that Sufis have long theorized as providing God's guidance to humanity on a permanent basis.[40] The beggar's status as someone with insight was not apparent but rather something hidden and easy to miss. And from this position as someone valuable but hidden, he could immediately see who it was that brought him the cereal, when even the teacher could not.

What is this thing that even a teacher could not see, that only a person of spiritual insight could see? What does Kamara narrate in an autobiography whose chief purpose is to identify its author as a friend of God? It is an augury. Auguries (*bishara*, pl. *bisharat*) are objects of hagiographic representation, units of saintly narratives. They are the indications of good news, of glad tidings. They are signs that come from a degree of prophecy, or *announcements*. In the first chapter, Kamara relates these auguries in the context of his youth, education, and travels and records the indications of his election from his dreams and those of others. The story of the beggar opens this important chapter and establishes the force of his election as a *wali* (a friend of God or a Muslim saint).

While Kamara's status as a friend of God might be understood as the straightforward point he is making—the takeaway, if you will—it is worth noting the *textual* quality of this augury as set in this work. By textual, I mean the excessive significance explored earlier in the close reading of *The Announcement*'s introduction. I understand this scene to be chiefly concerned with representing what Kamara understands of the textual attitude: the patient pursuit of insight, the looking into the meaning of signs in the text of creation.[41] We might consider this with two different literary frameworks in mind: Sufi poetics and ancestral African narrative.

Sufi hermeneutics relies on the distinction between the apparent or manifest (*ẓāhir*) and the inward or hidden (*bāṭin*). Interpretation becomes a matter of looking into what is on the surface of things in order to go beyond or beneath to find what is hidden inside. In much of Sufi literature, the image of the veil or the curtain becomes an important metaphor for that which separates the apparent and the hidden.[42] In his magnum opus on the doctrines and practices of the Tijaniyya Sufi order, the Senegalese Tijani leader Shaykh Ibrahim Niasse uses, for example, the metaphor in the title *Kāshif al-Ilbās*. According to the translator Zachary Wright, this title literally means the removal of clothing or garb but is understood by his disciples as referring to *al-iltibas* (confusion).[43] This play on words allows Niasse to deploy a core metaphor in Sufi literature while describing his objective in writing in the polemically charged context of Sufi and anti-Sufi debate. The

Sufi path and its techniques of self-cultivation through the annihilation of the ego become an important means of "lifting the veil." That the beggar, a conventional representation of the classical ascetic Sufi, passes the curtain that separated the outside of the house from the inside symbolizes this capacity to gain insight, to look into the real but hidden nature of things. Outside the house, the boy is just a boy, but inside he is revealed as a friend of God. The use of Sufi imagery in this augury, read in its generic context, shows that it is not simply the fact of Kamara's election that matters but also its form. This *literary* quality of the *bishara* is most noticeable when read not just for its meaning but also with an appreciation of its form.

Furthermore, the story of the beggar allows us to clarify another feature of Kamara's textual attitude. It is contemplative. The depiction of a scene of election, a story with Sufi imagery itself, has apparent and hidden meanings. The layering of this significance amounts to an invitation for contemplation. If we read the text simply as a fact, an event that happened, we miss what it does: It compels readers to consider the meaning of the scene and how it is achieved. The contrast between the two figures in the scene is evocative of this feature. The teacher, who was the first to teach the boy Musa the alphabet and parts of the Qurʾan, contrasts with the beggar. The teacher represents superficial knowledge transmitted from one to another as if it were a command: Learn these letters, memorize these verses, give the man the food. The beggar represents deeper insight that cannot be learned, God-granted knowledge that is revealed through contemplation. Importantly, the insight offered by the beggar is rejected by the knowledgeable teacher, who scoffs when he is told that the boy is a friend of God. In representing his own election in such a way, Kamara invites readers to contemplate for themselves, rather than accepting what is observable only on the surface of things and passed on through transmission. This scene thus represents an image of an authentic African Sufism that offers a considerable contrast with the stereotype, as common today as it was in the colonial period, of adherents who were completely gullible when faced with charismatic figures. As a humanistic tradition, Sufism, as represented in the story of the beggar, is an important resource for cultivating the capacity for individual contemplation.

For our purposes, it is relevant to note that the scene presenting the story of the beggar does not itself include any images of writing, as Kamara's textual attitude is a habit of mind that defies any opposition between the written and the oral. Moreover, the textual attitude cannot be contained by any simple opposition of the Islamic and the ancestral. On the surface, we might think of this text as being obviously and quintessentially Islamic. That it is written, that it is written in Arabic, and that its main theme is the author's saintly status all suggest that the text tells us something about a Muslim context. It certainly does that. Implied in such a reading, though, is that the text does not simultaneously tell us much about the ancestral dimensions of such a context with its persistent presence of so-called African traditional religions. This augury as an opening plot device, however, resembles narrative conventions of West African oral traditions in areas under the influence of imperial Mali. If we take the paradigmatic epic of Sundiata as a case in point, or Kaidara, or even Kamara's compilation on the life of Hajj Umar Tal, for that matter, the augury, or the foretelling of what a special hero is to become, is a standard feature.[44] Importantly, the future is always present in a story in the signs of what will eventually be, providing the very possibility of narrative in areas influenced by this tradition. Where there is a long legacy of reading Islam out of Africa by virtue of scriptural presence and literacy as some kind of Hegelian exception or of defending African ancestral religion against the encroachments of the *longue durée* of Islamization and reform, Kamara's *Announcement* refuses to comply with the easy dichotomies of modern thought.

Recognizing both Sufi literary and ancestral narrative conventions, we can acknowledge Kamara's inheritance of at least two traditions—Islamic and Sahelian—of self-reckoning that had been in conversation for several hundred years. Since at least the eleventh century, Muslims maintained a presence on the banks of the Senegal River, often forming semiautonomous communities that offered specialized services to rulers in trade, diplomacy, divination, and worship. As occupational specialists, they fit into the caste-like social structure that had characterized the lands of imperial Mali since the thirteenth century.[45] The system of endogamous occupational groups included griots, weavers, hunters, and servants. Each group maintained its own sets of practices and emphasized certain beliefs over others. For much of this history, then, Islam constituted one form of life among others. In the courts of rulers, Muslim scholars grew very familiar with griots, and griots became very familiar with Muslim scholars. Each group knew much about the other's methods of reckoning, stylistic conventions, and repertoires. Even as their oral performances privileged the spoken word, griots were familiar with Arabic writing, and some would eventually integrate it into their work. With the revolutions that swept West Africa from the seventeenth century on, Islam changed from being one form of life among others to being the paradigmatic form of life on which society would be organized. As a result, griots Islamized oral tradition, and Muslim scholars, reflecting their own societies, took on features of those societies in their work, even as they often maintained and even sharpened their commitments to renewing an Islamic normativity. The historian Shamil Jeppie has shown that by the twentieth century, griots and Muslim scholars in places such as northern Mali maintained close relationships and sometimes collaborated.[46] So the very exemplars of primordial African orality were at least sometimes conversant with written literary traditions, just as the Muslim scholars, as representatives of the written word in West African societies, reflected a social world profoundly influenced by an ancestral heritage.[47]

My argument here is not that West African Islam was syncretic. I am less concerned with the conventional preoccupations of defining religion than I am interested in how the diversity of resources for meaning making have come to shape a West African textual attitude. Against a proclivity to view African Muslim literacy as an exception, I insist that the textual attitude is not simply Muslim or a product of a written culture per se. Rather, as an orientation toward knowledge, the textual attitude reflects a long-held symbiosis. It is not unique to Muslim West Africa or even to Muslim contexts more broadly. Rather, the textual attitude is the classical orientation toward knowledge that has not originated in a particular religion or place but that has developed along different trajectories globally. The first augury in Kamara's autobiography reflects this textually inflected preoccupation with contemplation that developed from both ancestral African and Islamic African thought in his deployment of an oral traditional narrative convention in a written argument for his friendship with and proximity to God. To read Kamara appreciatively is to understand how he made sense of the world through contemplation and textual study.

A Marvelous Memory

The boy who would become Shaykh Musa maintained a peculiar relationship to study. He describes himself in *The Announcement* as having a prodigious memory. He needed only a glance at the charcoal etchings on a wooden board, the iconic medium of instruction in Muslim West Africa, to memorize the sacred writing. And when older students received a lesson on an advanced topic and were not able to copy down what the instructor had said or when they did not understand what they themselves had written, they would come to the young boy, and he would repeat what the teacher said or meant. He remembered what he heard, even if what was said was not intended for him. Whether it was speech or script, whether he heard it or saw it, Kamara had a gift for retaining transmitted knowledge in the form of words.

Such a capacity to remember has long been a deeply cherished skill in his geographic and cultural context. In Muslim West Africa, a steadily growing proportion of children over the centuries has been introduced to knowledge by memorizing the signs, their sounds, and their correspondence in divine script.[48] One of our earliest accounts of this comes from Ibn Battuta, who visited the empire of Mali in the late medieval period, after Mansa Musa's gilded pilgrimage to Mecca. Ibn Battuta observed that memorization of the Qur'an was such an important undertaking that religious teachers would shackle their own children who neglected their lessons.[49] Memorization of at least some scripture is a religious obligation necessary for the proper conduct of ritual prayer. In the process of fulfilling that obligation, students acquired literacy. The most gifted students devoted themselves to hundreds of hours of recitation of verses written on wooden boards by vigilant teachers who were ready to correct even the slightest error. The duration of this approach to education—which was folded into the struggles of everyday life, including working and securing food, attending to personal hygiene, and fulfilling social roles and responsibilities—ensured that learning was not an isolated affair but rather resembled an apprenticeship for life. Such devotion of both pupil and teacher ideally culminated with complete memorization of the holy text and the formation of a foundational relationship between the two. The student was then able to recite the venerable word from memory, thereby becoming a vehicle for scripture, a preserver of the recitation, a *ḥāfiẓ al-Qur'an*. In this way, memorization became a form of writing, a fixing of the holy text in the body of the believer.[50] This accomplishment was the foundation for all other scholarly pursuits. Some students might continue on to more advanced studies of the Qur'an itself, such as the art of recitation or interpretation. Others might proceed to study aspects of the law, the life of the Prophet, or perhaps language. Whatever the path taken, the study of the Qurʾan and its memorization were the paradigm of all subsequent study, and its performance in speech or writing has long ranked as one of the highest devotional acts.

As in the practice of Qurʾanic education, students progressed slowly through more advanced topics, focusing on a single text at a time. The teacher recited the work in question and sometimes provided commentary or clarified ambiguity. Each student copied the dictation and recited it back to the teacher, who corrected any errors, until they were satisfied with the student's recitation. Having successfully heard, written, and recited the text, the student was certified in this knowledge. Such license entailed the permission to teach the text, both what was written and what was said about what was written, to others. In this system, which was simultaneously oral and written, memorizing the Qurʾan constituted the first step on the scholarly path. More importantly, it was the paradigm for subsequent study, ensuring the self-regulation of the educational system.

And yet Kamara never finished the hallmark but elementary intellectual achievement of memorizing the Qurʾan in full. "I never completed in memorizing [the Qurʾan]," he says, almost in passing.[51] What might this apparently self-evident and seemingly transparent statement mean? It will be helpful to consider the ontological status of the Qurʾan, in addition to appreciating it as the principal source of knowledge. The Qurʾan is but one name of the uncreated speech of God. It is also referred to as the Book, or *al-Kitāb*. These are names of the scriptural text, not the specific material medium through which it might be transmitted. A particular material manifestation of the divine speech, of scripture, in codex form is called a *muṣḥaf*, an Arabic word whose etymology goes back to East African Abyssinia.[52] The word *Qurʾan* literally means, as opposed to referring to, the reading or the recitation. A verbal noun of the root *q-r-ʾ* (to read or to recite), the name of scripture comes from the first *aya* (verse) to be revealed to the Prophet Muhammad: "[1] Recite in the name of thy Lord who Created, [2] created man from a blood clot. [3] Recite! Thy Lord is most noble [4] Who taught by the Pen, [5] taught man that which he knew not."[53] There are several doctrinal reasons why "recite" is preferred over "read" in the translation of these scriptures. The Prophet Muhammad is unlettered, and when commanded to "*Iqraʾ!*," he first balks at the command because he does not know how. Then the angel Jibril instructs him. What I am interested in is the polysemy of the word *iqraʾ* and how that ambiguity connects the written and oral and ties both to knowledge. The Qurʾan is a divine speech act that instantiates itself as a sacred text that transcends its medium of transmission. Whether this speech is inscribed in the hearts of believers through repetition and practice or written on wooden boards, mausoleums, or paper, the recitation/reading of this command (*iqraʾ*) maintains this dual character of text and activity. In this tradition, memorization is a mode of writing, as it fixes and reiterates the fixing of the text. Moreover, there is no classical linguistic theory that distinguishes a sound and the letter that represents that sound in writing. The phoneme and the grapheme are one. To have never completed this fundamental and foundational task of writing the Qurʾan in his person, despite his prodigious memory, is significant.

Whether or not we appreciate the irony that Kamara has a photographic and phonographic memory and yet never memorizes the Qurʾan in full, this section of his autobiography documents his textual attitude. This unexpected admission comes in the first chapter of *The Announcement*, where he gives a detailed accounting of his intellectual development. He mentions all his teachers, what he studied with them, and where. He is precise in listing which chapters of which volumes of which works that made up the curriculum of a West African Muslim scholar.[54] Khalil's Abridgement on Islamic law and Abi Zayd's Epistle on epistemology are just some of the titles. He seems to have specialized in works on language and literature, such as works on grammar by the classic litterateur Hariri (1054–1122), the author of *Maqāmāt*.[55] Kamara describes the process of his education as "listening" to the text from his teacher. That Kamara did not complete the task of memorizing the Qurʾan and admits to it just after mentioning the texts he did study is unexpected.

Why would Kamara include such a detail? The obvious answer, when read with a hermeneutics of faith, is that he is honest and sincere, and when the task is to say what he studied, to omit the fact that he had not memorized the Qurʾan would be dishonest and inconsistent with his character.[56] Still, as a reader of similar texts—including Hajj Umar's *Book of Lances*; the educational excursus of the great political theorist and intellectual of the Sokoto Caliphate, Abdullahi dan Fodio: and the teaching text by the enslaved Muslim in Sapelo Island, Georgia—I am struck that without "I never completed memorizing [the Qurʾan]," we might presume that Kamara had accomplished this elementary step.[57] How else would he have been able to become the scholar that he was? Given that he had such an incredible memory, we would assume that he memorized the Qurʾan, if not as a child, then later when he became more serious in his commitment to study. This expectation forms one of the many prejudgments with which we approach such texts. It presumes that the normative is normal and provides a template of understanding, indeed of reading, before we have even opened the text.[58]

What makes Kamara's relationship to study even more interesting is that he maintained an intellectual independence. In explaining the reason he did not do well in his studies, he states that when he was young, he was distracted and not very serious. In the end, he did not learn much from his teachers. Instead, God granted him understanding in his own independent reading. This is remarkable because Kamara comes from an intellectual culture in which to study was to study with someone. It is often said among Sufis that "he who has no shaykh, Satan is his shaykh." To read independently was a moral hazard, as misunderstanding could lead the believer astray. Kamara does mention elsewhere his spiritual guide, Shaykh Saʿad Buh, discussed further in the following chapter, but this shaykh does not seem to be a teacher in a literal sense. This independence of mind is confirmed in the colonial surveillance file on Kamara, which notes that he had many disagreements with his various shaykhs and was known to have switched spiritual guides on several occasions.[59] In effect, Kamara's textual attitude, irreducible to the written or oral, developed from a particular relationship to knowledge granted, first, by God to him as an individual and, second, by immersion in the oral and written dimensions of the Islamic discursive tradition that nourished him. His textual attitude conditioned the possibility of a conversation with colonial philologists whose humanism prompted them to generate a native literature through a process of partial translation.

In this chapter, I first theorized the textual attitude as an orientation to the world disciplined by philological practice. Importantly, this theorization relies on my own performance of this attitude, in which I closely read with appreciation Kamara's textual life. These questions animated this reading: What is a text? And how might we read one? I chose Kamara's autobiographical *Announcement* because it provides both the content and the form of Kamara's textual attitude and illustrates the textual dimensions of his life. Reading it revealed that it is both wholly generic and totally unrepresentative.

My understanding of philology is neither as the technical discipline that is ancillary to the activity of the professional historian nor as the antiquated soft science that leverages knowledge of textual artifacts for elaborating and projecting religio-racial hierarchy into the world. I understand philology to be bigger and bolder than that, a human tradition across historical time and cultural difference—as indeed the love of study, a vitally human orientation toward the world. "Study" here refers to the contemplation of meaningfully composed texts, whether written or oral. This broader understanding of philology has obvious references in Erich Auerbach and Edward Said, but it is also inspired by the indisciplined curiosity of Malcolm X and the traditionalist commentary of Kamara. In appreciating the introduction to Kamara's *The Announcement* with a linear close reading, I practiced this philology to cultivate my own textual attitude, the orientation to making sense through reading.

Second, I considered the textual life of Kamara through close readings of two scenes of saintly election in his autobiography to understand the sources of his textual attitude. I argued that his philological practice drew on an intimate knowledge of Islamic and ancestral oral textual traditions but that it was not these traditions themselves that provided Kamara's ultimate understanding. Indeed, the beginning of his autobiography proposes that textual transmission is the necessary but insufficient means to knowledge. His individual contemplation and independent reading, not traditional transmission, were how he realized his friendship with God. These ideas made him peculiar for his context in ways that have not been fully appreciated in his reception.

All three passages I considered in this chapter, then, suggest an ethical dimension of the textual attitude. It is in the performance of philological practice that the subject develops a textual attitude that orients them toward the world of experience. The implication is that there is an important edificatory purpose of the classical textual attitude as exemplified by Kamara. Such a claim is by no means original in any absolute sense, only radical for its insistence on who I have identified as exemplifying this purpose. I locate the classical textual attitude not in the ancient Mediterranean but in early twentieth-century West Africa. My point is only to remind us of this religious meaning of reading, and of philology, as we use texts and dreams of Kamara's young adulthood to make sense of his saintly subjectivity.

TWO

A Degree of Prophecy

MANY YEARS LATER, after a full and prodigious life as a scholar, Shaykh Musa Kamara would reflect on what was intellectually the most important moment of his career: the moment when he abandoned youthful diversion for serious study. As discussed in the previous chapter, he showed signs that he had a remarkable intellectual ability and a strong memory and that he would become one of the close friends of God. However, he did not exert himself in the memorization of foundational texts or follow the direction of teachers. In fact, he regularly started and stopped working through texts and ended relationships with the teachers who taught him those texts. He had a mind of his own.[1] This lack of clear direction would come to an end when he was visited in his sleep by the prophets Ibrahim and Muhammad.

In this chapter, I explore the two forms of significance that shaped Kamara's life: texts and dreams. With the expression "forms of significance," I mean three things: (1) the shape in and around (the form) to which meaning coheres; (2) something that bears an importance that distinguishes the form's relative value; and (3) a particular type of either meaning or importance. The importance of texts, whether reading, writing, collecting, or discussing them, is obvious for a prolific author such as Kamara. They constitute the working material of an intellectual life. Most academic production about this remarkable scholar who enjoyed a rich reputation during the colonial period offers a list of the texts and genres—that is, the established forms—in which he worked.[2] Indeed, he presents himself in his autobiography as the author, and reader, of many texts. He includes their titles, some of their themes, and even endorsements for his own compositions by his Muslim peers and colonial correspondents alike. This textual dimension of his career has largely defined the attention he has received by academic scholarship. As I discuss in chapter 6, the resurgence of interest in him in the present, embedded in a wider interest in African textuality, particularly in Arabic script, continues the understanding of Kamara with reference to his texts[3]—and reasonably so.

However, dreams, as another form of significance, an important and meaning-bearing experience, also helped Kamara define himself. Interwoven with a listing of the works he authored in his autobiography, he includes accounts of dreams that he had or that others had about him. Scholarship has generally made less room for making sense of Kamara's dreams than his texts despite the fact they receive proximal treatment by Kamara.[4] One explanation for this omission is the difficulty of assimilating the intangible, immaterial, and subjective in classically historicist narratives that string together only verifiable facts. These facts are systematically established by a skeptical orientation toward claims in what has been described as a hermeneutics of suspicion.[5] In other words, dreams cannot be verified like events, which are objectively experienced by many parties. The inherent subjectivity of the dream would require a hermeneutics of faith, or at least an agnostic one, that takes the dream account at its word.[6] Another explanation is the diminished relative value placed on dreams in secular-modern modes of thought compared to Kamara's context, in which dreams were valued as a derivative but connecting form of prophecy.[7] Making space for Kamara's dreams, then, is a good strategy for understanding his life and his texts. This is especially true given the fact that academic research has yet to identify many sources for Kamara's life until around 1912, when he enters the colonial archive. The first dream Kamara shares is believed to have occurred sometime in the mid-1880s, allowing us to extend the narrative beyond the reach of the colonial-cum-national archive. The period between 1885 and 1912 was pivotally important, including the end of a series of jihads, the second wave of French military conquest, and the establishment of hybrid colonial-Islamic institutions alongside colonial infrastructures that reorganized space, reoriented patterns of extraction and accumulation, and redefined social life. Accordingly, attending to Kamara's dreams in addition to his texts allows us to narrate with texture—that is, with the sense of meaningfulness with which he lived.

While dreams constitute an underappreciated form of significance for Kamara's life and context that should be considered as evidence, their proximity to the discussion of texts in Kamara's autobiography raises a theoretical question: What is the relationship between texts and dreams in Kamara's self-understanding? I argue that Kamara's saintly subjectivity was shaped by texts and dreams as closely connected forms of significance that organized human beings genealogically. By "saintly subjectivity," I mean the sense of self as a *walī* (a Muslim friend of God). I develop this argument by first performing a close reading of a dream account that opens Kamara's *The Life of Hajj Umar*, a biography written in 1935 about Hajj Umar Tal, the militant Tijani scholar who transformed the religious, intellectual, and political landscape of the western Sahel.[8] I interpret this dream to make explicit a theory of text as disclosure that augments reality and as the mediation of presence and absence. This understanding of text as disclosure helps us better apprehend the textual life and afterlife of Kamara and their relationship to the fate of the humanities. Next, I apply this understanding to passages of Kamara's autobiography, *The Announcement*, that describe a pivotal dream that guided the course of his life and stimulated his development as an author well before his encounters with surveillance ethnography and colonial philology. Finally, I show the extent to which the disclosure of genealogical relationships as a structure of inheritance was a defining feature of both texts and dreams.

Texts and Dreams

For readers disciplined by the mental habits of the secular modern, the opening lines of Kamara's *The Most Delicious of the Sciences and the Tastiest of the News in the Life of Hajj Umar* are discomfiting:

> In the name of God, the Compassionate, the Merciful. O God, bless our master Muhammad and grant him salvation. Praise God who opened to his *awliyā'* the doors of his blessing and benefits and his most excellent of prayers and his acceptance upon the master of the people of his earth and his heavens, our master Muhammad, and upon his family, and his companions, and upon his children,

and upon his wives. And after: Musa bin Ahmad [Kamara speaking of himself], may God forgive his sins of the heart and the body, has chosen to serve the Shaykh al-Hajj Umar (may God be satisfied with him) by mentioning some of his *manāqib* and *karāmāt* to get him closer to God and hoping to return to him his *barakāt* and his *nafaḥāt*. Indeed, it was he (may God almighty be satisfied with him) that was my shaykh in my sleep, such that he taught me words from the Arabic language in a group of his pupils. At that time, I went to visit my shaykh, the shaykh Saʿad Buh (may God Almighty be satisfied with him and all his loved ones). I told said shaykh about this vision. So, he said to me "this Shaykh al-Hajj Umar is a saint without doubt. God almighty has given you Umar's hidden inheritance, if it be the will of God." And so, I saw the Shaykh al-Hajj Umar during the time I went to his son Agibu in Dingiray. I stayed there around a month. The shaykh came to me in my sleep every night. At that time, I was 24 years old. Perhaps these visions are what make me so close to him now.[9]

Beginning in the name of God, as one who has surrendered to God should, Kamara uses a specialist vocabulary that is at once poetic and cosmic. After these initial prayers and blessings bestowed on the Prophet, his companions, his family, and the close friends of God whom Christians would call saints, he introduces the subject of the text and explains his motivations for writing it. "Indeed," the polymathic Kamara writes of Hajj Umar Tal, the spiritual center of gravity of the preceding generation, "[his] shaykh in [his] sleep such that [Umar] taught [him] words from the Arabic language with a group of his pupils." In effect, Kamara begins by recounting a dream. Without knowing much about the text in question or its context, readers are, whether they know it or not, immediately faced with a dilemma of interpretation.[10] Will they interpret what is to follow faithfully? Or will they read with suspicion? Will they believe that Hajj Umar appeared to Kamara in his sleep? Or will they have to soothe their unease and uncertainty with the powers of explanation? Either decision about how to read such an incredible event will generate a distinct reading that will then generate other dilemmas of interpretation. Either choice or series of choices, conscious or otherwise, might be made for legitimate reasons, but it remains a choice. Choosing how to read this text using the text itself, then, is far from given, and the multiplicity of possible readings adds to the unease with which we begin—if we let it.

Sitting with the unease produced by the conflict when our habits of mind are confronted by another habit of mind is not so easy. This is particularly true for informed readers, who come to the text already familiar with the vocabulary, the formulas deployed, the references made, the individuals discussed, and so on. They already know how to read—or so they believe. They can quickly make sense of the text by way of other texts in the genre or tradition. Expert readers thus quickly identify the text as being wholly generic, characterized as it is by one of the most common narrative devices of Islamic hagiographical literature.[11] Their "making sense" relies on a sense of subject-area expertise to quiet any disquiet that may have crept up due to the invocation of a dream in this serious religious text.

Classical historians might disregard Kamara's account of his dream altogether. They would consider the dream unverifiable, an imaginary event that was not real. They would be more interested in what *The Life of Hajj Umar* offered by way of facts and figures, people and places. According to them, the text's introduction offers autobiographical details about the author. From it, they could glean that Kamara knew Shaykh Saʿad Buh, a notable Mauritanian religious personality known for his collaboration with the French;[12] that when he was twenty-four, Kamara traveled widely in the region and specifically through Dinguraye, the garrison town where Hajj Umar began his jihad; and so forth. Such details and sequence would be helpful for historians interested in reconstructing Kamara's life. But its utility in writing the history of Umar's life would limit this text to being a secondary source at best, removed as it was from Umar's death by some seventy years. The absence of this text in the definitive and exhaustive history of the Umarian movement by historian David Robinson is a case in point.[13] This observation is not so much a critique of a sterling example of professional African history as it is an observation that the rules of classical history have left this text, much like Kamara's dream that begins it, unread. If overly historicist readers picked up *The Life of Hajj Umar* at all, Kamara's dream would likely be ignored.

Read contextually, Kamara's dream might be appreciated at least for its historical irony. Although Kamara was born in 1864, the year of Hajj Umar's death, and the first third of his life was characterized by a degree of insecurity, he lived mostly in a period of relative peace, the so-called Pax Gallica, following French conquest and the establishment of French West Africa in 1895. Growing social inequality and political fragmentation that had resulted from the global slave trade and climatic change had been the conditions that defined an age of Islamic revolutions since the seventeenth century.[14]

Coteries of Muslim scholars and merchants began to assume political leadership and establish states around the principles of Islamic governance for all of society, whereas they had occupied only a circumscribed space since the eleventh century. From the seventeenth century, jihad became a new grammar for collective action, first directed against traditional elites, particularly those practicing ancestral African religions or accused of allowing ancestral practices to flourish despite their profession of the oneness of God, and eventually against European expansion. But this process folded back on itself with Hajj Umar's messianic movement, bringing two Muslim political bodies (the Umarian Tukulor Empire and Masina) into conflict,[15] creating a general regional insecurity. Kamara had experienced firsthand the aftermath of the waves of war that had left the region insecure and depopulated.[16] In the 1920s, he wrote approvingly of the impact of French governance and even wrote against the validity of jihad, citing Umar's jihad as the paradigmatic case of a jihad without prophetic leadership that resulted in the loss of Muslim life.[17] That he should be visited by Umar in a dream, given this context, is ironic to say the least. Moreover, the fact that Shaykh Saʿad Buh, who argued against his own brother's call for a jihad against the French, was the interpreter of the dream and said that God had granted Kamara Umar's "hidden inheritance" is especially curious. But readers can appreciate this historical irony only when the opening of *The Life of Hajj Umar* is read through context.

Applying a rhetorical strategy common for the genre of saintly narratives, Kamara uses his account of the dream to present himself as a direct student of one of the most consequential figures of nineteenth-century West Africa, a scholar whose written works and acts, miraculous marvels, and military maneuvers reshaped the region. This approach authorizes Kamara to write on a subject with whom he had no familial or direct intellectual links in a tradition that often favored such claims of descent in authorizing a person's speech on that subject. If the opening gambit of the text presents what is to follow as a service to Hajj Umar, the account of the dream provides the rationale. Such an opening is not particular to this text but is a common convention in writings about the friends of God. It is the trace of a standard textual practice in which visions and visitations are the key material with which narratives are composed.[18] Read in this way, Kamara's dream is simply a rhetorical device that allows the author to begin.

Critical readers might go even further in rendering Kamara's dream into familiar templates. They might argue that the dream is a classic case of mystification. The Marxist reader would say that the dream is a dulling distraction from the clerical exploitation of the peasantry whose labor provides the surplus value that makes Kamara's writing a possibility. The feminist reader might remark that women are absent from the dream and suggest that the dream's function is to affirm and naturalize patriarchal domination. And the psychoanalytic reader would seize on the dream account with glee as evidence of the symbolic order. To be sure, such caricatures illustrate vulgar forms of these critical theories, but they nevertheless demonstrate the point that we are confronted with a multiplicity of possible readings. They join some of the many incantatory explanations that informed readers might use to dispel the marvelousness of the text and render it comprehensible for secular sensibilities.

It is all too easy to dismiss Kamara's framing as a convenience, a convention, or a casual rhetorical gesture that allows him to begin.[19] Doing so enables us to get on with the work of processing the information the text has to offer. It is, after all, so obviously a text about the life of a friend of God. Reading it allows us to know something about such personalities or perhaps this person. We can rely on the one-to-one relationship between what the text says and what it means and can produce a reliable monograph on the topic as professional readers might. And thus, the responsible work of representation is accomplished.

But I want to pursue the slightly more challenging option and to take Kamara at his word—for a time at least. Instead of evaluating the truth of his claim that Umar came to him in a dream, I ask what Kamara's account of instruction and the text that is a product of that instruction teach us about the nature of reading and the possible methods of reading similar texts. After all, Kamara's introduction itself thematizes the work of interpretation. After he reports the dream, he writes that he described the dream to his shaykh, Saʿad Buh, who shares with him the dream's meaning: Kamara has received Hajj Umar's hidden inheritance. For Sufis such as Kamara, Hajj Umar Tal, and Saʿad Buh, the dichotomy of the apparent and the hidden is an all-encompassing framework for understanding. The world of mundane experience hides a far greater reality. ʿAli ibn Abi Talib—who was a cousin and son-in-law of the Prophet Muhammad and the fourth and final of the rightly guided caliphs and who is often claimed by Sufis to have been the first practicing Sufi—is remembered as describing this relationship in the following terms: "People are asleep as long as they are alive, when they die, they wake up."[20] The Sufi practices a methodology of peeling back the layers of what is apparent to access the truth of what is hidden. It requires a long and laborious path to see things as they are and not as they appear to be. Because of the contrast between the apparent and the hidden, it is only the true Sufi who can understand apparent contradictions and paradoxes. They, in fact, are in their bodies and in their persons a *barzakh* (a mediating bridge between what is hidden and what is apparent).

Read in this way, the dream in *The Life of Hajj Umar*, much like the text as a whole, is a disclosure. Let us return to the brief line of the text that concerns us here: "Indeed, it was [Hajj Umar] ... that was my shaykh in my sleep, such that he taught me words from the Arabic language in a group of his pupils." If we approach this statement with the question of its veracity, we leave it with one of two possibilities: Hajj Umar visited Kamara in a dream, or Hajj Umar did not visit Kamara. It is either true, or it is false. But if we suspend the question of veracity and approach the statement with the question of its meaning (in the sense of authorial intention, in the structuralist sense of the statement's relation to all the other statements in the text, and in the sense of the understanding that I bring to the text as a reader), we have a much greater and more interesting range of possibilities to consider.

For example, we might first note that for an account of a dream experience, there are very few details about what the dreamer saw, heard, or felt. We have some concrete nouns (*shaykh, me, words, pupils*) and a syntax that forms a relationship among them in the action of instruction. But as much as the sentence makes explicit what is reported to have happened, it leaves much about the dream implicit. Where did the instruction take place? How many people were present? Was the instruction purely oral, with the words of Arabic being transmitted from heart to heart? Or was the instruction conducted with a codex, with writing on a wooden tablet, or with writing in the sand? Was Kamara singled out in this instruction while Umar's disciples watched in a circle? Or was Kamara integrated into the rank and file of the students? The explicit statement of the author leaves room for the imagination of his readers. And when I read the sentence, my mind brings up the image formed by other descriptions of the traditional educational milieu and my own experience of seeing such scenes where an aged teacher sits before a young man, poring over a physical text, and pointing out words and discussing their meaning. If this image is even remotely accurate for the parts left unstated by Kamara, there are two implications. The first is that Kamara saw or heard, or saw and heard, an Arabic word in his dream that few others have seen or heard, as they have not experienced the dream. Given the sacredness of the Arabic language and the rarity of the word that Umar shares with Kamara, we are to understand that this is a powerful word hidden from most people. Kamara could have stated what the word was, but he leaves it hidden from the readers. The dream is thus an incomplete disclosure. The readers know there is a special, hidden word without knowing what it is. It is a secret.

The second implication of the statement is that unlike those of us who are limited to the physical temporal world in which either presence or absence is immediate and obvious, Kamara is in communication with and learns from people despite their location in time or space. The dream mediates the physical facts of presence and absence and augments physical reality for the dreamer. In this way, the dream helps us visualize a feature long associated with both written and oral textuality. To read, recite, or perform a text is to be with, learn from, and be touched by others who are not physically present.[21] While some meanings of the dream, such as the identity of a powerful word that Hajj Umar shares with Kamara, remain hidden and elusive, other meanings, such as Kamara's status as Umar's inheritor, are made apparent and manifest. The key insight of this Sufi text, then, is that as forms of significance, the nature of text in the most capacious sense and of dreams is one of incomplete disclosure.

In other words, we should read Kamara's *Life of Hajj Umar*, as we have here, and his autobiographical *The Announcement*, as we have in the previous chapter, not simply to learn about the putative subjects of those texts (Hajj Umar Tal and Shaykh Musa Kamara, respectively) but also to think about the problem of reading in general and of reading African Sufi texts in particular. In a moment in which university-based academics interested in Africa seek out decolonial approaches to thinking about Africa, this book insists on the value of slow, close, and multiple readings of texts, as it does for the work of the imagination. I argue that there is more than one way to read. Kamara's text, like the Arabic and Arabic-script texts that in recent years have become increasingly visible and subject to academic attention, is no exception. These multiple readings are essential to the work of understanding texts—and also dreams.

A Prophetic Dream

One dream that Kamara reports in his autobiographical *Announcement* stands out as particularly significant. Immediately following a discussion of the texts he studied as a part of his education but before presenting a list of texts that he himself composed, Kamara includes a collection of dream accounts. Some of these were dreams he himself experienced, which are generically typical. Others were reported to him by people who had experienced dreams in which he appeared. The inclusion of these dreams is less standard in the autobiographical form.[22] They are dreams in which prophets appear and other marvelous and hidden things are disclosed. The dreamers include one of his wives, his students, and his friends. They appear in no obvious order in the text, but they all support the overriding claim of *The Announcement* that Kamara is a *walī*. The dreams, as precious visions divinely inspired, are auguries that identify Kamara as a channel through which the emanations of God's grace from the invisible realm are manifested in the temporal world. In other words, the dream accounts testify to Kamara's status as an inheritor of the prophets and of the derivatives of prophecy. This status as a *walī* is not to be confused with prophethood itself. A saintly disclosure is to revelation what a marvel is to a miracle. The first of each pair is a derivative of the second insofar as it is similar, and yet the second maintains its theological distinction.

One dream account stands out for the role it plays in Kamara's actualization as a *walī*—that is, for giving shape to his saintly subjectivity. The dream is significant in both the sense that it provided him the meaning of his life and the sense that it was important. At the age of either twenty-one or twenty-two, he found himself, while sleeping, in the home of the Prophet Ibrahim, remembered in Qurʾanic stories for establishing the houses of monotheistic worship and having unshakeable faith. The text of this dream account is as follows:

> I saw while dreaming [*fīl-manām*] as if I had come to live in a house where the Prophet of God, our father Ibrahim, had appeared as if he were my father in old age. I greeted him. He said to me: "We thought that you were taking a path [*tariqan*] other than ours or you were pursuing a course [*taslik massalakan*] that was not ours either." I became anxious with this remark. . . . I said to him: "Oh Beloved of the Merciful, what is the path that I have taken and that is not yours?"

> I looked at him with reverence as he posed himself before me. It was at that moment that the Messenger of God [Prophet Muhammad] entered the room. Our father Ibrahim got off the bed and left without me knowing when or how or much less where he went. The Prophet, then sat down in the room next to the door facing me and asked: "What did this man say to you?" I said that he said to me: "You do not think I am taking your path." He started to reassure me, saying "you are safe. There is nothing wrong with you." He continued to say this until I sensed that I faced him as he approached me.[23]

We might first note that this dream represents Kamara as belonging to the same line as the most important prophets. "Our father Ibrahim," a title uttered in the liturgy of Muslim prayers, is designated as Kamara's own father. Kamara—who we should recall shares a name with the Prophet Musa, a descendant of Ibrahim in sacred history—finds himself in the house of Ibrahim. We should also recall that the house that Ibrahim built for his wife Hajar and son Ishmael was the Ka'aba.

Kamara's dream, as a scene of election, introduces readers to several affects that will come to define Kamara's saintly subjectivity. By "scene of election," I refer to the emplotted units of hagiographic representation. The motivating affects from this dream are anxiety, reassurance, and proximity. In the dream, Ibrahim appears worried about Kamara's direction in life, as fathers are wont to do, transmitting their own concerns to their children. But the Prophet Muhammad replaces Ibrahim, as he does in sacred history, and reassures the young Kamara. As a result, they face each other and draw closer and closer.[24] Where Kamara's sense of direction forms a question with the Prophet Ibrahim, it becomes clarified in the final sentence with the Prophet Muhammad. This increasing physical proximity of Kamara and the Prophet Muhammad is at once literal and figurative in its representation of *walāya*, a verbal noun whose generic meaning might be glossed as "closeness" but whose etymological use within the tradition signifies the state or condition of friendship with God, often through intercession.[25] It is literal in that the two find themselves facing one another; it is figurative in that this proximity has a whole host of consequences in the temporal world. Taken together, we might think of these affects of worry, reassurance, and proximity as forming a dialectic, in which the negative affect of human worry is counteracted by its antithesis of prophetic reassurance, which then synthesizes into proximity to God through the relationship with Muhammad. This dialectic is captured effectively in the title of Kamara's autobiography itself: *The Announcement of the Good News to the Fearful and Confused and His Reminder of the Breadth of the Mercy of God, the Generous Bestower*. Accordingly, we can say it is a key feature of Kamara's nascent saintly subjectivity.

As a *bishara* (an augury of election), the dream account bears a profound significance. We might distill the dream's significance in three ways, based on its formal, substantive, and functional meanings. The textual form of the dream account harnesses language to express something that was experienced and sensed, in large part, in images. Readers know the dream account is, in fact, a dream account by virtue of an explicit and implicit statement, by comparative conjunctions, and by a sense of disorientation and wonder. As for the explicit statement, Kamara writes that he "saw while dreaming." That the dream is a good dream divinely inspired, as opposed to a dream inspired by bad spirits (*ḥulm*) or a dream of a person's worries or wishes (*hadith nafsi*), is implicit by virtue of the tradition of dream interpretation based on a series of famous reports of hadith, or prophetic sayings. One of these reports is narrated by Abu Hurayra: "The Messenger of God, peace and blessings be upon him, said, 'When the end of time approaches, the dream of a believer can hardly be false. The dream of a believer is one of forty-six parts of prophethood and whatever is from prophethood cannot be false.'"[26] Because of Muhammad's presence, Kamara's dream is, in fact, a true dream, based on a hadith that attests to the impossibility of Satan taking the form of the Prophet.[27] Lastly, another hadith reports that while prophethood ended with Muhammad as the seal of prophecy, there remains something similar, as also reported by Abu Hurayra: "I heard Allah's Messenger saying, 'Nothing remains of prophethood except for things which give glad tidings [*mubashshirāt*].' They asked: 'What are these?' He replied: 'The true dream.'"[28] The dream account, then, is formally identified as a glad tiding or a true dream by the presence of the prophets. Furthermore, because the dream is divinely inspired, it is distinguished from prophecy only by degree and not by kind. Kamara's inclusion of the dream account establishes that as a friend of God, his dreams represent a degree, perhaps a very small one, of prophecy.

As for the syntactical form of the dream account, readers are alerted to the status of the dream as a dream by virtue of two comparative conjunctions. Kamara sees himself in the dream "as if" he had come to live in the

Prophet Ibrahim's house, and the Prophet Ibrahim appears "as if" he were Kamara's father in old age. These two conjunctions have a doubling effect in which a person or place is not simply themselves or itself but a shared form with other persons and places. The Prophet Ibrahim is not only the Prophet Ibrahim but also Kamara's father in the dream, thus visualizing the possibility of composite figures that can exist only in a dreamscape but that nevertheless connect distinct agents in the temporal world. Finally, readers know that they are reading a dream account by virtue of its sense of disorientation and wonder, induced by a string of adverbs. In the middle of this passage, the Prophet Ibrahim dramatically disappeared, and Kamara is left not knowing when, how, or where he went. This string expresses an ethereal quality characteristic of the dream experience in textual form. Together, these linguistic elements of explicit statement and implicit reference, comparative conjunctions, and disorienting adverbs give the dream account its formal meaning as a prophetic dream.

As the form of this dream account establishes the dream as divinely inspired, the substantive meaning of the dream deepens Kamara's connection to prophecy. All the action of the dream takes place in the Prophet Ibrahim's house—the home of monotheism, we might say. The domesticity of the setting suggests a sense of intimacy between Kamara and the two prophets. He appears as if he were a son of the prophets. I want to be careful here to highlight that the substantive meaning of the dream is not a symbolic meaning. The paternal relationship envisioned in the dream does not stand for something else but rather is literal. That Kamara appears as Ibrahim's son, converses with both Ibrahim and Muhammad, and senses close proximity to Muhammad means that he is indeed literally close to the prophets. Moreover, the matter explicitly discussed by Ibrahim is Kamara's path and course (*tariqa* and *massalik*). These are technical terms used by Sufis to refer to the method to achieve *maʿrifa* (gnosis, or experiential knowledge of the divine). This method includes accepting a master's guidance, reciting litanies at prescribed times, participating in spiritual retreat, and taking other ritualized actions that allow the Sufi to engage in a process of actualization, which presents many different challenges to overcome and stages of development to achieve. The substantive meaning of the dream, then, is that Kamara is a friend of God through the intercession of the Prophet Muhammad and therefore is a spiritual inheritor of the prophets.

While the dream account's formal and substantive meanings are closely aligned with a literal interpretation of Kamara's spiritual status beyond the text, its functional meaning deepens our understanding of Kamara's life *as a textual representation*. By this, I mean that the dream account represents an event in his life story: one that changes the shape and substance of time in its wake. Before and after the passage, as if they were a set of parentheses that sets the passage off from the rest of the text, are Kamara's statements that he had occupied his time with the amusements and games of youth. As a result of the dream event, he stops wasting his time with youthful diversion. Before the dream, he is a child; after the dream, he becomes an adult, one who takes responsibility for his own course. While the other dream accounts in the texts are rich in significance, they are simply marshaled as evidence of his election, as proof of his saintly status. They are not considered influencing actions. For this reason, we can determine that the dream that became a turning point in his life occurred sometime between 1885 and 1886. The prophetic dream marks a pivotal moment in the development of Kamara's saintly subjectivity.

In addition to being a dream event that allows for a subjective periodization of Kamara's life, the prophetic dream that Kamara reports functions narratologically as a motivation for his spiritual journey. However, as a young man still devoted to youthful diversion, he needs help in figuring out what the dream means. As a result, he strikes out to find a spiritual guide to make sure he is on the right path. While he has already traveled throughout the middle Senegal River Valley and the southern Sahara Desert for his elementary, secondary, and higher education, his need for a deeper knowledge takes him to the coast for the first time. In Ndar, or what the French called Saint-Louis after the small island in the middle of their own capital, Muslim scholars, Sufi masters, and merchants of all kinds maintained a foothold as a center of learning and trade. This is certainly the case for none other than Shaykh Saʿad Buh, a leader of the Fadiliyya network of the Qadiri Sufi order discussed further in the following section. Buh is less a teacher to Kamara than a guide on the path of spiritual contemplation that would shape the latter's life.

Most importantly, Saʿad Buh is able to inform Kamara of the significance of the dream—that is, both its importance and its meaning—that would become the turning point from immaturity to maturity. "From this date, I left the amusements and distractions of young students alone, and I directed myself to Shaykh Saʿad Buh, may God be pleased with him as well as his father. When I recounted this dream, he said: 'God only wants you to get rid of every impurity. Oh people of the house of the Prophet and wants you to purify yourself thoroughly' without adding anything, but God the most high knows more."[29] In response to Kamara's dream, Buh recites Qurʾan 33:33 without adding further commentary, making it a kind of "interpretation by Qurʾan." On the one hand, such a response might be seen as a conservative reading of the dream, as an admonition: Clean up your life! On the other, Saʿad Buh's use of this citation affirms Kamara's identity as a close friend of God, as it casts the dreamer as belonging to the people of the Prophet's house, a rare and special status. These possible readings of Buh's intended meaning suggest an ambiguity in his interpretation of Kamara's dream, which Kamara himself registers when he says, "without adding anything" and then invokes the supremacy of divine knowledge. If there was any ambiguity left in Buh's interpretation, Kamara immediately adds the interpretation of a renowned interpreter of dreams who is unambiguous. This unnamed person informs Kamara that his dream is an indication that people will bear him in their hands as he had borne the Prophet Ibrahim. When Kamara writes these lines toward the end of his life, he proclaims that this interpretation was correct.

Before moving on to consider the fateful encounter with Saʿad Buh and its place in Kamara's trajectory, we should keep in mind that *The Announcement* was written half of a century after the dream was reported to have taken place. The span of time between the dream event and its appearance in Kamara's text should be not so much a cause of skepticism about its reliability but as evidence of how profoundly significant it was for his own self-understanding as a friend of God, an inheritor of the prophets—that is, his saintly subjectivity. Where most dreams are forgotten by the time the dreamer wakes, Kamara's dream of the prophets remained in his memory over the arc of his life, gaining momentum, clarifying, and being clarified as it granted meaning to the trials and challenges of a Sufi friend of God. Perhaps most importantly for understanding the relationship between texts and dreams in the shaping of saintly subjectivity, the dream in which Kamara appears in the house of the prophets was the impetus for a series of events in the physical realm that would result in the composition of Kamara's first authored text.

A Fateful Encounter

Around a year after having the prophetic dream, Kamara finds himself in the colonial town of Ndar/Saint-Louis to meet Shaykh Saʿad Buh. It is useful here to discuss the latter's historical significance, an early "architect of accommodation."[30] He was the son of Muhammad Fadil, a disruptive spiritual figure in the nineteenth-century religious landscape of the southwestern Sahara, who challenged the dominance of the Kunta Sufi network by founding the Fadiliyya, a group that claimed sources of authority outside the region's established hierarchy of transmitted knowledge.[31] The Kunta had dominated this hierarchy, defined by affiliation with a Qadiri Sufi tradition, and had come to represent establishment political-economic interests in the region against the rising tide of Tijani Sufis such as Hajj Umar Tal from Futa Toro.[32] The Fadiliyya broke out of this two-way contest by claiming a Qadiri affiliation while deploying Tijani characteristics—such as independence from the chain of transmitted knowledge and the validity of inspired vision as knowledge—and even the Tijani litany. Free appropriation of different Sufi methodologies and practices was rejected by the Tijanis themselves, but such fusions and combinations made the religious, political, and intellectual landscape more complex in terms of the options available to an aspiring adept.[33] Notably, Fadil ventured to take the Sufi practice of *dhikr* (the congregational recitation of litanies) outside. The effect of this departure was to popularize what had been an elite and private affair, arguably contributing, along with Umar Tal's popular messianism, to a new Muslim publicity in the nineteenth century.

Saʿad Buh sought to take up his father's mantle in a crowded field of over thirty sons and possible successors. He would eventually rank among the most prominent, along with his future adversary and brother Ma al-ʿAynayn, who would advocate for armed struggle against colonization, a contrast to Saʿad Buh's message of mutual recognition with and support for the French. Saʿad Buh was by and large well respected in the southern Sahara as a scholar, a Sufi, and a *sharīf* (a biological descendant of the Prophet Muhammad). He was wildly popular south of the Senegal River, likely because of his reputation as a master of marvels, miracle-like events that indicated supernatural intervention.[34] He won the discipleship of some of the most prominent would-be political leaders whose domains were subsumed into the colony of Senegal with the entrenchment of French rule and was able to leverage his popularity to achieve several colonial objectives that he believed to be in Muslims' best interest (peace, security, and the promotion of trade). This view is effectively communicated in his *fatwa* (a nonbinding legal opinion) on the permissibility of living under Christian rule.[35] In exchange for his procolonial stance, he was allowed to exploit the infrastructures of the colonial economy to support his peripatetic practice of collecting alms north and south of the Senegal River. When Kamara sought him out in the mid-1880s, Saʿad Buh maintained a strategic presence in the colonial capital, where he kept current with markets, politics, and military power. That Saʿad Buh appears at such a vital juncture in Kamara's life, and life story, connects Kamara to a leading Muslim personality in a pivotal period of global history and the text of his autobiography to a renowned friend of God.

In addition to reading the appearance of Saʿad Buh in Kamara's autobiography historically, I want to emphasize his textual significance. He first appears in the introduction to *The Announcement*, where Kamara presents himself by way of a genealogy. As discussed in the previous chapter, the genealogy begins with the short sequence of Kamara's patrilineal descent: Musa is the son of Ahmad, who was the son of Mahmud, who was the son of Famodi. This genealogy of given names is then immediately followed by the statement that "Shaykh Saʿad Buh, may God be pleased with him, gave me the title Shaykh Musa."[36] The contrast of these two statements, sitting next to one another in the text, highlights the difference between a carnal genealogy of a given name—we do not choose our lineage—and a scholarly and spiritual title earned and granted, ultimately, by God through God's friends. The difference between the carnal and the spiritual lineages reveals Saʿad Buh to be something of a symbolic or spiritual father for Kamara, the person who gives Kamara the name that means the most. Saʿad Buh's textual significance lies in his representation of the alternative to carnal genealogies of flesh and blood.

Buh's second appearance in *The Announcement* renders him a spiritual guide, an object of desire, and a recipient of value. The story of Kamara's fateful encounter with him immediately follows a description of Kamara's studies and precedes the section of dream accounts where Buh appears as an interpreter of dreams, as already mentioned in the previous sections.

> After that I went to Ndar and met there with the perfect saint, Shaykh Saʿad Buh (may God purify his face on the day faces are purified). I took the Qadiri litany

from him, and he said to me spontaneously: "God will grant you abundant goodness, and if you come to me at my house, I will take pains for you." That is why I, after this remark, took pains to obtain something valuable to bring to him. It did not come easy in my going around except two bits of *filtur* and a worn white shirt. I went toward them for a span of six days, then I reached their neighborhood on the seventh day, which was a Monday during the siesta. Our Moorish companion informed them of my news. He sent a message to me, ordering me to be present with them that evening. I had composed a poem from the *ṭawīl* meter, mentioning all my desires from the divine closeness, which is to reach the lordly presence with the heart so that I do not occupy myself without it, and I do not see anything but it, and I do not look with my heart except to it, and I only think about it. When I came to them, I recited it in their presence. He was very happy with it. Then he said: "A camel-load and I am its guarantor!"[37]

If the dream itself serves as the turning point in Kamara's life, the fateful encounter with Buh reveals Kamara's new direction. Whereas the people he lists before this passage are the teachers of transmitted knowledge who failed to teach him very much, the people he lists after this passage are other Sufi friends of God. In taking the litany of the Qadiriyya from Saʿad Buh, Kamara inserts himself in a spiritual-social hierarchy of the Sufis. As a perfect friend of God, Saʿad Buh represents Kamara's point of intercession through which he is granted access to flows of God's grace. In return for this service, Kamara understands that he should offer something valuable. After almost a week of trying to find gifts, he comes up only with two coins and an old shirt, both of which should be understood contextually as currency, items of material value used in exchange. Having gathered so little, he offers his spiritual guide yet another form of currency, a poem.[38] The literary scholar of the Persianate context Mana Kia offers a thoughtful reflection on the implication of the text as a gift. Beyond being expressions of discourse, texts here are also "enactments of bonds between people."[39] For Kia, this recognition should compel us not only to read the literary lives of the Persianate past for what they meant in their own context but also to reflect on how the subjectivity of a *homo amicus*, her description of the presumed reading subject, might challenge our relationship to the interested and motivated *homo oeconomicus*, taken for granted at the center of modern capitalist market arrangements. Kamara's account challenges us similarly, for although his context of late nineteenth-century West Africa is different, shared commitments to the social and ethical dimensions of literature (*adab*) make it possible for a poem to be a valuable gift.

The poem that Kamara composes as a gift to his spiritual guide is the first of many texts he writes over his career. Regrettably, to my knowledge this poem has not been identified. What we can say about the poem from the passage is that it followed an established verse form of the *ṭawīl* and that its theme was the Sufi aspirant's desire for *walāya* (closeness or friendship with God). No matter the genre, Kamara would continue writing on this theme throughout his career, as I will discuss later. The description of the poem in this passage seems to follow an established meter form that is partially retained even in translation: "I do not occupy myself without it, and I do not see anything but it, and I do not look with my heart except to it, and I only think about it." What this passage highlights most is the role texts and textual production played in the spiritual, symbolic, and political economy of the region, where the literary had a tangible value—a "camel-load" of value, in fact.

The idea of poetry as currency reminds me of a moment during my research. While visiting members of Kamara's family in Mauritania, I was informed of a repository of oral-historical interviews held by the national archives. To my excitement, there was an interview with one of Kamara's sons Tourad, who had worked as a colonial employee. Eager to hear about things that happened that I could use as facts or as local color, something that might be of precious historical value, I listened to the interview, which took place in Hassaniyya, although I could not understand it very well. After the initial presentation of the interviewee, Tourad quickly begins to recite something. With some help from the Mauritanian researchers Baba Addou, Mariam Baba Ahmed, and Ahmed Maouloud Eida El-Hilal, I learned that the interviewer did not follow the script of a typical oral-historical or life-history interview. When Tourad described his early childhood, what the interviewer was most interested in was what poetry he remembered from that time. A good bit of the rest of the interview consisted of Tourad reciting poetry. I was struck because the interviewer did not ask the questions that might interest a historian. Instead, what was valuable to the interviewer and the interviewee alike was poetry. For Musa Kamara as well, when he needed to come up with something valuable to give to his new spiritual guide, the most important currency he could come up with was the first text he ever composed.

A DEGREE OF PROPHECY

Immediately after Kamara offers his first authored text, Buh appears as an elusive object of desire:

> Then he called me on the eve of that Thursday and said to me: "I fulfilled your need, no?" He commanded me to return to my family in Futa. But my intention was to relocate and devote to him and live with him forever. It was not my intention to return to Futa at all! So I said I do not like that, but I love to live with you forever. He said: "I have fulfilled your need, all and part. Do not doubt and you will see it, God willing." He repeated this statement to me several times. Then I spent the night with them on Friday and Saturday, and on the morning of Saturday, he commanded me to go out to travel and go back. He said to me: "Everyone who was there before you had needs, I fulfilled their needs for your sake." Among those who were with him at that time were those with needs, Siri Lamine Ceerno Sadik of Sinsou Bamambi and Ahmad Baba in Silune and others. We all returned together. Because of my excessive love for staying with them, I left my nephew, who is called Muhammad ibn al-Amin, with them, so that my heart would turn to them and become attached to them. At that time, I was twenty-two or three years old.[40]

This passage reveals the degree to which love as a spiritual quality defined Kamara's life on the Sufi path. Having had the prophetic dream, Kamara is prepared to turn himself around, a conversion of sorts, and commit to a radically different life course. When he comes to Buh, he intends to be as close to the spiritual master as possible, as he believes that proximity will bring him closer to God, a physical embodiment of what he saw in the dream. But after a few days, Saʿad Buh tells Kamara that he has done what the aspirant needs. Kamara is reluctant to receive this message and expresses his own intent instead. Buh repeatedly attempts to assure or get rid of him without success. Even when Kamara is refused and is ordered to return home with his companions, he leaves a nephew to serve the shaykh. Kamara believes that such an offering will cement the relationship with Buh and keep his own consideration of the spiritual master front and center in his own heart. Kamara does this for his own sake, to find an outlet for the excess of his desire to remain with the shaykh. He does not comment on Saʿad Buh's response to this last gesture, and we have little insight into how Saʿad Buh may have viewed Kamara's desire for spiritual and physical proximity at the time. Whether Saʿad Buh thought it excessive or saw it as a necessary attribute of a serious friend of God in training is hard to tell. Perhaps Kamara thought that his offerings of a few coins, a shirt, and a poem were still not sufficient and that the offer of his nephew was a placeholder for future gifts. After leaving Ndar, Kamara manages to obtain sixty coins in an undisclosed amount of time and returns, now accompanied by his own faithful disciple, Malick, to offer Saʿad Buh an even greater gift. Saʿad Buh accepts Kamara's gift before instructing him again to return home with his disciple and his nephew, but Saʿad Buh's refusal of Kamara's desire for proximity neither discourages Kamara nor makes him waver in his affection for Saʿad Buh's spiritual presence. If anything, his refusals seem to contribute to his status as an object of desire.[41]

Kamara's commitment to the path first shown to him in the dream of the Prophets Ibrahim and Muhammad and embodied by his relationship with Saʿad Buh is further evidenced by Kamara's offering his guide gifts over the course of his life, according to the text. After the subtle but repeated rebuffs from Saʿad Buh, Kamara decides to undertake the Hajj. This pilgrimage to Mecca had long been a cherished but challenging mission for West Africa's Muslim scholars.[42] To be successful, Kamara needs the financial and human resources to make it happen, so he travels throughout the Senegambia for a year to collect money from wealthy patrons, benefactors, and rulers who might support a promising religious personality such as himself. Kamara's fellow Futanke scholar Hajj Umar Tal had done the same to memorable effect.[43] Specifically, Kamara visits Almamy Ibrahim of Futa Djallon and Hajj Umar's son Agibu in Dinguiraye. The first recognizes Kamara as a friend of God just before a victorious military campaign.[44] The almamy offers Kamara his daughter for marriage and many captives, but Kamara refuses because of his overwhelming desire for the Hajj, an opportunity to fulfill a key religious obligation at the house built by Ibrahim, as well as a unique opportunity to be closer to the Prophet Muhammad's bodily remains in Medina. No doubt the memory of the Prophet Ibrahim's house from his dream has made him feel set in his course. As a consolation, Almamy Ibrahim gifts Kamara the value in silver of ten captives. Similarly, Agibu recognizes Kamara's spiritual station. He surprisingly tells his community— some of whom might have fought alongside or followed Hajj Umar or certainly were the children of those who did—that Kamara and Umar are essentially the same.[45] Their only difference is that Umar carried arms and Kamara does not. Agibu too offers a daughter and many captives, which Kamara refuses before accepting four servants. We should note here that both of these encounters are associated with the authoring of texts.[46]

By the time Kamara finishes his tour, God has turned him away "from his intention to go to Mecca."[47] Beyond divine redirection, such a trip was likely untenable with the level of insecurity in the region by the time he was twenty-four or twenty-five, which would have been around 1888 or 1889. The final jihad of the region, waged by Mamadou Lamine Drame, had only recently been repressed by the French, but Samory Touré still represented the possibility of conflict. Instead of keeping the gifts offered by the region's elite to establish himself, Kamara gave most of his accumulated wealth to Saʿad Buh. This extraordinary gesture, made after his own exploits and recognition as a *wali*, demonstrates how much Kamara valued the shaykh's intercession and how dedicated he would remain to him over the years.

In a subsequent chapter of *The Announcement* that includes endorsements and praise he had received over the course of his career, Kamara presents excerpts of several letters Saʿad Buh had written to him expressing the disciple's spiritual achievements.[48] Together, they suggest that Kamara's desire to attach himself to Buh as a spiritual guide and intermediary in the hierarchy of divine being, even when Kamara was at times pushed away or redirected, was a success.

Kamara's relationship with Saʿad Buh was part of a larger structure of relationships and patterns of practice. Saʿad Buh offered him tangible benefits. In a chapter on the love of the friends of God, Kamara discusses some of his own most loyal disciples, including Ousmane Ali, from a theoretical and personal perspective. He had dispatched Ali with a delegation to visit Saʿad Buh. Upon receiving the group, the shaykh says to them, "Come. I will write for each one of you something to protect you, and give you wisdom, secrets, and beneficial prayers."[49] Ali protests that Saʿad Buh's offering should not be for those present but rather for his absent shaykh who sent them. "As for me, I have no need other than my shaykh, Shaykh Musa. I am satisfied with him. If you write beneficial prayers, and wisdom, and secrets, then write them for him." Saʿad Buh responds favorably to Ali's request, as it expresses the disciple's love of his shaykh. This exchange resembles Kamara's first encounter with Saʿad Buh, in that the master receives visitors with a "need" that he satisfies before sending them on their way. The fact that Saʿad Buh receives Kamara's disciples years later in much the same way suggests a consistency in this practice over his life. But this time things have changed. Kamara, who is absent in this scene, is invoked by his disciple, who makes Saʿad Buh recognize Kamara's heightened spiritual station, as evidenced by Ali's devotion. Ultimately, Ali is indeed linked with Saʿad Buh but only through Kamara. This chain of intercession defined relationships among Sufis, while the practice of visitation maintained those relationships and ensured the flow of God's favor in the temporal realm. The chain of intercession constitutes the spiritual genealogy that Kamara outlines in his autobiography.

It is noteworthy that the encounters with friends of God and political leaders that Kamara includes all have some relationship with the production of a text. In the previous example, Saʿad Buh writes a short incantatory text that could be worn as a talisman or used in some specified way for effect in the material world.[50] After Kamara's first meeting with Buh, he composes a poem. And when Kamara meets Almamy Ibrahim, he writes two different works, one on the power of prayers for the Prophet Muhammad and another on asceticism. Finally, Kamara does not mention it in this text, but he would also credit the encounter with Agibu as corresponding with a dream that begins *The Life of Hajj Umar*, discussed in the first section.

Kamara's Career Through Texts

Kamara's disclosures, whether transmitted in the form of texts or inspired in the form of dreams, contributed to the esteem with which he was held. He developed a reputation as a friend of God with exceptional knowledge and insight who had few peers, and he makes this point forcefully in a chapter on the disciplines he studied and the works he composed.[51] The list of the disciplines he studied with a teacher is short: jurisprudence, Arabic language through literature, grammar, rhetoric, and logic. But his independent reading was far more extensive, especially in the field of Sufism. He also read independently in the foundational disciplines that he did study with others and included works on prosody, history, and prophetic biography. This self-directed reading was the basis for his own writing.

In this chapter, Kamara includes a nonexhaustive list of the works that he authored and that reflected his reading tastes. Many of the works listed also included endorsements by notable peers, attesting to the quality of his work. Take, for example, *The Wayfarer's Guide to the Meaning of Ibn Malik's*

Alfiyya, his commentary on an essential textbook of Arabic grammar written in rhymed prose.⁵² One ʿAbd al-Rahman al-Hasan calls *The Wayfarer's Guide* "a spark for beginners and a comfort for the initiated."⁵³ The work also received an endorsement from Hajj ʿAynayn Seck, from a notable Saint-Louisian family. While this more pedagogical work was received with appreciation, he also received endorsements for his works associated with Sufi devotional practices. These included *The Splendor of the Names and the Warmest Protection*, a treatise on the use of the names of God in prayers. These testimonials demonstrated the high regard in which he was held. For example, one of the endorsements reads in verse: "People are too good to praise a man without finding traces of excellence."⁵⁴

Despite the high regard that some of his peers expressed, Kamara was not universally celebrated. Oral histories in particular suggest a more controversial side of Kamara. Interviews conducted by Abdoul Malal Diop demonstrate some of the intellectual antagonisms that shaped Kamara's context.⁵⁵ When he arrives at the home of Thierno Tafsirou Balla, a jurist who took the position that tobacco was prohibited, a common one since at least Hajj Umar Tal's critique of the substance and its entanglement in a Christian political economy, Kamara sits out front of the house and begins smoking. Balla's students are shocked, and one goes into the home to tell Balla what is going on. He is reported as saying that Kamara is challenging him to a debate. But apparently, Balla does not want to engage, and he stays inside, refusing to debate him. This is such a precious detail for many reasons because it gives a sense of Kamara's personality. He was not afraid of his convictions and liked an intellectual quarrel. It also links Kamara to the Qadiri Sufi order, which famously took a favorable position on tobacco, in contrast to the Tijani position. This was one of the big issues up for debate that also touched on the region's place in the global economy.

On the theme of conflict with Tijani scholars, Kamara credits a dream with transforming his relationship to a Tijani peer. Ahmed Alpha Muhammad al-Futi al-Naʾari is a Muslim scholar who prefers study circles of transmitted knowledge over circles of *dhikr* (devotional worship). Al-Naʾari argues that the excessive practice of *dhikr* is not permitted and tries to prevent his brother Saʿid Alpha from participating in Kamara's *dhikr* sessions. This conflict is so contentions that his brother breaks ties with Saʿid Alpha. Al-Naʾari is reported to have regretted this position after his own fateful dream, in which he finds himself at a home inhabited by the

Prophet Muhammad and the founding Tijani saint Shaykh Ahmed al-Tijani and guarded by Shaykh Musa Kamara. Al-Naʾari gains access to the interior of the house without Kamara's approval, and Muhammad and Tijani ask al-Naʾari if he has entered with the permission of Kamara. Al-Naʾari admits to not having permission, to which they respond, "Return to him and ask for his permission because we only receive those that he permits."[56] Frightened by this dream, Al-Naʾari writes everything that he saw and heard in the dream and sends the dream text to Kamara, asking for his forgiveness. This dream reveals to al-Naʾari that Kamara has a superior station in the hierarchy of being, and his request to Kamara demonstrates his acceptance of Kamara's greater favor.

A close reading of Kamara's autobiography shows us that his dream of the prophets motivated his spiritual quest to be a friend of God. This quest would lead him to fateful encounters with his spiritual guide, Shaykh Saʿad Buh, and to form other pivotal relationships that shaped the middle period of his life between the mid-1880s and 1912, when he enters into the colonial archive. Having identified the pattern in the occurrences of dream events and the production of texts, in Kamara's self-understanding, and in the development of his saintly subjectivity, we have the occasion to reflect on the relationship of the two in Kamara's life. We did just that earlier in this chapter with the close reading of Kamara's dream during his visit to Agibu as it appears in *The Life of Hajj Umar*; it was the ideal dream narrative on which to base this reflection because of the place of text in the dream itself. We found that the relationship between the two is their performance of disclosure, a selective mediation of the hidden and the apparent. Kamara received and performed disclosure at key points of his life, including a prophetic dream in which the Prophets Ibrahim and Muhammad appear to him. This disclosure sets him on a spiritual path beyond the acquisition of transmitted knowledge where he develops a relationship with the guide Shaykh Saʿad Buh. Prior to his encounters with colonial officials, Kamara's career as an author, one that would both earn him esteem and cause ire among his contemporaries, develops from this point. Saintly subjectivity as a degree of prophecy and genealogical being were profound sources of meaning for Kamara in his body of work, which would hardly be regarded by either the colonial engineering explored in the following chapter or the colonial humanism discussed in chapter 4.

THREE

Islam Noir

Surveillance Ethnography and the Politics of Representation

CAPTAIN STEFF, the commandant of Kaédi, had a problem. The sons of Sammba Joom Bah (d. 1895/96),[1] the leader of eastern Futa Toro who had greatly facilitated French expansion in the middle Senegal River Valley during the nineteenth century, were at one another's throats. Each one claimed ownership of valuable land with harvests that were at least twice as large as those of the less-prized plots beyond the reach of the river's natural irrigation. The fraternal conflict within this noble lineage led to strife that threatened to disrupt public order. As the resident authority for the French colony of Mauritania, Steff was responsible for making sure such disruptions were limited. Moreover, each brother expected the state to resolve the matter in his favor. Steff was perplexed. Sammba Joom's landholdings were abundant, as he had confiscated much of the land of the fighters who migrated to participate in the multigenerational Umarian jihad. These holdings were more than enough to satisfy the needs of Joom's children, and yet the two brothers fought. Upon investigating the matter, Steff was confident that he had identified the source of the problem in his periodic district report in May of 1913, according to documents identified by the Senegalese historian Mouhamed Moustapha Kane. "Accord would prevail within this family if a cleric from the left bank, a freed slave of Sammba Diom's did not sow discord for his own advantage for, within the sharing out among the children of Sammba Diom, part of the land has been reserved and entrusted to the cleric's care."[2] Steff placed responsibility for the conflict squarely on Shaykh

Musa Kamara, who by this time had established his community at Ganguel, across the river in the colony of Senegal. Steff's accusation is complex and requires several layers of unpacking, which I will undertake in this chapter. For now, we should note that this incident highlights how much colonial knowledge and power relied on practices of partition, which sought to make the world cohere with dominant mental maps, and on the politics of representation—that is, the production and reproduction of identities through administrative institutions and research.

In this chapter, I argue that this middle phase of Kamara's life (1895–1926), which also coincided with the middle period of French colonial presence, was conditioned by the establishment of representation as a paradigm of both knowledge and power. To be sure, the emergence of representivity, the idea that a part of a larger body stands in for that larger body as if by synecdoche, was a global development that came with new expectations for knowledge and power. In Kamara's Futa Toro, which straddled the colonial administrations of Senegal and Mauritania, and in the broader federation of colonies known as French West Africa, representation as both an intellectual activity and a political mode came to be a paradigm shared by the colonial state and the colonized elites. The older French policy of assimilation, a system of direct rule in which coastal Africans could become citizens, had sought to make the African European and had signaled the impossibility of representing the African as African. But the shift in this middle period toward the policy of association, in which subject populations were governed indirectly through ethnic representatives, signaled the official recognition of African humanity and the validity of cultural difference. But this humanity had to be represented ideologically, conceptually, intellectually, literarily, and, most of all, scientifically. This representation was a complex process worked out in the struggles of everyday life by the interactions and interventions of colonized people (elite and common) and colonizers alike. It is in this period that ethnicity, race, and religion were defined in ways that are recognizable in our global present. The convergence of these processes of identification and the ideological elaboration of the categories of identity in ways that endow them with meaning can be understood as the politics of representation. One of the truly interesting features of Kamara's work is that while many of his peers participated in the politics of representation, he offered a compelling representation of politics—that is, a theorization of the political—so as to intervene in his historically specific problem-space.[3]

First, I describe the politics of representation that defined the micro-, regional, and global historical contexts of the period, which consisted of the shift toward a policy of association rather than assimilation, the pacification of anticolonial threats, Kamara's conflict over access to land, the scientization of colonial knowledge and power, and the carving out of a religious sphere in which Muslim scholars were able to maintain autonomy from colonial politics and the state. Then I demonstrate how Kamara became an important source of information through surveillance ethnography, a then-emergent form of colonial knowledge that resulted from the practical attitude. Finally, through a close reading of some of Kamara's critical work, including his invalidation of jihad as political, I show how Kamara engaged in the representation of politics that challenged the colonial delegation of decentralized despotism to Muslim scholars.

Partition and the Politics of Representation

Sometime around 1895 Kamara, then about thirty, settled in the village of Ganguel with his family and small entourage. Ganguel sits on the south bank of the Senegal River in the cluster of villages known as the province of Damga. The village bordered the village of Guriki, where Kamara was born and where his father had received land from Sammba Joom, the leader of the area, in exchange for divinatory and spiritual services.[4] The grant of land to Kamara's father followed a pattern that had existed in the region since the empire of Ghana, when Islamic religious specialists were granted land to maintain semiautonomous communities adjacent to traditional rulers.[5] Given the semiarid to arid conditions of the region, the thin strips of floodplains on both sides of the river were uniquely valuable.[6] The rich and well-watered soils could produce two harvests annually, as opposed to the single annual harvest for lands in the immediate highlands that depended on seasonal rains. Agriculture had long been the core productive activity, with most people throughout society participating in it to some extent. Land, and contests over it, was the factor of production that most defined political conflict and social life. As a friend, codisciple, and son-in-law of Sammba Joom through Joom's daughter Kuumba, Kamara was granted access to fertile fields around Ganguel and grazing lands on the north bank the same year as Joom's death.[7]

Kamara's claim to these lands would be at the heart of several conflicts he would experience over the course of his life—notably, with Aali Samba Joom and Abdou Salam Kane (1871-1955), the sons of his mentors Samba Joom and Mamadou Mamadou Kane (d.1890) and family members by marriage. The first was the case with which I opened this chapter. Joom's son Aali moved his immediate family and his many captives across the river from Guriki and founded the village of Faduwa in 1906.[8] This land north of the Senegal River was parceled out to Joom's heirs and fell under the administration of the recently established colony of Mauritania. But as disagreements between Aali and his half-brother Soulé intensified, the administrations of Mauritania, north of the river, and Senegal, south of the river, suspended the collection of taxes in the area and negotiated an agreement with the brothers with the facilitation of the chief of Damga, Abdou Salam Kane. Before this happened, however, Captain Steff of the Mauritanian administration conducted the investigation and recorded the words with which I opened this chapter. Kamara's students and other members of his entourage, who likely had a servile social status, worked some of the lands that were disputed by the brothers.

While this case might be read as a petty family squabble or as an economic contest, the specific context of the turn-of-the-century Senegal River Valley makes it chiefly a political struggle. In this period, politics had largely become the politics of representation—the production and reproduction of identities that would be the basis of territorial governance. This was the result not of a simple application of a colonial mode of thought but of a fusion of expectations from a long autochthonous history of political struggle over land and a scientization of knowledge as a precise instrument of power. This politics of representation should be understood in relation to the logic and operation of partition.[9] The drawing of the territorial border at the Senegal River divided Futa Toro between two distinct administrative structures. But partition was not limited to drawing lines on maps; it included material practices of division and conceptual distinctions that consolidated the categories of ethnicity, race, and religion in ways that cohere with hegemonically modern certainties about social identity and difference. Partition sought to make reality reflect the representations of reality as much as the representations sought to reflect reality.

A brief discussion of the context will help clarify this argument. The subregion had recently undergone so-called pacification, the violent process by which colonial domination was established. Before pacification, Islam in Futa Toro had provided the dominant justificatory framework for thought and action in collective life since the assumption of power by Muslim scholars in the imamate. Moreover, the French framework that justified the colonial enterprise—"civilization"—had recognized Islam and Muslim intermediaries as a civilizing force in what they considered uncivilized Africa. Pacification, however, changed this status of Islam in the region. The Umarian state in the neighboring upper Senegal and Niger River Valleys fell to Colonel Louis Archinard (1850–1932) in 1890, just as Colonel Alfred-Amédée Dodds (1842–1922) eliminated the threat of an African autonomy constituted by Abdul Bokar Kane (1831–1891) in the middle Senegal River Valley.[10] In both cases, and in others, resistance to French colonial domination assumed the grammar of jihad, a totalizing struggle in the path of God that relied on every means of resistance the Muslim community could muster. Jihad had both temporal and spiritual dimensions, in that it sought to preserve or make a space in which Islamic principles of governance as expressed in the *shariʿa* were upheld. While the politics of jihad in nineteenth-century West Africa had implications for the governing of territory, it emphasized a claim over people. As a result, migration for the cause of the struggle, whether voluntary or coerced, was a major occurrence.

Such movement, and the broader refusal to accept terms of colonial governance, made Islam a problem to be engineered. The resolution of this problem began with the defeat of Umar in 1864 and continued with the definitive defeat of his son Ahmad al-Kabir in 1893.[11] Islam would become a civilizing force by using Muslim intermediaries and encouraging the development of hybrid colonial-Islamic institutions. The elites who were at least recognized or at most authorized by the colony state were to manage the space now reduced and defined as religion by policing any undue enthusiasm that spilled over into the domain of politics.[12] This modus vivendi would also characterize indirect rule more generally, an order described by Mahmood Mamdani as decentralized despotism.[13] The body of knowledge that evolved from the practical attitude into an expertise in the engineering projects first Egypt, then Algeria, and finally the Senegambia was, accordingly, most concerned with surveillance and a mode of analysis that distinguished good Muslims from bad ones.[14] Regional elites who were aligned with colonial interests responded to migration for purposes of jihad by confiscating and redistributing land, as was the case with Sammba Joom. In the process, the Islamic framework that justified action was marginalized in society, just as the custodians of interpretation of that framework, the Muslim scholars, were marginalized as central actors. Captain Steff's words that describe Kamara as a slave-turned-cleric should first be put in the context of the marginalization of Muslim scholars following pacification.

Pacification set the stage for a shift in the French colonies from a policy of assimilation to one of association. Assimilation assumed that Africans needed to evolve from their state of nature to civilization to participate in politics. Successful assimilation into the "universality" of civilization granted them French citizenship in the system often described as direct rule. African Muslims were the exception to this practice in the four communes of Dakar, Gorée, Rufisque, and Saint-Louis, as they recognized a "law" (as in the *shari'a*) and had something recognizable to the French as "religion." Unlike the devotees of ancestral African worship who remained outside the category of the human and thus needed European law and religion, African Muslims could be admitted within the bounds of humanity. However, with the epistemic shift that occurred at the turn of the century, the French began to recognize the plurality of civilizations and the equality of cultural differences as knowledge grew in its secularity. Islam would no longer be privileged in colonial administration over other cultural (as opposed to religious) systems. Instead, colonial governance would be characterized by association, which consisted of governing populations based on "race," creating genealogically defined cultural unities that in many other cases would be defined as "ethnicity." The difference between race and ethnicity in this instance was one of scale and not of kind. This resembled the indirect rule most associated with British colonialism.

This shift can be dated to the implementation of the *politique des races* (racial policy) at the turn of the century. It sought to order space along racial-ethnic lines in the French colonial empire in Africa and thus undermine the organizing power of religious groups. These policies enacted different regimes of governance based on the underlying principle that subject populations should be governed according to their ethnic identities and local customs. The associationist policy of indirect rule followed the secularist doctrine of marginalizing religion in public life in the metropolitan center, in contrast to the previous assimilationist policy of direct rule that sought to use Islam as a civilizing force. In a departure from previous practice, William Ponty (1866-1915), the governor of French West Africa, restricted the delegation of administrative authority of Muslims over non-Muslims in 1909 and discontinued the use of Arabic as a language of administration in 1911. Additionally, he established a practice of censoring Arabic-language print materials and Islamic imagery from North Africa and the Levant.[15] The main goals of the new associationist policy were to limit the spread of Islam and to make administration more efficient by relying on ethnic elites, as opposed to Muslim scholars, to manage production, police order, and generally contribute to the colonial enterprise. Steff's siding with Sammba Joom's sons, as chiefs, over Kamara, as a cleric, should be read in this context of the new associationism.

Association as a "rational" policy of governing racialized subjects was consciously entwined with an assemblage of administrative practices, social scientific concepts, and expectations of representivity that sought to make colonial knowledge and power "scientific" and reflect precise representations of reality. At the turn of the century, interest emerged in a "scientific imperialism," which sought to integrate research and policy through the adoption of social scientific thinking. Surveillance became part and parcel of data collection, theory building, and social engineering in the colonial enterprise. General Joseph Gallieni (1849–1916), who led military regimes across the French colonial empire, described this relationship in the following terms: "The officer who has successfully drawn an exact ethnographic map of the territory he commands is close to achieving complete pacification, soon to be followed by the form of organization he judges most appropriate."[16] The positivist orientation of this process meant administrators could no longer prioritize unverifiable belief—a new definition of religion—in ordering the social world. Instead, race, and ethnicity as a subdivision of race, came to explain the kinds of human difference and hierarchy that religion had in the preceding period.

As a result, a racial theory of Islam emerged within the French colonial empire just as racial theory defined the social sciences, the disciplines, and common sense more broadly at the turn of the century.[17] This theory was developed by anthropologizing concepts in West and North Africa of Islam *noir*, Islam *maure*, and Islam *berbère*, which were coming to their full maturity. Separately, the concepts specified unique characteristics that distinguished local beliefs and practices from a classical Arab Islam as elaborated by metropolitan orientalist scholarship. They would also serve as the basis for later discourses on national forms of Islam, having been adopted as instruments of colonial governmentality.[18] Islam *noir* posited that Black African Muslims were less rational, were more inclined to ecstatic devotion than textual learning, were more docile than their relatively more white coreligionists, and still harbored beliefs and practices from ancestral forms of worship. Islam *berbère* suggested that the various Amazigh-speaking populations in Algeria and Morocco evinced a more democratic nature, offered women a higher status, and were superficially Islamized. In effect, they were more racially/culturally "white" than their Arab compatriots. Meanwhile, Islam *maure* represented the most "dangerous" and "fanatical" type, one that best explained Arab racial specificity, thus reworking classical representations that conflated the Arab with the Muslim as the essential enemy. Together, these concepts constituted an overriding racial theory of Islam that ultimately argued for the primacy of race in defining human community and explaining social phenomena.

Religion no longer offered the same explanatory power it once had as ethnological explanations of race usurped its place. Wolof-speaking Muslims in Senegal, for example, could no longer be understood as analogous with or related to North African Muslims; rather, they were viewed in comparison to and connection with other Black ethnic groups, no matter their religious adherence. Similarly, in Morocco, General Louis Herbert Lyautey employed a colonial social science to gather social facts that would serve as the basis of the "making" of modern Morocco.[19] Notably, these concepts were formed in relation to the surveillance activities mentioned previously and served as the basis of policy described later. The most important writer in the West African phase of this new French sociology of Islam tradition, Paul Marty (1882–1938), discussed in more detail later in the next section, wrote several volumes on Islam in the French colonies using the documentation collected by the Muslim Affairs Service, highlighting for us the relationship between state surveillance and the adoption of the social scientific framework of ethnology.[20] The form and content of Captain Steff's colonial report that communicates his findings should be understood in relation to this scientization of colonial knowledge and power.

Finally, we should consider how this period was shaped by the increasing competition among the elites of Futa Toro to influence colonial knowledge and power through the strategic relay of information.[21] The case that implicated Kamara in the Joom brothers' conflict is a great example. As masters of the land, a meaning of *joom* in Pulaar, the sons of Samba Joom competed first and foremost to claim their father's mantle and the power, prestige, and wealth associated with it. As they could not win this contest outright, they sought recourse from the colonial administration, each hoping to buttress his claim as the rightful heir to the land and to the right to represent that land and the people on it to the administration. Their peer Abdou Salam Kane, the son of Mamadou Mamadou Kane, had succeeded in this struggle to represent the province of Damga by being granted the title of colonial chief. The Joom brothers' case was settled in an hours-long negotiation between the two brothers and the two colonial administrations through the facilitation of the younger Kane.[22] Around this time, Abdou Salam Kane had several of his own land disputes and would go on to author two essays on land tenure in Futa Toro in French publications. While the stated intent of the brothers' agreement was to share the land among all of Sammba Joom's descendants, oral reports collected by Mouhamed Kane indicate that the brothers were eventually able to take possession of the lands of their siblings. This outcome should make us read Steff's description of Kamara as a former slave with some skepticism, as it suggests that that was likely a strategic choice to marginalize his claim to the land. My interest here is not to determine whether Kamara was indeed of low status, as is commonly believed by many Senegalese scholars but resolutely disputed by the Kamara family and in the work of Abdul Malal Diop.[23] Rather, I am interested in how the representation of Kamara as being a slave or of slave descent did political work in this period. The coordinated efforts of the Joom brothers, along with Kane's recurring role in defining custom, law, and tradition and in determining ownership of land, demonstrate that politics in this period consisted of the representation of a demarcated and partitioned population through claims of land.

What the case that brought Kamara into the colonial archive shows is that representation as a paradigm of both knowledge and power came to define the context of his intellectual maturity. The partition of Senegal and Mauritania was a symptom of a broader historical development, in which the expectation of an exact correspondence between reality and its representations characterized both intellectual work and political activity. By focusing on a specific contest over land in which Kamara was implicated, we have seen the way representation operated up and down the scales of organization from the micro to the global. But partition describes not only the division of land but also the categorization of human difference in putatively scientific racial terms—across the Du Boisian color line, if you will—as well as the differentiation of the spheres of religion and politics. Together, I describe these processes as partition and the politics of representation. In the rest of this chapter, I develop this argument by showing how Kamara became vitally important for the development of a field of expertise known as the sociology of Islam, which was based on surveillance ethnography, before considering Kamara's attempts to speak back to this regime of knowledge and power.

Muslim Affairs and the Rule of Experts

Building on the experience of distinguishing good Muslims from bad ones from the interested point of view of the colonial state and of managing the consequences of that distinction, a group of officials, many of whom had deep ties to the engineering project in Algeria, developed a form of applied knowledge, or expertise, best described as Muslim affairs. This expertise was battle hardened, poorly resourced, and honed over decades of volatile change. However, at the turn of the century, it still relied on individual intuition developed from time in the field and yielded inconsistent results. If such expertise was to become a truly useful tool in colonial administration, it needed to be thoroughly documented and implemented in policy. The need for a more institutionalized and rational approach became apparent after the death of Xavier Coppolani (b. 1866) in 1905.[24]

Coppolani had been a civil servant in Algeria, where he had a lasting impact on colonial policy toward Islam by developing surveillance ethnography and direct action while an operative on the frontiers of colonial control. This influence is enshrined in *Les confréries religieuses musulmanes*, an officially commissioned study of Sufi orders in Algeria that established a preoccupation with Sufi networks as institutional and ideological threats to colonial order.[25] Coppolani spent his teenage years in Algeria and was competent in vernacular Arabic. His outsider status in the colonial administration and his tireless ambition suggest, however, that his education at the École Normale of Constatine did not grant him an elevated education associated with orientalist scholarship. One of the last self-styled explorers in a moment of increased professionalization of administrators, Coppolani traveled south through the Sahara to Timbuktu, seeking to ally with the most important forces in the region. He dreamed of connecting France's North and West African conquests through the negotiated—as opposed to military—domination of the Sahara. Although he had seemed to successfully negotiate a way forward for French dominion in the Sahara, he was killed under questionable circumstances.[26] This reversal of fortune, along with a widespread colonial paranoia about Muslim uprisings, posed several questions for the administration to take up systematically: Who was actually friend, and who was foe? Who could be trusted with the mandates of indirect rule, and who would need to be managed as a risk to colonial order? In other words, who, from the French perspective, was a good Muslim, and who was a bad one?

Robert Arnaud (1873–1950), a protégé of Coppolani who traveled with him through the Sahara, was dispatched to definitively determine which Muslims could facilitate the pacification of Mauritania and which ones might impede it.[27] Moreover, he was tasked with developing a system that would provide answers to this question on an ongoing basis throughout French West Africa. Born in Algiers in 1873 to a colonial translator, Arnaud studied Arabic and attended the colonial school before joining the administration in 1898. While in school, he studied the basics of Islamic law, theology, and history as the curriculum mandated. His first assignment was to accompany Coppolani in the surveying of the lands and cultures of the Sahara, and they visited Timbuktu and what was to become Mauritania. After his mentor was killed during these efforts, Arnaud was dispatched on a fact-finding mission that would be the basis of French policy. This report would become the *Précis de politique musulmane*.[28]

It was this policy that focused on surveilling Muslim notables. The first article of the section entitled "Maintaining Security of the Territory" calls for surveillance of religious personalities as potential enemies. "Another job that the posts have to accomplish is to prevent the departure of dissidents and to keep a very close watch on the actions of the enemy, both beyond and within the border, which is usually ideal."[29] This job is accomplished by operation of a "complete intelligence service, by official agents or others; this service doubles as a service of enforcement (proceeded by cross-checking). The natives do this gladly, especially when they know they will be paid for their services. A corollary to this service is the creation of individual reports attributed to principal political personalities, both within and beyond the area." Religious personalities and religious activity are read as identical with political personalities and political activity in this policy. The different terms are used in separate articles, but no substantive distinction between the two is ever made.

Arnaud would later refine and extend his influence on Muslim policy with his *L'islam et la politique musulmane française en Afrique-occidentale française* in 1912. He reported on the implementation of the *fiche de renseignement*, an intelligence report, that each officer was to keep on prominent Muslim personalities in their district.[30] These had been developed through several colonial decrees made over the course of 1906 and 1907. Arnaud's update gave a more precise and standardized form to the practice of surveillance. The statement on this policy, which appears as the second chapter entitled "Our Policy Towards Islam" and a section described as the "Fight Against the Spirit of Caste," reads as follows:

> It has been prescribed to carry out, in each colony, the census of the religious personalities who stay there, either permanently or temporarily. Each of them is the subject of a file in which is written his place of origin, his age, his family relations, the brotherhood to which he is affiliated, the attitude towards the authorities, the quality of his teaching, the trips he makes, his description, and, in general, all the information that the *commandant de cercle* can collect on him. A duplicate of this form must be kept and kept up to date at the capital of the colony. The surveillance to which the marabout is subject is, of course, exercised with all possible tact and prudence. It allows the superior authority to have, on occasion, precise details on a given religious personality and on his moral value.[31]

In this passage, Arnaud outlines at the broadest level the form and practice of the surveillance of Muslim scholars, such as Kamara. It evidences the practical attitude in action. The ultimate point of surveillance is to establish a relation of value. Although described as moral value in the passage, the context suggests that it is their utility to the colonial enterprise that defines a particular Muslim's worth. The gathered facts are in service to the ultimate designation of value, whether positive or negative. From the colonial perspective, this meant whether the religious personality could support the moral (read: ideological) project of colonization or whether they might be an obstacle in its achievement. The census becomes a technique and a technology in this practice of determining value. It refers to a certain totalizing relationship to a territory; it is a will to know exhaustively and rationally. The census is a way of knowing that is not at all textual, which is the way we saw Kamara write about himself in the previous two chapters. It is based on the observation of externalities and constituted a kind of accounting.

It is significant that Kamara appears in an early articulation of the policy I have been describing. It enshrines his place at the very foundation of colonial expertise on Muslim affairs. Already almost fifty, he has spent decades tilling the land, teaching his students, and leading a large and sprawling family and entourage. He had become known among his peers as an intelligent scholar and as a possessor of special spiritual insights, a reputation attested to by his autobiography, explored in the previous chapters. This notoriety brought him to the attention of a developing web of surveillance that encompassed both an anxiety about Muslim resistance to colonial rule and an interest in leveraging the Sufi orders as institutions of quasi governance. At this time, Kamara thus appeared to be a useful interlocutor on two levels: first, in the theorization of Islam as a phenomenon to be governed and, second, for the more practical information tied to intelligence and governance. Arnaud mentions Kamara in the 1912 text as a part of a section dedicated to explaining "Muslim propaganda"—that is, the appeal and spread of Islam in the region. After arguing that the devotee of ancestral traditions, whom he describes as fetishist, does not have a belief system and that Islam thus constitutes a veritable opening in the "psychology of the Black races," Arnaud describes the "maraboutic system," in which religious practice is centered around the learning of a few individuals who stand out for their knowledge. It is at this point that Kamara becomes the source to substantiate what would come to be a core colonial idea about the superficial nature of Islam in West Africa:

At Padalal, the cheikh Moussa Kamara, important Kadrya [sic] talibé of Cheikh Saâd Bouh, said to me: "In the Canton, religion has only been professed for three generations, and already the people are returning to disbelief; They prefer their material interests to the concern of their soul, and then also, the *grands marabouts*, ask them too often for gifts and this contributes to distancing believers from God!" Moussa Kamara had besides broken with his old master; He had lost a lot of his first's influence in marrying, against the religious law, nine wives, in neglecting Ramadan, etc.[32]

Kamara's appearance here is as the student of a trusted Muslim scholar and as someone who was critical of the excesses of the maraboutic system; the French often assumed that the master-disciple relationship that structured so much of religious life in the region was an exploitative one.[33] These two points were of vital importance for the administration's view of Muslim scholars, both those with whom they wished to cultivate relations and those whom they wished to manage as a threat. The first concern was loyalty to the French cause. Shaykh Saʿad Buh, whom Arnaud was referring to, had taken a position favorable to colonial rule and had personally intervened on behalf of Arnaud's mentor, Coppolani.[34] As for the second, the growing consensus in the first decades of the twentieth century was that Islam represented either an exploitative *ancien régime* similar to prerevolutionary feudal Europe or a modernizing pan-Muslim threat emanating from Turkey and Egypt. Either way, gullible West African Muslims had to be protected from traveling religious leaders who could exploit them economically or cause trouble politically. Finally, the discussion of the violation of the religious law represented the laxity of even the marabouts, the representatives of Islam in this context. Taken together, these were core pillars of the theory of Islam noir discussed later. Even if Kamara was not aligned with the colonial engineering project, he could be useful to it. His independence, moderate influence without political ambition, and familial connection to colonial employees led officials such as Arnaud to see him as an asset. Such a regard had as much to do with Arnaud's practical attitude as it did with anything about Kamara.

Soon after Kamara's appearance in the originary statement on colonial expertise in Muslim affairs, this body of knowledge took an institutional form as the *Service des Affaires Musulmanes*. The office collected and reviewed the reports sent in by colonial officers throughout French West Africa and oversaw the dragnet of surveillance. Paul Marty, the first director of the service, used these reports to further elaborate the expertise as a body of objective knowledge. This expertise was objective only in the sense that it was not based on individual experience. It was not objective in the sense that it was value neutral or free from bias. Marty also had personal links to Algeria and seemed to have inherited the practical attitude of the engineering project the French established there and continued to develop in West Africa.

Marty's work culminated in territorially organized monographs on all the West African colonies in France's possession.[35] These works were distinct from the type of works produced by orientalist scholarship based on philology and edition. Building on the foundations laid by Arnaud, Marty's major works on Islam in Senegal, Mauritania, and other regions came to be organized by personalities. Ironically, such a structure was not wholly different from the biographical profiles we see in the *tarjama* literature discussed in the previous two chapters. But the meaning—that is, the purpose—of these works was entirely different. Far from the exemplary function of the *tarjama* for a Muslim audience, these biographical surveys performed an informational function. They allowed the surveillance of the social terrain in a search for potential assets to be leveraged by the colonial officer seeking to govern, extract, and transform. Taken together, these monographs held the field of documentation, the library in the Foucauldian sense, from which the theory of Islam noir would be expounded.

A discussion of colonial knowledge production on Islam would be incomplete without a more focused consideration of the theory of Islam noir. Its emergence constituted a historical break in the way in which colonial power in French West Africa understood Islam and in the way the one related to the other.[36] It sought to explain, from the colonial perspective, three great displacements in terms of time, geographic space, and race. To the colonial theorists of Islam noir, the dramatic increase in the rate of Islamization of West Africa that occurred during the eighteenth and nineteenth centuries, in areas remote from the presumed Islamic center and cut off by a supposedly uninhabitable Sahara Desert, meant the experience of Islam in West Africa by and large fell outside of the time and space of the orientalist-constructed "golden age" of classical Islam. The spread of Islam in Africa came after Islamic civilization's supposed decline into decadence. Furthermore, a shallow rate of Arabization meant that these Black Africans—already understood as lacking intellectual capacity in a white supremacist ideology that needed to justify chattel slavery and colonial conquest—had only limited access to the superior culture of supposedly white Arabs. The "whiteness" of these Arabs meant that they could be learned, orthodox, and rational, although their religious difference supposedly made them violent, fanatical, and dangerous. Often credited with the initial phrasing and propagation of the theory, Marty used the phrase *Islam noir* to articulate the ensemble of ideas that the colonial administration had started to develop about Muslims in the region. These ideas included an emphasis on a personal, charismatic model of devotion manifested in the master-disciple relationship and institutionalized in Sufi orders; a nontextual orientation to religious practice; an intermingling with preexisting African animism; and a docile governability. Marty presented these ideas in his report on the Muridiyya Sufi order but used the opportunity to offer a much more general abstraction about the nature of Islam. "As Islam distances itself from its cradle . . . as races and conditions change, it becomes increasingly deformed. Islamic confessions, be they Malaysian or Chinese, Berber or Negro, are no more than vulgar [counterfeits] of the religion and state of the sublime Coran."[37] Although Islam had long been known for a universalism similar to that of Christianity, the notion of Islam noir broke the world religion up into a plurality of particulars that could no longer be known from its principal texts; Islam now had to be known from direct observation in either of its twin forms: surveillance or ethnography.[38]

This theory had at least two implications. First, it both described a geographic imagination projected by French colonialism and its interests and proscribed a specific relation of areas defined by that geographic imagination. With this theory, Islam did not overly complicate the racial logics that partitioned Africa into white populations north of and Black populations south of the Sahara Desert. The obviousness with which the desert functioned as a natural barrier would not be betrayed by the inconvenient facts that documented millennia of trade and circulation through the space. Such a border was useful to a French understanding of the world that saw a strategic need to keep French subjects away from the other Muslims of the world, who might resist the colonial state's imperialist designs. The fact that religious affinity might cause Muslims in West Africa to identify with the German-aligned Ottoman sultan caused considerable anxiety. Insisting on a natural difference between Black African Muslims and other Muslims, and reinforcing that difference with policy, was one product of the theory of Islam noir. West African Muslims, as French subjects, needed to have a general orientation to France to allow for the fulfillment of French interests. In that way, the theory of Islam noir was an instrument of colonial governance.

Second, the theory accompanied a major shift in policy practice. As Christopher Harrison has pointed out, William Ponty's *politique des races* encouraged a kind of ethnic particularism. Encouraging ethnic particularism, and in some ways producing ethnicity, was part and parcel of the transition from an assimilationist to an associationist policy. Under French assimilationism, the colony was tasked with making subjects, Muslim or otherwise, French citizens, and the four communes, particularly Saint-Louis, had certain models for making that happen. For the Senegalese historian Mamadou Diouf, the civility of the sons of Saint-Louis, or Ndoom Ndar, is an important example of making colonial subjects into French citizens.[39] One of the consequences of the participation of Muslim intellectuals in public life in Saint-Louis was that they played critical roles as intermediaries in the functioning of the colony, and Arabic was an important medium of communication. Even in areas that were not primarily Muslim, the French would sometimes use Arabic to communicate with diverse ethnic groups who spoke different languages. The region saw an increase in the rate of Islamization during the period of colonization because being Muslim and speaking Arabic facilitated movement through colonial space and access to the colonial state. Commenting on such developments, Alfred Le Chatelier, the editor of *Revue du monde musulman*, a major French orientalist journal he founded in 1906, said: "Saint-Louis was ... before the period of Muslim policy inaugurated by Faidherbe, a town of merchants who were indifferent in religious matters. Today it is an Islamic center, learned, devout, and restless."[40] Concerned with this Islamization, the secularist Ponty wanted to disfavor the spread of Islam through colonial channels. At the same time, he needed to oversee a policy akin to indirect rule in the rural areas. Instead of using Muslim intermediaries, as the colony had done in the past, he determined that ethnicity would be the basis of representation. Village chiefs would be named according to the ethnic identity of the majority of the inhabitants of each village. It is worth noting that the *politique des races* preceded the elaboration of the Islam noir theory but that both are part of the paradigm shift that occurred in the first two decades of the twentieth century. In this new paradigm of interrelated policymaking and knowledge production, empiricism was foundational, and the visibility of racial difference was the object of that empiricism.

Importantly, the theory of Islam noir and the strategy of the *politique des races* implied a colonial understanding of the nature of West African social relations and their relationship to Islam. Ponty and other administrators thought that West Africa was a feudal society on the verge of a social revolution that France had to help actualize.[41] They argued that Islam had encouraged rampant slavery in the region and that Muslim clerics had supported the institution. Islam was therefore synonymous with the aristocracy, and the diverse and numerous forms of servitude, understood as slavery *tout court*, would end only by neutralizing Muslim leadership and limiting the process of Islamization. The insistence on the analogy with Europe has long characterized historical thought and, in this case, made the fundamentally different experience of the ancien régime serve as a model of theory and practice in the colonial present.[42] The result was the suppression of Islam, although there were, in fact, no analogous structures between the Catholic clerisy and the Muslim ʿulamāʾ (a horizontal body of scholars). The idea that Islam was a cause of slavery, or its key culprit in the region, comes from the largely Christian abolitionist discourse that, following the orientalist tradition, presented Islam as a barbarous and totalitarian enemy of freedom.[43] Ponty inherited these views, and they informed his understanding of the role of Islam as a tool of the aristocracy that had to be isolated and marginalized. The characteristics of Islam noir favored the eventual marginalization of Islam in the colonies' urban political life while centralizing Islam in the administration of rural areas.

Kamara makes his second appearance in the colonial library by way of Marty's influential work *Islam in Senegal*. That appearance indicates Kamara had become a well-known entity to the colonial surveillance-cum-knowledge apparatus. Colonial officials had noticed him. It is worth citing the entry in full:

> Chek [sic] Moussa Kamara of Gouriki, at Ganguel (Damga). This last one, born toward 1864, intelligent and educated, runs a Koranic school and professes the rudiments of Muslim laws. He is both a Qadri and Tijani moqaddem and possesses a large influence. He has 50 or so talibés who work for him. His influence does not go beyond Demga where it is only partial. He is the uncle of the senior assistant of Indigenous Affairs Iba N'Diaye.[44]

There are a few things to note about this brief entry. While the beginning of the report seems positive—Kamara is intelligent and educated—it raises a question as to the degree of sophistication of his legal knowledge.

Developing ideas about Islam noir relied on stereotypes of racial incapacity. Noting that Kamara knows the rudiments of Islamic law presents him as exceptional in that he was learned, but it qualifies the extent of that learning as being elementary. American historian Rudolph Ware's research suggests that it was Marty who had the more rudimentary grasp of classical Islamic knowledge and thus was likely in no position to make such an assessment.[45] All the same, the entry provides an indication of how colonial expertise sought to order Muslim notables racially according to an assessment of intellectual capacity.

The passage also states that Kamara is a *moqqadem* (Arabic: *muqqadim*), a sort of lieutenant, of both the Qadiri and the Tijani Sufi orders. Based on our current knowledge of the period, this is odd. The literature on Islam in Africa presumes a long-standing antagonism between these two Sufi orders in West Africa. The Tijani claim of having a stronger, more powerful litany to be recited in ritual practice and of having a greater proximity to the diffusion of *baraka* (spiritual blessing) was hotly contested by the older, more entrenched Qadiri Sufi order. Moreover, Kamara's descendants do not remember him as having a Tijani affiliation. He is thought of as being a Qadiri, especially given that his primary spiritual guide was the Qadiri personality Shaykh Saʿad Buh. What could explain such an anomaly? The easiest answer is that Marty was mistaken, thus adding to the argument for discrediting the validity of colonial expertise. The other explanation is that Kamara did not consider the litanies to be exclusive; rather, as in much of the broader Sufi tradition, one might be initiated into many different esoteric methods.[46] He, in fact, expresses such a position in *The Clear Truth in the Brotherhood of All Believers*.[47] The Tijaniyya, after all, was distinct at the time for its claim of exclusivity. Perhaps Kamara collected these affiliations without discrimination, and Marty's surveillance reflected this ecumenicalism even though these affiliations have not been remembered today. Such a possibility is made more plausible if we consider that colonial expertise was preoccupied as much with tracking the relationships among scholars as with accurately describing the substance of their beliefs. Association with a subversive figure could make a Muslim scholar come to the attention of the experts as much as anything they said or did. Because of a colonial construction of the Tijaniyya as a source of troublesome activities from Hajj Umar Tal, the prototypical "bad Muslim," to Shaykh Hamallah (1882–1943), a Tijani affiliation might invite greater scrutiny.[48] In other words, the designation of Sufi affiliation in this surveillance report categorizes this Muslim scholar by his potential level of threat.

The report continues from a statement of affiliation to an assessment of Kamara's influence. Paradoxically, it states that his influence is large just before saying that it is limited to the administrative district of Damga. Moreover, even within that district, Kamara's influence is said to be partial. Perhaps both statements cancel one another out, suggesting that Kamara only had a modest influence. But why include two contradictory statements if one could simply say that Kamara had a modest influence? We should situate "influence" within the criteria of the colonial expertise on Muslim affairs. The first use of "influence" appears in the sentence describing Kamara's religious affiliations. Here it refers to the impact he might have on a given network of Muslim scholars. Kamara could be leveraged, for example, to influence both Qadiris and Tijanis to accept, support, or encourage colonial policy. In other words, influence is about the degree of integration into different networks and the extent to which this can be used to impact others. The sentence that follows refers not to social affiliation but to Kamara's relative position in economic production. He has some fifty people working for him, presumably cultivating his fields. This "influence" makes Kamara a manager of workers whom he could compel to contribute to the colonial economy. These social, spiritual, and economic senses of influence are closely related in the report and are the central criteria of colonial expertise.

The sense of influence in the report shifts when the emphasis on people and economic production changes to an emphasis on territory. The report states that Kamara's "influence" is limited to Damga, a unit of colonial administration. The surveilling official might have decided that Kamara's utility was limited to a particular area. He could not be mobilized for colonial ends beyond his district. This observation suggests that the expertise on colonial affairs qualified its findings by situating itself in a particular space.

Finally, the report closes with the observation that Kamara is related to a colonial employee. This relationship may have indicated loyalty or at least a social imbrication with the engineering project. Such a connection might be used to apply leverage, but one wonders who would be considered leverage for whom. Could Kamara be used as leverage against the colonial employee Ndiaye, or was Ndiaye the leverage for Kamara? Or perhaps the social division being implied here is with those unnamed. Having a family relation with an employee of the administration makes Kamara distinct from that mass of people who have no direct connection to the administration at all. Thus, he is a part of that small segment of the population who participates in and ensures the success of the colonial engineering project.

Of course, the autobiography of Kamara that we read closely in the previous chapter was written decades after the surveillance report. It was therefore not available to the authors of the report. All the same, the contrasts between the two clarify the expanse that lies between Kamara's concerns and the preoccupations of colonial expertise. The intelligence report is all external, instrumentalist, and governed by a principle of efficiency, thus exemplifying Edward Said's description of orientalist discourse.[49] His autobiography, in contrast, is contemplative, expository, and interested in the interiority of that which cannot be seen.

No matter the analysis of the surveillance report, the broad impression we are left with is that Kamara was, from the perspective of Muslim affairs, a good Muslim. This determination was the product of the theory and practices of colonial expertise. The interest in Kamara for practical reasons of surveillance and control, as a source of information, was distinct from the reasons held by a different group of colonial humanists, who appreciated Kamara for a shared commitment to philology, which I will discuss in the following chapter.

The Representation of Politics

I have shown that after the establishment of French West Africa in 1895, politics under the colonial administration was by and large the politics of representation, a process in which elites chosen through the system of chieftaincy stood in as if by synecdoche for the populations associated with their landholdings. The implementation of this system coincided with the application of a policy that sought to organize the population along ethnic lines so as to justify the processes of representation as being natural and rational. Representation here refers not so much to the kinds of democratic process that had long existed in the four communes[50] as it does to the mechanical functioning of the state via an intermediary that mediated between a subject population and the colonial state.[51] Surveillance ethnography constituted an applied science that participated in this politics of representation by producing identities through discursive elaboration.

Kamara's peer Abdou Salam Kane embodies the convergence of the paradigm of representation in the colonial state's functioning by way of chieftaincy and the paradigm of representation in scientific work with his publication of works on land tenure that were written in the period in question but not published until sometime later in 1935.[52] In much the same way that Kamara found himself in conflict in relationship to access to land, we can read him to be engaged in a very different kind of intellectual work. Where Kane embodied the politics of representation in his effort to stand in for the communities who lived on lands that he claimed, Kamara practiced the representation of politics, which I understand to be an intellectual activity of critique. I take this turn of phrase from David Scott, who is interested in debates in postcolonial theory and a certain depoliticizing direction that he sensed in the work of contemporary criticism by the late 1990s.[53] The contrast of these two activities and their relationships to power offer me an effective way of describing Kamara's particularity in his context. Where many of his peers were invested in the politics of representation by presenting themselves for possible roles mediating between the colonial state and the subject society and between its organs of both knowledge and power, Kamara's "constrained engagement," in the words of Senegalese-American political scientist Mbaye Lo, consisted of a critical representation of politics.[54] In what follows, I show this through a close reading of Kamara's *Most of the Would-Be Jihadists*, but my analysis is also grounded in previous arguments about *The Life of Hajj Umar*.[55]

Most of the Would-Be Jihadists is a long essay that treats the topic of jihad in the context of nineteenth- and early twentieth-century West Africa.[56] While it is difficult to date the text precisely, Lo has reasonably estimated a composition date between 1926 and 1930.[57] Kamara argues that armed struggle in the name of religion is not valid for his historical context because of the resulting loss of Muslim life, the lack of prophetic leadership, the absence of divine conditions, and the corrupting effect of political power on religious piety. Using his personal experience, archival documents, historical works, and examples from the sources of Islamic normativity, he makes a compelling case against a practice that was incredibly attractive to many of his immediate predecessors and contemporaries. In a show of exemplary coherence and intellectual consistency over the arc of his career, the central theme here is the tension between the desire for political power and the devotion to religion for Muslim scholars, a theme that he returns to in his biography of Hajj Umar. For our purposes, two features of the essay stand out for their representation of politics: He circumscribes the domain of the political by attention to historical specificity, and he categorically empties modern jihad of its religious content.

Before I turn to Kamara's text, I believe it helpful to note that there is a robust debate about the validity of the categories of *religion* and *politics* in both classical and modern Muslim societies. One side argues that the separation of distinct spheres identifiable as religion and politics is historically conditioned and that these should not be taken for granted as universal anthropological categories. This argument is built on a scaffolding of critical postcolonial religious studies that has come to interrogate what Talal Asad calls "formations of the secular."[58] It is also informed by theoretical discussions of political theology proposing, on the one hand, that religion persists in political forms, institutions, and practices and, on the other, that religion has always had political effects.[59] The other side raises this counterargument to the invalidation of the categories of religion and politics: Not only are these categories valid, but also Muslim societies are perhaps among the first in human history to distinguish the two.[60] Among those holding this view, their works, often of a historical bent, insist on the necessity of conceptual translation to identify emic terms such as *dīn* (religion) and *dunya* (world). This debate is by no means academic because it raises a question that has animated Muslim thought and action around the world in the twentieth and twenty-first centuries and lies at the heart of understanding the place of Islam in political modernity. Islamist reformists of various stripes famously reject the description of Islam as religion—if, by religion, we mean the absence of the political—because it is a colonial imposition. The postsecular position first described produces an echo of this understanding. In contrast, other Muslim intellectuals and activists have identified the utility of a secular orientation.

The study of Islam in Africa has not ignored the more general theme of the political and the religious. While early work often took for granted the terms that organize modern academic knowledge such as *religion* and *politics*, there has been a sustained interest in contextualizing their meanings and internal theorizations. The debate on whether Muslim West Africans have historically embraced the unity or the separation of the political and the religious has been expressed as the Maghilian tradition and the Suwarian tradition.[61] Muhammad al-Maghili (1440–1505) was a North African jurist who spent time in major courts of West African states. He is known for a rigorist interpretation of the *shariʿa* that called for the harsh treatment of non-Muslims. His legal opinions offered to Askia Muhammad of Songhai are cited in the following centuries by many of the intellectuals who advocated for jihad as armed struggle in West Africa, such as Sokoto's Fodiwa and Hajj Umar Tal. Hajj Salim Suware represents the inverse mirror image of al-Maghili. A Mande speaker who lived sometime between the thirteenth and the fifteenth centuries under the auspices of the empire of Mali, he advocated restraint and tolerance of non-Muslims by Muslim scholars, particularly those who lived as minorities.[62] This emphasis on coexistence became an influential strand of Islamic thought in West Africa, especially among Dyula scholars and merchants who would make a Muslim distinction between religion and politics in the region possible. More recent work has carefully considered these distinctions and interrelationships of the political and the religious by looking closely at the texts in which the debates are documented.[63] The interest in classical themes of political theory such as sovereignty, legitimacy, and authority in texts and sources that had otherwise been overlooked for their putative religious character has encouraged this examination of the religious and the political.

Drawing from the broader postsecular theoretical literature and the historiography of Islam in West Africa, I refrain from taking an either-or position on the identity of or difference between the religious and the political. Instead, I like to approach this question from the point of view that power is not reducible to either the political or the religious. I am particularly influenced by Talal Asad's description of the religious today as an effect of power, as well as by Claude Lefort's argument that the "theologico-political" is permanent—that transhistorical continuities bind the religious and the political but that their forms, expressions, and interrelationships are historically contingent.[64] Practically, this means that neither the religious nor the political are stable absolutes. Rather, they are arguments made and remade, forming a spectrum that must be read, contextualized, and read again.

Most of the Would-Be Jihadists begins with a strong sense of historical specificity. Although historical specificity, or an awareness of the similarity and difference of a given temporal context, is not explicitly named in the text as an operative concept, it can nevertheless be discerned with a careful reading. The introduction discusses the political culture of Futa Toro with explicit reference to the state's history. "Among the political habits of the people of Futa Toro, following the demise of Deeniyanke rule, was that the royal prerogative was not exercised by a particular family but rather was given to people who, through luck in life, attained a position of prestige, knowledge, or wealth or, through their generosity and courage, or eloquence, were able to gain support; such individuals were elected as the sovereign king."[65] This opening line of the introduction demarcates two eras in Futa Toro's political history. The first was the era defined by heredity kingship under the Saitigis, who traced their lineage from the leaders of the empire of Mali but who ruled this satellite state after the empire's fragmentation.[66] The second was the era of the imamate, led first by Ceerno Sulayman Baal and then, after the Toorodo revolution in 1776, by Almamy Abdul. While Kamara does not date this rupture in the text, its consequence for understanding a change in political life is clear. There is a transition from an era that operated by a political logic of tradition to one that is based on something like merit. As the text progresses, Kamara takes care to show that the imamate did not simply result in the "political" leadership of the almamy but rather was a dual system in which the almamy, who was elected, coincided with political rulers who were also elected. This awareness of historical difference between two periods of Futanke history allows Kamara to identify a clearly political structure that resembled but was separate from a structure of religious leadership that operated by the same logic.

Kamara then elaborates his understanding of Futa Toro's historical specificity as he explains an important feature of Futanke collective life in comparison to the situations in contemporary neighboring states. Kamara points out that as a result of the system of electing both political and religious leadership, membership in the class of scholars was no longer strictly inherited, as had been the case in Futa in the earlier period and in neighboring countries of the Saharan *Biḍan* and Futa Jallon.

> This practice specifically constituted an obstacle for the development of a hereditary class among the *ulama*. For, once one of their scholars was installed

as Almamy and, further, in most cases, was made a sovereign king, his children would be preoccupied with affairs of governance and conducting prestigious public duties, such as accompanying ministers, raising money, and entertaining the griots. Consequently, these children would disregard the fact that knowledge is the true source of real authority and the fact that other elements, such as raising money, and rewarding ministers and other peoples in order to control them, are actually less important sources of authority.[67]

What Kamara describes in this introduction, by way of comparison, is a transition from a caste-like social structure to one of classes.[68] Where the hereditary identity of scholarship that characterized pre-imamate Futa Toro and contemporary Moorish and Jallonke societies resembled the system of occupational specialization so common in areas under the sway of the Mali Empire,[69] the revolution initiated by Baal resulted in a surprisingly modern social mobility. To be clear, Kamara does not argue that this was a positive development. Instead, he enjoins his readers to take this as a lesson to preserve the pursuit of knowledge over the preoccupation with wealth. All the same, his comparison with neighboring contemporaries allows him to use historical specificity to analyze a social logic that differentiated the domain of the political and the domain of the religious.

To further demonstrate the distinction of the political and the religious, Kamara uses the amount of land to which a scholarly family has a claim as a measure of the likelihood of political aspiration. He gives as an example the scholarly family of Thierno Tilléré, which was known to maintain a scholarly identity over several generations. The inventory of the family's lands, its emic categories, and the amount of seed needed to cultivate those lands, cited from a named source in the family, together make the point that the family had a modest amount of property.[70] This modesty extended to the relative prestige associated with rendering everyday religious services such as daily prayers and funerary rites. While the requisite knowledge for these religious services was relatively valuable, it was not the kind of religious knowledge that made a scholar a candidate for the most prominent offices in the country associated with affairs of state. Kamara suggests that the continuity of the scholarly identity of the Tilléré family can be accounted for by the constraints of their material conditions and their social function as occupational specialists. The family still lived as scholarly families as they had lived before the Toorodo revolution, when the caste-like social structure contained scholars' ambitions and social mobility, making them the exception to the postrevolutionary rule in Futa Toro. "Because the people of Futa Toro prefer to designate a scholar to lead them as Almamy and sometimes become their king, an irresistible desire to become king has developed among their scholars. Few scholars are the exception to this rule."[71] For Kamara, the historical specificity of Futa Toro during his lifetime is such that scholarly ambition has excessively blurred the borders between the religious and the political.

Having distinguished the political and the religious through the analysis of historical specificity, we can also discover a surprising comparison made over the course of Kamara's work between the protagonists of arguably anticolonial jihad and procolonial African employees of the state. The first group is best exemplified by the historical example of Hajj Umar. Kamara develops his chapter on Umar through archival research in colonial offices and includes excerpts from the *Naṣīḥa*, written by his mentor Shaykh Saʿad Buh.[72] Kamara's argument is that the dramatic loss of Muslim life and the destruction of Muslim wealth violate core principles of Islamic governance. Besides Umar, Kamara includes several personal examples of his contemporaries, intended to show that public interest requires the acceptance of French rule. What is surprising comes in the ninth chapter, which appears to have been written after the rest of the main text. There Kamara describes the great lengths that certain African colonial employees have gone in order to use state power for their personal gain or to weaponize the state against their enemies.[73] Mbaye Lo convincingly argues that the employee described as "the envious one" refers to none other than Abdou Salam Kane, whom I have described as Kamara's antagonist in the politics of representation. After showing Kane's machinations against Kamara and the familial conflict of Kane and his family, Kamara argues that just as desire for power corrupted the leaders of an anticolonial jihad, it corrupts the class of colonially named chiefs. Politics, then, whether militant or administrative, is not only distinct from the religious but also detrimental to it.

For Kamara, the representation of politics constituted the performance of critique. This critique was historically specific to his context in both the form and the content of *Most of the Would-Be Jihadists*. This historical character is made explicit when he invites his readers to "consult history books, biographies on kings and sultans and their encounter with the *ulama*, and the righteous and pious people who challenged their political authority by rebelling against them. The number of these pious people who were killed in such conflicts from the time of the companions of the Prophet to our time defies approximation or estimation."[74] Such descriptions of politics depart from those of many of his peers, whose politics consist of representing the subject population. By standing in for Futanke society at large, in Kamara's point of view the elites risk their moral integrity by engaging in a competition to harness the power of the state for personal gain.

The German-Jewish philologist Erich Auerbach wrote *Mimesis*—which many consider to be one of the greatest masterpieces of literary criticism—between 1942 and 1945, while in exile in post-Ottoman Turkey. This was the same period in which Kamara would struggle, as we shall see in the following chapter, to get his own work published by a colonial state that was preoccupied by the same fascist war that made Auerbach flee Europe. The tradition that has celebrated Auerbach's accomplishment, best captured in the writings of Edward Said,[75] has emphasized the incongruence of the ambition of the work—the representation of reality in Western literature—and the lack of libraries and references to which its author had access while residing in the so-called Orient. Kamara too struggled with such limitations. But the practice of philology, the slow and meticulous attention to language and texts, enabled Auerbach to plunge headlong into the project, starting not with a synthetic, bird's-eye view of the phenomenon that interested him in the confident tone of the expert but with the readerly attention to detail of the scene in which the hero of the Homeric epic is recognized by a "scar on his thigh."[76] There are many ways, of course, that *Mimesis* has been read; but I am interested in the historical appearance of the text during World War II as a symptom of a major global epistemological transformation, one that involved an entanglement of colonial powers and colonized lands. If the ambition to describe the representation of reality in Western literature was available to Auerbach, it was because literature was no longer tasked with the socially useful work of representing reality. That task had, by the war, been definitively delegated to science. Literature could no longer be expected to offer the most accurate representations that might be useful from the perspective of the practical attitude. *Mimesis*, then, is an elegy to the textual attitude, a requiem for an order in which the arts of representation yielded to the sciences of identification.

In this chapter, I described the ways in which Kamara navigated this transition and the emergence of representivity as a paradigm of scientific knowledge and of political power as an expectation of both metropolitan and colonial spaces. I first showed how the micropolitics of land management in the Senegal River Valley following partition rendered Kamara vulnerable to peers who sought to mediate the relationship between the colonial state and colonized society. I then showed the development of a field of expertise in Muslim affairs, with Kamara appearing both in its originary conceptualization and in its archive of surveillance, in ways that differed greatly from his own self-definition. Finally, I contrasted Kamara with his context by showing how his representation of politics constituted a historically specific critique of power. The invocation of Auerbach's *Mimesis* here is intended to describe the character of a global moment that Kamara shared. It is also intended to underscore the value of a commitment to close reading that eschews the systematic and authoritative posture shared by the engineer and the social scientist, whose practical attitude helps in part to explain what happened to Kamara's masterpiece, *The History of the Blacks*.

FOUR

A Monumental Text in an Orientalist Season

SHAYKH MUSA KAMARA grew frustrated. The Muslim scholar who had spent most of his life on the banks of the Senegal River had toiled for years collecting and consulting Arabic manuscripts, listening to griots, and posing questions to village chiefs and clerics. He had painstakingly composed hundreds of pages of a monumental work on the history and customs of the land of the Blacks. He expected this work—*Flowers from among the Gardens in the History of the Blacks*—to be translated into French and printed in a bilingual edition.[1] After all, his friends, the colonial administrators-cum-scholars had published his peer Siré Abbas Soh just as they had published the previously impossible to find *Chronicle of the Seeker*.[2] Had Kamara not written an even more thorough account of the West African past? Had he not submitted several shorter works for publication after the French governor announced a prize for indigenous authors? Had he not faithfully responded to the queries about custom and Islamic law to aid in the work of colonial governance? What's more, he had grown old and frail. The demands of a large family and entourage in an increasingly cash economy in an increasingly marginalized corner of colonial French West Africa had made compensation for his efforts even more urgent. And yet, after years of waiting, he would have to send another letter. Maybe he could write yet another text.

I pose two key questions in this chapter: How did late colonial officials read, or fail to read, Kamara? And why did he bequeath his intellectual work to a colonial institution despite this disregard? By narrating the story of Kamara and his *History of the Blacks*, which begins with energy and enthusiasm before yielding to frustration and disappointment, I tell the story of the opening and closing of an orientalist season in the period of France's colonization of West Africa. Borrowed from French historian Jean-Louis Triaud, the expression "orientalist season" refers to an unexpected opportunity in the relations of knowledge and power that made the philological encounter between Kamara and a small group of colonial officials possible.[3] This was a moment when the textual attitude, as an orientation toward the world through the mediation of meaningfully composed texts, managed to carve out a space for itself in the ever-present battle with the practical attitude of colonial engineering. While I argue that the orientalist season was one of possibility, I also show that it was undermined by the contradictions of colonial humanism and the transformation of philology into a technical discipline ancillary to history and religious studies. I base this argument on Kamara's surveillance file, close readings of his autobiographical *The Announcement* and *The History of the Blacks*, and relevant secondary literature.

Kamara in the Generation of a Native Literature

In contrast to the practical attitude that characterized the expert colonial regard toward Kamara, explored in the previous chapter, there existed a countervailing textual attitude that characterized a more humanist engagement with him. This attitude was held by a small group of philologists who, though fully implicated in the engineering project, devoted themselves to a form of study and contemplation that defied the mandates of instrumentalist value and the criteria of efficiency. If the practical attitude of surveillance and expertise in Muslim affairs is best embodied by Xavier Coppolani, Robert Arnaud, and Paul Marty, the colonial textual attitude is best exemplified by Octave Houdas, Maurice Delafosse, and Henri Gaden.

Houdas was a prolific translator and professor at the School of Oriental Languages in Paris. His singularity within the history of French orientalism was his move away from the study of the classical languages and texts of the Muslim world and toward the vernacular languages of North Africa. While we might see in this development the impact of the evolution

A MONUMENTAL TEXT IN AN ORIENTALIST SEASON

within turn-of-the-century European philology toward a more empirical linguistics—that is, toward a knowledge of languages as they are actually used in everyday life and not as they are recorded in writing—Houdas's interest in colloquial Arabic coincided with his interest in an underappreciated West African textual tradition.

Born in France but settled in Algiers with his family while young, Houdas had an unconventional path to philology.[4] He made his way to the work of translation from the demands of working in French schools in Algeria as a teacher first of French and then of vernacular Arabic. Having published several teaching texts, he eventually turned toward works of greater scholarly interest, including a treatise on law and Maghrebian histories. He was named to a position at the School of Oriental Languages in 1884. His 1900 edition of Abd al-Rahman al-Sa'adi's *Tarikh al-Sudan*, the manuscript of which he had received from a team of colonial conquerors and explorers who had famously captured Hajj Umar Tal's library, which held some four thousand pillaged documents and texts, might be considered an event in the history of the French academy.[5] The seventeenth-century chronicle testified to an African historicity that had been ignored and denied. Houdas would also be associated with the publishing of several other West African chronicles that have been key references in the African library, having provided the core of what is generally known of precolonial West African history.[6]

The introduction that Houdas wrote for the *Tarikh al-Sudan* is characteristically orientalist in several ways. Perhaps most charitably, the text is orientalist in its technical method; it presents the textual scholarship of a particular Arabic text. Houdas's method included the collection and comparison of several versions of *Tarikh al-Sudan*, from which he established an imagined urtext that he then translated into French. But the introduction is also orientalist in the sense that it features many of the clichés and habits of mind associated with the group of scholars and their tradition devoted to such work in the West. This is seen in phrases such as the "period of decadence" (i) when describing the moment of the text's composition and in the dismissive evaluation that "the scribes attached less importance to the exact reproduction of the text than to calligraphy" (iv). We often associate this second sense of orientalist with Edward Said's critique: the condescension that accompanies the interested and strategic will to know the Orient as an object of power.

[117]

A MONUMENTAL TEXT IN AN ORIENTALIST SEASON

But there is an even deeper sense in which the work is orientalist: It produces only a partial translation. While Houdas methodically determined the language of the text and then translated it into French, his commentary evaluates the text only in terms that are relevant and important to his own intellectual context. The absence of a preconceived organization in the writing of *Tarikh al-Sudan*, in the style of Arab chroniclers, contributes to his dim assessment of the text. Such a desultory organization offended modern French readers, who, no doubt, were anticipating a Cartesian logic. Moreover, the absence of both an explanation of the causes of facts and an examination of their consequences left the text just on the edge of historical scholarship (iv). These largely negative evaluations are based on implicit comparisons with the orientalist's own intellectual milieu and suggest a relative lack of curiosity that he held for the milieu of the author he was studying.

An explanation for this refusal to translate fully is found in the final sense we might use in describing this introduction as orientalist. In discussing the ultimate value of *Tarikh al-Sudan*, Houdas makes explicit the paradigm of evaluation:

> Despite its faults and lacunae, the History of the Sudan is full of new or unpublished facts of the greatest interest; it sets from now on the principal stages of the national life of a portion of the natives of the Sudan. It shows that these populations, to whom one is tempted to refuse any initiative in matters of progress, had their own civilization which had not been imposed on them by a people of another race and that the disappearance of this relatively prosperous State is due largely if not solely to conquerors of the white race. Finally, it connects to the general history of humanity a whole group of nations which hitherto had been almost completely excluded from it. (ix)

In other words, *Tarikh al-Sudan* is valuable because, not to be too tautological given the title of the work, it renders Africa historical. The text provides a periodization by which the African past could be known, despite colonial claims as late as Hugh Trevor Roper's 1965 statement that the African past was nothing but "the unedifying gyrations of barbarous tribes in picturesque but irrelevant corners of the globe."[7] This history was one of self-asserted agency and progressive movement, and the vehicle for that movement was a nation that was unique and a state that was sovereign. These criteria of historical development, national identity, and cultural genius proved some core tenets of the modern humanist's worldview to be true: People make history, and that history is progressively better. Civilization is a process in which all societies can partake—and all have done so.

The consequence of such universalism was not solely positive though. By placing West Africa in "history," in terms that are legible to modern colonial thought, it also situated West Africa in an inferior stage of development. Such a framing aligned with the colonial humanist case for colonization, often described as the civilizing mission.[8] If the colonial practical attitude characterized the sober engineer who busied himself with extraction, this colonial textual attitude was premised on a rationale of partial translation. Houdas in many ways opened within French African studies the orientalist season, a period of time when African manuscripts received serious textual scholarly attention, even if their translation of the work was only partial. But he was not alone in these efforts.

One of Houdas's star students at the School of Oriental Languages was Maurice Delafosse, who studied vernacular Arabic with Houdas and eventually married his mentor's daughter. Instead of applying his university studies "in the field" in North Africa, Delafosse was first assigned to Cote D'Ivoire. He eventually climbed the ranks of the administration, and on the side, he developed an interest in African languages. Jean Schmitz has argued that Delafosse's study of African languages is filtered through his study of Arabic.[9] Delafosse eventually published several influential texts on Mande languages and also popularized basic knowledge of France's West African colonies in *Haut-Senegal-Niger*, often considered to be a foundational text for French Africanist scholarship.[10]

Henri Gaden was yet another student of Houdas who engaged in the philological work of publishing texts by native authors and reference works. But where Delafosse worked on the Mande-speaking milieu, Gaden explored the Pulaar-speaking context. He was noted for the scholarly endeavors he conducted alongside his responsibilities of administration. He once served as the lieutenant-governor of Mauritania. Aided by a vast social network through his unrecognized Senegalese wife, Coumba Cissé, he acquired many manuscripts and developed a solid scholarly profile.[11]

Together, these three embarked on a project of generating a native literature. While an abundant literature existed well before this trio, we cannot accurately describe it as a *native* literature. As explored in the first two chapters, West Africa is home to varied and overlapping traditions of textual production in both oral and written forms. Some of these traditions explicitly referenced a self-consciously ancestral identity in opposition to Islam, while others were more Muslim in flavor or were hybrid in nature. But this literature, in the sense of both aesthetically oriented textual forms and a coherent body of intertextually referenced writing, was not "native." The native was produced in the colonial encounter and was both the continuation of what had come before and a screen for colonial projections of difference. In other words, the native was a colonial institution. Before that, what could be described as native existed otherwise.

An important example of the will to generate a native literature is the story of the famed phantom text of the Sudan, *Tarikh al-Fattash* (Chronicle of the Seeker). For much of the twentieth century, it was considered one of the great sources of precolonial African history. Along with the *Tarikh al-Sudan*, it comprised what is often referred to as the Timbuktu Chronicles. Long believed to have been authored by Mahmoud Ka'ti, *Tarikh al-Fattash* presents the history of the Songhai Empire before the Moroccan invasion of 1591. In the 1970s, Nehmia Levtzion questioned the authorship of the text, suggesting that the text published in 1913 by Houdas and Delafosse was, in fact, a forgery by Ahmad Lobbo, the nineteenth-century leader of the Hamdallahi Caliphate.[12] Mauro Nobili has since substantiated this claim, proving that the *Tarikh al-Fattash* was a nineteenth century creation that combined the seventeenth century chronicle by Ibn Mukhtar with another document to legitimize the reign of Lobbo.[13] This discovery, along with arguments by Paulo Farias that use epigraphic evidence from the Sahara and show that the chronicles were intellectual interventions in their own times, has forced a rewriting of late medieval and early modern West African history.[14] But what is even more interesting for our concerns here is the story of how the text was created. In the late 1890s the French explorer Felix Du Bois (1862-1945) was traveling the Saharan-Sahel zone, many people knew about *Tarikh al-Fattash*, but nobody had seen it, let alone read it. To create his forgery, Lobbo had all the known manuscripts collected, all those that foretold his reign were copied, and all those that did not testify to his coming dominion were destroyed. This was not known at the time by Du Bois, who was committed to acquiring this fabled manuscript. The problem, as he would discover, was that it did not yet exist—so it would have to be generated. Eventually, the colonial explorer Albert Bonnel de Mézières (1870-1942) acquired several manuscripts that together were used by Houdas and Delafosse to establish a text that otherwise did not exist in physical form prior to the philological intervention. Its circulation had been an oral phenomenon. In so establishing the text, Houdas and Delafosse generated a native literature that could define the colony in terms legible to the administration and the academy.

As a colonial institution, "native literature" required translation. In addition to the chronicles already mentioned, the team of Houdas, Delafosse, and Gaden translated and published such works as Siré Abbas Soh's *Chroniques du Foûta sénégalais* (1913), *Légendes et coutumes sénégalaises: Cahiers de Yoro Dyao* (1912), *Tedzkiret an-nisyan* (1913–1914), *Proverbes Peuls et Toucoleurs* (1931), and *La vie de el Hadj Omar* by Muhammad Ali Caam (1935). The publication dates of these titles suggest two periods of publishing intensity: one in the years leading up to World War I and another in the interwar period. At stake in the generation of a native literature was the recognition of African humanity. This recognition went beyond the preoccupation of the engineering paradigm embodied by Louis Faidherbe and routinized by the surveillance apparatus that initially facilitated Kamara's entry into the colonial archive. Nevertheless, it grew increasingly necessary, given the evolution of a Black politics and metropolitan-colonial dynamics.

There was, however, a degree of ambivalence in this recognition of African humanity. It is worth considering the testimony from the preface of a work on which Delafosse and Gaden collaborated: *Chroniques du Foûta sénégalais*. Authored by Siré Abbas Soh, a famous genealogist from the Senegal River Valley, the text was as close as the team could come to finding a historical chronicle like one of the Timbuktu Chronicles. And even it was written on demand after Gaden asked Soh to write it. But it paled in comparison in Delafosse's view: "Fundamentally, [Siré Abbas Soh's] chronicles do not constitute, from our European point of view, a well-filled nor very interesting history of Fouta, but it seemed to me useful to give the translation, given that we have no other historical document on this country and that we have no chance of finding anything better than what Sire-Abbas has done. It is very curious that, in this region which has been Islamized for so long, we find absolutely nothing analogous to what was found in the middle Niger region."[15] This quote suggests that there was a certain desire for or expectation of a historical chronicle. In the absence of such a text, Soh's work was made to stand in its place. But the translators were dissatisfied with what the text had to offer: It was too fantastical, and the facts were too uncertain. This dissatisfaction generally accompanied the interest in West African texts.

A MONUMENTAL TEXT IN AN ORIENTALIST SEASON

We might better understand the orientalist ambivalence by considering how Delafosse's philology was embedded within a broader theory of developmental humanity. In the final paragraph of his short prefatory note, Delafosse discusses the value of the text and its translation. The chronicle had no literary or historical value in his mind. Furthermore, it featured too much of the miraculous in human affairs. But it was precisely this feature that was to be found among all peoples "at the beginning of what we call the 'historical period.'"[16] To be sure, Futa Toro had just begun its historical period with the occupation of European powers within the colonial paradigm. In other words, the inhabitants and cultures of the Senegal River Valley were indeed like all other humans and their cultures; it just so happened that they were still in an earlier stage of human development, one that Europe had long ago moved past. This denial of coevality is, of course, a central feature of modern thought generally.[17] But it also operated by virtue of a discipline of orientalist philology that elaborated both the universality of the human category and its internal hierarchization based on religio-racial lines grafted onto the stages of development.

Having embraced this strange orientalist ambivalence, defined by both the desire for the historical text and the denial of coevality, the colonial humanist team of philologists would undertake one of its most ambitious projects: the generation, that is the solicitation, edition, and translation of *The History of the Blacks* by Shaykh Musa Kamara. In what follows, I will retrace the colonial humanist project that supported and validated Kamara's monumental history and the effort to translate it. However, the seeds of the project's failure were already sown in the internal contradictions of a colonial humanism that was limited by the partial translation of orientalism and by the competition between its own textual attitude and the practical attitude explored in the previous chapter.

The History of the Blacks

The History of the Blacks is a monument of historical memory and geographical imagination. Written in a Maghrebi-Sudani script, the version held today at the Institut Fondamental d'Afrique Noire (IFAN) contains over 1,700 pages. It offers a survey of the major personalities, genealogies, narrative histories, anecdotes, cultural practices, and ethnic formations that had come to define the western Sahel, that "coast" between the sea of the Sahara Desert and the more verdant lands farther south, during the peak of colonial rule.[18] Herein lies one of the many peculiarities of this staggering work. The history that Kamara covers is a long one that reaches well beyond the history of colonial conquest of the Senegambia and the western Sahel in the latter half of the nineteenth century. It even reaches beyond the revolutionary age in which the region's Muslim scholars and merchants seized the dominant role in society amid the amplified ravages of the Atlantic and Saharan slave trades in the eighteenth century. It stretches back to a sacred history that is barely historical at all. And yet this past is made to speak to the actuality of a colonial present in which Kamara wrote. The work does not merely transmit an African antiquity as if it simply reflected that tradition. It links its own colonial modernity with a deep past, one beyond historical time. Organized geographically by the densely populated village clusters and lands then subject to French rule, *The History of the Blacks* reflects an understanding of space that had been defined as much by a long arc of autochthonous historical development as by colonial administration. As much as Masina, Segou, Xasso, and Futa Toro, for example, were precolonial political formations, they were also administrative units that colonial officials might recognize as being under their authority.[19] In that way, the organization of *The History of the Blacks* would not have been totally unfamiliar to a *commandant de cercle* (district officer), who might reference, for example, Delafosse's *Haut-Senegal-Niger*, which brought together a historical overview and a discussion of customs for the subject population in a monograph on the communities in his district.[20] But as much as the organization of *The History of the Blacks* would have been familiar to colonial employees, its Arabic language, its traditionalist values of the culture of documentation, and its style would have been inaccessible to all but the most specialized, and interested, bureaucrats.[21] The excess produced by a text that responded to a colonial demand for practical knowledge for governance, as well as to a colonial humanist demand for inclusion in a universalist narrative of humanity, has proved to be at the heart of its monumentality.

When Kamara first sent off his monumental work in May of 1924, he did so with a sense of urgency, according to the French historian Anna Pondopoulo.[22] Gaden had asked Kamara to write a history of the region and encouraged the undertaking.[23] Kamara worked past his initial reluctance to write such a book and embraced the opportunity to have his writing circulate beyond his immediate network of friends with whom he shared locally produced and hand copied works and occasionally print works from North African traders. The urgency of his efforts comes across in his decision to send the unfinished manuscript to Gaden to begin the onerous editorial work for its publication. Gaden responded enthusiastically, asking Kamara to send the rest without delay. Receiving this endorsement, Kamara wrote the rest and sent it off just a few months later. But as Gaden had taken leave in France, Kamara sent the missing section directly to Gaden's intellectual collaborator Maurice Delafosse. The urgency that animated Kamara's and Gaden's attention to the manuscript fed into an enthusiasm for establishing and elaborating an autonomous field of knowledge about African colonial subjects who happened to be Muslim.[24]

Over the course of the sprawling work, three themes emerge that Kamara would eventually elaborate on in subsequent texts.[25] Primary among these themes is the struggle of religious leadership burdened with the demands of temporal power. The paradigmatic case for this interest is that of Almamy Abdul, so named as the most influential leader, or imam, of the revolutionary Muslim state of the late eighteenth century. Once a Qurʾanic teacher who lived a strict and withdrawn life of study, he succeeded his teacher Ceerno Sulayman Baal as the head of Futa Toro. However, his personal direction, which he had developed successfully at the small village scale, failed in the state and regional arenas. A second theme that emerges in the work is a concern for the invention and abuse of genealogy to obtain power. Using everything from grammatical criticism, cultural critique, rational disputation, documentary evidence, to appeals to Islamic normativity, Kamara highlights the weakness of the claims by many of the region's elite that they were linked genealogically to the first generation of Islam. He gives as an example the claim by rulers of the Deeniyankooɓe dynasty that they were descendants of Bilal, the once-enslaved Abyssinian who was the first muezzin to call the Muslim community at Medina to prayer. Finally, the third theme is the human price of war, conflict, and insecurity. Repeatedly in discussions of the jihads of Ceerno Sulayman Baal (d.1776), Almamy Abdul Qadir Kan (d.1807), Hajj Umar, and Mamadou Lamine Draame (d.1887), Kamara highlights the loss of innocent Muslim lives, a violation of a chief principle of Islamic teaching. Together, these themes run throughout the work. Eventually, Kamara would articulate these ideas in more explicit and focused terms in shorter, more topical works such as *The Precious Collection*,

A MONUMENTAL TEXT IN AN ORIENTALIST SEASON

The Life of Hajj Umar, *Most of the Would-Be Jihadists*, *The Purification of Thoughts from Delusional Doubts*, and *The Announcement*, having used *The History of the Blacks* as a sort of first draft for the development of his ideas.[26]

It is worth discussing the form, style, and what we might call the mode of *The History of the Blacks*. The two terms that come to mind when describing these features are *compilation* and *commentary*. Kamara appears, above all, to be a consummate collector whose authorship should be understood as acts of composition, the bringing together of disparate traces of human and community life in a meaningful sequence. Long excerpts of letters, treaties, and chronicles are preserved in their entirety in the text alongside oral accounts and family and clan genealogies. They are often presented as Kamara encountered them, reflecting the culture of documentation that is part and parcel of the manuscript tradition, in which the bibliographic infrastructure of modern publishing is absent and thus a text must carry its references with it. Preceding, following, and only occasionally interrupting such documentation is the commentary, in which Kamara explains, expounds on, introduces doubt about, or confirms some feature of a reported utterance.

The features of compilation and commentary also give us an indication of Kamara's method. Central to his approach was the collection and recording of the most diverse set of documents available from multiple perspectives, on the one hand, and the evaluation of the authenticity, normativity, and reasonability of those documents and what those documents represented, on the other. Kamara's "documents" are both written, such as letters, chronicles, treaties, and classical works from the Islamic tradition, and oral, including reports by participants and traditions transmitted orally. To collect the written documents, he conducted archival research in the personal libraries of his scholarly peers and in the files of colonial offices in Saint-Louis and Dakar.[27] He also maintained a robust correspondence with other Muslim scholars of the region through which they identified and traded works of interest in both manuscript and print form.[28] In addition, he dispatched some of his students to copy and trade these written works. Finally, he interviewed griots, Muslim judges, village chiefs, and other notables, recording their testimony. The language of these written and oral documents often appears in their entirety. Kamara's practice of compilation contributed to the great scale and sometimes the redundancy of his work, but the payoff is that he records unique and valuable information and perspectives otherwise unavailable in the historical record.[29] Thus, it might be useful to think of *The History of the Blacks* as a metatext and an archive of the West African past as much as the product of a single authorial voice.

Nestled around the documents, and only occasionally within them, are Kamara's commentaries. He will make a brief introductory and descriptive statement about the document, sometimes already announcing his view of its contents. Most of the commentary, however, follows the document, where he explains any of its obscurities and evaluates the content. His evaluations generally follow a pattern of thinking that reflects the hierarchy of Islamic epistemology. First, he compares what the document says to the norms and understandings expressed in Qurʾanic scripture and sayings and behaviors of the Prophet's Sunna. Then he includes any transmitted knowledge relevant to the document, such as a consensus position of Muslim legal scholars or proverbs and poetry that might give any insight. He next considers the plausibility of a document's claims in light of his own reasoning. To do this, he might tap into the vast reservoir of linguistic and cultural knowledge he had acquired through a lifetime of study. While the normative thrust of Kamara's evaluation might have been alienating to an intended colonial readership, his methodical approach to commentary demonstrates a historical skepticism, which was what Gaden and Delafosse likely appreciated most about his work at the time and which would excite a later generation of Senegalese scholars, explored in the following chapter.

One can perceive many models and influences of this work through its citation of content and form. Some of these models came from classical sources of Arabic historiographical prose. Here the prosopographical tradition of biographical dictionaries exerted a particularly strong influence, with the lives of saints, scholars, and rulers depicted in ways that often sought to instruct, edify, and exemplify the ideal Islamic form of life, whose paradigm, of course, was the biographical literature of the Prophet Muhammad.[30] Hadith scholarship, which had developed a robust system for the authentication of transmitted reports and source criticism, also had an influence here.[31] And, of course, classical masterworks of history, such as those by al-Tabari and Ibn Khaldun, and of geography, such as those by al-Masʿudi and Ibn Battuta, are both sources of information and conceptual models.[32] There was also, however, a notable influence from modern sources. There are citations from *The Complete Lesson in General History*, the late nineteenth-century history textbook from Al-Azhar University in Cairo, and from the eighteenth-century Moroccan historian Ahmad al-Nasiri.[33] Kamara's personal library also included print copies of works such as *The Arabs Before Islam* by Jurji Zaydan, an Arab Christian Nahda intellectual.[34] Together, the classical models and modern references show Kamara was both fully situated within the broad and deep tradition of Arabo-Islamicate thought and relatively current with contemporary scholarly debates, despite material, political, and infrastructural limits that disfavored, without preventing, West African connectivity with the rest of the Muslim world.

According to correspondence in colonial archives and Kamara's autobiography, the lieutenant governor and amateur philologist Gaden solicited *The History of the Blacks*. The request was part of a broader effort to generate a native literature and a colonial science for both humanist reasons and administrative purposes. In the second chapter of *The Announcement*, Kamara presents a list of his authored works and their endorsements by his peers and concludes with a discussion of the works he wrote with a colonial audience in mind: "The motive of [the] composition was the governor M. Gaden's request of me."[35] In the context of a discussion of his body of work, *The History of the Blacks* represents a pivot. All his previous texts—such as pedagogical texts on the foundations of law, grammar, and rhetoric; works on literary theory and criticism; polemical works on Sufism; and devotional works on the names of God—fit within well-established genres of Arabo-Islamic writing. But the final texts presented in the chapter all fit the rubric of the kinds of texts the colonial administration was interested in, such as histories, works on genealogy, and a treatment of law and custom, and all are described by Kamara as being requested by the French. Accepting this information that Gaden asked Kamara to write this text as true, we are still left with the question of why he agreed to such an undertaking.

The introduction to *The History of the Blacks* introduces a wrinkle in our understanding of Kamara's motivation for the work. We learn that his acceptance of Gaden's request was not a straightforward matter. He, in fact, expresses several reservations about writing a history, a less valued but not wholly absent genre in the Arabo-Islamic tradition in general and in Muslim West Africa in particular. In the opening remarks of at least one version of the text, Kamara makes clear that Gaden asked Kamara repeatedly to write a history of Futa Toro: "He [Gaden] sought after the widest benevolence toward me and affection for me with favors. Then he beseeched [me] on his behalf that I gather for him the history of Futa Toro."[36] But Kamara demurs for religious reasons. He writes that the endeavor would constitute a moral hazard for him because writing such a history would mean potentially engaging in slander, lying, insulting the friends of God, and gossiping. It would also expose the inadequacy of his language, as such a text would need to be fit for kings. He justifies the first four of these reservations with references to the sources of Islamic normativity, including the Qur'an and hadith. Here he expresses the reasons why there had been no major "histories" of the Senegambia like the famed Timbuktu Chronicles, a lack that was a source of frustration to Delafosse, who had translated and edited the chronicles with his father-in-law, Octave Houdas.[37] In fact, Kamara's key insight explains why the Timbuktu Chronicles were more exceptions to the rule of scholarly writing in the postclassical period of West Africa's Islamic tradition. Ultimately, however, Kamara acquiesces to Gaden's request for religious reasons as well. After citing yet another hadith—"Whoever is hostile to a friend of mine, I have declared war on him"—Kamara explains that because Gaden is in power as determined by God, he owes the nominally Christian colonial administrator obedience.[38] The fact that Kamara mobilizes religious reasons to explain both his reluctance to write a history and his eventual acceptance of such an undertaking speaks to the profoundly religious motivation for a text that has typically been understood in more secular terms.

Regardless of any ambiguities in Kamara's views of the endeavor, the orientalists first tasked with assessing the value of *The History of the Blacks* within the rubric of colonial humanism were unambiguously favorable. These assessments are captured in the correspondence between Kamara and the amateur philologists Gaden and Delafosse, who, in turn, were in conversation with professional orientalists in Paris. Kamara had sent several hundred pages of the text to Gaden in May of 1924, and several months later Gaden wrote to Kamara that he had sent the manuscript to Paris, where it had been well received: "They responded that after consultation, examination, and review, they find it interesting and very satisfying. They have promised to make it into an excellent edition. I credit, dear master, their appreciation towards your *History*, for which I am enthusiastic."[39] Eventually, Delafosse, one of the people Gaden was referring to, wrote to Kamara directly: "It is in my opinion a beautiful production, excellent and invaluable. I have even begun its translation from Arabic into French, hoping to finish it one day, God willing. In fact, my goal is that your book be published in Arabic, in French, so that the people of our region and yours can all refer to it." Delafosse then informed Kamara that he had participated with his father-in-law, Octave Houdas, in the publication of the famous Timbuktu Chronicles and that Kamara's work belonged next to those works. He believed that it constituted in all its monumentality— that is, its scale and its relationship to memory—a reliable West African transmission of the classics, thereby earning its place in the orientalist's library, if they could manage to find the time to translate it.

A History Lost in Translation

The History of the Blacks encountered the first challenge to its translation and publication with the death of Maurice Delafosse on November 13, 1926. The former colonial administrator's liberal views on governance in the French colonial empire had estranged him from the colonial service after World War I, but his appointment in Paris meant that Kamara had a well-respected representative in the metropolitan academy.[40] While at the Special School of Oriental Languages and the Colonial School, Delafosse had published many works that would serve as a foundation for scholarly and popular African studies in France.[41] This activity grew from, elaborated on, and encouraged the belief among a certain segment of colonial administrators that a robust understanding of local history, language, and custom had to be the foundation of a system of colonial governance if it was to be both effective and respectful.[42] It was a minority colonial humanist position that defied the antihumanist common sense that privileged the power of engineering. As long as he was alive, Delafosse supported Kamara and his writing, promising the broadest possible audience for the somewhat reclusive village dweller in the far reaches of the French colonial empire. The primary challenge for Delafosse in realizing his goal of seeing *The History of the Blacks* on library shelves was the overwhelming scale of the undertaking and the complexity of its translation, which required a specialist skill set and competencies not only in Arabic but also in other languages such as Pulaar and Mande. Though Delafosse had some familiarity in this regard and a broader knowledge of linguistics, he was not fluent and needed considerable time to look up terms in reference works. When he had confronted this problem before World War I in his efforts to publish the Timbuktu Chronicles and *Chroniques du Foûta sénégalais* by Siré Abbas Soh, he had collaborated with Houdas and Gaden, who was a specialist in Pulaar.[43] Peacetime granted Delafosse the opportunity to return to his project of translation. He made great efforts to translate the work, but progress was glacially slow. In the meantime, he communicated the importance of the project and his special regard for Kamara. With Delafosse's untimely death, however, the project was faced with an indescribable loss: Not only was the text's translator no longer alive, but also the manuscript on which he worked had disappeared.[44]

Despite this incredible setback, the translation project was back on track by 1931, and Kamara had many reasons to be optimistic about the whole endeavor. Gaden had been in touch with the top orientalists of the day, including Louis Massignon, to find a translator.[45] A letter from Gaden to Kamara suggests that the latter had agreed to writing the work a second time and over the course of the intervening seven years had sent the work in sections organized geographically.[46] Gaden informs Kamara that he has enlisted the help of Maurice Gaudfroy-Demombynes, a leading orientalist at what had become the National School of Living Oriental Languages who had participated in the development of a program in African languages and civilizations.[47] Gaudfroy-Demombynes's own doctoral thesis was on the fifteenth-century Egyptian encyclopedist Ahmad al-Qalqashandi,[48] and this familiarity with the tradition of compilation and commentary proved useful in his initial favorable assessment of Kamara's work. According to Gaden's letter, Gaudfroy-Demombynes notes that Kamara's introduction has accurately cited al-Qalqashandi, an observation meant to communicate that Kamara had a perfect knowledge of the tradition. For the orientalists of this era, value was still assessed, at least in part, in relation to fidelity to classical works. What made *The History of the Blacks* and Kamara valuable during this orientalist season was the degree to which he represented the broader Arabo-Islamic tradition. Gaudfroy-Demombynes's intervention promised to make the text's worth legible to the French academy.

In the same year, Kamara was inducted as a knight in the French Legion of Honor, the highest award for either civil or military merit given by the French government. The award was established by Napoleon Bonaparte in 1802, after the French Revolution's abolition of the aristocracy, to recognize individuals who embodied the highest ideals of the republic.[49] Because these ideals included the democratic principle of equality, anyone from any background that made a valuable contribution to society deserved recognition from the state. Instead of landed gentry who had inherited privilege based on blood or saints recognized by the Catholic Church for their exceptional holiness, the award identified individuals whose meritorious contributions to the republic were to be emulated. Legionnaires were new secular "saints of the republic."[50] Interestingly enough, some of the most radical republicans resisted the entire idea of the legion, as its hierarchy, structure, and privilege resembled the aristocratic order of the *ancien régime*. They believed that in making social distinctions, the legion created and managed a new system of rank, which the revolution had sought to abolish.[51] The award thus quickly became, or perhaps always was, both a technique of governance that encouraged certain behaviors and temperaments over others and a political instrument within mainland France that was highly regulated by the state bureaucracy. While Kamara's induction certainly represented a boon to his fortunes, the contradictions between the legion's expressed ideals and its inherent pragmatic application of the award reveal some of the broader ambiguities of the translation project. After all, the fact that Kamara, a Muslim saint, was named a "saint" of the secular French republic presents a delicious irony.

In the overseas empire, the instrumentality of honor and merit can be considered even more important for the mechanics of colonial power, which sought to extract the greatest benefit at the lowest cost. It is likely no coincidence, then, that before World War I, there were only 45,000 living honorees. But as a result of World Wars I and II, embedded as they were in imperialist competition that provoked great material and ideological strain to hold on to the colonies, that number grew to 320,000 by the end of Algeria's liberation struggle in 1962.[52] More than ever, the last half century of French colonial rule saw the Legion of Honor working to attract and reward "native" participation in the civilizing mission. As much as the honor was an achievement for Kamara, we should consider what it meant for his undertaking. While I have not identified the text of Kamara's commendation or anything he said or wrote about the award, the example of Mademba Sèye, an African employee of colonial Senegal who would become a king in what is now Mali, provides a compelling illustration of the award's function.[53] Because he had successfully risen through the ranks of the telegraph service and had fought anticolonial elements on the colony's frontier while installing the telegraph line, Mademba was recommended for induction in the legion in 1883. In his approval of this recommendation, the director of colonies made it clear that the honor was not simply a matter of recognition but was also awarded for its subsequent effects. "Bestowing this honor has the power to produce the best results."[54] According to American historian Richard Roberts, many of Mademba's "bargains of collaboration," in which he made colonial rule possible in return for power, prestige, and wealth, can be organized around the colonial induction and promotion of him to the legion and his leveraging of this honor to his own ends, which included a public relations blitz in France to encourage investment in French Sudan's cotton industry.[55]

To be clear, the similarities between Mademba and Kamara are only superficial. Born and raised in the colonial town of Saint-Louis and mentored directly by Louis Faidherbe, Mademba masterfully used the power of the colonial state to devastating and morally objectionable ends. Also, his Islamic learning was limited. Kamara, in contrast, geographically and practically maintained a pious distance from power, and the few objectives he pursued in interacting with the state—publishing his work and building a school, for example—were principled endeavors that rarely came to fruition. Still, the comparison with his predecessor highlights the colonial instrumentalization of honor and merit in a perpetually resource-strapped enterprise that relied on attracting enthusiastic participation. Kamara's enthusiasm for the translation project was channeled through the bureaucratic institution of the Legion of Honor. The consequence of this social engineering and instrumentalization was ultimately to undermine the sincere attempts of the colonial humanists such as Gaden, as the effort required to understand Kamara's immensely complex work overwhelmed any practical value it might offer.

Also in 1931, the colonial government announced a literary prize for native authors that included an award of Fr. 3,000, suggesting its interest in and potential support for an accomplished author such as Kamara.[56] The scale of this interest was by no means negligible. In the 1930s, colonial subjects, particularly those trained as teachers and translators, were encouraged to document as much of native culture, language, and history as possible.[57] There were several venues for this work, including the *Bulletin de l'enseignment de l'Afrique occidentale française*. The literary prize was but one means to encourage this work. It followed the French Enlightenment tradition of using literary competitions to encourage cultural flourishing while at the same time meeting the practical needs of information gathering. In that way, the literary prize functioned as a sort of microinstitution that, similar to the Legion of Honor, could potentially produce, or at the very least contribute to the making of, a hierarchical social order through the equal opportunity of merit based on the identification of exemplary talents of the ideal colonial subject.

A MONUMENTAL TEXT IN AN ORIENTALIST SEASON

While the colonial state had clear interests in awarding a literary prize that reflected a desire for the native text, authors such as Kamara had their own motivations for submitting their works for consideration. By this point, Kamara had written several works and enjoyed an Arabophone readership, which would have included mostly elite and learned Muslim scholars, but this readership was severely limited by both language and materiality.[58] Evidence for the lack of circulation of Kamara's works is his near absence from most Arabic archival collections of West Africa.[59] There are few textual witnesses outside of manuscripts held by IFAN or in the family collection in Ganguel. The only evidence we have of his circulation is the endorsements that Kamara himself includes in *The Announcement*. While the elite echelons of the Senegambia developed a superb knowledge of Arabic, they were the exception and not the rule during the colonial period, especially for any Arabic used outside specifically liturgical activities. Moreover, the circulation of his work was limited by the manuscript medium of his works, which required time, materials, and skilled labor to reproduce. The chapter of Kamara's autobiography that includes endorsements of several of his works by his Muslim peers reveals a network of correspondents who were consistently trying to identify, copy, and trade both manuscripts and print books.[60] The literary prize represented the possibility of getting his work in print, thereby growing his audience, getting him some compensation, and granting him recognition for his special saintly status.

The literary prize represented the most visible expression of a broader competition among Senegambian intellectuals, particularly those from leading families in the Senegal River Valley, to produce, frame, and generally mediate the knowledge necessary for colonial governance. Having already published a work produced on demand with Henri Gaden in 1913, Siré Abbas Soh was considered an authority.[61] After a long period of inactivity due to health reasons, in 1935 Soh requested funding to support new research on Futa Toro, according to French historians Céline Labrune-Badiane and Etienne Smith.[62] The interim Governor-General M. Boisson approved a modest monthly allowance and provided precise instructions to gather documents relating to castes, family origins, property, and customs. Ultimately, the allowance was grossly insufficient for the intellectual efforts and physical demands of the work requested, making all parties unhappy with the project's progress. Also in 1935, a treatment on land tenure in the middle Senegal River Valley written decades earlier by Abdou Salam Kane appeared in the *Bulletin du Comité d'études historiques et scientifiques de d'Afrique occidentale française*.[63] He also published a work on legal customs in 1939.[64] I am unaware of any direct relationship between Soh and Kamara that would suggest they were rivals. But the fact that both struggled to receive just compensation for their labors from the same entity in the same period demonstrates that they were competing to attract limited resources for research support. Kane and Kamara, on the other hand, were clearly rivals. In addition to being Kamara's son-in-law and the son of Kamara's mentor Shaykh Mamadou Mamadou Maqami Kane, Abdou Salam Kane found himself in direct conflict with Kamara over questions of access to prized land and in competition for colonial recognition for religious and legal authority, as discussed in the previous chapter.[65] That Kane published short essays on land tenure and legal custom as Kamara sought translation and publication on the same subjects highlights the broader environment of intellectual competition that characterized this period.

These developments encouraged Kamara to enter a new period of scholarly productivity that coincided with greater engagement with and initiative in the broader life of the colony. He began to write shorter, more topical works that would be of interest to a colonial readership. Some of these works included direct responses to inquiries by colonial administrators about regions or ethnic groups under their authority. Others about important historical figures of the region were of broader interest. Still others pertained to Kamara's own commitments to religious knowledge and practice. Kamara also began to circulate among the Muslim elite in areas that were more central to colonial rule. In 1935, for example, he represented the Muslim community at the opening at the Cathédrale du Souvenir Africain, built by the Catholic Church in Dakar. His speech raised the topic of the unity of the Abrahamic religions, a subject he would later expound on in yet another text, which I discuss later. It seems that Kamara's relationship with Seydou Nouru Tal (1880–1980), Hajj Umar Tal's grandson and a representative of a domesticated Tijaniyya, and with Boghé Ahmadou Mokhtar Sakho (1867–1934), a colonial Muslim judge, may have facilitated such a prestigious opportunity.[66] In 1937, Kamara submitted his 1935 biography of Hajj Umar for the literary prize announced in 1931.[67] Taken together, his new textual production and his mobility in colonial urban spaces and with the new Muslim elite reflect his eagerness to use his scholarship and writing to influence the world around him, which had become a largely Muslim colonial society.

A MONUMENTAL TEXT IN AN ORIENTALIST SEASON

The best illustration of Kamara's efforts to use his writing to impact religious life in the colony is his attempt to reform the system of indigenous education. Qur'anic education in what had become French West Africa maintained the practices, materiality, models, and objectives of antiquity.[68] Teachers, who embodied the revealed message of the Qur'an, first taught young children the sounds that corresponded with letters written in charcoal or other pigments. Eventually, children learned to connect those sounds into words that made up the revealed text, which was then memorized to varying degrees of completion. Memorization was a holistic activity facilitated by the practice of ritualized gestures; the development of emotional bonds of affection between the teacher and student, as well as between the student and their peers; and the overcoming of the physical hardships of pain, discomfort, and hunger. Qur'anic education was not simply the absorption of an objective knowledge or the acquisition of a skill. It was also an initiation into a symbolic universe, a moral order, and a social network.[69] The late medieval traveler Ibn Battuta noted the seriousness with which West African Muslims approached education and the extent to which parents would go to ensure their children's success.[70] The culture of Qur'anic schooling was widespread by the beginning of the nineteenth century, causing one observer to note that literacy levels among Muslim residents likely exceeded those of European contemporaries.[71]

However, this holistic approach to schooling was time and labor intensive, ensuring that only the most gifted, the highest achievers, and the most well-positioned in society gained the greatest benefits. Where many students may have learned to recognize letters and would have memorized enough of the Qur'an for recitation in ritual prayer, few, relative to the total population, could hope to have an intermediate level, let alone an advanced level, of learning. This system worked well enough as long as the hierarchy of Muslim scholars was responsible for the life and the afterlife of the community of believers, a situation best represented by the leadership of an imam, as had been the case for much of nineteenth-century Futa Toro. By the 1930s, however, the unevenness of these results began to appear patently obvious in the face of new expectations for education. What's more, the emergence of modern conditions—in which individuals were increasingly responsible for their own conduct, religious authority and political authority were divorced for the first time, and greater competencies were required to meet the labor needs of economic development—made the need to reform

Qurʾanic education equally apparent to both the thoughtful Kamara and the utilitarian colonial state engaged in its project of social engineering.

Kamara envisioned a place for religious education within a secular French system. In a letter dated April 8, 1938, the Office of Indigenous Affairs notified the governor general that Kamara wanted to participate in the reorganization of Qurʾanic schooling. This reorganization, which the French had been considering since at least the previous year, would introduce the instruction of the French language and eventually the instruction of other subjects, with French as the language of instruction, alongside the classical curriculum. This model eventually came to be known as the *école franco-arabe* and was championed by Senegal's Muslim modernists from the 1950s onward.[72] Kamara wanted to author a textbook with all the essentials of religious obligations so that all students could gain the minimum knowledge necessary for their religious practice. Interestingly, his request to author what the letter describes as a "sort of catechism" was embedded in yet another text that he hoped the colonial state would publish.[73] An elaboration of the speech that he gave in 1935 at the Cathédrale du Souvenir Africain, entitled *The Coming Together of Christianity and Islam*, reflects an ecumenical spirit that the Kamara family today claims presaged the contemporary discourse on interfaith dialogue.[74] In it, Kamara identifies the gestures, material culture, and discourses shared between Muslims and Christians. Unlike the many texts that Kamara eventually donated to IFAN, a copy of this one sits in his surveillance file with a partial translation into French and a summary in which the portions that caused the administration's concern are underlined in red. Kamara's request comes from the following passage, which is translated into French from the chapter entitled "Good Advice Addressed to the Senegalese":

> It would be good if the French Government ordered the Senegalese to teach their sons, as soon as they start speaking, the letters of the alphabet and a few short suras from the Qurʾan. They would also teach them the fundamental principles of religion. I beg the superior authority to have the kindness to order me to compose a book neither too long nor too short which would contain all the sacred duties (theology, Muslim law, etc . . .) . . . It remains of course that the study of religious sciences and Arabic literature should only be done outside of French classes, because France is the nation to which God has entrusted our affairs.[75]

A MONUMENTAL TEXT IN AN ORIENTALIST SEASON

As ever, Kamara's text was read with a view to the practical implications of colonial governance in mind. On the one hand, the bureaucratic exchange around Kamara's request noted that giving Kamara authorization would give the appearance that his manual was linked to the colonial administration, which was out of the question, as they did not want to risk being perceived as meddling in religious affairs. But Kamara was free to do as he pleased if what he pleased did not upset public order. On the other hand, Kamara could be pulled into ongoing efforts to legitimize colonial intervention. The note directs officials to encourage Kamara to hold off on his project until the opening of the colonial *médrasa* in Dakar, where Kamara could meet with "other marabouts of merit" and develop something that would have more weight in the community. Between Kamara's request and the colonial response, we can see Kamara's embrace of colonial rule for its beneficial outcomes for the Muslim community, as well as a colonial ambivalence about the nature of that power. Kamara recognizes French power and wants it to be used for moral benefit. But understanding its power as secular, the colonial state avoids the appearance of interfering in religious life, even as it invests in the development of hybrid colonial-Islamic institutions and encourages certain religious actors (those "of merit") over others. On June 11, 1938, the colonial administration decides to suppress Kamara's proposed textbook. The original text in which the request was made, *The Coming Together*, is permitted to circulate—but with the language of the request removed. There is no indication of the channels in which the text was approved to circulate or if it was to be printed in the original Arabic or translated to French. There is no evidence that the text was published while Kamara was alive. All the same, the correspondence around *The Coming Together* testifies to Kamara's desire to intervene in the colonial context with his Arabic writing and to an ambiguous colonial entanglement in the production, circulation, and preservation of some of the most significant Arabic textual production of the region under its domination.

The ambiguities of colonial support have already begun to turn Kamara's enthusiasm into frustration by 1936, when new conditions of disregard started to emerge. Kamara has grown frustrated with the lack of progress on the publication of *The History of the Blacks* and with the lack of compensation for his labors. He writes a letter requesting payment for his work and a consideration of his hardships encountered in his old age. After this letter goes unanswered, Kamara writes to Marius Moutet, the minister of the colonies, in

Paris the following year: "I sent, a number of years ago, several manuscripts to M. le Governor Général in Dakar who had announced in the Official Journal that a payment would be given to anyone who wrote books on the history of the country. Now, I have written books that I sent to Dakar. Until now, I have received no response. I will give the titles of the manuscripts to the new Gouverneur Général, M. de Coppet who can give you all the details."[76] This letter from Kamara appears in a flurry of correspondence between 1936 and 1939, at which point those in a new cohort of personnel are not as familiar with Kamara and the native literature to which he contributed. The bureaucracy, primarily the Office of Political Affairs, which is preoccupied with the work of social engineering, has to inquire about the status of the work and what possible financial resources might be used to satisfy the request of a pacifist Muslim scholar who has been loyal to the French cause. The office discovers that little progress has been made on Kamara's manuscript but that there is room in the budget for a modest political gift of Fr. 500. Growing exasperated with the process, Kamara declares that he will send a third copy of the manuscript if that is what is needed to get the work published.[77]

It's hard to describe the disappointment Kamara likely feels at that moment. The fate of his most significant intellectual undertaking, which he has entrusted to the French to translate and publish, is unclear. What's more, now in old age and facing the demands of a large family and an increasingly cash economy, he is finding it difficult to support himself and his entourage. His submission for the literary prize should be understood as Kamara's new strategy of recognition where the previous attempts to circulate his work had failed. Citizenship is yet another of his strategies.[78] He applies for French citizenship in 1938 as a means of getting a reprieve from taxes. But he is denied, due to his practice of polygamy. Nevertheless, he continues to write. During this period, he writes more distilled essays: *The Precious Collection* and *The Purification of Thoughts from Delusional Doubts*. Both are works of genealogical criticism in which he uses the primary research conducted for *The History of the Blacks* to challenge the claims of noble birth of Saharan and Sahelian elites.

Frustrated and disappointed, Kamara also turns to writing himself into the region's memory of the religious elite once and for all. He pens *The Announcement*, which has furnished much of the material in chapters 1 and 2 of this book. It is a writing of the saintly self, charged with sentiment and spiritual striving. The story that Kamara tells about himself in the twilight of his life, sometime between August 1937 and his death in 1945, with its inclusions and exclusions, may or may not have been the story that he would have told at a different moment. The story he did write, as we have seen in the earlier chapters, is that as a friend of God, Kamara had inherited a degree of prophecy that the community of Muslims needed for their well-being. Beyond *The Announcement*'s explicit message of Kamara's saintly subjectivity, the text provides insight into his mood following colonial disregard toward the end of the orientalist season. I consider it a sentimental text because it documents several of Kamara's affective motivations toward the end of his life. In the chapter on the praise he has received from "elite scholars of action and righteous friends of God," he informs readers of these motivations: "I had been having a lot of depression and dread, little joy and hopefulness.... However, a state of hope and delight ran over me. I said to myself, it would be better if I wrote glad tidings [*bishārāt*] to strengthen my hope in God. So, I wanted to write here what I have left of the letters which contain praise for me."[79] One pictures an aging Kamara looking through his papers to remind himself of the support and enthusiasm with which he had been received over the course of his life. This passage and its sentimental excess offer a key to reading the autobiography as a part of the hagiographic process.[80] In collecting these letters and recollecting his own memories, Kamara is sincerely making sense of his life as a friend of God, someone who through emulation and proximity has a subjectivity that approaches the ideal Islamic form of life. Whether or not that means something to his colonial interlocutors or whether his achievements are as widely recognized as he thinks they should be is irrelevant. All that is left for him is to leave a trace of his legacy—and to leave it all to God.

We can mark the final blow to Kamara's translation project with the death of his longtime collaborator Henri Gaden. Since their first communications, which likely came sometime after World War I through the hybrid network of the learned Muslim elite of the Senegal River Valley and the colonial experts, Kamara and Gaden maintained a robust correspondence.[81] In Gaden, Kamara had a reliable sponsor for his endeavors within the colonial administration. Kamara's period of activity that opened the 1930s was accompanied by Gaden's efforts to find resources and people to facilitate the beleaguered translation project. Gaden was himself familiar with the double challenge of securing state benefits in retirement while writing his own work on the Pulaar language and Peul culture.[82] His final years were

A MONUMENTAL TEXT IN AN ORIENTALIST SEASON

mostly spent in a modest room in Saint-Louis, where he labored with failing eyesight over index cards for a Pulaar-French dictionary. In 1937, Gaden had managed to secure Fr. 10,000 to pay M. Benhamouda of the Collège Sadiki in Tunis to translate *The History of the Blacks*, but this came to nothing.[83] Before his passing, Gaden handed off stewardship of the translation project to the naturalist Théodore Monod, who in 1938 had been named the first director of IFAN, the center for colonial scientific research.[84] Six months before Gaden's death, Monod declared to him that the "poor manuscript" did not have a chance.[85] Gaudfroy-Demombynes, who had initially reviewed the manuscript for Gaden, never got around to the undertaking and suffered from failing health, prompting him to suggest to Monod that he contact Vincent Monteil, a young military man.[86] All the same, Monod would try for many years to get Kamara's works translated, including an attempt in 1958 when he solicited Bachir Ly of the École Arabe in the Cape Verdean neighborhood of Dakar. Although Ly made an effort at translation, he eventually abandoned the work because the compensation was too low.[87]

Just one year before his own passing, Kamara wrote a letter to Monod, reviewing the entire saga of the translation project, according to Pondopoulo.[88] Kamara had kept a copy of a chapter of *The History of the Blacks*, but he encountered a problem that symbolizes the general threat faced by the scholar confronting the vastness of the past, the paucity of its traces, and the fragility of its evanescence. At first, he could not find the text among his many books, and by the time he did find it, he discovered that it had been eaten by termites.[89] While Kamara held out hope for the translation, offering his son who was a colonial translator to help with the project, the termite-induced decomposition of his text served as a reminder of the deaths of his collaborators Delafosse and Gaden and his own impending demise.[90]

Despite the early interest in Kamara's work, the translation project never got far. Translators based in France eventually received far more compensation for their aborted attempts to render it accessible to the French academy than Kamara did for composing it. Feeling the urge to leave an intellectual legacy all the same, upon his death he bequeathed tens of his works to IFAN, right at the peak of his last efforts to get translated and published. At the time, the institute employed a new generation of African writers more aligned with ethnology, such as the prolific Amadou Hampâté Bâ. But the epistemic chasm between the older orientalist paradigm that read texts and the newer ethnological one that surveilled populations and promised obvious applications for social engineering was too great; the work of translation between them had become too tedious, time consuming, and ineffective for the demands of colonial governance. The symbolism of this shift is striking. One of Amadou Hampâté Bâ's (1901–1991) first tasks was to organize the papers that Kamara had donated—and that remain a cornerstone of IFAN's archival collection.[91] Philology had finally and definitively become obsolete.

Viewed from the perspective of our contemporary common sense about the relationship of Islam and modernity, as well as the assertion of African sovereignty in the world since decolonization, it seems curious that Kamara would have written anything at all for a colonial readership, let alone that he would donate his priceless intellectual legacy to a state that disregarded his work and broken its promises. The irony of such a decision is heightened when we consider assessment of his work during the transition, discussed in the following chapter, between the colonial and national period, which dismissed Kamara altogether.

Had it been only a matter of his place in colonial knowledge production, Kamara's fate of obscurity would have been sealed. Two factors prevented this from happening. Because he was a Sufi master who practiced contemplation and strived for spiritual excellence as modeled by the masters that preceded him, many of his contemporaries recognized his accomplishments and accordingly his disciples and descendants have remembered him for his saintliness. This tradition of Kamara has long existed beyond the confines of the colonial archive removed from cultural circulation and the colonial library as a field of documentation that founds modern knowledge. Moreover, Kamara would eventually make several returns. After independence, Senegalese scholars retrieved Kamara for the development of a national literary canon and as an authentic voice for an true African history. And more recently, the convergence of the African Renaissance and the Global War on Terror have renewed an interest in Kamara for his religious teachings that emphasize quietism, tolerance, and political noninvolvement. Therefore, his religious significance and the historical conditions in which he and his work have been transmitted inform his meaning beyond the limits of colonial humanism, which I will explore in the rest of this book. Perhaps this Muslim scholar's bequest to colonial institutions was not so paradoxical after all. Perhaps he saw something about the future that few others could.

FIVE

The Pitfalls of National Literature

BY THE TIME the African American historian Constance Hilliard found herself in the archive of the Institut Fondamental d'Afrique Noire (IFAN) in the early 1970s, Senegalese academics had recognized Shaykh Musa Kamara as a valuable resource for writing an *African* African history. This recognition, however, was by no means inevitable. Just a decade before, Kamara's monumental text, *The History of the Blacks*, had been dismissed as gibberish by Vincent Monteil, the French Islamicist and former director of what had been the Institut Français d'Afrique Noire. But with the intervention of Amar Samb, a French-trained Senegalese scholar of Arabic who served as the director of IFAN between 1971 and 1986, Kamara's writing had become literature. A cohort of young Senegalese scholars had begun to read and translate the treasure trove of Kamara's writings that he had bequeathed to the colonial research center upon his death in 1945. Finally, Kamara's work began to circulate in translation as he had wanted. This scholarly activity, along with a broader African historiographical project that included mining archives, collecting oral histories, and performing archaeological research into the past's material remains, provided a new documentary foundation for the historical memory of the paradoxically young nation with a deep past.

Hilliard, like many in the tradition of Black thought, was interested in precolonial African history. Young scholars at IFAN, such as Rawane Mbaye, directed her attention to one of Kamara's later works, *The Precious Collection*.[1] This 1938 text, one of the last he would author, is a critical essay on the social organization of the western Sahel that challenged colonial common sense about the region's caste-like hierarchy and its historical becoming. It also provided substance to precolonial African identities that had been transformed in the Americas, a topic of great interest to a blossoming diasporic historiography. Hilliard would produce as a part of her dissertation the first complete English translation of one of Kamara's texts—and until 2023 the only one available. In doing so, she contributed to a Pan-African project of decolonization that viewed the written text in general and the text of historical writing in particular as indispensable resources for thinking the human as African.

This sequence of colonial denial, African nationalist rewriting, and diasporic engagement is but one iteration of a broader pattern in which the negation of racial and colonial discourse is answered by intellectual work that seeks to affirm African humanity. A careful reading of the production of this period with this context in mind highlights the broader set of stakes that shaped both Kamara's afterlife as a *literary* figure and the meaning and substance of decolonization. Following Senegal's independence in 1960, Kamara and his textual production returned as a rejoinder to colonial and racist representations of Africa as lacking civilization, as needing guidance, and as being the home of a diminished or immature humanity. The task for the first generation of Senegalese, like many African scholars at independence, was the affirmation of a humanity that had been negated by these discourses. The construction of a national literature out of an Arabo-Islamic written heritage was one response to this problem. Kamara was featured prominently by a generation of historians and Islamic studies scholars working from the late 1960s to the 1990s who saw in the colonial-era intellectual an invaluable resource for making this literature. And for them, history was the genre of literature to which Kamara made his greatest contribution. In this chapter, I argue that efforts to make Kamara a pillar of a national literature in the period we now associate with decolonization is characterized by an ambivalent African humanism.

The Denial of Kamara as an Author

Vincent-Mansour Monteil (1913–2005) was something of a transitional figure in the history of the forms of knowledge that have claimed to represent Islam in Sahelian West Africa.[2] On the one hand, he was the quintessential orientalist identified in the critique of Edward Said. Monteil completed a doctorate in modern Arabic after a career in the French military that took him to North Africa, the Middle East, and Southeast Asia. While still a student at the famous military college of Saint-Cyr, he also studied at the Parisian École Nationale des Langues Orientales Vivantes, the institutional hub of French orientalism in his day. It is there that he befriended one of the most important orientalists of the twentieth century, Louis Massignon, who is known for introducing the Persian Sufi mystic Mansur al-Hallaj to the French academy and public. Monteil combined area expertise, language capacities, and battlefield experience with the vocation of scholarship, epitomizing what Said meant when he argued that the will to know the Orient was embedded within the will to obtain power over it. Beyond his own commitment to the marriage of knowledge and power, Monteil had a familial orientalist pedigree few could claim. His father, Charles Monteil, was an influential colonial civil servant who had military experience, taught African languages in Paris, and worked under Maurice Delafosse, a founding figure of French African studies. The elder Monteil's contribution to colonial knowledge/power included an insistence on colonial administrators' positivist orientation to the territories under their administration through the study of history, language, and custom.[3] He also, according to the younger Monteil's dedication in his influential *L'islam noir: Une religion à la conquete d'Afrique*, taught his son "to love Africa."[4]

As much as the younger Monteil typifies the tradition of colonial knowledge and power, however, it would be a caricature to present him as simply an embodiment of that tradition. His earliest academic positions were as the head of the Islam department in 1959 and then as the director of IFAN after independence between 1963 and 1968, the period that saw the change in the research center's name in 1966.[5] While at IFAN, Monteil set about consolidating the accumulated knowledge of Islam in Africa, paying particular attention to a hitherto neglected manuscript heritage. While he is best known for his book *L'islam noir*, which has long attracted critiques for its racializing discourse, he was a more complicated figure than these critiques would suggest. Having commanded Muslim soldiers in Morocco, Palestine, and Vietnam, he demonstrated a relative degree of sympathy for Muslims throughout his career. Especially considering his public embrace of Islam in Nouakchott in 1977, his body of work reveals that he saw in Islam a universalism with many expressions, as captured in the title of his work *Aux cinqs couleurs de l'islam*.[6] Most importantly, he saw Islam as a vector of modernization, the actualization of human potential. Accordingly, Monteil both typified a tradition of the colonial sociology of Islam discussed in chapter 3 and gestured toward a postcolonial Muslim modernism.

Despite the colonial-Islamic duality Monteil represents, his 1964 assessment of Kamara was unambiguous. Over several publications, Monteil appeared primarily concerned with the question of Kamara's originality, the perceived lack of which led him to deny Kamara as an author. He expressed his frustration with reading Kamara's monumental *The History of the Blacks* in his field-shaping *L'islam noir*:

> The content of the Arabic manuscript is quite characteristic of the rambling aspect of this kind of work. 866 recto-verso folios contain a vast compilation in which, in the greatest disorder, the author mixes his own knowledge with information gleaned from works sometimes difficult to identify....
>
> Nothing is therefore more disappointing than a reading of this kind of work, and it requires deciphering never-ending digressions to pull out some useful nugget of the text. They are books of sorcery (grimoires) that the Portuguese call alfarrabios: that is to say, "gibberish."[7]

Although Monteil's remarks are brief, a close reading of them reveals much. For him, the manuscript that languished in the archive was useless. Far from being a literary monument of great merit, *The History of the Blacks* was a desultory stack of papers that failed to meet the criteria of originality, rational organization, and transparent citation, qualities that conform to the expectations of a modern reader. Echoing the orientalist tone we observed in chapter 4 but sharpening its pitch, he bemoans the amount of effort that the text demands. "It requires deciphering never-ending digressions to pull out some useful nugget of the text." The image here of a nugget being pulled out of a text is not arbitrary. It speaks to a theory of reading that is extractive, thus exemplifying a broader philosophy of knowledge that sought to pull value out of the colony. Moreover, that the nugget should be useful—as opposed to beautiful, or meaningful, or any number of qualities we might imagine for a precious ore—demonstrates Monteil's preoccupation with use value. From the point of view of the practical attitude, this commonsense expectation barely warrants attention and will probably bore or frustrate the good readers whose own investments in the social sciences make them wonder what exactly my point might be. Nevertheless, it indicates that even for Monteil, a reasonably sympathetic scholar of the Islamic tradition of letters who had written about and translated canonical Muslim authors such as the mystic poet Abu Nawas and the polymath Ibn Khaldun, the classical textual attitude exemplified by Kamara, which was the basis of a colonial humanist project of translation discussed in the previous chapter, was hardly available in the same way. Dissatisfied with the equation of effort divided by utility, Monteil outsourced the labor of making sense of Kamara and of identifying any originality that might be useful in the project of modernization to Abdallah Djenidi, an Algerian scholar of Arabic who had come to work at the University of Dakar.[8] The irony of Monteil's dismissal of *The History of the Blacks* is especially acute when read alongside the positive assessment of the orientalist Maurice Gaudfroy-Demombynes, also discussed in the previous chapter. The very feature that made the text valuable to an earlier generation of colonial philologists—that it accurately cited older texts—made a later generation think that the text was useless. In both instances, the text remained the same; it was the mode of reading that changed. Clearly, the orientalist season was over.

At the risk of putting too fine a point on this discussion, let me be explicit in framing Monteil's dismissal of Kamara as a denial of him as an author. There are several implicit ideas that frame and support Monteil's commentary. That *The History of the Blacks* could be read as a compilation of other works and not an original composition undermined Kamara's status as an author in the modern sense. This modern definition of the author includes the idea of the individual lone genius who is inspired and who, through the masterful use of language, brings into being that which did not exist before—the author as a demigod of sorts.[9] Also, the author's imaginative writing is definitive of literature. The inability of readers to easily hear Kamara's voice as an individual apart from the echo of tradition rendered *The History of the Blacks* a document in technical terms perhaps but not a text—a form of intention—and certainly not literature. Then again, even its status as a document in the historical sense of a record attesting to something that occurred or was said at a specific time and place was tenuous. What of the manuscript reflected the historical specificity of Kamara's life and environment? Without clear indications of what was original and what was repetition, the modern historian was at a loss as to how to use such a document.

Monteil's designation of this monumental work as a *"grimoire"* does a particular kind of work. Where the philology of the orientalist season entertained works such as Kamara's, those versed in the form of colonial knowledge that came to be known as the sociology of Islam, even when put at the disposal of the new nation for the work of development and modernization, read Kamara's text as a derivative work lacking an authorial voice. Associating it with books of sorcery, Monteil relegated Kamara to the premodern even though he was a contemporary, making him another case of what was becoming known as the magico-religious function of a restricted literacy in Africanist research.[10] Such a restriction of literacy in the anthropology articulated by Jack Goody nullified the primary function of writing as a medium of human communication. The secularity implied in the modern conception of the author who expresses their humanity as opposed to communing with the divine is thus shown to be absent in Kamara's works. And the perceived meaningless quality of the writing ("gibberish") evidenced an incompetence of language, not its mastery, that sine qua non of literature. Accordingly, Monteil's reading, or nonreading, of Kamara constituted an act of epistemic violence, despite all his sympathy for Muslims, insofar as it reduced the rich texture of the work and assessed it by standards external to it.[11] *The History of the Blacks* resembled the Islamic tradition of letters with its Semitic script, but under the theory of Islam noir in the new sociology of Islam, the blackness of its author reduced it to something not much more than the speech of barbarians. For this influential orientalist working at the dawn of independence in a Senegalese institution, the form, style, and content of Kamara's writings disqualified them from being considered literature. The negative evaluation of the literary quality of one of West Africa's most prolific writers in the Arabic language would become the target of a corrective decolonizing African humanism.

The Affirmation of African Humanity

It is all too easy today to speak of African independence as an empty signifier marking the passage from one period of domination and uneven development under the aegis of empire to another period of subordination in the world system within which national sovereignty can be only a disguise for "power without responsibility" or "exploitation without redress."[12] Indeed, even before the end of that hopeful decade of the 1960s, Kwame Nkrumah, Ghana's first prime minister, famously made such an argument, describing the postindependence period as the period of neocolonialism. But to return to the time of independence is to make space for just how meaningful independence could be. Aimé Césaire's preindependence description of colonization as "thingification" is but one example that highlights colonial rule's dehumanizing effects and its reliance on the erasure of African presence in world history and on the obliteration of its unique possibilities.[13] Humanity here is understood, in a fashion profoundly influenced by Romanticism, as the accumulated achievement of human history in the form of civilization, and possibility is understood in philosophical anthropological terms as genius, creativity, and agency. In much the same way that *Négritude* as a literary and cultural movement can be read as an antiracist racism, political independence promised to negate the negation of African humanity; that is, it promised affirmation.[14] Above all, it promised the affirmation of African humanity at a moment when the nation had become the container and vehicle of mature, actualized agency in the world. Independence was as much a normative ideal in post-Enlightenment thought as it was a description of a political order. To be human meant having one's own nation. That Africans could claim to fulfill this ideal after a long century of being subjected to colonial rule and an even longer period of being subjected to the ravages of the slave trade was monumental. But independence required intellectual work to establish and elaborate. The affirmation of African humanity was a goal that had long existed in abolitionist and anticolonial thought and that became a chief concern of national African thought on a Pan-African scale.

We can describe this body of thought as African humanism: a set of ideas, figures of thought, patterns of thinking, and styles of reasoning that have provided the intellectual foundations that justify, rationalize, organize, and give meaning to the assertion of African sovereignty after empire. Its defining feature is an appropriation of the values and forms associated with modernity.[15] Similar to the colonial humanism discussed in the previous chapter, African humanism locates humanity in the hierarchical chain of being between nature and divinity. Humanity's creative capacity and agency in historical development distinguish it from the environment. The means by which humanity acts, culture, provides humanity with a power over nature. It is this value relative to nature that gives humanity inherent dignity, a value relative to what just is, in nature. In contrast to colonial humanism, African humanism refuses the racial hierarchy within the human species that represents Black peoples as being closer to a "state of nature" than white peoples, whose godlike condition allows them to self-actualize. It demands equality and inclusion within the category of the human while dismissing the implication of colonial humanism's racial hierarchy that normalized the so-called civilizing mission. The practices and disciplines that gave expression to this African humanism can be described as the African humanities, which were often proclaimed in the early decades of decolonization but remain a project to be achieved.

What decolonization as the affirmation of African humanity would mean at that time was an open question. Would it consist of wholly new forms created organically from a mass culture, as advocated by Frantz Fanon; forms retrieved from precolonial forms; or simply Black faces in high places, as was so comically captured in the famous opening scene of Ousmane Sembene's *Xala*?[16] At least two strategies were available to African intellectuals committed to responding to the negation of African humanity central to colonial modern thought. One strategy consisted of rendering perceived absence as difference. According to this view, it was not that civilization—as the progressive achievement of culture in complexly structured societies—did not exist in Africa; it was that African civilization was *different*. It reflected a different character or type of human being. It was not that there was no tradition of history writing; it was that history writing, so to speak, was oral. It was not that there was no African philosophy; it was that philosophy was collective wisdom discernible in folk sayings and cultural practices. The task for those engaged in the first strategy of African humanism was to translate what was present by way of cultural forms into terms that were legible to modern thought.

None other than Léopold Sédar Senghor, Senegal's first president, was the grand theorist of African humanism as the translation of difference. In countless speeches and essays over the course of his poetic and political career, he elaborated this view. Celebrated and vilified for his aphorism—and the cultural politics it implied—that reason is Greek as emotion is Negro, his project was to make a place for blackness in the humanist tradition.[17] For Senghor, *Négritude* as a philosophical and literary movement was, in fact, a variety of humanism.[18] Against (mostly Anglophone) critics, who saw *Négritude* as a racialism that accepted the idea of Black inferiority or who perhaps took an exclusivist view of humanism as a European idea, and therefore not an African idea, Senghor claimed that Négritude was a "confirmation of one's *being*" in that it recognized *"the sum of the cultural values of the black world."*[19] The point of this clarification of the African personality is to identify the basis of an African contribution to that "empire of the spirit," the "Civilization of the Universal."[20] If one starts, as Senghor did, from the point of view that the modern world inherited a classical tradition that affirmed the place of reason in ordering society and privileged the individual as the agent of history and the site of meaning, there remains the need for other qualities to make an integrated human being. African ontology provided this contrast that could make the human whole:

> Far back as one may go into his past, from the northern Sudanese to the southern Bantu, the African has always and everywhere presented a concept of the world which is diametrically opposed to the traditional philosophy of Europe. The latter is essentially static, objective, dichotomic; it is, in fact, dualistic, in that it makes an absolute distinction between body and soul, matter and spirit. It is founded on separation and opposition: on analysis and conflict. The African, on the other hand, conceives the world, beyond the diversity of its forms, as a fundamentally mobile, yet unique, reality that seeks synthesis.[21]

What is important to note in Senghor's argument is that what had been the basis of denial and exclusion is translated into valuable difference. Where in a white supremacist, civilizational, and colonial discourse Africa had been constructed as absolutely Other for its perceived lack, Senghor asserts positive difference. African ontology for Senghor was a comprehensive philosophy that complemented what Europe was, or even compensating for what it was not. Where dichotomy, conflict, and stasis favored the emergence of the individual in Europe, African communalism with its emphasis on unity, balance, and harmony offered the modern world virtues for an interdependent world. Senghor made his case by reference to the humanities: ethnology, African art, and grammatical analysis of African languages. Instead of lack, Senghor thus identified a human value of difference. It must be said here, though, that the difference Africa represented for Senghor, with his emphasis on emotion, rhythm, and harmony, could already be found in the alternative values embraced by Europe's counter-Enlightenment, best described as Romanticism and validated by the vitalism of Henri Bergson and Pierre Teilhard de Chardin, a connection Senghor often made throughout his career. The difference that Senghor highlighted therefore was not an absolute difference but one that could already be accommodated by humanist thought more generally. His translations of African difference therefore sought legibility by mobilizing marginalized ways of knowing within modern Euro-American society. Much of Senghor's work and cultural policy as a politician can be understood as translational in this way.

Senghor articulated his version of African humanism in a 1973 address to an academic society of classicists in Rome, named after the influential French humanist Guillaume Budé (1467-1540) who institutionalized classical language study. Invited to speak about the place of the study of Latin and the classics in general in Senegal's recent educational reform, he explained that the fundamental purpose of education was to provide the human being with culture:

> But what is Culture? By definition, it is comprised of the acquired knowledge and disciplines that allow the mind to develop critical thinking, taste, and judgment. And what else? It is comprised of the theoretical knowledge and practical disciplines that allow us not only to know each other better, as well as our environment, but also to adapt to the world as a human and physical entity. Culture is therefore knowledge, but formative knowledge, because it is critical and sympathetic. It is oriented towards action because it develops taste and judgment. In other words, it is Man, and he alone, who, through his culture, can exercise his "generic activity" as man by acting on his environment as a reaction to it. He makes himself by acting. But, in truth, it is by creating that he recreates nature. In short, Culture is the self-creation of man. I said "Culture"; I could have said Humanism. As a Wolof proverb from Senegal goes, *Nit, mooi garab u nit*: "Man is the remedy of man", that is to say, his measure and solution. Is it not significant, this negro proverb, which synthesizes Plato the Greek and Terence the African? For the former had told us that "Man is the measure of all things," and the latter, that none of what is human is foreign to him.[22]

In this passage, Senghor collapsed the category of culture with the project of humanism. Culture does not simply exist. Rather, it is the means by which humanity relates to its environment, or nature, on the one hand, and accedes to the divine-like qualities of creation, on the other. Echoing famous humanist formulas from Plato and Terrance, the Wolof proverb allowed

Senghor to squarely situate the African within the classical tradition and its reflection on the human condition. But as much as we see that Senghor asserted equality through an embrace and a valuing of difference, we can also observe a liability of this perspective. The humanism that he described is one that rests on a hierarchal ontology, in which ascending categories of the mineral, the vegetal, and the animal are at the service of the relative dignity of the human, who alone can articulate with the divine. Racial thought takes this hierarchy as a model for a racial hierarchy within the category of the human. In other words, human difference is nestled within the greater inequalities of being more generally. The disgraceful "missing link" thesis that tried to "explain" blackness reflects this view. Senghor wanted to accept the relative value of the human against nature, but he also wanted to insist on utter equality within the category of the human even though the notion of racial hierarchy rests on the human distinction from nature. His great effort to elaborate essential difference sought to achieve this inclusion in the humanist vision but had to remain silent on the humanist premises that contributed to the racist thought he rejected. We might describe this silence as emanating from an ambivalence of African humanism.

We might also read the body of work by Amadou Hampâté Bâ, a Malian man of letters, in this way. As a trained ethnologist and folklorist, he asserted that oral literary works such as *Kaidara* and *Njeddo Dewel* were distinct African expressions of humanity[23] and that African historicity should be understood as being expressed in orality.[24] Finally, at a moment when modernization was the goal of most serious intellectuals, he insisted on the value of tradition in defining what it meant to be African.[25] A critical view of accepting "African" as a sign of difference would argue that such translations adopt the same negating function of anti-Black modern discourse in general or that they are simply conservative attempts at naturalizing patriarchal gerontocracy in Hampâté Bâ's case in particular.[26] All the same, his academic production, his literary works, and his cultural activism on a world stage exemplify the strategy of articulating African difference as the affirmation of humanity, a strategy that was similarly available to Amar Samb and used in his framing of a national literature.

The other strategy of African humanist affirmation was to accept the hegemonic terms of what constituted humanity to show that by the very criteria of evaluation that had denied and discredited African presence, contribution, and so on, the negation of African humanity was simply incorrect, a technical error explainable only by the irrationality of white supremacy as a political project and an ideology. If history was history by virtue of the presence of writing, then Africa could, by virtue of Egyptian hieroglyphics, Abyssinian Geʻez, and Arabic Timbuktu manuscripts, for example, not be excluded. The scholar's task in this strategy was to document the histories and civilizational achievements that, in fact, belonged to Africa but that had been attributed to foreign agency, explained as an aberration, or erased altogether.

The work of Cheikh Anta Diop, a Senegalese polymath and political rival of Senghor, exemplifies this corrective strategy within African humanism. After receiving a traditional Islamic education in a rural area of Senegal among the Murid Sufi order, known for its unique articulation of Black consciousness within an Islamic register,[27] he studied the hard sciences and philosophy at the University of Paris after World War II. He wrote prolifically and sought to mobilize the humanities and the natural sciences for the purpose of development. Famously, he argued that the ancient Egyptians were Black, using cutting-edge carbon-dating techniques on mummified remains. He also used linguistic evidence to demonstrate the cultural unity of the African continent. Moreover, he asserted that the African origin of civilization had been falsified because of hegemonic racist ideology. The "meaning of [his] work" was to correct this irrational error. "Our investigations have convinced us that the West has not been calm enough and objective enough to teach us our history correctly, without crude falsifications. Today, what interests me most is to see the formation of teams, not of passive readers, but of honest, bold research workers, allergic to complacency and busy substantiating and exploring ideas expressed in our work."[28] These ideas included the core thesis that civilization, in the singular, was "Negro"; the monogenetic thesis that humanity originated from a single source in Africa; the possibility to discern laws of historical development from African cases (as opposed to making Africa an area of application of laws developed elsewhere or, worse, a simple chronology of facts); the influence of Africa in making the "Mesopotamian Semitic world"; the origins of Christianity and Islam in pharaonic religion; the capacity of African languages to communicate complex thought; the creation of an African literature worthy of the name; and the generation of a true African modernity without psychological complex. Diop argued that only by virtue of this corrective work would it be possible "to build African humanities, a body of African human sciences."[29]

Diop penned an influential essay on the African Renaissance while he was still a student in Paris and before he had managed to fully articulate his corrective approach to African humanism. It is of interest here for the way in which it frames the issue of African renascence as a *literary* question. To contextualize this essay, it is useful to reflect on the title itself: "When Can We Talk of an African Renaissance?"[30] This question suggests that there already existed a conversation in which the African Renaissance was up for discussion. The critical tone of the essay, which begins with the observation of two traditions in Africa—one untouched by colonial modernity and one profoundly shaped by it—indicated that Diop's intervention sought to subject an emergent discourse to rigorous scrutiny. Indeed, he regularly attended the same literary salons that nurtured the growth of the *Négritude* movement.[31] Furthermore, the year this essay was published, 1948, was a germinal moment in the history of diasporic Black thought. A wave of fresh Black representation in the French Parliament following the sacrifices of the colonies in the war, an increase in the number of colonial students in the metropole, the presence of African American soldiers and artists, and the hallmark publication of *La nouvelle poésie negre et malagache* contributed to a robust conversation among members of the African diaspora, in which the Harlem Renaissance had been an important reference.[32]

Diop's putting the African Renaissance in question takes on significance when contextualized in this moment, even as its implications would continue to be realized in the decades following decolonization and beyond, as explored in the following chapter. Importantly, he asserted that a real African literature, and therefore the African Renaissance, would not come into being without the development of African languages through writing in those languages, the enrichment of those languages through a project of mass translation, and the study of classical African languages such as Egyptian in order to "build our humanities on Egyptian foundations—the same way the Greek language is at the foundation of humanities in Western civilisation."[33] Using Wolof as a case study for his thesis that literature was a vector of development, he began with a correction: "Let me first of all state that contrary to current opinion, there are written African literatures, not just oral, which represent a well defined poetics. Valaf [Wolof] epic literature, for example, is in no way inferior to European epic literature. In fact, its form is in a way superior to that of the European model. Its development continues even today in the works of Moussa Ka for example.

Valaf literature is already very varied. Apart from the epic, there are such other genres as satires, epistolary forms, historical forms, narratives, etc."[34] We take from this passage a sense that literature in an African context is identified by the same measures used in a European context and that, when juxtaposed, the works of African literature do not come up short—and, in fact, are superior. Literature, as understood in the Western tradition as the sum of particular forms and genres, is, in fact, present. The problem is that this Wolof literature is unfamiliar to those who have received a hegemonic Western education. The mentioning of Moussa Ka is significant here, as he authored a number of celebrated poems about the Murid founder, Shaykh Amadou Bamba Mbakke, writing in Wolof and using the Arabic script known as *Wolofal*, now increasingly referred to as *Ajami*.[35] Despite Ka's prolific literary production and robust reception in Murid spaces, Diop's reference to him in 1948, as far as I am aware, might be the first time his name appears in a French academic publication.

Diop's assertion of African literary equality, if not superiority, rests on correcting this exclusion of African literature from the canon of literature. After addressing this erasure, Diop goes on to show how this literature, understood as authentic expressions of a Wolof African culture, stands to be enriched by using concrete words for abstract meanings, using an analogy with European languages' communication of geometrical concepts. What Diop needs is not the creation of a Wolof literature but its development. Importantly, the comparison with Europe is intended to be one illustrative analogy among others. Ultimately, African cultural production needs to be a continental and diasporic conversation that can freely adopt foreign matter for its own purposes. Implicit in his argument is the same kind of universalism in Senghor's assertion of equality within the category of the human. However, instead of arguing for the value of difference and communicating that for a European audience, Diopian humanism was universalist in its rigorous application of reason, which Europe failed to embrace for thinking about the colonized. In this essay, Diop articulated an early anticolonial and then decolonizing African humanism and argued that literature and literary study in African languages form a key axis of activity in the corrective strategy.

No wonder, then, that embedded in Diop's argument for the African Renaissance is a critique of a Senghorian African humanism that hinged on the translation of difference:

THE PITFALLS OF NATIONAL LITERATURE

> We believe that whoever writes has a definite objective; in which case, African writers must first ask themselves the following question: Why and for whom are we writing? If it is admitted that their writings are, in a way, the answer to this question, then one cannot but note that it is essentially a European public that they address; that their aim is to impress Europeans while incidentally defending an African cause. It is easy to see when a writer is mainly trying to express himself correctly in French, to demonstrate an unexpected literary talent or to exhibit his mastery of grammatical subtleties rather than expressing ideas that are useful to his community. French is not only an instrument for the acquisition of knowledge but also a corpus of knowledge in its own right: one is obliged to show that one has a total grip on it, the rest is secondary. This explains the reason for so much pedantry on the subject and enables one to appreciate the full significance of the expression *djvaya degi nasarann*, "Oh, how well he has assimilated French" used by the Senegalese elite. It also explains why such writers devote their efforts to making their writings intelligible, not to Africans, but to Europeans, as if their sole aim was to solicit respect from the latter; which to say the least is childish.[36]

It is hardly a stretch to read Diop's description of an emergent group of African writers in the French language as a critique of *Négritude* in general and of Senghor in particular. Who else viewed French as "not only an instrument for the acquisition of knowledge but also a corpus of knowledge in its own right" other than France's first African *professeur agrégé* of grammar and future immortal of the French Academy? Moreover, the strategy of the translation of difference, as described by Diop, presumes a European audience. Who else would need to have Africa's difference translated? The African audience of a literary work in an African language would not need translation and would not find difference relevant. According to Diop, then, literature within the translation of difference was simply the performative demonstration of linguistic mastery, not a civilizational achievement that might express a people's genius. Echoing a famous work of literary criticism by Leroi Jones speaking of the American context, Diop asks this question: "How does it happen that all modern Black literature has remained minor, in the sense that no Negro African author or artist, to my knowledge, has yet posed the problem of man's fate, the major theme of human letters?"[37]

The corrective strategy of Diopian African humanism organically grew out of the classic critiques offered up by modern Black and antiracist thought discernible from the work of Olaudah Equiano and Henri Grégoire, through that of W. E. B. Du Bois and even Maurice Delafosse.[38] Kamara's use of Arabic writing enabled a classical mode of textual humanistic scholarship, thus favoring Amar Samb's adoption of the classic strategy of postcolonial African thought, which sought to correct the oversights and falsifications of racial ideology. The presence of a monumental written text could not be denied, and Monteil's dismissal of Kamara's work as useless to the historian could be corrected using a more inclusive literary approach, in contrast to the practically minded empiricist sociology of Islam. But to fully appreciate Samb's project, which we consider in more detail later, it is necessary to situate him between Senghor and Diop.

Much like Senghor, Samb saw the need to relativize and translate difference or perhaps across difference. Samb's work consisted by and large of translating works in Arabic, French, and Wolof, as well as demonstrating an ethic of translation in explaining differences in literary form. Moreover, he valued the idea of cultural contact and complementarity, as we will see shortly, a practice Senghor advocated for African writers working in the French language. Much like Senghor spoke of the African contribution to the civilization of the universal, Samb framed his work as highlighting the contribution of Senegalese writers, their *Négritude*, to the literature of Arabic expression. However, Samb's work focused precisely on making known to the world of academic research and scholarship the "tradition that has remained intact and continues to survive despite modern influence" that Diop announced.[39] Samb, like Diop, asserted African humanity as expressed in an already existing African literary heritage, one that might be a legitimate foundation for the development of a national literature, albeit one that had yet to be achieved. Curiously though, both Senghor and Diop offered only elliptical references to Senegal's Arabo-Islamic heritage; they warrant a fuller treatment but are regrettably beyond the scope of this chapter. All the same, it would be left to Samb, and his work on and through Kamara, to find the place of the Arabic writing of Senegal in articulations of African humanism.

A final word is needed about the affirmation of African humanity before investigating Samb's body of work. Whether through the strategy of difference or that of correction, affirmation was typically limited by the disciplinary vocabulary that negated African humanity in the first place. For the American religious studies scholar Robert Orsi, the "disciplinary vocabulary of modernity" refers to the way in which terms such as secularization, modernization, and globalization in intellectual production propose to describe the world but actually prescribe the way the world *ought* to be by establishing what constitutes the "good" in contemporary human life.[40] Orsi, of course, is concerned with the globalized twenty-first century. But the insight is still valuable for thinking through the time of African independence. While genuinely reflecting sincere and legitimate political desires, the terms of nationalization, Africanization, development, and modernization were accompanied by a colonial inheritance that would continue to discipline, in the sense of coerce and order, African life, through the knowledge forms of the modern academic disciplines, which privileged European measures of humanity. Samb's strategy to affirm African humanity by establishing a national literature, complete with a historical consciousness, simultaneously embraced the mantle of autonomous maturity contained in the nation-state as enshrined in the postimperial United Nations charter and risked actualizing the civilizing mission's goal of creating self-policed subjects of colonial power.

Toward a National Literature

A portrait of Amar Samb and his body of work provides a compelling model with which to sketch the broad contours of the first phase of decolonization, one that was characterized by a profound ambivalence. Such a portrait will animate for us the stakes of the intellectual project of making Kamara a pillar of Senegalese national literature. This portrait then reveals the tension within the postcolonial intellectual project, which needed to valorize the inheritance of precolonial tradition for the purposes of modernization without making modernity appear as a total break from that tradition. We can describe this need as the need for a national literature.

This task is aided by a reading of Samb's thinly fictionalized novel *Matraqué par le destin: Ou la vie d'un talibé* (*Bludgeoned by Fate: Or, the Life of a Talibé*).[41] This 1973 coming-of-age memoir recounts the experiences of Omar, a gifted boy from the same inland rural town between Dakar and Saint-Louis as Samb. Despite the greatest odds, the fictional Omar, much like the real Amar, moves from a traditional Qur'anic education to the colonial school, where he excels before being granted a scholarship to study in France. *Matraqué par le destin* shares themes such as the dilemma of colonial education and the cost of European migration with the classics of postcolonial African literature, such as Cheikh Hamidou Kane's French-language *L'aventure ambiguë* (*Ambiguous Adventure*) and Tayeb Salih's Arabic-language *Mawsim al-Hijra ilā al-Shamāl* (*Season of Migration to the North*).[42] However, unlike his Senegalese peer Kane, who represents tradition and its custodians romantically, Samb represents the figure of the Qur'anic teacher, or marabout, and the experience of being a Qur'anic student (*talibé*) critically. And unlike Salih, who carefully tracks the psychology of the colonial migrant and his impossible returns, Samb unambiguously celebrates the protagonist's move to the metropole. Omar, the thinly veiled Samb, faces unexplainable violence and abuse at the hands of the marabouts, who appear as dim-witted brutes who abuse good faith. The title itself announces Samb's basic idea: To be a *talibé* is to be doubly bludgeoned—first by the marabout and then by destiny. It is not without reason that *Matraqué* has not found its place in the canon of African literature. The prose approaches tedium, densely packed as it is with historical information and ethnographic explanation. Its plot could be presented as a table of contents of a thesis. And sometimes the narrative breaks down completely in favor of essayistic diatribes against the cultural practices of popular Islam in Senegal and the structures of Sufi orders that dominated social life there at the time of the book's writing and that still do. The Senegalese literary scholar Mbye Cham has usefully situated Samb's fiction on a political spectrum of engagement with Islam that ranges from the promoters of Islam embodied by the likes of the poet Moussa Ka on the right to the apostates like Ousmane Sembene on the left.[43] Cham situates Samb as an iconoclast who offers a critique of religious organization, making him left of the Muslim humanists such as Cheikh Hamidou Kane and Aminata Sow Fall and of the irreverence of the oral tradition but still just right of Sembene.

Even if a reading of Samb's novel illustrates the nature of his literary intervention as an author, his greatest contribution to developing a national literature relied upon the country's manuscript heritage. At independence, the new nation-states in West Africa inherited physical archives of Arabic writing and less tangible structures of knowing Islam outside of the Sufi orders that were generated in the encounters I discussed in chapters 3 and 4. This inheritance accompanied the other state apparatuses that required decolonization. Similar to the nationalist historians of the Ibadan school of History in Nigeria who were exploiting Arabic sources to write precolonial histories and narratives of anticolonial resistance and the political leaders like Kwame Nkrumah who had a Pan-African ideological interest in Arabic manuscripts at the Institute of African Studies at the University of Ghana, scholars and politicians in Senegal were eager to define decolonization as nationalizing the country's Arabo-Islamic tradition in order to make a literature.[44] For Senegal, this intellectual, institutional, and infrastructural inheritance is reflected in the conveyance of the archival collections to the new government and the deployment of the hybrid methods of French *islamologie*, an empiricist sociology of Islam that nevertheless featured the study of texts, albeit in a more extractive and empiricist manner. Samb sought to nationalize Senegal's Arabo-Islamic written heritage through three activities that constituted the pillars of his research agenda: his individual scholarship, the collection and preservation of manuscripts, and translation.

Samb would lead this effort, first and foremost, by surveying the nation's Arabic literature. His *Essai sur la contribution du Sénégal à la littérature d'expression arabe* (Essay on Senegal's contribution to literature of Arabic expression) was published in 1972, making it one of the earliest such works for a West African country.[45] It was a peculiar work at the time and in many ways inaugurated a peculiar field. While its empirical focus on Senegal made it a work of African studies, the Arabic language of its material linked it with the study of the Middle East. Although the framing clearly makes the case for the inclusion of Arabic written heritage in the study of Africa, it was and remains an argument that must be justified to non-specialists. Furthermore, Samb's intervention faced the challenge of defining a body of texts whose religious, pedagogical, and sometimes prosaic nature would not be reflected in the curricula of most twentieth-century departments of literary studies.

Those peculiarities aside, what is conventional about the work is its methodological nationalism. In *Essai*, Samb takes the Senegalese territory and its organization into administrative units for granted as intellectually coherent, even though most of the authors he writes about crisscrossed the broader region. He limited the volume's scope to the colonial-cum-national borders of Senegal and organized it by "schools" of writing, representing

THE PITFALLS OF NATIONAL LITERATURE

the various regions of the country. For Samb, "schools" referred both to the abstract sense of thematic and stylistic tendencies and to the physical institutions where writers were educated, often under the auspices of the various Sufi orders that dominated Senegal's religious establishment. They were also largely defined by the textual production of a leading personality. The schools surveyed span what is sometimes called the golden age of Arabo-Islamic learning in Senegal, which almost exactly corresponds with the period of French colonization, from the "school of Guédé" of Hajj Umar Tal in the mid-nineteenth century through the "school of Touba" of Shaykh Amadou Bamba Mbakke (1853–1927) in the early twentieth century. By bringing together intellectual genealogies of "Senegalese" writers of Arabic with descriptions and excerpts of their work, Samb affirms a spatial, territorial logic for understanding Muslim intellectual life, which was, if not alien to the tradition, made more pronounced by the pragmatics of the colonial system of surveillance explored in chapter 3. Samb's chief aim in producing this nationalist survey of Arabic literature was to demonstrate to the world "Negro genius" and its capacity to participate in a world civilization. In doing so, however, his inheritance of an autochthonous tradition relied on colonial assets: both the archives and the frameworks for understanding their contents, expressed in a transparently nationalist paradigm of modern knowledge. His canon of Senegalese Arabic literature was defined by the territory demarcated by the firepower of colonial cannons.

Relative to his impact on the religious, political, and social history of Senegal, Kamara enjoys a prominent position in Samb's tome. The work, which sought to define the young nation's literature as an authentic expression of blackness in the Arabic language, reasonably begins with the militant Muslim scholar Hajj Umar Tal, as his millenarian movement in the mid-nineteenth century and his abundant corpus of juridical, mystic, and poetic work have made him a cornerstone of a national canon. It then features a discussion of Tal's primary rival, Bou al-Mogdad Seck, who, as the first salaried African employee of the colonial state, oversaw the interpreter corps, through which France governed the colony in Arabic as an official language until the turn of the twentieth century. Just after these two figures, who would otherwise not be remembered primarily for their literary contributions, Samb provides Kamara one of the most extensive treatments of any author in the volume. Samb's concluding words in the chapter provide a sense of why Kamara enjoyed such pride of place in the work:

> This anthologist, this historian, this defender of the revealed religions, this writer who is a bit of a jack of all trades, with a generous heart and who knew how to cultivate friendship with all races, with the great as well as with the lettered men of his time, also knew how to express himself in simple, correct words, never vulgar, but polished, with a clear outline scrupulously followed, with short, well-balanced sentences, a permanent concern for good composition in sober but flowing prose, lyrical, elegiac, but never cluttered with assonance or artistic affectation. The prevailing quality of his style is a marked taste for grammatical correction and appropriate expression. He remains, if not the greatest prose writer, at least one of the most remarkable Senegalese writers of Arabic expression. With him, Senegal can be proud of having produced a genius man of letters.[46]

This passage states in no uncertain terms that Kamara was a fine author who deserved a leading place in the canon of Senegalese literature. The variety of his interests, the quality of his written language, the stylistic prowess he demonstrated, and the sense of taste he cultivated distinguish him and his body of works as an achievement of literary importance. Samb's reading of Kamara could not have been more different than Monteil's dismissive description discussed earlier. Where Monteil characterized Kamara's writing as useless, unorganized, superstitious, derivative, and generally unimpressive, Samb declares that Kamara contributed to many fields, featured a unique voice, and was systematic, rational, and ecumenical. He further asserts Kamara wrote in short expressive sentences that could be crafted only by a real talent, that were far from the "endless digressions" of sentences encumbered by ornate prose or scholastic formulas that the orientalist stereotype of Arabic letters might lead one to expect. In providing such a reading and situating him as prominently as he did, Samb sought to correct Kamara's relative obscurity in both legacy colonial knowledge production and popular narratives about Senegalese culture, in which Kamara was marginal.

Samb's summative statement on Kamara reflects both the literary nature of the former's work and its character as a humanist project. One wonders upon reading this description if Kamara was not Senegal's own version of the men associated with the European Renaissance such as Petrarch, Erasmus of Rotterdam, and Lorenzo Valla, whose supposed break with scholasticism enabled more spontaneous use of language, encouraged polymathy, and insisted on an inherent human worth and dignity that should be cultivated in the practice of virtue. Like these authors, the literary and humanistic Kamara in Samb's treatment engaged with many fields and genres, balanced reason and emotion, and sought to perfect his humanity through language. In contrast to Monteil's almost tactical treatment of Kamara, which ends before it even begins, Samb's specifically literary study of Kamara's writings and appreciation of their form, in effect, brought Kamara back from the death of the colonial archive.

Samb's humanism is highlighted not only in the implicit comparison between Kamara and the canonical figures of Renaissance humanism but also in the description of what one infers from the text to be a unique sociality for his context. Here Kamara's humanity is captured in the idea of his compassion, his goodwill toward his fellows, and even a sort of antiracism. Samb argues that Kamara's "cult of friendship," an idea that has had profound staying power in Kamara scholarship, is a leading indication of his open and humanistic spirit.[47] Reflection on friendship can be identified in classical thought, but it achieved the status of celebration with this phrase in eighteenth-century Enlightenment-era France as a kind of social relation outside of erotic or familial relationships, as well as beyond the relationships of obligation of a feudal context. Readers do not need a vivid imagination to see how the historical emergence of this concept coincided with the emergence of a sociality that undergirded the development of modern civil society. But what did it mean in Samb's description of Kamara? As an intellectual of the young African nation, Samb is interested in elaborating exemplars and the ideal forms of social belonging that would help develop the nation. "The man was generous, honest, good, tolerant, open to everything, a humanist, because what is humanism, if not a sincere love for everything that touches man, whether he is White or Black?"[48]

Samb writes of Kamara: "He placed friendship above all; this was for him a cardinal virtue. And to hear him talk about his friends, one gets the impression that he had a Platonic conception of them."[49] The Platonic conception of friendship here refers to the idea that friendship should be based on a shared pursuit of wisdom and on innate character traits. Samb makes this claim based on the voluminous correspondence that Kamara kept and reproduced in his autobiography. Curiously, Samb reports in a footnote that the quotation that he includes in the body of his text to make his point about Kamara's Platonic conception of friendship was supported by a prophetic statement, making Kamara's conception of friendship as much Muhammadi as it was Platonic. That the translation ties Kamara's view of friendship to the classical tradition while subordinating its Islamic reference to a footnote reveals the likely audience addressed in this work. To a French-speaking audience educated in a Western canon, Samb shows that there exists a humanism nourished from Islamic sources. And no one in Senegal's canon embodied this Muslim humanism more than Kamara.

This discussion of Samb's treatment of Kamara demonstrates that the former read him in literary and humanist terms that emphasized Kamara's status as an author and his works as a human achievement and presented him as a subject to be emulated in the modern nation of Senegal. This was a novel way of reading Kamara at the time but one that has had an influential impact on the scholar's reception. To better situate this literary afterlife of Kamara within a consideration of Samb's work more broadly, we should consider Samb's understanding of humanism.

Samb viewed humanity as intimately linked to historicity—that is, the capacity to create changes in the conditions of life—which was, in turn, directly linked to the course of Islam in Senegal. Samb's 1971 article on Islam and history effectively demonstrates these relationships. In it, Samb argues that Islam is a traditional religion in the sense that it is constituted of inherited meanings and forms, thoughts and actions. The article begins with an epigraph from Félix Brigaud, which reflects the Hegelian theory that attributes to Islam Africa's entry into history, humanity, and civilization. Samb addresses the quote early in the work to highlight Islam's role in African history—that is, its development. He qualifies this role in a footnote by saying that Africa has a pre-Islamic history, but this remark seems to be an afterthought, and he does not elaborate on it. What remains clear is the place of Islam in the humanist theory of African history. After citing the Arab geographer al-Bakri, Samb says:

> The importance of these lines is that they reveal three elements that form the basis of history: man, land, and time. History is only the unfolding, the evolution of the synthesis of these three entities from a more or less determined point in space and time. Indeed, the *Blacks*, established on both sides of a *river*,

count among their kings a Muslim sovereign, Waar Diaabé who died in 1040 AD after having spread Islam in his kingdom dependent on the empire of Ghana (790–1076).... It is from there that events take their course, that the Senegalese man defines himself progressively throughout the centuries without ever separating himself from Islam which can be said to be also a traditional religion for this country.[50]

Here Samb shares with the paradigmatic African humanists Senghor and Diop a view of history in which humanity is central to its unfolding by interacting with an environment over time so as to allow culture to achieve ever higher forms and levels of sophistication. What is emphasized in Samb's presentation of this view is the link between Islam and sovereignty over a territory in the person of Warjabi b. Rabis, as well as humanity's capacity for self-definition. Unlike nature, which just is, human beings have the power to name, giving meaning to existence with the help of divine revelation. In this way, Samb mobilizes a humanist understanding of the deep Senegalese past to authorize a national memory and imagination in which Islam is core to national identity.

Samb's African humanism is profoundly influenced by the humanism of the French orientalism in which he was trained, as well as by his contemporaries discussed in the previous section. He was a student of Charles Pellat, whom Samb described as "one of the pillars of European orientalism,"[51] and mastered the disciplinary conventions and bodies of literature and scholarship relating to the secular study of Islam through Arabic texts in the French academy. Since Silvestre de Sacy, metropolitan orientalists, from their institutional locations in Paris, represented Islam to the rest of the academy and to French society through the secular concept of Islamic civilization, situating the study of Islam within the humanist tradition but locating Muslim societies at an intermediate stage of human progress, one that was thought to be more advanced than Black African civilization.[52] We might, following literary theorist and critic R. A. Judy, describe this view as the humanist ambivalence toward Islam, the idea that Islam had a positive civilizing effect on Africa but that Islamic civilization was an inferior competitor to the civilization of European modernity.[53] Inflected by historicism and the formalist study of canonical texts, French orientalism generated ideal types that became the foundation of social theory disbursed through the disciplines and more popular representations. This form of study was not simply antiquarianism. The tradition of French orientalism produced public intellectuals who established discourse well beyond their fields of expertise, such as Ernest Renan, who famously developed anti-Semitic ideas in his theorization of nationalism and whom Samb cites for very different reasons in his discussion of Kamara's autobiography.[54]

The humanism of French orientalism provides Samb with a ready-made interpretative grid for thinking Senegal. The corrective work to be done simply requires applying the same measures and patterns of civilization found in European history to that of Senegal. For example, Samb describes the center of learning at Pir in Senegal as a university that rivaled those in Timbuktu, Jenné, and Gao, where all the great religious leaders "did their humanities before founding each in his village, a center of studies, a 'dara', or school of teaching and education in which all the religious and secular disciplines of Arab-Muslim civilization were taught."[55] To describe this system of learning as a university is a particular translation that is neither totally false nor fully complete. The model of the university suggests a degree of institutionality in a place that was less important than the social network of master-disciple relationships that crisscrossed the landscape. To describe the studies themselves as "the humanities" papers over important differences between the religious character of traditional education and its modalities of instruction and the secular philosophy of the modern liberal arts. These partial translations, while clarifying, miss an opportunity to rethink the assumptions of humanist thought. By and large, Samb does not challenge the frameworks or methodologies offered by humanism as articulated by French orientalism, electing only to expand its reach to include a literary tradition and an attendant national identity and will, which until his intervention had largely been ignored.

If humanism provided Samb the overarching theory of his intellectual work, comparative literature provided its concrete realization. On the title page of his *Essai*, Samb included an epigraph from an undergraduate handbook on comparative literature by the authority Marius-François Guyard: "In every era, a type sums up the aspirations and embodies the ideal of elegance or morality or of a generation or a class. Sometimes this ideal is indigenous, sometimes it is *borrowed from neighboring nations* which thus assert a certain supremacy; sometimes again, the national hero will define himself in reaction against a foreign model."[56] Though only an epigraph, these lines are suggestive of Samb's literary paradigm. First, there is the

THE PITFALLS OF NATIONAL LITERATURE

idea that literature embodies and expresses human qualities that are not captured in materiality. These qualities include the aspirational, that which humans desire and strive to achieve, as well as the beautiful and the good. These qualities might also represent the unique character or genius of a group (generation or class). Second, literature reflects a period of time—that is, it is historical. Third, what ultimately defines the "type," which is probably something like personality or character, is a duality, being both native and organic, as well as being both foreign and borrowed. The work of the comparatist in this framework is the history of international literary relations as determined by formal and thematic connection and circulation, captured most succinctly by the idea of influence.[57] As an imperative of literary research, the literary comparativism that guided Samb's reading of a Senegalese national literature in Arabic is defined by the tension between formal influences from elsewhere and the expression of Black cultural authenticity.[58]

But what exactly was literature for Samb? And what was its place in the broader humanist vision? It is noteworthy that he begins a discussion of the influence of Islam on Wolof literature with a discussion of the phonetics of Wolof transcription.[59] While it might be considered a simple transliteration note and not a part of the text proper, it nevertheless suggests an understanding of literature as the rendering of sounds in writing, as opposed to, for example, imaginative creation.[60] Moreover, his descriptions of various phonemes are made with reference to Europhone sounds in German and Spanish alongside the technical linguistic description. Implied in this note is an understanding of national literature as the development of a particular language that is occasioned by the technology of writing and the forms of complexity that it alone engenders in politics, society, the economy, religion, and philosophy, as established in European tradition. This view of literature seems unorthodox in the field of African literature, but he states his case fully:

> One of the most interesting aspects of this original element of Wolof is its literature, which is Negro-African. But is it not too ambitious to use the word literature, which broadly designates a set of writings aimed at communicating, with or without aesthetic intention, facts, ideas, teachings, etc.? We deliberately emphasize *writings*, but Wolof, like almost all Negro-African languages, is not written. Does this mean that literature can do without writing? Just as the arrow

cannot do without the wood and the string of the bow, so literature, as its name etymologically indicates, cannot really exist without the writing that materializes it, that brings it to life, that transmits it from one generation to another, from one era to another, and which, in short, makes it a literature worthy of the name. There is no question of denying the primacy that must be given, in this domain, to oral tradition, nevertheless this cannot be the whole of literature; it is a system of signs (litterae) adopted to reproduce the words of a given language, to express with letters the sounds of speech and the meaning of discourse, which constitutes the sine qua non condition of the existence of a true literature. Precisely, it is Islam which has furnished the Wolof its system of writing.[61]

In other words, the quality of having been written defines literature. The gift of Islam to the Wolof language is the possibility of writing, which also is what inaugurates civilizational history. Samb tries to carefully balance a notion of literature that would exclude most premodern African societies with a claim of the exceptional status of Wolof society, which stands in as a statement about Senegal more broadly because of its Islamic history. The result of this tension is an implicit ambivalence toward the civilizational discourse that accepts the value of an African literary expression on the condition that it orient itself outward.

Samb, however, claims that there is no ambivalence in this historical fact, only the tensions that pull on human beings over the course of their lives. To return to the article on Islam's impact on history, he writes: "His contribution in the form of writing in Arabic characters for Wolof and Pular, the enrichment of the vocabulary of these two languages, the method allowing prose writers and poets speaking these two idioms to express their thoughts and feelings, their sorrows and their joys, their despairs and their dreams, their loves and their disappointments, their anger and their pride, constitutes one of the most beautiful titles of pride that the religion of Mohammed can, without complex, claim."[62] In this passage, he takes up classical humanist ideas about the function of literature, which is to express humanity through the use of language, the collocation of reason and affect. Ultimately, he argues that the relationship between an Arabo-Muslim civilizational heritage and Senegalese society is a symbiotic one. Senegal receives script, history, and religion (with its law). In effect, it receives a factor of progress and unity. In return, Senegal gives the tradition new proofs of its universal applicability, as manifested in the uses of classical Arabic poetic meter to convey a Wolof vocabulary. The result is an enrichment of language. In contrast to Senghor, who presents Arabic as a classical, dead language, Samb concludes that this legacy of influence makes Arabic a national language that must be supported by the state, an argument that would only build in its momentum and validity in the following decades.[63] Viewed in this way, Samb's scholarly project had overwhelming stakes, for Senegal's Islamic past and Arabic literature were the very means by which the Senegalese people could make an equal claim on the category of the human.

Samb's scholarship would be joined by his practical work in collecting, cataloging, and preserving several manuscripts not already in the state's possession. This activity constituted another pillar of the nationalization of the Arabo-Islamic heritage and the construction of a national literature. Prior to his intervention, IFAN already featured several collections with Arabic materials. Except for Kamara's collection, these consisted of Arabic-script documents and texts gathered by colonial officials such as Henri Gaden, Jean Henri Cremer, Jules Brévié, Colonel R. Figaret, and Gilbert Vieillard that reflected their personal interests.[64] With the support of Senghor and IFAN's institutional resources, Samb conducted two extensive collection trips throughout Senegal in 1966 and 1974. This process of collection greatly diversified the contents of what had become a university archive, covering a near totality of the Islamic sciences.[65] The organization of Samb's collection, when compared to that of the older collections, suggests an intention to make the archive representative of the range of genres of Arabo-Islamic textual production, as well as the regional diversity of the nation. Whereas in the older collections there is a noticeable absence of Senegal's major religious personalities in favor of texts that were useful for administrative purposes, Samb's collection features writing by renown Sufi leaders organized by the disciplines and genres of Islamic knowledge.

While these collection trips yielded many documents, Samb and many who followed him were baffled by how often families resisted the surrender of Arabic texts despite the obvious urgency presented by decaying texts and the exciting opportunity represented by decolonization. Religious leaders and their descendants have been reluctant to offer their wealth of written heritage to both the colonial and the postcolonial states. Many researchers have tried to rationalize this refusal in passing by citing colonial legacies of archival seizure, lack of faith in the functioning of the neocolonial state, and economic incentives for maintaining ownership.[66] There are, however, other immaterial benefits of maintaining possession of the manuscripts, such as *baraka*, or the aura of the text. Samb expressed a frustration with what he understood as a parochial and irrational obstacle to a simultaneously African and Islamic claim on universal reason and its accompanying projected public good. That Samb was able to collect any of these works at all, though, represented an advance in the nationalization of the tradition.

A third pillar of Samb's nationalization of Senegal's Arabophone tradition was the translation of the texts of that tradition, making them available to the Senegalese public and to a broader international audience. First for IFAN's academic journal, *Bulletin de l'Institut fondamantal d'Afrique noire*, and then for publishers of mass-market paperbacks, Samb, along with other scholars such as Moustapha Ndiaye, translated many sections of Kamara's *The History of the Blacks*, *The Life of Hajj Umar*, *The Clear Truth*, *The Coming Together of Christianity and Islam*, and *Most of the Would-Be Jihadists* from Arabic into French.[67] While Kamara's autobiography, examined in chapters 1 and 2, demonstrates that he did enjoy a positive reputation as a scholar during his lifetime, it was only during the 1970s that his scholarship became more widely available, even to the region's Muslim scholars learned in Arabic. The first citation of Kamara's work in an Arabic text that I have been able to identify does not appear until after Samb's intervention. Kamara's *The Life of Hajj Umar* is referenced in what is generally considered the official biography of Hajj Umar Tal, written by the Tijani leader's grandson Muntaga Tal.[68] This intervention was invaluable to the project of decolonizing Senegal's history in the decades immediately after independence and was an essential precondition for making Kamara available for critical thought today. By publishing Kamara in French-language print publications, Samb and others sought to insert him into public discourse, where access to him had otherwise been denied by a complex web of institutional, familial, and scholarly relationships. Kamara's writings were documents only as long as they remained in the archive. Putting them in circulation made them literature.

Relative to the other authors in *Essai*, Kamara was especially important for Samb's humanist project, as his historical writing demonstrated progress in the form of literature. Where most of the other authors surveyed were poets or jurists who wrote in a scholastic mode, Kamara was evidence of a development of prose. This is important because poetry is often seen as a first literature in civilizational developmentalist terms. Whether it is Homer or the pre-Islamic Arabs or the famous griots of West Africa, whom

THE PITFALLS OF NATIONAL LITERATURE

Samb seems to avoid in his discussions, primordial literature is associated with these forms and their performance. We must immediately point out that these are oral forms. Poetry subsequently grows in sophistication with its own theory as it becomes written. Then, as the civilization "develops" with the technology of writing, history as a form of writing becomes the next stage of writing. Poetry is superseded when history takes over. This is why Samb is more interested in Kamara: his development of historical writing signals important progress in the history of Senegalese literature. It represents an advancement in the civilizational terms Samb deploys. It also announces the possibility that historical consciousness, associated with modernity, will emerge, even if it is not yet fully actualized. Obviously, Samb is thinking in the colonial humanist terms that he has inherited. Kamara for him is proof of literary progress and evolution, even if he is not fully satisfied with what that literature has achieved. He is a modernist and is committed to developing the tradition.

Kamara provided Amar Samb with the ideal resources with which to elaborate the documentary basis of an African historiography, resources that harnessed the inheritance of tradition while demonstrating the features of modern thought as an organic development of Senegal's historical specificity. The foundation of Kamara's contribution to Samb's project of writing a nationalist African history was Kamara's collection of raw historical information absent from other sources. Kamara's treatment of the experiment of an ideal Muslim community at Maghama, for example, includes details on the background of its leader, Ceerno Braahiima, and the early days of the community.[69] This information was not available in either colonial archives or oral traditions collected in the 1970s and includes testimonies not found elsewhere, according to American historian David Robinson. Kamara's original research in the 1920s recorded valuable information that otherwise would have been lost to historical memory. For Samb and others engaged in writing a Senegalese national history, such information facilitated their work incredibly. That such information came from an African intellectual and was not filtered through the perspectives of European observers vindicated their efforts even more.

Beyond Kamara's raw historical data, Samb used his historical method as proof of a Black historical consciousness that did not rely on European tutelage. The stakes of this argument were nothing less than a claim of an organic Black modernity, a mode of thought that was built at least partially on empirical observation and that recognized historical difference between the present and the previous eras. In the framing essay of his translation of Kamara's *The Life of Hajj Umar*, Samb defines Kamara's work as good history:

> His qualities as a historian are not difficult to demonstrate: it only suffices to browse his book on The Life of El-Hadji Omar. Starting with material testimony, written and oral, the Cheikh proceeds, armed with a critical sensibility, always with an eye for discerning the authentic from what is not, the natural cause of legend, and the rationally admissible facts of miracles. . . . [He cites Kamara speaking about the spurious claim that Umar was a descendant of the Prophet]. Such is the method of a real historian, that is to say, reasoning from real facts or from reliable information, or in the absence of the two, putting forward hypotheses that are not repulsive to a sane and rational explanation. This proves the intellectual honesty of a critical mind, which refuses any dogmatic endeavor.[70]

Samb appears to be successful in his argument: Yes, we have our historians too. The methods, concerns, and kinds of arguments that Samb's representation of Kamara uses make him an ideal historian, one who might as well have lived and written in nineteenth-century Europe. Framing Kamara as a historian in this context followed an understanding of decolonization as the assertion of an already existing indigenous modernity, the emergent way of thinking about humanity.

For Samb, Kamara's self-conscious method puts him in a class of modern European historians in the tradition of Leopold von Ranke, Thomas Carlyle, and Gustave Le Bon. These references are as literary as they are historical. Samb makes much of Kamara's introduction, which declares the contents of the text and its primary sources. Commenting on Kamara's opening statement, Samb says: "This is, we see it again, the same method of investigation: real facts, verifiable information and reasonable hypotheses. Yes, it is this method, this care for a clear outline and this bare style, which explains the superiority of the Cheikh. These are the literary virtues that good Arab writers envy in Senegal, and it is with these qualities that one creates if not a masterpiece at least originality, this being the capacity to know how to invent, order, and express one's thought in a personal, unique way."[71] Use of such a mundane statement to illustrate exceptionality reveals an underlying tension in Samb's interest in Kamara. On the one hand, Kamara represents an entire tradition of Arabic historical writing in Senegal and puts this tradition on par with European and Arab historical writing. On the other, Samb's preoccupation with finding an exceptionally great writer of a uniquely Senegalese tradition divorces Kamara from that tradition. Samb appears stuck amidst Romantic notions of the artist and his relationship to a tradition, a valorization of the Arabic language as a vehicle of nationalism, and an insistence on the need to develop tradition into something modern. It is unclear precisely who Samb's intended audience is. If he was writing to European scholars, we might say that his reading of Kamara portrays him as a genius in whom Europeans could identify the embodiment of an entire tradition. But for a Senegalese audience, Samb uses Kamara to show everything that the countless marabouts were not.[72] And for a prospective Arab audience, Samb presents Kamara as a writer to be seen as an equal, if not a scholar to be envied. As a result, we are left with an ambiguous assertion that only Kamara's blackness sets him apart from modern historians, and yet his rationalistic approach to history puts him among their rank.

In addition to Kamara's modern rationalism, his narrative style made him a modern historian, according to Samb. He cites at length Kamara's description of the battle between Umar and Ahmad b. Ahmad, the ruler of Masina, a neighboring Muslim state: "It is at last the style of the epic in the action, the subject, the adventure, the *dénouement*, the protagonists, the setting, and the moral. See the sumptuous and emphatic vocabulary, the colors, the personification of the mountains.... We must admit that we have a fresco worthy of the brush of Delacroix."[73] Throughout this work, Samb insists on the literary quality of Arabic writing from Senegal, so he stresses those features that appeal to such an assessment, such as epic style, elements of literary form, and use of literary devices. Notably, Samb says that the drama of the moment around which *The Life of Hajj Umar* is in many ways organized is worthy of a painted representation by Eugène Delacroix, the famous painter of such oriental scenes as *The Entry of the Crusaders in Constantinople*, *The Women of Algiers in Their Apartment*, and *Fanatics of Tangier*.[74] This assertion by Samb inserts Kamara, after the fact, into the field of representation that Edward Said characterized as orientalism, which itself insisted on a certain *literariness* of the Orient. For many of Samb's readers, the representation of Senegal as being a part of Europe's Orient was likely tenuous because of its location in so-called Black Africa. But his insistence on the literariness of Kamara's work, and his representation of the confrontation between Hajj Umar Tal and Ahmad b. Ahmad in particular, puts that work on a stage of history that it could share with civilization, broadly construed. In this way, Samb uses Kamara the historian-writer as proof of Senegalese participation in world civilization and as the basis for a Senegalese modernity. No matter how degraded and criticized, it was still seen as being worthy of literature and art. Without history, one could not be considered a worthy subject of art and literature.

Beyond the literary qualities that evidenced Kamara's modern sensibilities, Samb emphasized his ecumenism and spirit of tolerance. Citing *The Coming Together of Christianity and Islam*, Samb presents a Kamara who is concerned with all the gestures, material culture, and idioms shared between Muslims and Christians. "A curious and critical mind, Cheikh Moussa was also an open, indulgent, conciliatory and tolerant man," Samb writes, before adding that "not only is it rare to see his equal among the Senegalese marabouts but it is still difficult to find his peer among the Muslim Arabs."[75] In short, for Samb, Kamara was an enlightened Muslim who was exceptional within the Arabo-Islamic tradition. However, it was not Islam that elevated Kamara; it was Kamara's special spirit of modernity, a spirit apart from his religion and perhaps even despite it. The texts highlighted in this essay on Kamara would eventually be translated and published in full by Samb during the following decade. In that way, the essay serves as a précis of Samb's publishing to come, which would emphasize Kamara's literary humanity, historicity, and Enlightenment character, and contribute to the modernization of Islam and the nation.

Contradictions of Nationalization

Samb's nationalist project is not free from some crucial contradictions. In disproving Monteil and the broader idea of African lack by furnishing the example of Kamara's historical writing and its associated historicity, Samb falls into a common conceptual trap confronted in Black and antiracist thought. By accepting the terms of a loaded question, Samb is backed into a damning admission despite its falsity. Either he responds unacceptably that, no, Africa is not historical, and the implication is that the absence of history is evidence of European supremacy. Or he responds that, yes, Africa is historical, and the implicit measure of that historicity is defined by past historical experiences in Europe, thus making the ancestral home of whiteness the universal measure against which other experiences might be judged. While Samb manages to assert African historicity, he reaffirms historicity as understood from the historical specificity of Europe. This challenge that faced the project of affirming African humanity has long plagued earlier generations of Black thought more generally. In responding to negation, one is faced with a choice of either accepting that some part of the negation is true or accepting how that negation has happened. As much as Samb has sought to negate the negation, so to speak, of the colonial inheritance of intellectual, institutional, and infrastructural assets, he carries on the potential of the original negation. As the Black feminist poet and thinker Audre Lorde reminds us, the master's tools will never dismantle the master's house.[76]

Even more troubling is that the assertion of African humanity through a nationalization of Arabo-Islamic heritage is locked into a profound Hegelianism. To revisit Samb's framing remarks of *Essai*, he believed that it was "time to show the world what Black genius is capable of producing in contact with a civilization, or a foreign culture."[77] This statement, read ungenerously suggests that although there exists Black genius, it has not found its expression in its own civilization, that it might find form only through contact with other civilizations. Implicit in this suggestion is that with the exception of the Arabo-Islamic heritage that Samb dedicated himself to nationalizing as a literature in the affirmation of African humanity, what was essentially African was indeed uncivilized. The status of Islam as the exception to African absence was a central tenet of Hegel's thought. If Hegelianism describes the colonial and racist idea that Africa is "no historical part of the world," Samb is caught in a sly Hegelianism he seeks to disprove.[78]

Black and postcolonial thought has often noted that Hegel manages to represent Africa and blackness as negation only according to his own logic because he cuts Africa off at the Sahara, naming it Africa proper, as opposed to European Africa and Asian Africa. In effect, Hegel makes Africa a geo-racial entity, as opposed to a rationally defined pan-continental landmass. This critique follows the common logic of the second strategy of affirmation, that the negation of African humanity was simply incorrect, discussed earlier. Far less appreciated in this tradition, however, is the appearance of Islam in Africa as the exception to the negation of African history. After the part of the text just cited, Hegel mentions the place of Islam in Africa as an afterthought: "Mahommedanism appears to be the only thing which in any way brings the Negroes within the range of culture."[79] Presumably, the "range of culture" here refers to the Germanic idea of *kultur*, one that is closer to the Anglo-French notion of civilization, which emphasizes a particular history of political formation, the development of technology, certain theological and philosophical ideas, and, of course, writing. Given the context of the argument, Hegel is suggesting that Islam, in its religiously endowed universality, its scripture, and its law, gives Africa proper its only access to humanity and the possibility of the political, of connectivity to world history. If Hegelianism describes the still too common idea that Africa is no historical part of the world and that the African is not fully human, Samb's acceptance of modernity's disciplinary, and disciplining, vocabulary traps him in the negating Hegelianism he seeks to refute.

This contradiction can be fruitfully understood in what Partha Chatterjee has called the contradiction of the thematic and the problematic in postcolonial nationalist thought.[80] The problematic for Chatterjee consists of the claims of a social ideology—in our case, African humanism. The thematic is the justificatory structure for those claims—in our case, the intellectual, institutional, and infrastructural inheritance from colonial thought and practice that conditioned and made possible Samb's work on Kamara. The contradiction of nationalist thought consists of the problematic, asserting an African historicity and humanity distinct and apart from the colonial enterprise, and the thematic, adopting the colonial "islamological" and empiricist approach that had been responsible for rendering Africa ahistorical in the first place. As much as Samb's work of collection, preservation, and translation has made an invaluable contribution to knowledge, making further work possible, we would be remiss in not pointing out this fundamental, broader contradiction of knowledge production in the first generation of African decolonization.

Other Readings and Other Possibilities

Building on the work of scholars such as Amar Samb, the American historian David Robinson elaborated Kamara's utility for professional African history. Robinson's dissertation and first book on Futa Toro in the second half of the nineteenth century relied on Kamara's archival collection at IFAN, fieldwork collecting oral traditions in the Senegal River Valley, and long stays with Kamara's descendants in and around Matam. Much like Hilliard, Robinson was encouraged by fellow young Senegalese historians—in Robinson's case, by Oumar Ba,[81] who recognized in Kamara a fount of African history.[82] In addition to writing his own historical works, Robinson identified, collected, copied, and published many invaluable sources for use by other historians. He did this with both written works and oral traditions for Muslim scholars such as Kamara and Hajj Umar. The multinational team that worked on translating Kamara's *The History of the Blacks*, discussed shortly, credits Robinson with providing much of the foundation for the project.[83] Robinson also contributed to the team's translation project itself. He rounded out his contribution to professional African history—in particular, the history of Islam in Africa—by writing a widely used undergraduate textbook on Muslim societies in African history. That Kamara was so important to the development of the career of such an influential historian of Africa is no coincidence. The professional historians of African within Senegal, as we saw with Amar Samb and beyond, largely understood their task in the first generation of decolonization as identifying and valorizing sources and methods that had been invalidated or deemed impossible from the colonial period. Kamara, and the scholarship concerning him, represents a paradigmatic example, then, of what the decolonization of history meant in the first thirty or so years after independence.

To complete the discussion of the first generation of Kamara studies, we must consider the ongoing effort to make Kamara available in translation. In the early 1990s, a multinational team of scholars associated with the University of Dakar, IFAN, and the Centre National de la Recherche Scientifique in Paris undertook a massive effort to translate the monumental *History of the Blacks* into French. The director of the project, French anthropologist Jean Schmitz, has highlighted the complex set of competencies in Arabic and Pulaar, textual scholarship, and regional history and geography that this required.[84] The first of four volumes of the translation, done by Moroccan-French historian Saïd Bousbina, appeared in 1998. The other volumes, translated by Bousbina, Khadim Mbacké, and Abdoul Malal Diop, have yet to appear. Since publication, the first volume has been an important reference for historians of West Africa. Interestingly, much of what circulates as the oral tradition of Futa Toro today is already present in this colonial-era text. One new aspect of the reception of Kamara associated with this project is his emergence as a geographer. In addition to providing valuable historical information, the translation serves as a resource for a better understanding of the human geography of the middle Senegal River Valley, with a particular attention to Kamara's knowledge of the region's riverine system.[85] While this facet is clearly present in the original text, it is worth noting the conjunctural conditions that made it visible to scholars for the first time. The conflict in this border zone between Mauritania and Senegal and the prominence of a certain area-studies paradigm that privileges place-based knowledge in the knowledge production of Africa must be considered key parts of the context in which Kamara the geographer began to accompany Kamara the litterateur and historian.[86]

There is perhaps a third strategy of affirmation of African humanity yet to be realized for the works of Kamara and the broader field of Arabic writing from West Africa. If Amadou Hampâté Bâ's exploration of an oral folk culture of Muslim-majority West African societies replaced absence with presence and Amar Samb's nationalization of Arabo-Islamic written heritage made a contradictory and self-negating bid for inclusion in the category of the human, a third possibility might be embodied by the novelist Yambo Ouologuem. His 1968 *Le devoir de violence* constituted a radically critical and creative reading of the Sahelian self in the way it combined oral tradition, features of Arabic chronicles well-known in the region, and strategic poaching of contemporary novels written in several languages, all while fearlessly regarding the tragic violence, self-inflicted and otherwise, that characterized collective life.[87] Born in Bandiagara, in the very cliffs where Hajj Umar Tal is said to have left this world in an explosion of gunpowder, Ouologuem was concerned with the legacies of power that also interested Kamara when he wrote *The Life of Hajj Umar*.[88] While Ouologuem was initially celebrated as offering a radically new possibility for post-Négritude and postcolonial letters, accusations of plagiarism based on a superficial reading of the work undermined his place in publishing. Facing such lack of regard, Ouologuem returned to Mali to eventually become a Qurʾanic teacher associated with the Tijani Sufi order, notoriously turning his back on the literary world.[89] In both his imaginative reading of his complicated inheritance and his eventual refusal to engage the international publishing market, Ouologuem offers a model for a third strategy in the affirmation of African humanity: what has come to be known in the body of work of Toni

THE PITFALLS OF NATIONAL LITERATURE

Morrison as self-regard, a theory of the literary that rejects the politics of representation. It is a strategy of reading Kamara that is yet to be pursued.

By refuting an essentially colonial reading of Kamara's uselessness for the historian and ushering in an active period of translation and popularization, the first generation of scholars interested in Kamara after Senegalese independence sought to perform intellectual decolonization through the affirmation of African humanity by means of work in the humanities disciplines. While the work of decolonization was shared by an entire generation, Léopold Senghor, and polymath Cheikh Anta Diop represent two distinct strategies of translating difference and correcting distortions of racist thought. Many Senegalese scholars participated in this work, but it is the national literature project of Amar Samb that integrates these two strategies, and captures the Senegalese national project to decolonize knowledge emblematically. Samb framed Kamara as Senegal's historian-as-litterateur par excellence, that many intellectuals took up. The work these Senegalese scholars did on Kamara encouraged broader participation by professional historians beyond Senegal in the development of resources and scholarship needed to make African history truly African. The raw material for these efforts is certainly present in Kamara's body of work. However, I argue that Pan-African nation building, committed as it was to decolonization as a political and intellectual project, was at the heart of a preoccupation with Kamara's literary framing that made him vital for establishing Senegalese historicity and humanity. We have seen this by paying attention to scholarship not simply as the attempt to uncover truth or a series of contending arguments but as a set of discursive practices. A reading of these discursive practices reveals a set of contradictions that is not totally dissimilar to what Frantz Fanon described as the "misadventure" of national consciousness led by the postcolonial middle class and the "cosmopolitan mold" in which its mind is set.[90] It is also an attention to discursive practice that allows us to perceive a more recent shift in the reception of Kamara toward one that emphasizes religion as a new vector of decolonization.

SIX

The Secular-Religious Afterlife of Shaykh Musa Kamara

THE STREETS OF DAKAR, Senegal, teemed with Gaza solidarity protests during the onslaught of Israel's Operation Protective Edge in the summer of 2014. Talking heads met on the top news show to discuss the matter. Bakary Sambe, a Senegalese professor of Islamic studies and a consultant on "countering violent extremism" initiatives, and Tariq Ramadan, a once-major figure of global Islam who has since fallen from grace following accusations of sexual assault, faced off.[1] The debate quickly descended into an exchange of verbal fire after Sambe declared that Hamas was not a political party like any other.[2] Ramadan accused Sambe of having a colonized mind. At a momentary loss for words, Sambe hit back at Ramadan, saying "It is you who are the first colonizers, you Arabs."

Once tempers cooled, Sambe used his blog to provide context to the heated debate and to clarify the statement that solicited Ramadan's insult.[3] First, Sambe contextualized the exchange by referring to a long-standing debate between the two men about the nature of the French-led military intervention to secure Northern Mali after Islamist insurgents had held vast amounts of territory under their control. Ramadan had referred to it as a case of imperialism. Sambe countered that "Arab paternalism" needed to be equally addressed because it was this view that animates "Salafi" and "Wahabi"—terms that describe a rigorist interpretation of Islam that is associated with the Arab Gulf in popular culture—efforts to "Islamize" African Muslims despite Islam's millennial history in the region. As evidence,

Sambe invoked the destruction of tombs in the fabled city of Timbuktu that had been occupied by militants for some ten months.

Pivoting from the global concerns invoked in the television debate and the subsequent reference to Timbuktu as a case study in an Arab and European contest for influence, Sambe refuted Ramadan's claim that the public intellectual had a colonized mind. He spoke neither from Paris nor from Washington, as Ramadan had suggested, but from Ganguel, a village on the southern bank of the Middle Senegal River. This very, very small place, that is only reachable by a long, rough dirt road, is a far cry from the centers of "Françafrique" or of American empire. It had only recently been connected to the electrical grid when I first visited that year. Yet for Sambe, Ganguel represented a site of an autonomous Senegalese tradition of an enlightened and modern Islam—an Islam that was peaceful, tolerant, and learned. This association between a quintessential Senegalese village and a vision of a modern Islam that appropriately distinguishes religion from politics was made possible because that place was the longtime home of Shaykh Musa Kamara, a colonial-era Muslim scholar best known for the monumental *History of the Blacks* and increasingly for an Islamic critique of religious violence.[4] While Sambe's invocation of this remote locale and allusion to a relatively obscure figure in a discussion of pressing world affairs may seem out of place, it fits perfectly well within an ongoing process of making Kamara a secular-religious icon, an embodiment of modern virtue.

Across two distinct generations since Senegal's independence in 1960, Kamara and his textual production have returned as a rejoinder to colonial and racist representations of Africa as lacking writing, history, and civilization; as needing guidance; and as being the home of a diminished or immature humanity. As I explored in the previous chapter, Kamara's first textual afterlife was characterized by his literary qualities and historical consciousness. These characteristics were very much shaped by the demands of nation building and the developmentalist imperative to mobilize patrimony for cultural and economic progress. In this chapter, I show how Kamara's second afterlife consists of a *religious* concern since at least 2012, when the occupation by transnational Islamist militants in neighboring Mali made local references as urgent as ever. Sambe's invocation of Kamara as a rebuttal to an accusation of colonial thinking—in a debate about the fortunes of Timbuktu and the subordinate role of religion to politics—is part of an effort to make Islam in Senegal, and Sahelian Africa more broadly, cohere with a secular, modern concept of religion. This project occurs in two key contexts: (1) that of the African Renaissance, which asserts the humanity of global blackness, and (2) that of the Global War on Terror (GWOT), Islamist political violence, the fragmentation of authority, and the rise of military, economic, and cultural multipolarity. In this chapter, I argue that Kamara has been undergoing a process of secular-religious iconization as the result of a complex dynamic consisting of an affirmation of religious selfhood and intellectual autonomy, the GWOT and the securitization of Islam, and a process of secular religion-making. The framework of secular religion-making highlights the ways in which the secular is less the absence of religion than the active defining of what constitutes the religious in modern life. I do so with a place-based and conjunctural reading of Kamara's reception and circulation in the present that privileges the production of contemporary Senegalese intellectuals. The chapter is based on a corpus of Arabic editions of Kamara's major works, French translations, and other works about him published between 2013 and 2023, as well as on my observations and conversations from extended and periodic visits to Senegal for language study and archival research between 2014 and 2024. This grounded and situated reading reveals that the most recent afterlife of Kamara is as a scholar-saint, a secular-religious icon, in which he is fashioned as the embodiment of exemplary behavior, the subject of emulation for a mode of being religious that is compatible with political modernity.

The African Renaissance

Timbuktu is a synecdoche of African civilization.[5] It sits on the desert's edge, around ten miles from one of the world's great rivers, which over millennia has attracted populations to settle and engage in agriculture and participate in trade. Once thought to be a part of the Nile River by the geographers of the Mediterranean world, the Niger River was the central artery of densely inhabited urbanism that would become the basis of the medieval and early modern West African empires of Ghana, Mali, and Songhai. Timbuktu's strategic location near natural resources and between geographic zones made it an important hub for transregional commerce and culture.

From that prosperity, it developed a global reputation for being the source of great wealth and for being extremely remote since at least Mansa

Musa's (d.1337) pilgrimage to Mecca in 1324. Accounts of Timbuktu from fourteenth-century Ibn Battuta (1304–1368/9) and sixteenth-century Leo Africanus (1485–1554) increased its global fame.[6] The city's so-called golden age would come later, during the Songhai Empire, when the Askiyas recruited and attracted great minds from other parts of the lands of Islam, including the Iberian Peninsula and the Muslim East.[7] Its native scholars would develop their own tradition of scholarship in classical disciplines that also enjoyed considerable fame, as was the case with the jurist and author Ahmad Baba (1556–1627), leading Ousmane Kane, a Senegalese scholar of Islam in Africa, to describe its epistemological specificity as the Sankoré paradigm, so named for the city's central mosque.[8] Timbuktu took on mythic significance in the age of European colonization, as it remained inaccessible to explorers until 1830. At the same time, it took on new meanings for diasporic Africans in antebellum America as a source of dignity and sense of worth amid a more general environment where classical antiquity provided a source of identity for the young nation.[9] In New Jersey and New York, diasporic Africans, both those who had been freed and those who had liberated themselves, named their communities after Timbuktu.[10] They participated in the Underground Railroad and aboveground abolition work and, in the case of the New York community, attracted abolitionist John Brown to become a resident.

The history that connects the transformation of natural resources into commodities, the accumulation of wealth that supported the growth of a complex society, the projection of political power, and the achievement of high levels of culture and intellectual pursuits inspired the abolitionist association with Timbuktu as a synecdoche of African civilization at the very moment when colonization and slavery were justified by the gospel of European civilization that represented Africa as a continent of barbarism. It is of little wonder then that this small place stood in for a much greater African whole that harkens back to a notable past, thus elevating African identity and propelling it toward a desirable future of possibility.

Such metonymic work is on view in two well-known documentaries about African civilizations produced by the literary critic Henry Louis Gates Jr.: *The Wonders of the African World* (1999) and *Africa's Great Civilizations* (2017).[11] In these projects, Timbuktu represents a priceless precolonial African legacy that exposes the racist lie of an African lack of history, writing, religion, or science—the sum total of "civilization." The sixteenth-century savant

THE SECULAR-RELIGIOUS AFTERLIFE OF SHAYKH MUSA KAMARA

Ahmad Baba, a prolific scholar who wrote a critique of the racialization of slavery, is invoked in these productions as an exemplar of a precolonial African intellectual history. As a result, Timbuktu's manuscripts emerged as yet another level of synecdoche for African civilization. Baba's writings were neither the first nor by any means the last of West Africa's Arabic heritage, but one can argue they became something of an inflection point in recent history when the Timbuktu manuscripts were recovered and used for a Pan-African project.

The synecdoche that allows Timbuktu to stand in for African civilization was also grasped by Thabo Mbeki (b. 1942), a former president of South Africa whose intervention in 2001 made the recovery of Timbuktu's manuscript heritage a Pan-African priority. Even before South Africa maintained a diplomatic presence in Mali, Mbeki committed to supporting the preservation of and research in an archive of some 300,000 documents. The Tombouctou Manuscript Project at the University of Cape Town, led by the historian Shamil Jeppie, has carried out this work since its inception. In the introduction to an edited volume that presents state-of-the-art information at the time of publication on the Timbuktu manuscripts from an African perspective, Jeppie situated South Africa's support within the discourse of the African Renaissance.[12] Contrary to the idea of an Afro-pessimism that saw no hope for Africa's future following political and economic setbacks in the 1990s, Jeppie wrote that "Mbeki's argument is that the revival of the continent is clearly necessary and this is not possible without Africans engaging in regional and continent-wide coordination and exchanges to transform their conditions. The intellectual and cultural exchanges are as important as the political and economic collaboration needed to strengthen African capacities."[13] Mbeki followed this up with resources dedicated by the highest levels of his government and made it the first cultural project of the New Partnership for Africa's Development (NEPAD), the economic development plan of the African Union. Such investment has been one of the factors that have contributed to the flourishing of academic work on Islam in Africa. The fact it has coincided with its other factor, the GWOT, speaks to an ambivalence on the status of the religious in this political project.

Much in the way Timbuktu and its manuscript heritage have operated at the Pan-African scale, Kamara and his textual production, along with the manuscript heritage of Senegal's Muslim scholarly families, have been subject to attention, care, and investment amidst Senegal's pioneering role in the elaboration of the African Renaissance. The idea of this renaissance could be described as an expression of African humanism, defined as a set of ideas, figures of thought, patterns of thinking, and styles of reasoning that have provided the intellectual foundations that justify, rationalize, organize, and give meaning to the assertion of African sovereignty. Its defining feature is an appropriation of the values and forms associated with modernity. On the one hand, it embraces the ideas of humanism—including the idea that the human is one who is a uniquely endowed agent of historical change composed of thought and feeling; who is due rights, responsibilities, and freedoms; and who pursues their interest in free association—as the virtues associated with civilization broadly construed. On the other, it rejects the hierarchization of difference of race and ethnicity and instead insists on the equality of social differences as a value in its own right. Colonial humanism, however, haunts African humanism, as it has often set the terms of possibility for the forms and practices of human flourishing so that they closely correspond with the historical experience of Europe. In practice, the most common way African humanism has been expressed is through the inversion of colonial discourses. Egypt, not Greece, becomes the source of civilization. The "Dark Ages" of medieval Europe become Africa's Golden Age, as testified to by Timbuktu. The European Enlightenment and its accompanying march of civilization through colonization become Africa's dark age, from which the continent must be reborn. The Sambe-Ramadan exchange discussed earlier has as its background a muted ambivalence about Islam's place in African history and civilization and its relationship to Muslim terms of possibility.

Mbeki is most closely identified with reinserting the idea of the African Renaissance into African discourse and institutionalizing it at a continental scale. He first began to articulate this African humanist project in his "I am an African" speech, delivered in 1996, following the adoption of the postapartheid South African constitution.[14] Speaking to the constitutional assembly, Mbeki opens at what he calls the beginning, a declaration of identity. It is an identity linked to the natural geographic features of a "native land." But as if following the civilizational discourse, the speech turns to history with the presence of humanity. The hunting-gathering ancestors of the Khoi and San and their confrontation with genocide are followed by European settlers in search of home and enslaved Malay in this overview of the defining statement of "African" identity. The names of southern

African warrior kings and a Xhosa prophetess are also invoked. This inclusive vision of African identity demonstrates where African humanism breaks with colonial humanism. Where colonial humanism sought universality through a hierarchy of difference, Mbeki's universality insists on equality and the invalidity of race as a basis of identity. His expression of African identity recalls the famous words attributed to Terence the African, the manumitted Berber who became one of the most important playwrights to have written in Latin: "I am human; I consider nothing human alien to me."[15] The next part of Mbeki's speech describes the inhumanity of humans toward other humans as the denial of universal dignity and worth, a state of affairs that was an actuality. But this negative portrayal then gives way to a discussion of democracy as a human achievement. Here he explicitly addresses the core tenants of liberalism: the freedom of expression and conscience, the freedom from fear of oppression, the rule of law, and the state's role of supporting human flourishing. But perhaps most importantly, there is the freedom to cooperatively define the self: "It also constitutes a tribute to our loss of vanity that we could, despite the temptation to treat ourselves as an exceptional fragment of humanity, draw on the accumulated experience and wisdom of all humankind, to define for ourselves what we want to be."[16] Rejecting exclusivist notions of identity, or of cultural particularism, or of essentialism, Mbeki's articulation of African humanism integrates a history of bitter conflict, colonization, slavery, and apartheid with a will for self-definition.

This new self-definition of the African as human would come to be known as the process of rebirth invoked by the term *African Renaissance*. The idea of a revival of African history has been a durable one, dating back at least to Pixley ka Isaka Seme (1881-1951), a South African lawyer and one of the founders of what would become the African National Congress, whose 1906 speech "The Regeneration of Africa" won an oratorical prize at Columbia University.[17] That speech would influence two Africans in particular: Kwame Nkrumah (1909-1972), future prime minister and president of Ghana, and Nnamdi Azikwe (1904-1996), future president of Nigeria, both of whom sought to elaborate the intellectual foundations of African autonomy.[18] Chiekh Anta Diop, whom Mbeki quotes directly in the speech, is also associated with the idea of the African Renaissance, as discussed in the previous chapter.[19] All of these formulations shared the idea that the catastrophes of slavery and colonization, the "colonial episode," were interruptions of a glorious African past, the embers of which were needed to make a bright future.

Mbeki elaborated on this theme in his "African Renaissance Statement," delivered on August 13, 1998.[20] He opens with a description of the conjuncture in Africa at the end of the millennium—but in sweeping epochal terms. That conjuncture is one of dehumanizing poverty, irrational violence, a lack of dialogue, corruption, and avarice. In short, it is the condition that has nourished Afro-pessimism, the skepticism about Africa's prospects for development. In response to this state of affairs, Mbeki shifts the tone and flow of the speech with the invocation of Timbuktu:

> As we recall with pride the African scholar and author of the Middle Ages, Sadi [sic] of Timbuktu, who had mastered such subjects as law, logic, dialectics, grammar and rhetoric, and other African intellectuals who taught at the University of Timbuktu, we must ask the question—where are Africa's intellectuals today!
>
> In our world in which the generation of new knowledge and its application to change the human condition is the engine that moves human society further away from barbarism, do we not have need to recall Africa's hundreds of thousands of intellectuals back from their places of emigration in Western Europe and North America, to rejoin those who remain still within our shores?[21]

In this speech, the historical memory of civilizational achievement constitutes a turning point from a present of barbarism. The rest of the speech gains momentum and explains the barbarity as a result of the imperial domination and the enslavement of the mind and soul. This speech would usher in a new period of Afro-optimism, institutionalized as policy in a number of initiatives, including NEPAD and the African Renaissance Institute. Taking Mbeki's statement as a whole, we can read his vision as a Pan-African project of self-affirmation, self-assertion, and sovereignty, expressed politically and intellectually. The South African project to preserve and research the Timbuktu manuscripts does just that. Let us recall that Timbuktu's fortunes ultimately declined after the 1591, when Moroccan forces under Ahmad Mansur (1549-1603) brought an end to the Songhai Empire at the Battle of Tondibi. Feeling the pressure of a growing Iberian naval dominance and facing bankruptcy from expenses incurred by fighting that dominance, Mansur made a play for the trade routes along which West African gold and enslaved people traveled. The fall of Songhai, with its attendant disappearance of an African sovereign with global reach was a precondition for the gradual racialization of slavery at the global scale. Mbeki's memory of Abd al-Rahman al-Saʿadi (1594–c. 1656), who authored *Tarikh al-Sudan* in the aftermath of the Moroccan invasion, speaks to this pivotal historical moment that ties together sovereignty and intellectual production.

The idea of the African Renaissance and eventually of the related "Africa rising" discourse would be taken up by many of the continent's intellectuals. Notably, the International Decade for People of African Descent took as its theme the African Renaissance. Africa 2063, a sort of fifty-year plan created by the African Union, also uses this idea.[22] One of the more interesting elaborations of the African Renaissance can be found in Ngũgĩ wa Thiong'o's 2009 book, *Something Torn and New: An African Renaissance*, in which he expounds on its origins, development, and prospects of realization.[23] While he identifies the term's recurrent use throughout the twentieth century, he defines it as an ongoing process that began with the emergence of the "African idea"—that is, African self-representation as African, which began in the diaspora during the period of bondage and then traveled back to the continent. The defining characteristic of the African idea was the expanded horizon of self-identification from clan, ethnicity, or location to meaningful global categories of Africanity and blackness.

For Ngũgĩ, the comparison of the African Renaissance with the European Renaissance is unavoidable—not because the European Renaissance preceded the African Renaissance but because the "monumental historical shift" that constituted the European Renaissance relied on an emergent capitalist modernity that was rooted in slavery and colonialism, the cause of the "hiatus" of organic African development. He describes this hiatus as the African Middle Ages, the period of so-called darkness.[24] Ngũgĩ advances a debate that otherwise proposes either that following a European historical model is desirable for its achievements of modernity or that applying such an idea to an African Renaissance is inappropriate because it reinforces Europe as a standard against which Africa might be measured. In identifying the connection between the European and the African Renaissances, Ngũgĩ shows that the first caused the need of the second. The fall of Timbuktu in the sixteenth century, described earlier, was inherently connected to Europe's rise. Moreover, his use of the "African idea" allows him to extend the reach of the African Renaissance to include the experience of Afro-modernity in an ongoing process.

THE SECULAR-RELIGIOUS AFTERLIFE OF SHAYKH MUSA KAMARA

But we should press the analogy between the two renaissances further. The explicit analogy compares the slave trade and the colonization of Africa to the "Dark Ages" of an intellectually backward Europe. Here we should note that the idea of the backwardness of the Middle Ages was itself a creation of the European Renaissance. Petrarch, one of the towering figures of this movement, successfully constructed the Middle Ages as a period of backwardness through a tripartite division of human history: antiquity, the medieval, and the modern. For him, backwardness was caused by the loss of access to the ancients, which only language study, what we now call philology, could reestablish. It was not until the secular age of the nineteenth century that this backwardness was associated with the dominance of "religion." But it is important to recognize that this was a construction. In the analogy between the two renaissances, African antiquity was a flourishing period of civilization, followed by interruption and then retrieval. Ngũgĩ's elaboration of the African Renaissance is generative in that it begins with the limits of comparison that are the result of connection. If the European Renaissance relied on the conditions that made the African Renaissance necessary, it is clear that the means of accumulation and violence that were available for the first are not so available for the second. This allows Ngũgĩ to explain predation, corruption, and tyranny in contemporary Africa as a product of this structuring historical relationship. This argument pushes us to consider the implications of this explicit analogy, which puts history in a tripartite structure of greatness, backwardness, and reemergence. What benefits does it offer? And what might it foreclose? Might not the future be something other than a destiny of repeating unchecked growth, on the one hand, and unending immiseration, on the other? Might not a different understanding of African relationships to time help us imagine different goals? Finding answers is all the more urgent given pending climate catastrophe, which will likely change humanity's orientation to growth as the means and ends of modernity.[25]

There is also the implicit analogy with the European Renaissance yet to be articulated. That analogy does not yet exist, but one we might offer through the prism of how Kamara relates to Petrarch again. Petrarch originally offered *Studia Humanitas* not as a secular form of study—that is, an atheist form of study—but rather as a form of study that focused on the lives of exemplary men, as opposed to the formalistic, arcane, and esoteric study of Christian scholasticism. It was the study of great exemplars of how humans *should* live. This was not inherently a break from religion, even if the eventual Enlightenment break from religion would reconstruct Renaissance humanism as its first development. But in fact, Petrarch used the study of the lives of men in order to redefine them as pagan Christians, so to speak. His project was to incorporate them into the fold of grace by saying that through their works and deeds, left in words we can read, they exemplified what scripture was really about. Renaissance humanism proposed that the study of lives was more important than the study of doctrines. Similarly, I think there is an analogy to be made about the move to study the lives of "saintly men" in Senegal. The rise of the biographical Kamara, explored shortly, seeks to elaborate the study of actual lives under the oppressive conditions of colonialism, conditions that unfortunately endure, to provide meaning for contemporary life. Therefore, the implicit analogy between the European Renaissance and the African Renaissance reveals that the process of iconization we observe by reading recent publications by and about Kamara has a role to play in the African humanist project.

If the discussion of a South African political discourse and a critical-theoretical intervention by a Kenyan author demonstrates the Pan-African quality of the African Renaissance, it is important to identify its relevance in the specifically national context of Senegal. Nothing evinces this relevance more than the African Renaissance Monument in the seaside suburb of Ouakam, outside of Dakar. The massive brown metal work, Africa's largest statue, features a burly man with stereotypically African features who holds a voluptuous and scantily clad woman, who looks like she might be fainting, in his right arm while he holds a small boy aloft in his left. Together, the nuclear family faces in the direction in which the boy is pointing, northwest across the Atlantic Ocean toward the Statue of Liberty in New York, according to tour guides at the monument. The statue's meaning is ambiguous: Is it the promise of the future of the African boy oriented to American freedom, or is it the paradox that freedom should be associated with the land where enslaved Africans were taken? Its signification probably lies somewhere in between romance and tragedy, like so much Black thought of the twentieth and twenty-first centuries.[26] Perhaps it lies somewhere in the ambiguous refrain that no Black person anywhere will be free until Black people everywhere are free or in the idea that the future of both continental and diasporic Africans requires that the dismembered African body politic be healed through the work of re-membering the past.[27]

THE SECULAR-RELIGIOUS AFTERLIFE OF SHAYKH MUSA KAMARA

Inside the monument, there is a small exhibition. The story it tells is almost identical to the one that is told in the larger and slightly newer Museum of Black Civilizations in central Dakar, as if it was a dry run for what was to come. The exhibit starts with the emergence of the human species, its authentic culture, which begin in Africa; civilization and monotheistic religion start in the African Nile Valley; the glory of African antiquity is diffused throughout the continent but becomes fragmented; eventually, the slave trade and colonization count as a dark age; finally, Black consciousness is born in diasporic encounters in the Black Atlantic, and the subsequent flourishing of art and culture anticipates free Black nations that usher in the African Renaissance. These exhibits reconcile the proto-Afrocentrism and political radicalism of Cheikh Anta Diop with the literary Négritude and Francophilia of Senghor, making the kinds of accommodations between them that would have been impossible when two of Senegal's most influential intellectuals were alive and bitter political rivals. In effect, the African Renaissance Monument seeks to demonstrate the humanity of blackness.

There is a temptation to read the scenography, symbolism, and narratives of the African Renaissance Monument as the successful culmination of a national intellectual project. The painful past is remembered as the basis for a promising future, political independence is the proof of a people's achievement, and that people is represented comprehensively in the national story as much as it is in parliament by their representatives. But such a reading has to avoid the breaks, the internal divisions, the conflicts, and the silences found throughout the national discourse and its memorialization. Take, for example, the many controversies surrounding the monument itself. It is situated on land traditionally held by Lebou communities that was socialized by the state under Presidents Senghor and Abdou Diouf, whereas later liberalization under President Abdoulaye Wade meant the privatization of property. The privatization of land around the monument—highly desirable suburban beachfront property—dispossessed many of the local inhabitants. Meanwhile, the iconography and immodesty of the statue's listless woman have long since been a sore point for more conservative residents, to say nothing of an obvious feminist objection.[28] In addition to the controversies surrounding the building of these sites of public memory expressed in humanistic terms, their very content suggests internal tensions in that project.

THE SECULAR-RELIGIOUS AFTERLIFE OF SHAYKH MUSA KAMARA

From the western tip of the African continent, then, to the halls of the South African parliament where Thabo Mbeki supported research into West Africa's Arabic-script heritage, politicians and philosophers loudly proclaim the dawning of an African Renaissance. It is the idea that crystalizes Africa's emergence in a new age of political and economic liberalism in the twenty-first century. Similar to nationalism and Pan-Africanism from the moment of decolonization, the African Renaissance depends on an African humanism that makes claims on a precolonial past and a civilization beyond European hegemony. However, unlike in that earlier moment, when Islam was often marginalized as an alien Arab influence, African intellectuals are seizing on a certain kind of "good Islam" and its accompanying written heritage in order to present to the world a precolonial civilization that can serve as the basis of a pluralistic modernity.[29]

Despite an investment in preserving this manuscript heritage for the sake of exploiting these intellectual resources to produce African humanistic knowledge, a number of apparent contradictions require us to question the discourse of the African Renaissance. At the very moment that some African leaders and intellectuals are calling for a new humanism for the implicit purpose of participating in a global liberalism, neoliberal economic forces have decimated African universities' ability to produce knowledge about their own societies beyond the exploitive interests of global actors.[30] Furthermore, the African Renaissance depends on the discourse of the Enlightenment, which calls for an instrumental and calculative rationality of science even as the family owners of many Arabic manuscripts refuse to render visible what is in many ways a spiritual inheritance. The conflicting regimes of knowledge and power come into even greater relief when we take into consideration the role those Arabic manuscripts played in the conflict in Mali, where militant Islamists menaced the manuscript libraries of Timbuktu, the symbolic center of Islamic knowledge south of the Sahara.[31]

The Iconization of Kamara

Timbuktu, the jewel of Islam in Africa, has often been called the "City of 333 Saints" because of the Muslim scholars and teachers buried there. In 2012, militants said to be mostly Tuareg and Arab violently took control of the city, and when they were forced out the following year, they left a path of destruction. The images of charred manuscripts and demolished shrines infuriated many of neighboring Senegal's Muslim intellectuals; commentators said that such destruction of the priceless cultural heritage was anti-intellectual and a caustic and callous affront to Muslims and Africans everywhere and in particular to the Muslim Africans of the region who identified as part of a peaceful and tolerant tradition. The identification of the militants as Arab and Tuareg in popular discourses, even though many of the militants were, in fact, local, added a racial dimension to the event. On the one hand, this inflection allowed some to frame Islamist politics as emanating from outside the region and external to organic local development, a trope inherited from colonial discourse that is over a century old. On the other, because of the association of the militants with racial Others, the attack took on the meaning of a racial insult. The Timbuktu manuscripts represented African contributions to knowledge and proved a precolonial historicity for a continent supposedly without writing. At the same time, the shrines of the saints represented a particular West African spirituality and its model of structuring the contemporary social world.

The symbolic value of the manuscripts, which appealed to universalist ideas favored by Enlightenment thought, directed itself outward toward a global audience, while the significance of the shrines, which appealed to a spiritualist understanding of the world, oriented itself inward toward local sensibilities. Together, the apparent and hidden values of what was understood as a priceless heritage went without questioning, and the condemnation of their destruction went without saying. The acts of iconoclasm were beyond the pale of civilization, beyond the limits of anything that could be considered a political act, and therefore would eventually be considered a crime against universal culture by any reasonable person—indeed a crime against humanity to be prosecuted in the International Criminal Court.[32] That these acts, and others like them, have so often been described as barbaric suggests that globally Islam is awkwardly teetering on the limit of political possibility, sometimes leaning inside toward liberalism, sometimes leaning away toward liberalism's Other.[33] In the wake of this event, African Muslims could assert they belonged on the side of universal civilization as good Muslims, whereas Arabs could be disavowed as enemies of civilization. The exchange between Sambe and Ramadan with which we began this chapter was conditioned by these inherently racial dynamics in the negotiation of Islam and politics. That Kamara was eventually invoked in the debate speaks to his availability for thought among contemporary Senegalese intellectuals, particularly as a reference for defining religion in secular terms.

This secular-religious afterlife of Kamara follows the first generation of intellectual decolonization that shaped his literary and historical afterlife. It reads him in new ways that respond to the demands of the present. Squeezed between the civilizational and racial supremacies of both the West and the Arab world, many a Senegalese intellectual has looked into an autochthonous past to respond to the negative claims made about Islam in Africa. In the present, the international system, sometimes described as the Washington Consensus, keeps a heavy hand on fiscal and budgetary policies that directly determine the form and quality of life for millions of people in Africa, compelling them to denounce the major organs of the global system as neocolonialist. Meanwhile, Arab-sourced capital and philanthropy channeled through Senegalese social entrepreneurs appear to be destabilizing the structure of society and transforming culture, giving rise to denunciations of Arab racism, paternalism, and even imperialism such as that by Sambe. Both extremes of this spectrum of influence and domination, Euro-America and the Middle East, promote ideological representations of African societies and African people as lacking capacity and needing guidance, a construction profoundly tied to the histories of global slavery and political colonization in the nineteenth and twentieth centuries.

This is the spectrum of coloniality today, as viewed from Senegal. Forced into a position between these two civilizational forces, intellectuals within Senegal have oscillated between fusing the two into an African-centered capitalism with Islamic characteristics and strategically playing one against the other. The economic enterprise of the vibrant and dynamic Muridiyya Sufi order is an example of the first response. Invocations of Kamara today reflect the second. His prodigious intellectual production proves Senegalese participation in civilization to the West and proves local sources of religious authority to the Arabocentric Muslim world, opening up an understanding of an autonomous tradition that is fully modern. This project might be found in a recent body of work.

Several publications either by or about Kamara appeared in Arabic, French, and English in the decade after the 2012 insurgency in Mali. Most of these have been authored or edited by Senegalese scholars who are residents of Senegal or part of the global Senegalese diaspora. The number of publications, the frequency of their publication, and the number of people involved in publication exceed such statistics for any other period of the same length since Kamara's death in 1945. The number of publications also exceeds what Kamara managed to circulate during his lifetime. Accordingly, the dynamics that made this current state possible warrant our attention. One key element in this process has been the affirmation of the religious self in public life.

A conference held at the Islamic Institute of Dakar (IID) on July 13, 2013, played an important role in igniting the spark leading to the renascence in Kamara scholarship. The IID is a public religious institution attached to Dakar's Grand Mosque and administered by the Ministry of Education. It offers courses of study, sponsors research, and provides religious programming related to Qur'anic recitation, Ramadan, and pilgrimage to Mecca. The Kamara family, led by the current head, Thierno Mouhamadou Bassirou Camara, in concert with a research committee, organized panels and an exhibition as a part of what was described as a "cultural day around the works of and life of Shaykh Musa Kamara."[34] The event attracted a large crowd consisting of the general public, religious dignitaries, academics, and government officials, including President Macky Sall's chief of staff, according to a video of the event posted online.[35] Speakers at the conference, which was covered by the national television station (Radiodiffusion Télévision Sénégalaise, or RTS), emphasized the value of Kamara's singular intellectual contribution, as well as the urgency of preserving his legacy and deepening understanding of him and his work. Ismaïla Camara, the family spokesperson and one of Shaykh Musa's grandsons, made a direct comparison between the manuscripts in Ganguel and those that had been threatened during the Islamist occupation of Timbuktu—namely, they were vulnerable to loss. Speakers also expressed a great appreciation for President Sall's support of the Kamara family's attempts at preservation. Ismaïla reported that the family had made great efforts to get support from the previous president, Abdoulaye Wade, but to no avail. One speaker went as far as to say that Sall was both the guardian of the constitution and the guardian of Senegalese patrimony. These words were later followed up with deeds.

Within a year, several publications appeared that came out of the conference or could be tied to the activity of members of its research committee. The inaugural issue of the institute's journal, *Revue d'études arabes et islamiques*, featured a partial translation and summary of Kamara's treatment of jihad alongside institutional histories of Islamic studies in Senegal.[36] The proceedings of the conference were then published in a special issue by the IID. Thierno Kâ, the director of the institute, described this publishing activity as the first of its kind undertaken by the institute.[37] Subsequently, the institute released an Arabic-language edition of Kamara's autobiography in 2014, followed by a French translation in 2015.[38] In 2014, Kâ also published a slim Arabic paperback edition of a biography: *Shaykh Musa Kamara: His Life and His Ideas*.[39] In the dedication of the book, Kâ notes that he decided to write it after presenting at the 2013 conference. He realized that there was a "need to continue the studies around this singular scholarly personality" and "to spread it in book-form to benefit teachers, researchers, and those seeking knowledge in the world."[40] Abdoul Malal Diop, a professor of Arabic, former diplomat, and member of the research committee, defended his dissertation on Kamara in 2014.[41] He had been working on Kamara for decades before the conference, having been a member of the multinational team that was translating Kamara's magnum opus discussed in chapter 5, but the coincidence of his dissertation's completion at this time is striking. It speaks to the consolidation of a conversation about Kamara after 2013 and the various human and material resources devoted to facilitating it.

Since the conference, several other publications have appeared. In 2015, an Arabic-language edition of Kamara's historical and genealogical account of the western Sahelian elite, *The Precious Collection*, edited by the Mauritanian scholar Nani Wuld al-Hussain, was published by a Moroccan press.[42] The Senegalese American political scientist and Arabist Mbaye Lo began publishing and presenting work in English on Kamara in 2015, an effort that would culminate with the 2023 English translation of Kamara's work on religious violence, the same text that appeared in the first issue of the IID journal.[43] And the editorial team behind several of Kamara's Arabic-language editions from the 2000s, the Moroccan historian Ahmad al-Chokri and the Senegalese Islamicist Khadim Mbacké, published an edition with what they claimed to be a missing chapter of Kamara's critique of jihad originally published in 2003.[44] The Senegalese codicologist and editor of Arabic books Ousmane Diaw wrote a sophisticated review of this edition in 2019, questioning the inclusion of this chapter in the jihad text and thus demonstrating the development of a robust debate on the scholarship on Kamara.[45] And finally, Muhammad Said Bâ, through the newly minted Kamara Research Center, published a rigorous scholarly Arabic-language edition of Kamara's *The*

Announcement in 2022.[46] All of these publications focus on making Kamara directly accessible either in his original Arabic words or in translation.

Suspending the question of Kamara's invalidation of jihad, which took on an obvious relevance that I will discuss later, the appearance of these works reflects a new emphasis in Kamara's reception. Where Kamara the native informant and native author had grown to be the Senegalese historian and litterateur previously, the autobiographical Sufi "saint" Kamara now emerged. The emphasis on Kamara's *The Announcement* is the most important feature of this shift. Indeed, as discussed in the previous chapter, Amar Samb used Kamara's autobiography for his research. Although he had translated parts of Kamara's historically oriented works, his commentary on jihad, and his treatise on the ecumenicalism of the Abrahamic faiths, Samb did not make *The Announcement* directly available to either a scholarly or a popular readership. One might infer that for Samb, the subject of Kamara's life was incidental to the textual monuments that he produced. In contrast, the current reception of Kamara insists on the incontrovertibility of reading Kamara's autobiography as a precondition of reading his other works. Abdoul Malal Diop made this argument to me directly after patiently listening to some of the arguments in my dissertation, which focused on Kamara's biography of Hajj Umar Tal.[47] He insisted that Kamara's *The Announcement* was a guide for reading all of his other works and that I should start there to better understand the larger body of work. This approach is probably the correct one. But as my readings of Kamara's texts in previous chapters show, this is one approach among many possible ones, and the fact that it has emerged as the preferred way to read him suggests a new tradition of reception. This broader shift is also reflected in the fact that while Kamara has been an incredibly important source for the historiography of the Senegambia, relatively few works have focused on his life.

The shift toward an autobiographical Kamara is reasonable, but the elaboration of Kamara as a subject of research proper also tells us something about the time in which this shift is happening. A closer reading of these paratexts is thus instructive. Take, for instance, the booklet published by the director of the Islamic studies archive at the Institute Fondamental d'Afrique Noire (IFAN). Given its historic relationship to the University of Dakar, IFAN had long been the organ associated with research on Islam and the Arabic literary heritage in Senegal, as discussed in the previous chapter. As a part of a series to popularize knowledge about Senegal's Muslim scholars, Thierno Kâ published several short biographies of notable figures, including *Shaykh Musa Kamara: His Life and His Ideas*, in which Kâ describes Kamara as one of the most prominent "Islamic and humanist thinkers" in Senegal's history. Most of these books have been printed as bilingual French-Arabic works, but the book on Kamara is only available in Arabic. This publication is unique in the academic reception of Kamara for its classical mode and its emphasis on the esoteric elements of Kamara's oeuvre.

Kâ's short biography of Kamara can be understood as a précis and a commentary. What strikes me about this publication in relation to others is how closely it adheres to a classical, scholastic mode that resembles Kamara's writing itself. I mean this in several ways. First, the primary objective of this booklet is to transmit what was in *The Announcement* and complement it with other sources, particularly the sources of Islamic normativity. These complements seek to verify what appears in the original text. The objective of transmission is distinct from the objective of analysis, that totem of contemporary academic scholarship. Furthermore, Kâ does not try to retell the story of Kamara in a narrative mode adapted to the present, as is sometimes the case with modern renditions of classical literature. Kâ's work presents facts, their validity, and the permissibility of reported actions and attitudes from a normative perspective based on what Kamara says as determined by using classical tools of Muslim textual scholarship. Another way that Kâ's work is classical is that it is most interested in commentary. It is not fundamentally skeptical of the text it is transmitting. In other words, there is no "hermeneutics of suspicion." While such a hermeneutics has long been prized as a mode of reading in academic scholarship, a "hermeneutics of faith" has begun to emerge in postcritical religious and literary studies in the Euro-American-dominated academy.[48] Kâ's use of commentary, whether as a theory or as a practice, aligns with this development. The mode of commentary in the text is here already present, taking its cues unselfconsciously from its own tradition. In other words, Kâ explains and clarifies the text that precedes him. He does not "put it in question," that highly valued activity in modern scholarship.

In the opening paragraphs of the preface to his book, Kâ makes two points that are otherwise omitted or made marginal both in previous works by Samb and in the colonial archive: that Kamara was a savant without having been a good student and that his major marvel was that he met people from before his birth.[49] These are details that largely have not been a part of Kamara's reception. In a section entitled "Divine Marvels," Kâ considers the marvels I read closely in chapter 1, including the story of the beggar who announces Kamara's election and Kamara's photographic and phonographic memory. Before discussing the three stories that Kamara includes in his autobiography that attest to his status as a friend of God, Kâ affirms the Sunni doctrine that Muhammad is the seal of prophecy but that the door to marvels is still open to the righteous and to the friends of God. He then narrates the story of the beggar as the second marvel. Finally, he describes Kamara's achievements in the domain of lettrism, the knowledge and use of the alphabet for supernatural ends. Kâ's inclusion of these accounts is the first instance of it, or of anything like it, that I have found in my research. To be sure, I am not including the largely oral and less official ways in which Kamara has been circulated and has been remembered by his descendants, disciples, and detractors. Those have indeed focused on the marvelous attributes of the shaykh.[50] While we might quickly describe this preoccupation with Kamara's friendship with God, his marvels, and his secret but powerful knowledge as part and parcel of a Sufi milieu that has come to be associated with Senegal, I find it important to recognize the implications of that description. As a mode of religiosity, Sufism encourages the elaboration of the aspirant's interiority through ascetic practices, spiritual discipline, and personal devotion to a guide. These features have an individualizing thrust to them that we can describe as a kind of subjectivation, the making of a particular kind of agentive subject. That Kamara is presented as a model of such subjectivization through the classical themes and form of this publication prefaced by a statement of doctrinal legitimacy speaks to the religious nature of the new readings of Kamara since 2012.

Another example of recent paratexts that reframe Kamara's work in religio-biographic terms is an Arabic edition of Kamara's *Announcement* edited and introduced by the public intellectual Muhammad Said Bâ. In this superb, systematic study of the original manuscript, Bâ provides a treatment of Kamara's autobiography of the highest scholarly quality. The introduction is of interest for how it frames the work of recovering Kamara and his texts as the work of recovering an inherently religious identity. Bâ first situates Kamara's life within the generation that was defined by the fall of the imamate of Futa Toro, a political formation best known for its making Islam the central paradigm for collective life, and the imposition of French rule. Bâ then says of the colonial enterprise: "It began to implement its project, one of the most important foundations of which was cultural alienation, in preparation for obliterating the identity of the peoples of the region and separating them from their glorious history, because they were certain that they would not be able to establish a foothold on their land if these peoples remained under the protection of this cultural system derived from Islam, which had become the primary tributary for forming the values, concepts, ideas and orientations of the region's population."[51]

For Bâ, this historical context of Kamara's life was thus defined by a set of stakes that were nothing less than a people's identity, the sine qua non of collective historical agency. The drama of this historical backdrop then becomes the setting for a description of an exceptional life: a seeker of knowledge, who, despite relative social marginality, rose to become a singular example of a pious figure who was intellectually prolific, exercised his freedom of conscience no matter the social cost, practiced independent reasoning over traditional compliance, was active and productive in the realm of work, and left a precious testimony of cultural history. In other words, Kamara's autobiography tells the story of the development of a modern subjectivity achieved through the cultivation of a religious identity. Instead of associating the religious with tradition from which there must be a break, Bâ frames Kamara as being modern *because* of and not despite his religion.

The corpus of recent publications by and about Kamara, particularly read against the backdrop of the colonial and nationalist periods, reveals an emergent process of iconization. Icons in the Orthodox and Catholic Christian traditions are generally associated with the use of stylized and sometimes abstracted images of holy people, such as Jesus, Mary, and the canon of saints. The icon in those traditions is an object of devotion and contemplation that facilitates a pietistic state and provides models of comportment and gesture. Islam is generally thought of as an iconoclastic religion that prohibits the depiction of living beings, but in practice, iconography has a long and vibrant history in Muslim contexts.[52] This is particularly true in Senegal.[53] However, my use of *icon* here is inspired by the expanded meaning of the term, now used to refer to any major cultural referent or symbol or even celebrity that stands in for a complex of ideas, attitudes, and memories held in common. Most importantly, the expanded meaning of icon makes it a relevant term beyond images. While in Senegal the depictions of the friends of God associated with the major Sufi orders, such as Shaykh Amadou Bamba Mbakke, al-Hajj Malick Sy, Shaykh Ibrahim Niasse, and Baye Fall, are so common as to define the graphic landscape of most cities, I am less interested in the actual image of Kamara, which does exist and circulate modestly, than I am in the composite representation of him as a discursive construction in the present. He is at once the intellectual who exerted his own reasoning through *ijtihad*, or individual interpretive effort, exercised his freedom of conscience, and was critical of "backward" superstition, as represented in the essay by Muhammad Said Bâ. And Kamara is the Sufi mystic who as a friend of God is a channel of divine blessings and who has secret knowledge. This composite renders Kamara a legible icon that embodies modern virtues from the perspectives of both the rationality of the state and the spirituality of society.

Secular Religion in the Time of Terror

The Kamara family representative's invocation of Timbuktu at the 2013 conference invites us to contextualize the iconization of Kamara with the religious dynamics engendered by the Global War on Terror, in addition to the African Renaissance. The more visible features of the GWOT and the subterranean process of the conjuncture described in this section highlight both relations of power and a structure of feeling. From a top-down perspective, the securitization of Islam, beginning after the attacks on American embassies in Tanzania and Kenya in 1998 and accelerating after 9/11, has subjected it adherents to a new wave of techniques, practices, and technologies of surveillance, control, and instrumentalization.[54] From a bottom-up perspective, Islam has increasingly provided the languages, spaces, and symbols that enable a growing population of Muslims from Senegal to Somalia, from Cairo to Cape Town, to express their personal commitments and to engage meaningfully in private and public life.[55] Economically, a network that orients parts of Africa to the rest of the Muslim world competes with the circuits of capital, aid, and philanthropy that have long ensured flows between African countries and their former colonizers, thus disrupting the ethno-, techno-, finance-, media-, and ideoscapes that so defined the twentieth century.[56] For example, Islamic finance and Islamic philanthropy have emerged as new vectors that orient and connect Africa to the rest of the Muslim world. Deep histories of Islam on the continent have been remembered, imagined anew, or rejected in an embrace of both ideas of traditional continuity and radical rupture in order to narrate Africa's place in a divine ordering of human experience. As a result of these processes of securitization, Islamization of society, and reorientation, Islam is made visible, worked on, and made essential by a wide range of conflicting actors, forces, and sensibilities. Studying Islam in Africa today, then, allows the thinking through of pertinent global questions that both exceed Islam and Africa and fail to encompass the meanings and possibilities of either. Among many expectations of modernization theory that have not come to fruition, the assumption that religion and religiosity would disappear has proven to be patently false. These conditions and processes, which we might date schematically to the period of structural adjustment, have made Africa a world leader in living in and with austerity, precarity, and insecurity, increasingly the features of the global human condition. The historical specificity of the religious in this conjuncture and any readings that might be performed in it can fruitfully be understood in relation to these developments.

Given the political and academic significance of Timbuktu and its manuscript heritage, it is easy to appreciate the symbolic potency of the occupation of Timbuktu by a coalition of Islamist militants for ten months in 2012 and 2013.[57] It is a potency that has resonated in the return to Kamara since the occupation of Timbuktu. Within two months, the armed groups defeated the Malian army in the north and claimed control of some two-thirds of Mali's territory, naming it the Islamic state of Azawad.[58] This existential challenge to the Malian state was precipitated by a military coup that has fundamentally reshaped life in the western Sahelian country, and the region, ever since. Most notably, these militants meted out punishment for crimes following a rigid and rigorist interpretation of Islamic law, destroyed Sufi shrines that had been recognized as UNESCO World Heritage Sites, and committed other acts defined by international convention as war crimes.[59] In addition to the obviously political dimensions of the militants' direct challenge to state power, their occupation of Timbuktu had major religious implications in the region. In the immediate sense, it amplified the urgency of debates in the public sphere about the place of religion in public life amidst the ongoing Islamization of society.[60] More fundamentally, the event motivated a profound effort to define Islam as a secular religion, a form of life that accepts the normative expectations associated with political modernity. As much as the recent reception of Kamara cannot be appreciated outside the organic development of the African Renaissance, it should also be situated in ongoing religion-making projects defined by dynamics of the GWOT.

Let us describe this conjuncture, then, as the time of terror, the period in which war on a planetary scale became the defining feature of everyday life, what we would otherwise describe as peace. I take this description from the more common Global War on Terror, which is the expression most associated with the American response to the September 11, 2001, attacks on the World Trade Center and the Pentagon by operatives of the militant Islamist network al-Qaeda.[61] It was a figure of speech used to signify a total mobilization of resources and forces to address an intractable problem: the use of violence in the name of religion directed toward civilians and nonmilitary properties, especially those with symbolic meaning. What made this problem so exceptional from the hegemonic view of global order was that the violence conducted by groups like al-Qaeda was performed not by the legitimate monopolizers of violence, states, but by nonstate actors. Furthermore, as they were not recognized as states by other states and therefore not subject to policing by the "international community," these nonstate actors disregarded the rules of war, human rights, and national sovereignty. Most of all, the violence perpetuated by organizations such as al-Qaeda produced, from the hegemonic view, terror, a destabilizing feeling of insecurity that threatened all order and sense. Pulling a page from a politically conservative playbook, the figurative "war" on terror was inspired by the wars on crime and drugs, which included such political, economic, social, and cultural initiatives and strategies that extended the state's mobilization beyond a sphere of formal war to create a total sphere of activity.[62] If war is the continuation of politics by other means, as Carl von Clausewitz's famous aphorism would have us believe, the war metaphor redeploys the use of legitimated violence for political ends. This means that the GWOT was not simply a figure of speech; it was an illocutionary speech act that authorized the extension of military action, personnel, and logics into the fabric of everyday life through the infrastructures, practices, and techniques of surveillance and securitization. And, of course, nothing about this violence for the people targeted—who were and are overwhelmingly non-European, non-Western, and Muslim—has been figurative. It has meant death. The transformations that this war, with its total front, wrought for the planet have indelibly marked reality, possibility, and imagination to such an extent that we should describe the GWOT as a structuring condition of feeling.

While we can reasonably periodize the time of terror to the first use of the phrase "Global War on Terror" in the immediate aftermath of the September 11 attacks, a conjunctural reading favors redirecting our focus toward events in Africa. Africa, we might say, is where the GWOT begins.[63] The bombings of American embassies in Nairobi, Kenya, and Dar es Salam, Tanzania, in 1998 opened a new period of asymmetrical political violence by Muslim militants, described as jihad, which would soon find its center of gravity in Afghanistan and Iraq with the deployment of American military forces. That the present conjuncture begins in Africa highlights the underappreciated but central place of the continent in the transformations in securitization that have defined global order since the late 1990s.

Africa's importance in the GWOT increased after the season of Arab revolutions in North Africa that saw cycles of hopeful promise of democratic rule, followed by Islamist party politics, the return of dictatorial despair in Egypt, monarchial consolidation in Morocco, and the debacle of the ouster of Muammar Gadhafi in Libya in 2011. Libya's political fortunes were intimately tied to the continent's security. With Gadhafi gone, arms and militant groups flooded the greater Sahara region. Mali was the first West African country to succumb in the new environment, with the convergence of a secessionist movement, jihadist organization, and a military coup. Since these events, the broader Sahel, the arid and semiarid region between the Sahara and the savannah and stretching from Senegal to Somalia, has become one of the most important theaters in the GWOT, with a degree of military activity not seen since colonial occupation. As a result, the greater Sahelian region has been subject to a transformative assemblage of military, intelligence, political, philanthropic, and intellectual activity.

The recognition of the greater Sahel, sometimes appearing discursively as the Sahara-Sahel, as a distinct region in academic production signals the development of the conjuncture as a moment of regional containment. If the Sahara appeared as either a barrier for much of the twentieth century or as a bridge since the global turn of academic research in the 1990's, this disciplinary moment is defined by the appearance of the unit Sahara-Sahel as a space of concern.[64] The Sahara-Sahel now appears as a space onto itself—that is, as its own space of economic production and social reproduction, not simply as a thoroughfare, as was previously the case.[65] However, the Sahara-Sahel does not correspond to a single political claim to sovereignty over territory. Politics in the Sahara is seen first and foremost as insurgency, which must be securitized through metrics of risk, warning, and threat and, of course, by military presence and sociocultural and economic strategies of deradicalization. The Sahara-Sahel also becomes a space of concern in this disciplinary moment because of the gathering of interests in making the space a matter of fact, a unit of urgent attention and analysis. It no longer simply connects North and West Africa as a transregion through which people, goods, and capital move, as it was in the heyday of the globalization discourse; rather, it is emerging as a discursive-cum-material object made through the gathering of forces, institutions, and actors of various stripes that make it globally important. The return to Kamara in religious terms should be contextualized by the new concern in defining religion in the Sahara-Sahel, where Senegal is the most extroverted, developed, and politically stable of the region's nation-states.

The present is defined by anterior processes and less visible forces that lie beyond developments we can easily link to the GWOT. Among the preceding events that have marked the present is the Iranian Revolution in 1979 and the new horizons of possibility that it ushered in with the idea of a modern Islamic state.[66] The resulting implementation of broad-ranging structural adjustment programs in Senegal (including the gutting of the university, the forced early retirement of public employees, and the devaluation of the CFA franc) has had a crucial impact on defining the present. Political and media liberalization too has had profound impacts. All together, these processes have made it such that in Senegal today, as in much of the Muslim world, Islam has replaced the nation as a horizon of consciousness.[67] It provides the repertoires for dominant and marginal modes of social performance and to great extent for the institutions and practices of public life.[68] Economically, Senegal is a fast-growing hub for Islamic finance, punching well above its weight as it competes with much larger economies, including Cote d'Ivoire, Kenya, and South Africa. In June 2014, for example, Senegal became an innovative pioneer in this industry when it attracted the equivalent of $200 million in *sukuk*, a kind of shariʿa-compliant bond, from local and international investors, according to a report on the Islamic economy in Africa by Economist Impact.[69] Also, Senegal's historic relationship to Morocco through the Tijani Sufi order has facilitated considerable diplomatic and business activities over the last decade in ways that supported the inclusion of Morocco in the Economic Community of West African States and the African Union. And the discovery of oil and natural gas off the coast of Senegal will likely increase the stakes of national debates, which tend to invoke religious symbols and appeal to Islamic sensibilities.

After the encounter that descended into an exchange of crypto-racial insults between two Muslim public intellectuals—one global, the other local—Bakary Sambe expounded on why Kamara is important today. The reference to Kamara constituted both a continuation of the project of intellectual decolonization inherited from a previous generation and a break in how that decolonization should be understood. Where decolonization had meant recovering Kamara's literariness and historicity for the first generation, reading Kamara in religious terms has come to characterize the second generation of decolonization.

On his website, Sambe writes: "At the end of the debate, inspired especially by Cheikh Ahmadou Bamba, Cheikh El Hadji Malick and Cheikh Moussa Camara in my critique of jihadism and violence in the name of Islam, I reaffirmed that in Africa we have the appropriate resources for Islamic religious discourse and have no need to be Muslims supervised by others. I even believe that our Arab friends might be invited to be inspired by the successes of the African experience of Islam, notably the harmony between social reality and religious principles that I call 'the critical assimilation of Islam.'"[70] By referring to three notable saintly figures from Senegal affiliated with locally based religious fraternities with a global reach, he identifies an autonomous tradition that provides intellectual resources and normative examples. The exemplary quality of this preceding generation is captured in the Wolof expression *sunu maam yu baax yi*, meaning "our good grandparents."[71] This rhetorical move is intended not only to assert equality but also to insist on an unexpected, even ironic, superiority. In this, one hears an echo from Amar Samb's project to demonstrate Black genius by showing the Senegalese contribution to Arabic literature. Like Amar Samb, Bakary Sambe refers to Kamara's intellectual output to enable his rejection of the globally hegemonic view that in Islam—as in all matters of political, economic, and social consequence—Africa is derivative, unlearned, and dependent on others. In insisting on Senegalese Islam's substantive modernity—what he calls the critical assimilation of Islam—Sambe uses a disciplinary vocabulary that is different from Samb's "civilization" but that nevertheless means something similar: the affirmation of an African humanity.[72] The takeaway, if you will, of the argument is that Black African Muslims and their history offer valuable insight into how to make Islam a secular religion.

THE SECULAR-RELIGIOUS AFTERLIFE OF SHAYKH MUSA KAMARA

The expression "secular religion" might appear as an oxymoron from the perspective of everyday speech, even as common representations of Islam globally render the idea of a secular Islam absurd. It is precisely this oxymoronic absurdity that offers us a critical wedge with which to think. An important current of religious studies has challenged the idea that religion is a universal category with a meaning that is stable across time and space. This theoretical literature has shown that the category of religion is itself constantly in contestation and that the normative distinction between the religious and the political in modern thought does not adequately serve to describe social reality. For Talal Asad, the designation of something as religious, as opposed to secular, is itself an effect of power.[73] That which is described as religious today is that which is subject to a power that defines itself in opposition to religion. In this strand of thought, secular is not so much the absence of religion or an antagonism toward religion as it is a relegation of that which gets marked as religion to a subordinated role in collective life.[74] Another way of putting this is that the category of religion becomes obvious only when a power external to it supersedes and limits it.[75] The antipathy with which Islam as religion is viewed from this hegemonic perspective results from a perceived Muslim reluctance, or perhaps refusal, to appropriately distinguish religion from politics. The more Muslims can make that distinction, the more they appear as "good Muslims," whereas the less they can make that distinction, the more they appear as "bad Muslims." The fact that Kamara offers materials and models, particularly in his *Most of the Would-Be Jihadists*,[76] with which to define Senegalese religion as identical to a secular theory of religion has made him a privileged reference in the time of terror.

Like the more well-known contemporaries that Sambe mentions who are affiliated with large transnational Sufi orders (Bamba and Sy), Kamara has been mobilized and interpreted to justify Senegal's place in the world. When Kamara is invoked today, mostly either by his descendants or by a network of Islamic studies scholars in Senegal and France, commentary revolves around material in his work that appeals to modern, rationalist, liberal-democratic values. Typically mentioned are his critical position on violence, his ecumenicalism, and his maintenance of a pious distance from political power. In other words, Kamara is now an example of and a resource to define and objectify religion in secular terms for the Muslim-majority country. It is in his intellectual output, his saintliness, his esoteric mysticism, and so on that a particular theory of what religion is, what it should do, and how it should be in the world is stabilized. This is, in fact, a secularized version of religion that is being endogenized—that is, identified as a phenomenon that was already present before colonial rule.

A key indication of the shift toward a "religious" Kamara is a new emphasis on his treatise on jihad. In *Most of the Would-Be Jihadists*, he argues that jihad is not an acceptable practice because of the loss of innocent lives and the lack of prophetic leadership to authorize it. This text is familiar to a Senegalese audience, mostly because of Amar Samb's translation, entitled "Condamnation de la guerre sainte."[77] The immediacy of the threat posed by Islamist political violence makes Kamara's arguments critical in the sense that they respond to a present crisis in which the scale of the militarization of the western Sahel is as great as it has ever been since it was occupied by the French military during the colonial period. That such a timely argument is made in Islamic terms against Islamist violence by a Senegalese thinker makes claims against Arab paternalism and imperialism, like those voiced by Bakary Sambe, possible and compelling. The unique value of Kamara's Islamic critique of jihad is captured explicitly in the Mbaye Lo's title of the first published translation of Kamara into English: *Sheikh Moussa Kamara's Islamic Critique of Jihadists*.[78]

My close readings of Kamara's autobiography that highlighted his status as a friend of God in chapters 1 and 2 are inspired by the way Kamara is increasingly discussed in more formal settings within Senegal. This stands in stark contrast to both the colonial and the nationalist receptions of him. It is in this context of needing to define Islam as a modern, secular religion that this reading of a mystical Kamara (or perhaps an esoteric Kamara, to be true to local parlance) has emerged. In addition to the new emphasis on Kamara's treatise on jihad and his autobiography, other parts of his body of work and examples of his life have begun to circulate more broadly. His views on the relationships among the major monotheistic religions, for example, are also often used to explain and justify a popular Senegalese discourse on ecumenicalism and tolerance. Any visitor to Senegal today will likely encounter a discourse about how religiously open the country is, about how, despite religious differences, the Senegalese people are united by some underlying stratum of cultural practices—even the first president, Léopold Senghor, was Catholic, while most of the population was Muslim, one will be reminded. These same discourses are echoed globally in various representations of Senegal's exceptionalism. During my stays in Senegal, Kamara's speech delivered at the opening of the Cathédrale du Souvenir Africain in Dakar in 1935 was often referenced as an embodiment of the Senegalese exception.[79] The use of Kamara's texts gives Senegalese secular modernity its scholarly legitimacy while providing the ideology of tolerance its historical authenticity.

Another example of the circulation of a religious Kamara is a discussion of his relationship to political power. His pious distance from politics is often taken as a normative model for the relationship between religion and politics. Today, the Kamara family insists that their forefather had no interest in politics, that he was part of a quietist tradition.[80] This position, also emphasized by academics such as Amar Samb, would seem to be confirmed by Kamara's own account of himself in *The Announcement*.[81] Kamara could have been an inspector of Arabic instruction or a Muslim judge, and yet he decided to stay in his small village to cultivate the land, teach the Qur'an, and devote himself to God. Such a representation is often accompanied by a criticism of contemporary religious leaders who appear too interested in obtaining political power and accumulating wealth. While this representation might very well be true, what is most interesting is how smoothly it aligns with the modern premium placed on the separation of religion and politics and offers itself as a normative measure against which to judge Muslim leadership today.

We should also add information about the recent debate over the *laïcité*, or secularism *à la française*, to our consideration of Kamara in relation to contemporary "religion-making" in Senegal.[82] A possible objection to my argument here is that there has been a significant resistance in recent years to defining Senegal as secular. In 2016, then President Macky Sall proposed a referendum to modify Senegal's constitution to assert the immutability of the secular character of the state. Opposition to this proposition was swift, massive, and diverse. Intellectuals from the major Sufi orders, which have long benefited from the modus vivendi in which the state recognized their autonomy in matters of religion—understood as domestic family relations and ritual practice—joined with smaller, less powerful Muslim reformist organizations, which did not want to abandon the potential for harnessing the powers of the state to achieve the Islamization of society. Sall quickly abandoned the project, but the controversy and the debate that it engendered constitute a part of the story of the efforts at defining and making religion. A common claim is that Senegal is not, in fact, *laïque* in the anticlerical and atheist sense associated with French republicanism but is instead closer to American secularism, in which the public is profoundly religious and even religious actors play a significant role in politics. One argument even asserts that Senegalese secularism consists of the state's equal *protection* of religious communities.[83] What these critiques share is that whatever the relationship between the religious and the political, a French colonial inheritance of secularism should not continue to define the Senegalese state, its society, and their shared moral order. As much as this resistance to the normative separation of religion from politics would seem to suggest that the secular in Senegal is fragile, it explains why Kamara would become so attractive for secular religion making. In Kamara, with his irrefutable credentials as a Muslim scholar, contemporary intellectuals have a model of an authoritative Islam that coheres with modern religion without reference to a colonial legacy of influence. Pious distance from power, ecumenical tolerance, rejection of political violence in the name of religion, and internalized experience of the divine are features of Kamara's life and works that model a religious comportment aligned with the modern order.

As much as Kamara may be invoked as the embodiment of the virtuous reconciliation of Muslim belief and practice with the globally hegemonic forms of life of the modern world, I would be remiss in not acknowledging that he is but one example of a much broader practice of iconization. In fact, from a more general perspective on contemporary Senegal that privileges influence and impact, that is, one that seeks the most representative case, Kamara remains a relatively marginal figure in popular memory and imagination. The most common example of a Sufi saint who has negotiated the subordinated status of Islam as religion to a secular politics is Shaykh Amadou Bamba Mbakke, who refused the strategy of armed struggle during the colonial period, preferring instead "the greater jihad of the self," and who emphasized using vernacular modes of expression to provide religious education for the masses. Several works have framed Bamba as embodying modern religious virtue.[84] Unlike Bamba and others such as Sy and Niasse, who all attracted mass followings, resulting in the development of organizations and microinstitutions to regulate collective life, Kamara attracted only a modest following that did not require the social infrastructure that the colonial and postcolonial states would try to leverage in their practice of indirect rule. Today, the Kamara family would likely argue that this lack of discipleship is evidence of Kamara's commitment to a classical model of the pious ascetic Sufi whose spiritual value was a hidden truth that only other spiritual masters might recognize.[85] All the same, a comparison of their respective followings illustrates Kamara's relative marginality. The Grand Maggal of Touba, the Senegalese city where Bamba is buried, is an annual pilgrimage that commemorates his persecution and exile by the French to Gabon. It draws millions of people each year, making it the largest event of any kind in Senegal and one of the largest religious gatherings in the world. The annual visit to Ganguel where Kamara is born was attended by several hundred when I attended in 2017. The order of magnitude is hardly comparable. The difference that we might note between the invocation of Bamba as an exemplary modern religious figure and that of Kamara is that the circulation of Bamba in contemporary discourse is often sectarian insofar as it is often Murids who offer Bamba as a model. While the family and followers of Kamara might also use him in similar ways, most of the intellectual work concerning him and his writings is done by Senegalese scholars who do not claim such affiliations. What is unique about Kamara's iconization, then, is that it is as motivated by secular reason as it is by religious attachment.

In sum, Kamara is made a key symbolic and substantive resource by which a Senegalese modernity can be articulated. This alternative modernity is both distinct from and compatible with global political modernity: It is an African-Islamic liberalism with "good" public Islam as the source, and it is beyond the influence of the West or the experience of colonialism. Kamara is an attractive figure for such a liberalizing project because his example seems to encourage the type of political structures and relationships palatable to liberal democracy: tolerance, a pious distance of religion from the state, and the controlled exercise of reason. At the same time, he gives the unique and specific cultural content needed to make modernity in a Senegalese image. In short, new readings of Kamara have permitted the formulation of a secular Islam.

Some eighty years after his death, Kamara has returned as a secular-religious icon, an exemplar of Senegalese Muslim virtue in the modern world. This secular-religious afterlife appears at the intersection of the African Renaissance and the Global War on Terror. The African Renaissance as a process of self-representation in the political and intellectual sense has underscored the necessity for Africans to reclaim their heritage and perfect it for the future. Like the sixteenth-century scholars Abd al-Rahman al-Sa'adi and Ahmad Baba invoked by Thabo Mbeki and Henry Louis Gates Jr., Kamara has been made available for Senegalese intellectuals in the ongoing struggle for self-definition and sovereignty. Just as was the case in the European Renaissance, when humanists developed textual scholarship and the study of classical languages to access the lives of exemplary men—and regrettably it remains a male-dominated enterprise—Senegalese intellectuals laboring in the shadow of the African Renaissance Monument are elaborating a field of study on the lives of local Muslim saints as subjects of emulation. The Global War on Terror constitutes the other, if contradictory, context of the return of Kamara. The affective terrain that has emerged from a combination of total war at the planetary scale, the retreat of the state in providing for the well-being of its population, and the Islamization of society has necessitated meaningful, local references for the definition of religion in terms that align with modern subjectivities. The occupation and cultural destruction of Timbuktu in the early days of Mali's last decade of instability marked a new set of conditions to which Kamara's life and works might be offered in response. The convergence of these two discourses does much to contextualize the new emphasis in the reception of Kamara's autobiographical *The Announcement* and antijihad treatise *Most of the Would-Be Jihadists*. Kamara is no longer simply a figure who is useful, whether as an informant (as was the case for the French) or as an author and historian (as was the case for nationalist scholars after independence). Current discursive practices have now made him a religious scholar-saint, someone legible to both the rationality of the state and the spirituality of society.

While I hope my exploration of the two contexts has been clarifying, I do not want to suggest a relationship of causality. Neither the new secular-religious reading of Kamara nor the contexts of reception explain one another. Rather, as I have done in each chapter, I have discussed Kamara's textual life and textual afterlife in the hope that this serves as a prism to throw light on changing contexts and the relations of knowledge and power therein. If the arc of this book is any indication, new conjunctures in the future will invite new readings of and new afterlives for Shaykh Musa Kamara.

Coda

Long Live Philology!
Or, Remembering the Future of the Humanities

AROUND TWO HUNDRED STUDENTS came to an amphitheater at Gaston Berger University in Saint-Louis, Senegal, on a Saturday morning to hear an American speak about a Senegalese intellectual that most had never heard of. To be fair, their attendance was compulsory as a part of the departmental program for students at the Center for Religious Studies, ranging from first-year undergraduates all the way to doctoral candidates. After a generous introduction by the interdisciplinary scholar Abdourahmane Seck, the host and department chair, they turned their respectful attention, and perhaps curiosity, to me. What did I have to tell them about their own intellectual heritage? I had struggled for weeks to prepare what I had hoped would be a successful talk. Ironically, for several years I had been thinking of my project as a translation of Shaykh Musa Kamara's life, works, and legacy for an American academic audience, one that not only moved meaning across linguistic divides of Arabic, French, and Pulaar but also conveyed forms, styles, sensibilities, and contexts across time, space, and culture. But now I needed to translate my translations back into idioms and registers that would be recognizable at the source.

I planned my talk to follow the emotional arc of this book. I would open with the hopefulness and goodwill that accompanied Kamara's submission of his monumental *The History of the Blacks* to colonial administrators who also fancied themselves as philologists. Then I would share how I as an African American came to such a project, and narrate the saga of the long-delayed publication of Kamara's major work. I would finish by arguing, on the one hand, that the story of Kamara—with all of its accomplishments, disappointments, and misunderstandings—shows us that the so-called crisis of the humanities, in which disciplines like literature, history, religious studies, and art appear imperiled in an increasingly technocratic world, was always the colonial enterprise that was its foundation. On the other, Kamara's story shows us that, perhaps paradoxically, we can be optimistic, for the humanities, at their core, have a persistent textual attitude that perennially returns or, at the very least, retains the potential for a return.

I decided to disturb the sense of decorum that I had grown familiar with in Senegalese universities, in which the professor, on their elevated dais, offers truths in the magisterial course. Instead of lecturing, I immediately posed a question for them to answer: What exactly was colonization? I climbed the stairs in the hall and handed students the microphone to collect responses. And from there, I tried to enter into the story of Kamara. I was able to cover much less ground than I anticipated, but at the very least, I shared the tragic arc of Kamara's publication. The most basic point that I wanted to leave with them was that as we return, again, to think through what it means to decolonize—as many of the students were, given the rise of movements for popular sovereignty in the region—thinkers such as Kamara, who lived, worked, and thought in a historically specific condition of colonization, are an important resource.

This had been neither my first talk on Kamara in Senegal nor my first talk at the Center for Religious Studies. In 2017, I presented what would become the first chapter of my dissertation. At that point, I still did not know that I would eventually write a book on Kamara. I had only just begun to appreciate how much there was to say about him as I still tried to make sense of a broader discursive formation around the historical personality of Hajj Umar Tal, who had reshaped the greater western Sahel in the nineteenth century. Kamara's biography of Tal had taken up so much space in my thinking that I began emphasizing Kamara over Tal in my presentation. I was most interested in Kamara's way of thinking about the past and his method for recovering it. That audience was far smaller and more patient than the present group, as I recall saying a lot without knowing very much about my topic.

But much had changed since my last talk. The feeling on the campus then had been very different. Where I remembered the grounds to be well ordered, with students in their place as they disciplined themselves to

CODA

enter into the world of the formal economy dictated from elsewhere, I now saw student initiative everywhere I looked. An unruly and beautiful self-assertion was everywhere apparent. Whether it was a guerrilla student garden behind a dormitory village built by young women or a simple mosque built by students adjacent to a slick athletic field, the campus revealed the signs of student agency. This made sense, given the struggles the students had accumulated in the years since my previous lecture. They had had their martyrs. In 2018, Fallou Sène was killed by the forces of order in a student action demanding scholarship payment and better learning conditions.[1] In 2022, Seynabou Ka Diallo fell on "this battlefield called life," murdered by her intimate partner when she refused to abort her pregnancy.[2] And Alpha Yero Tounkara and Prosper Clédor Senghor were killed during the national protests supporting the election of Bassirou Diomaye Faye as president and Ousmane Sonko as prime minister just three months before my talk in 2024. Signs of these battles, with their losses and victories, were abundant.

Senegal has long nourished a robust culture of student activism with rapid mobilizations and periodic strikes in support of bread-and-butter demands for scholarships and housing. But the years between my two talks saw a wave of protests that changed a culture of student activism into a youth movement in and beyond the university. I am unsure of any explicit connections in tactics or strategies or consciousness with other student and youth movements in Africa such as Rhodes Must Fall, Fees Must Fall, and *Le Balai Citoyen* (The Citizen's Broom) or with the solidarity protests organized by the Movement for Black Lives after the murder of George Floyd, but one cannot help but note the simultaneity of these movements. Indeed, the globally shared context of the COVID-19 pandemic and its aftermath might be said to have created a new global terrain characterized by both popular protest and what political scientists call democratic backsliding toward authoritarianism. However, the Senegalese youth movement has been catalyzed by some very specific conditions, even if the resulting unrest may have resembled and coincided with broader currents.

Beyond the campus in the city of Saint-Louis, there were several other differences that make the mantra of decolonization more than a metaphor. The discovery of natural gas and oil off the coast of Senegal in 2014 set off a development bonanza. Infrastructural projects, including the opening of a small airport with commercial flights to Dakar and the completion of a new highway to the capital, signal a new era characterized by the business of resource extraction. And as a result, land theft has been rampant, and the price of real estate has greatly increased. This new industry, however, will likely result in an uneven development, as it attracts expatriate labor, while local labor works in languishing industries like fishing. The resulting rise in the cost of living can be felt in every domain.

These changes in the local context are profitably put in a broader national frame.[3] The difference between 2017 and 2024 in Senegal is, in part, the difference between former President Macky Sall's first mandate, which was characterized by infrastructural development, constitutional reform, and efforts to attract foreign investment, and his second mandate, which featured rampant profiteering by elected officials and the president's attempt to hold onto power. The selling off of public goods is captured well in the common complaint that Macky Sall had "sold the sea."[4] As is often the case, the tragic irony of the enrichment of the few was that it happened alongside the immiseration of the many. This period saw declining economic growth, rising inflation, and food insecurity, according to the World Bank's 2023 economic update.[5] Sall's long-standing strategy of isolating and suppressing political opponents was particularly evident when his government leveraged allegations of sexual assault against the charismatic Ousmane Sanko in order to jail him and bar him from running in national elections. Public health restrictions associated with the COVID-19 pandemic became a laboratory for repressive tactics as those in power responded to the increasingly acute social crisis. The imposition of curfews, for example, hampered the movement of workers who spent hours every day to get to their place of employment. Such repression of the average citizen took an explicitly political form when thousands of young men and women were jailed, and some killed, in connection with protests that rocked the nation. Another key difference was the movement from the margins to the center of the slogan "France Dégage!" or "France, hands off!" I recall friends attending fringe protests against the deep-seated investment interests of the former colonizer in the years before 2017. Today, through the alchemical transformation of popular struggle, one might see anti-imperialism as a policy aspiration of the state.

These shifts in the national context follow a broader regional pattern in West Africa that amplifies the urgency of rethinking the colonial. An increasing anti-France discourse has been exemplified by the popular critique of persistent French influence based on the monetary policy of the

CFA franc in formerly colonized countries and has been enacted by military coups in Niger, Burkina Faso, and Mali that have expelled Western military elements. Paradoxically, this period of popular anti-French sentiment has been accompanied by the robust cultural diplomacy of Emmanuel Macron, directed to middle-class intellectual, entrepreneurial, and activist Francophone Africans and Afropeans whose mobility makes them a force on the continent and within France. This diplomacy has included support for programs such as Les Ateliers de la Pensée, Africa 2020, and, most notably, the drive to restore art objects to African countries. That Faye and Sonko and their movement for popular sovereignty have come to power through elections that almost did not happen makes Senegal an exception to the broader regional pattern only in form and not in substance. The differences I observed on campus that make decolonization a contemporary project are wholly coherent with these developments at every scale of context.

After finishing my talk at Gaston Berger University, students intervened with questions and comments that I think effectively organize the major issues this project highlights and to which it responds. I did not have time to respond in the way I would have wanted to on that day. I include their interventions here and offer the responses I would like to have given as a way of closing this work.

Intervention 1: What Was the Quality of Kamara's Religious Knowledge, and What Were the Controversies Associated with Him?

The question of the quality of Kamara's religious knowledge posed by a religious studies student in a Senegalese university strikes me as particularly interesting. Near the beginning of my talk, I asked if the students had heard of Kamara. Unlike during my 2017 talk, when I saw a few hands raised, in 2024 I did not see a single hand raised. This surprised me; while I did not expect most to raise their hands, I assumed the great efforts to popularize Kamara that I discussed in chapter 6 would have made some inroads. For example, former President Sall himself attended the opening of a research center devoted to the shaykh in Kamara's village of Ganguel to much fanfare in 2021. Alas, no one admitted familiarity with this personality. But when I heard this question about religious knowledge, I quickly assumed that this student was at least familiar with Kamara and knew of the controversies surrounding him, for he was indeed a controversial figure—perhaps most controversial for his interpretations of Islamic norms around marriage, tobacco consumption, the validity of jihad, and ritual observance, as well as his views on Sufi orders and his relationship to colonial power. Concerned as I have been with how Kamara read himself, how the colonial administrators read him or failed to read him, and how nationalist scholars working to forge a national literature and history read him, I have only just begun to attend to the *religious* Kamara in my work. This is unfortunately all too common in the field of Islam in Africa, from which religious studies training is conspicuously absent. The student's question very well may have been an expression of sincere curiosity. From this perspective, we might see the student's question coming from a degree of skepticism. Why was Kamara not more well-known, like the leaders of the mass Sufi organizations such as the Muridiyya and Tijaniyya, if he was indeed such a towering intellectual? Perhaps his obscurity could be explained by a flaw on Kamara's part that undermined his reliability as a transmitter of sound religious knowledge.

Indeed, the side of the debates upon which Kamara fell that I have mentioned might in many ways be considered unpopular, or at least uncommon, by the religious establishment. His intellectual positions reflected something of an idiosyncratic, if not dissenting, voice. It is of little surprise, then, that Kamara, to the extent he is invoked today, is accompanied by accusations of his servile status, as I discussed in chapter 3. When I bring Kamara's name up with Senegalese intellectuals, I often notice a degree of discomfort or a desire to situate him as something of an outsider. His family name, I am often told, suggests that he was not of noble birth, and I am reminded of how hierarchical the society of Futa Toro can be, with its system of caste. Abdoul Malal Diop has refuted the claim of servile origins, highlighting the genealogical account that Kamara himself gives in his autobiography.[6] This argument is convincing enough. But there is something I find even more interesting about Kamara's status in relation to his reliability as an authority. An accusation of servile status, whether true or not, sought to disqualify a speaker as a legitimate scholar. It was a common accusation in the region, as by the colonial period, the proportion of the population that could be said to have servile origins was as large as 50 percent in certain parts of West Africa, and the religious sphere had for some time been a space of social mobility. The accusation could be credibly launched against many scholars—and indeed was—and could be used as a way to marginalize a critical voice. Kamara, with his critiques of claims of nobility by the region's elite, was particularly susceptible to disqualification by a religious establishment that, in practice, often kept leadership in the family.

Kamara's supposed caste status presents what might be called a limit of global Black studies. For a Senegalese audience such as the one with which I shared my work at Gaston Berger University, having been a slave or a descendant of slaves would likely be a mark against Kamara, rendering what he had to say negligible. In an African American context, such humble origins, if true, would make what he had to say all the more worth listening to. The very attribute that might enable a discourse about Kamara in an American context is also the attribute that disables it in his own geographic setting. Here lies the central irony in the story of Kamara: Even as he may be mobilized for the purpose of racial vindication in global discourses—as we saw in such diverse work as the colonial humanism of Maurice Delafosse and Henri Gaden, the nationalist literature and history of Amar Samb, and the secular religion making of Bakary Sambe—the logic of caste renders him unworthy of reading locally.

All of that said, we can confidently state that Kamara was, in the best possible way, a peculiar figure. While he remained stylistically and epistemologically traditional, he was undeniably modern. He was incredibly pious, but he believed in the importance of history. He relied on individual reading, undirected by a teacher, and inspiration over transmission. Whether he was of supposed low birth or not, his outlook made him an outsider. He was therefore not representative of the tradition but is fundamental in our efforts to think it through all the same. The fact that one of his last works, his autobiography, frames him as embodying that tradition indicates that it is an argument he himself had to make. Though he had many admirers, there is little evidence to suggest that he was seen as authoritative. Perhaps his autobiography should be read as a final attempt to make the case despite all odds. But we should not take his being unrepresentative as a reason not to read him. In fact, his singularity makes him all the more worthy of being read.

CODA

Intervention 2: What Is the Meaning of Colonial Humanism?

This was a clarifying question that a student posed to invite me to define my terms. I am glad that he did, as I had yet to consider consciously what this term meant even though I had used the expression throughout the book. Here is what I should have said at the outset: Colonial humanism refers to a set of ideas, figures of thought, patterns of thinking, and styles of reasoning that provided the intellectual foundations that justified, rationalized, organized, and gave meaning to the European enterprise of settlement and extraction beyond Europe from about the 1880s until the beginning of World War II. Its defining feature was a contradiction.[7] It proposed, through an elaboration of new disciplines, the universal applicability of conceptual categories and methods for systematically understanding a subject defined by biology, as opposed to religion: the human species.[8] The "human," as this talking animal was known, was best understood as the agent of historical change who was due rights, responsibilities, and freedoms and who pursued their interest in free association. An endless range of possibilities could be understood in relation to this. But while colonial humanism was premised on universal inclusion, it nevertheless had to confront the fact of human difference. It did so by insisting on a hierarchy of difference, in which humans were categorized by races—according to supposedly visually observable traits—that could be placed on a scale of historical development. The degree of adherence to the qualities of the "human" defined where in the hierarchy one stood and the degree of applicability of the universal framework. The disciplines that came to be understood as the humanities over the course of this period oversaw the elaboration of colonial humanism in the day-to-day work of research and teaching, to be sure, but also in that wide arena of social reproduction that is ideology in both the metropole and the colony.

Importantly, colonial humanism can be understood in religious terms. Much like religions we would more readily identify as such, colonial humanism was a wellspring of meaning. An action was undertaken or not undertaken or an event or a community was understood or not understood in relation to the set of ideas that saw the human experience as structured by a hierarchy, historically defined. A scholar looked for a manuscript and deciphered it because its contents could provide evidence of humanity—that is, of belonging to the universal category of the species—but did so on a hierarchical scale of historical evolution. The production of Delafosse is a case in point. The work to generate a native literature was motivated, on the one hand, by a desire to demonstrate African humanity and African contributions to civilization but also, on the other, by a need to create a measure of lack that placed Africans lower on the scale of development and historical evolution. This double move of inclusion through subordination was always the point of an intellectual work within the paradigm of colonial humanism and gave it its meaning. Colonial humanism was also religious in that it had its norms of elaboration and ideas of comportment for the scholar. But perhaps most importantly, colonial humanism offered its own sense of secular morality. Those societies, peoples, and individuals who were more civilizationally and historically advanced were obliged to develop, guide, and mentor the supposedly more backward races. While this can indeed be understood as the justification for colonial settlement and extraction that was, and is, ongoing, it is insightful to recognize it as a moral imperative that somehow transmogrified the otherwise dirty work of colonization—an enterprise that relied on murder, rape, and pillage—into something noble.

In the tragic story of Kamara's struggle to publish a monumental history, we have seen that the textual attitude—an orientation to the world mediated through the reading of texts—was shared by the deeply religious Muslim scholar and a few colonial humanists, such as Delafosse and Gaden. We saw over the course of the first and second chapters, through a reading of Kamara's autobiography and his biography of Hajj Umar Tal, the texture of a textual attitude that was nourished by the contemplative tradition of West African Sufi Islam, one that privileged disclosure and emulation. We saw in chapters 3 and 4 two distinct attitudes among colonial administrators that led them to either read or not read the works of colonized subjects. The practical attitude of getting things done, associated with an engineering paradigm, was preoccupied with identifying good and bad Muslims and the "human resources" best positioned to facilitate the work of extraction. This attitude generally dominated the colonial enterprise and was characteristic of bureaucrats like Robert Arnaud and Paul Marty. Ultimately, the textual attitude of the colonial humanists was undermined by the contradictions of a colonial humanism that expressed itself more explicitly in the practical attitude. All the same, it was the shared textual attitude that made reading Kamara even a possibility.

CODA

Intervention 3: Because of the Coloniality of Knowledge, European Models of Knowing and Being Persist in Formerly Colonized Spaces

This comment by one of the Senegalese students in attendance indicates the relevance of a contemporary global conversation about the ongoing need to decolonize knowledge. The decolonial discourse has many references from the long history of anticolonial struggle around the world and enjoys widespread engagement in diverse contexts. There is a paradox though. In some ways, decolonial theory represents an antitheoretical theory. It resists the imperative to generalize and make universal claims, a practice associated with post-Enlightenment thought, choosing instead the particular lifeworlds of Indigenous peoples and the lands they inhabit. And yet its popularity, its capacity to travel, its use in diverse settings and circumstances, and its tendency toward metaphorization appear to generalize all the same. What I understand from the comment is that the student saw in my presentation yet another instance in which Indigenous knowledge gets discounted, and suppressed, both in the past by the colonizers and in the present by the inadequacy of university-based research efforts to understand colonized peoples. There is a bit of that in the story I tell in this book. But it is worth thinking the claim through.

I understand coloniality of knowledge and being to describe the persistent relations between knowledge and power in global domination, a situation best exemplified by the historical experiences of societies that have undergone and continue to endure settler colonial projects, particularly in the Americas, Australasia, parts of Africa, and Palestine. In these places, knowledge has been and continues to be premised on and elaborated through the removal and erasure of the Indigenous populations, their modes of life, their languages, and their ways of knowing that it authorizes. Beyond these sites, in places subjected to imperial domination but not necessarily settlement, the populations remain, but their societies and economies are reorganized for the sake of extraction and the creation of captive markets. Part and parcel of this process is a "reformatting" of minds to support this transformation.[9] Here the coloniality of knowledge becomes a figure of speech to highlight paradigms and patterns of fundamentally unequal relations at the planetary scale. There is value to such an ahistorical and ontological description: It clarifies the stakes of intellectual labor.

However, the decolonial approach in a strict sense is not very helpful in understanding the life of Kamara, appreciating his texts, or making sense of his reception. For one, Senegal was not a settler colony. Unlike Algeria, let's say, Senegal was first an outpost of mercantile capitalism that gradually came under French control through a mix of negotiation and violent coercion. There was never an attempt to displace the native population; rather, the French incorporated Senegal and its resources into its colonial empire. Knowledge, therefore, was not needed for the brute mechanics of genocide or for the mechanisms used to steal land on a large scale and distribute it to settlers. Indigenous knowledge, however, was needed for a more efficient management of the population. Inequalities that were already in place such as supposedly traditional regimes of land tenure could be used in the management of production and the policing of order. In that way, indigenous knowledge was incorporated into what became colonial knowledge, as it was *essential to the operation of power*. For this reason, an analytical approach rather than a figurative one is crucial. Instead of painting all knowledge with the broad ahistorical and ontological brush of coloniality, we need to ask what forms of knowledge are used for what ends, by whom, and in what modalities. My reading of Kamara goes in this direction. I read his work and its reception carefully to think through the inequalities that were instrumentalized and redeployed in the operation of the colonial state. It is a way of insisting on historicity without being overly historicist. In returning to the scene of actual colonization, we are better positioned to evaluate the inheritances of the past and to strategize for a future beyond empire. To rephrase la paperson, I am less interested in decolonizing knowledge as I am in knowledge that decolonizes.[10]

Intervention 4: What Can This Information Do for Us Today?

This question expresses what I have described as the practical attitude, an instrumentalist orientation toward the world preoccupied with getting things done. Reasonably, the practical attitude emerges from the fact of scarcity and is a feature of all social life—and one felt acutely in this contemporary African context. What can knowledge of Kamara's story do? The question also probes for a sense of value—in particular, use value. One might rephrase the question to be more explicit: In a society in which scarcity is a primary and driving concern and in which most waking hours of the majority of the population are preoccupied with the struggle to satisfy the needs of life to a historically appropriate standard, what is the value of a work about a religious scholar who died almost a century ago? From the perspective of the practical attitude, which we considered in chapter 3, the content of Kamara's works, like much in the humanities, has little value because it is a knowledge that does little. It is "use-less." This negative assessment of the humanities is today as common in Senegal as it is in the United States, perhaps more so. And it is an assessment that lies at the heart of the so-called crisis of the humanities. According to Helen Small in *The Value of the Humanities*, scholars tend to respond to such questions about the value of the humanities in at least one of five ways: They focus on meaning and meaning making in ways that are different from other forms of knowledge, they are indeed useful but in ways that trouble the hegemony of the paradigms of use value and exchange value, they feel good, they teach citizenship, and they are intrinsically valuable.[11] One might imagine a response to this question along these lines. But before we rush to respond with the sense that is genuinely due, it is worth noting that much like the request for justification that accompanies the so-called crisis of the humanities in a Euro-American context, the student's question is a symptom of the crisis of the African university embedded in a broader social crisis.

One often gets the impression that in Senegal the categories for understanding that are generally available from a global perspective never quite match social reality, that it is an imaginary world that is superimposed on a real world.[12] The first world gets the label and prestige of formality, of the official and the institutional. It enjoys the recognition and the resources and wealth that accompany formality. The other world receives the label of informality. But if you spend much time doing much of anything, it is clear that the formal is artificial and fictive, corresponding to nothing that is actual and real. This is all the more true when it comes to the university and its inheritance of forms and traditions that were established in the period of colonization and that have been maintained by ongoing relations of domination ever since. The continued reliance on the French language in Senegalese universities is but one example of the mismatch between university-based knowledge production and a society in which French is a minority language. The crisis of the African university, with the perceived inutility of the humanities at its center, is therefore a crisis of relevance and legibility.

There seem to be two options available in face of this crisis: disruption and decolonization. Disruption of the African university through the intervention of venture capital represents a quiet revolution that threatens to quickly transform the higher education landscape in Africa. Various "education providers," many of which are multinational corporations of one kind or another, promise a direct pathway to employment through a business school–inspired curriculum that emphasizes professional training in in-demand hard skills, problem-solving, and the soft skills and literacy necessary to operate on today's global teams. On an individual basis, the offer is seductive, as it promises access to the best and most cutting-edge job opportunities, often compensated in foreign currencies worth relatively more than national currencies paid to strictly "local" workers. It's a straight shot to the good life. But viewed on a social level, such initiatives compound the already cascading accumulation of disadvantage set off by the global racial empire.[13] They further entrench Africa as the site of a cheap labor reserve, a new digital Bantustan to serve the global settler colony, or the source of raw materials to support the world's electronic infrastructure.

The other option for transforming higher education in Africa is decolonization. I understand decolonizing higher education as securing epistemic autonomy, the freedom to think through one's own conditions, using categories that correspond to one's conditions.[14] This requires the interrogation of the durable structures of knowledge and power that allow for reconfiguration and adaptation so that they earn their legitimacy through legibility. Ultimately, epistemic autonomy depends on political autonomy, which is extraepistemic. It is not voluntaristic in this way. All the same, academic work aligned with African political autonomy on the continent and beyond needs to think through conditions with the aid of organic intellectual resources in order to formulate categories that emerge from those conditions.

What can this information do for us today? From the perspective of the practical attitude, an attitude that is aligned with the imminent disruption of the African university, Kamara's writings are relatively worthless. Reading Kamara will not create many jobs. It will not make you a better employee. But from the perspective of decolonization, Kamara's story highlights for us that the crisis of the humanities was always colonialism.

CODA

The goal of colonial humanism to include was undermined by the impulse to subordinate. Its textual attitude, while virtuous, was invalidated by an antagonistic practical attitude that coincided it. Furthermore, this information helps us identify resources for thinking about the present and the inheritances from the past that have had durable effects in ordering and structuring our present. Let us be clear: The call for epistemic autonomy is not a good in and of itself; its purpose is emancipation.[15] This work is useful insofar as it identifies resources for critical thought that have emerged from and respond to the historical specificity of Senegalese society. Its use is to develop critical thought, one that seeks not to do the work of representation but to enable the interrogation of power. In the effort to elaborate references for epistemic autonomy, thinkers such as Kamara are essential. He is not incontrovertible simply because he was a Senegalese or a Muslim intellectual; he is essential because he practiced critique as a Senegalese Muslim intellectual. Kamara provides models for thinking that emerge from the historical specificity of his context, that correspond to it much more closely than do some of the models that we get from academic social science and its world-making project.[16] If knowledge is to serve society, it must reflect that society and be legible to it, and vice versa.

In the vein of legibility, the question that I struggled with in the weeks before my talk was, in fact, the most important question: Can I translate my translations of Kamara for an American academic audience back into idioms and registers that are recognizable at the source? It remains a work in progress. In many ways, this book can be considered only an introduction to Shaykh Musa Kamara, his work, and his legacy. There remains much to do to provide a robust account of this singular figure. For example, a more conventional biography might give a more detailed description of Kamara's daily life, a fuller exploration of his personality, and a more thorough examination of his myriad social relationships. Or a more focused literary-critical work could consider his Pulaar language poetry and his commentaries on versification and classical Arabic poetry, as language and literature appears to be an area toward which he gravitated most often, especially early in his life. Finally, more should be done on Kamara's philosophy of history and on his work as a social theorist who thought through the caste-like social formation of Sahelian West Africa. Kamara's own texts housed at Institut

Fondamental d'Afrique Noire and in the family collection in Ganguel are indispensable resources for this work, but they need to be better situated in a larger body of sources where they can be compared with and studied in relation to the work of contemporaries, predecessors, and successors. There are enough source materials and questions to pose to occupy an entire group of scholars. My intention in this book has been to contribute to that field by synthesizing the excellent work that has already been done, opening it up to broader theoretical discussions, and extending it to an Anglophone audience. Beyond research on Kamara specifically, this book offers some methodological and theoretical insights that the broader field of Islam in Africa and the African diaspora might pursue. Instead of always searching for the most representative case or the most authoritative voice, there is great value in searching for insight from the margin, the exception, and the ignored. Moreover, identifying *the* meaning of a text is often a missed opportunity. Differential reading, a mode of textual engagement concerned with plurality and antagonism *within* a given work, promises to offer richer and more textured understanding.

I see the best way forward for developing a humanities worthy of its name comes out of work I have been doing for several years with Abdourahmane Seck and the decolonial collective Groupe d'Action et d'Étude Critique—Africa. Conceived as a third space between an African university and the community that surrounds it, GAEC has been thinking from and acting upon the web of nestled antagonisms between knowledge (understood narrowly as research output, only 1 percent of which comes from Africa)[17] and life (understood expansively as always present, always abundant, refusing measure, and evasive).[18] Seck has used *mémographie* to describe an emergent collective form of study, experimentation, and experience—that is, of living in history. It is something of an antimethod of testimony that seeks to make sense. One of the concepts that has emerged from this practice is *mbokk*, a Wolof word that refers to something like "kinship" but that emphasizes what is shared, solidarity, and the possibility of inclusion rather than a limited notion of exclusive belonging.[19] When Kamara writes at length, particularly in his later works such as *The Precious Collection*, about genealogy and critiques the abuse of genealogy to make claims to temporal power, he is thinking about *mbokk* as a way of making sense as a person situated within the set of social relations about which he writes. In that way, Kamara is, or can become, a theorist of *mbokk*, enabling the elaboration of a decolonized humanities in the place where GAEC is situated. My commitment is to continue this work of translation.

Despite the air of dread that often accompanies discussions about the humanities, I am hopeful. The story that I have told in this book speaks to the persistence, if only *in potentia*, of the textual attitude, an orientation toward the interpretation of meaning. Despite the challenge Kamara faced in getting works such as *The History of the Blacks*, *The Announcement*, and *Most of the Would-Be Jihadists* in circulation, the fact that they remain waiting to be read, and to be returned to, as they are now by Senegalese intellectuals, suggests the permanent possibility of cultivating the textual attitude—to interpret, to read deeply. If the humanities have a real value, it is to be found in this *commitment to read again*, or *relegere*, one of the classical etymologies of *religion*. As long as we learn from Kamara this commitment to return to the text, to practice philology, the fate of the humanities remains promising.

Notes

Overture: Philology as the Love of Study

1. Malcolm X and Alex Haley, *The Autobiography of Malcolm X: As Told to Alex Haley* (Perfection Learning, 1987), 423.
2. Malcolm X and Haley, *The Autobiography of Malcolm X*, 176.
3. Malcolm X and Haley, *The Autobiography of Malcolm X*, 400.
4. Julia Fields, "Aardvark," in *Black Out Loud: An Anthology of Modern Poems by Black Americans*, ed. Arnold Adoff (Macmillan, 1978), 33.
5. Stuart Hall, "Through the Prism of an Intellectual Life," in *Culture, Politics, Race and Diaspora: The Thought of Stuart Hall*, ed. Brian Meeks (Lawrence & Wishardt, 2007), 268. For an incisive commentary on the detour through thought and its connections to Antonio Gramsci and Edward Said, see the essay by Asad Haider, "Politics Without Guarantees," *The Point* 25 (August 15 2021), https://thepointmag.com/politics/politics-without-guarantees/.

Introduction: Deaths of Philology

1. Kamara uses three titles of this work interchangeably: *Zuhūr al-Basātīn fī Tārīkh al-Sawādīn* [Flowers from among the gardens in the history of the Blacks], *Intiṣār al-Mawtūr fī dhikr qabāʾil Futa Toro* [Victory of the wronged in the memory of the tribes of Futa Toro], and *Iḥyāʾ mā ʿAfā wa Andarasa min ʿUlum Tārīkh al-Sūdān wa Inṭamas* [Revival of what has been effaced and extinguished from the historical arts of the Blacks and obliterated]. "Zuhūr al-basātīn fī tārīkh al-sawādīn" is the most common title used in the scholarly literature. I translate it here literally, but it is worth noting that "Anthology of the Gardens in the History of Blacks"

would work as well, as the etymology of "anthology" suggests a gathering of flowers, with flowers being figurative language for poetry or other written wonders. A more liberal and poetic rendering might be something like "A Bouquet from the Garden of Black History." I will refer to this work in this book as *The History of the Blacks*. Throughout the book, I use English translations for Arabic titles in the main text and full citations of the original language in the notes. I recognize this might not be so common a convention, but it is a part of my broader project to render the strange familiar for an Anglophone readership.

2. David Robinson, "Abdul Qadir and Shaykh Umar: A Continuing Tradition of Islamic Leadership in Futa Toro," *International Journal of African Historical Studies* 6, no. 2 (1973): 286, 287, https://doi.org/10.2307/216779.
3. Abdoul Malal Diop, "La vie et l'oeuvre de Cheikh Moussa Kamara de Ganguel (1864–1945)," (PhD diss., Université de Cheikh Anta Diop, 2014), 21.
4. Diop, "La vie et l'oeuvre de Cheikh Moussa Kamara de Ganguel," 21; David Robinson, "Un historien et anthropologue sénégalais: Shaikh Musa Kamara," *Cahiers d'études africaines* 28, no. 109 (1988): 96.
5. David Robinson, *The Holy War of Umar Tal: The Western Sudan in the Mid-Nineteenth Century* (Clarendon Press, 1985); Farah El-Sharif, "Kitāb al-Rimāḥ of 'Umar Fūtī Tāl: Sealing Muhammadan Sainthood in Nineteenth Century West Africa" (PhD thesis, Harvard University, 2022), https://www.proquest.com/docview/2643966044/; Amir Syed, "Al-Hājj Umar Tāl and the Realm of the Written: Mastery, Mobility and Islamic Authority in 19th Century West Africa" (PhD diss., University of Michigan, 2017), http://search.proquest.com/docview/1917831465/.
6. Abū 'Ubayd al-Bakrī, "Kitab Al-Masālik Wa'l-Mamālik" [Book of Routes and Realms], in *Corpus of Early Arabic Sources for West African History*, ed. J. F. P. Hopkins and Nehemia Levtzion (Markus Wiener, 2000), 77.
7. Nehemia Levtzion, *Muslims and Chiefs in West Africa: A Study of Islam in the Middle Volta Basin in the Pre-Colonial Period* (Clarendon Press, 1968), http://hdl.handle.net/2027/heb.02619; Roman Loimeier, "Patterns and Peculiarities of Islamic Reform in Africa," *Journal of Religion in Africa* 33, no. 3 (2003): 77–107, https://doi.org/10.1163/157006603322663497. For an example of how this worked out in a different subregion, see Levtzion, *Muslims and Chiefs*. For general patterns, see Loimeier, "Patterns and Peculiarities."
8. Tal Tamari, *Les castes de l'Afrique occidentale: Artisans et musiciens endogames* (Société d'ethnologie, 1997).
9. Boubacar Barry, *Senegambia and the Atlantic Slave Trade* (Cambridge University Press, 1998); James L. A. Webb, *Desert Frontier: Ecological and Economic Change Along the Western Sahel, 1600-1850* (University of Wisconsin Press, 1995), http://www.gbv.de/dms/bowker/toc/9780299143305.pdf; Philip D. Curtin, *The Atlantic Slave Trade: A Census* (University of Wisconsin Press, 1972); Paul E. Lovejoy, *Jihād in West Africa During the Age of Revolutions* (Ohio University Press, 2016), and *Transformations in Slavery* (Cambridge University Press, 1983).
10. Toby Green, *A Fistful of Shells: West Africa from the Rise of the Slave Trade to the Age of Revolution* (University of Chicago Press, 2021).
11. Philip D. Curtin, "Jihad in West Africa: Early Phases and Inter-Relations in Mauritania and Senegal," *Journal of African History* 12, no. 1 (1971): 11–24, https://

INTRODUCTION

doi.org/10.1017/S0021853700000049; Michael A. Gomez, *Pragmatism in the Age of Jihad: The Precolonial State of Bunda* (Cambridge University Press, 1992).

12. For Malik Sy's (d. 1699) Bundu, see Gomez, *Pragmatism in the Age of Jihad*. For Ibrahim Sori's (d. 1791) Fuuta Jallon, Sulayman Bal's (d. 1776) Fuuta Tooro, and Usman Dan Fodio's (d. 1817) Sokoto Caliphate, see Yusufu Bala Usman, *Studies in the History of the Sokoto Caliphate*, (Ahmadu Bello University, 1979). For Ahmad Lobbo's (d. 1844) Masina Empire, see William A. Brown, "Toward a Chronology for the Caliphate of Hamdullahi (Māsina)," *Cahiers d'études africaines* 8, no. 31 (1968): 428–34; Bintou Sanankoua, *Un empire peul au XIXe siècle: La Diina du Maasina* (Karthala, 1990); Mauro Nobili, *Sultan, Caliph and the Renewer of the Faith: Ahmad Lobbo, the Tārīkh al-fattāsh and the Making of an Islamic State in West Africa* (Cambridge University Press, 2020);.
13. Franz Rosenthal, *Knowledge Triumphant: The Concept of Knowledge in Medieval Islam* (Brill, 2007).
14. Wael B. Hallaq, *Sharī'a: Theory, Practice, Transformations* (Cambridge University Press, 2009), 1–6.
15. Ahmet T. Karamustafa, *Sufism: The Formative Period* (University of California Press, 2007), 19–26.
16. See Mohamed Labib Nouhi, "Religion and Society in a Saharan Tribal Setting: Authority and Power in the Zwâya Religious Culture" (PhD diss., University of Alberta, 2009), 73–105, 134–49; Louis Brenner, "Concepts of Tariqa in West Africa: The Case of the Qadiriyya," in *Charisma and Brotherhood in African Islam*, ed. Donal B. Cruise O'Brien and Christian Coulon (Clarendon Press, 1988), 33–52; Aziz A. Batran, "Sīdī Al-Mukhtār Al-Kuntī and the Recrudescence of Islam in the Western Sahara and the Middle Niger, c. 1750–1811" (PhD diss., University of Birmingham, 1971). On the economic bases of Kunta authority, see E. Ann McDougall, "The Economics of Islam in Western Sahara: The Rise of the Kunta Clan," in *Rural and Urban Islam in West Africa*, ed. Nehemia Levtzion and Humphrey J. Fisher (Lynne Rienner, 1987), 39–54.
17. As Marcus-Sells has shown, *ṭarīqa* is a concept subject to historical change. In particular, exclusivity as a key marker of the corporate identity of Sufi orders, though taken for granted today, was not nearly as common in the nineteenth century, let alone the eighteenth. Ariela Marcus-Sells, *Sorcery or Science? Contesting Knowledge and Practice in West African Sufi Texts* (Pennsylvania State University Press, 2022), 46–53.
18. See the similar case of Shaykh Siddiya in C. C. Stewart, with E. K. Stewart, *Islam and Social Order in Mauritania: A Case Study from the Nineteenth Century* (Clarendon Press, 1973), 78–108, 109–30.
19. Muusa Kamara, *Florilège au Jardin de l'histoire des Noirs: Zuhūr al-basātīn* (CNRS Éditions, 1998), 317; Rudolph T. Ware III, *The Walking Qur'an: Islamic Education, Embodied Knowledge, and History in West Africa* (University of North Carolina Press, 2014), chap. 3.
20. Kamara, *Florilège au jardin de l'histoire des Noirs*, 317.
21. Kamara, *Florilège au jardin de l'histoire des Noirs*, 323.
22. Green, *A Fistful of Shells*; Lovejoy, *Jihād in West Africa During the Age of Revolutions*; Jean Schmitz, "Islamic Patronage and Republican Emancipation: The Slaves of

the Almaami in the Senegal River Valley," in *Reconfiguring Slavery*, ed. Benedetta Rossi (Liverpool University Press, 2009), 85–115, https://www.jstor.org/stable/j.ctt5vjf4h.12.
23. Tamba M'bayo, *Muslim Interpreters in Colonial Senegal, 1850-1920: Mediations of Knowledge and Power in the Lower and Middle Senegal River Valley* (Lexington, 2016), 39–46.
24. David Robinson, *The Holy War of Umar Tal: The Western Sudan in the Mid-Nineteenth Century* (Clarendon Press, 1985).
25. ʿUmar al-Fūtī Tāl, *Rimāḥ Ḥizb al-Raḥīm ʿalá Nuḥūr Ḥizb al-Rajīm* [Lances of the Party of the Merciful One against the Necks of the Party of the Accursed One] (Bayrūt: Kitāb - Nāshirūn, 2020); Farah El-Sharif, "Kitāb al-Rimāḥ of 'Umar Fūtī Tāl: Sealing Muhammadan Sainthood in Nineteenth Century West Africa"; John Hunwick, "An Introduction to the Tijani Path: Being an Annotated Translation of the Chapter Headings of the Kitab al-Rimah of al- Hajj 'Umar," *Islam et Sociétés Au Sud Du Sahara* 6 (1992): 17–32.
26. Iza R. Hussin, *The Politics of Islamic Law: Local Elites, Colonial Authority, and the Making of the Muslim State* (University of Chicago Press, 2016).
27. Donal B. Cruise O'Brien, *The Mourides of Senegal: The Political and Economic Organization of an Islamic Brotherhood* (Clarendon Press, 1971).
28. David Robinson, *Paths of Accommodation: Muslim Societies and French Colonial Authorities in Senegal and Mauritania, 1880-1920* (Ohio University Press, 2000).
29. Diop, "La vie et l'oeuvre de Cheikh Moussa Kamara de Ganguel," 24n1.
30. Diop, "La vie et l'oeuvre de Cheikh Moussa Kamara de Ganguel," 51–59.
31. Muusa Kamara, *Sheikh Moussa Kamara's Islamic Critique of Jihadists*, trans. Mbaye Lo (Lexington, 2023).
32. Barry, *Senegambia and the Atlantic Slave Trade*.
33. Leland C. Barrows, "Faidherbe and Senegal: A Critical Discussion," *African Studies Review* 19, no. 1 (1976): 95–117, https://doi.org/10.2307/523854.
34. Kazuo Kobayashi, *Indian Cotton Textiles in West Africa: African Agency, Consumer Demand and the Making of the Global Economy, 1750-1850* (Palgrave Macmillan, 2020); Jody Benjamin, *The Texture of Change: Dress, Self-Fashioning, and History in Western Africa, 1700-1850* (Ohio University Press, 2024).
35. Leland C. Barrows, "The Merchants and General Faidherbe: Aspects of French Expansion in Sénégal in the 1850's," *Revue française d'histoire d'outre-mer* 61, no. 223 (1974): 236–83, https://doi.org/10.3406/outre.1974.1757.
36. These reflections are greatly influenced by Timothy Mitchell, who argues that modernity is not simply a stage of historical development but the physical staging of difference. This difference takes two forms: the difference between the West and the rest, or the modern and the traditional on the one hand, and the difference between reality and its organization as a space of representation, on the other. Timothy Mitchell, *Colonising Egypt* (University of California Press, 1988), and *Questions of Modernity* (University of Minnesota Press, 2000).
37. Mitchell, *Colonising Egypt*.
38. Edward W. Said, *Orientalism* (Vintage Books, 1994), 77–83.
39. Said, *Orientalism*, 92–94.

INTRODUCTION

40. Gil Anidjar, "Secularism," *Critical Inquiry* 33, no. 1 (2006): 52–77, https://doi.org/10.1086/509746.
41. Hallaq uses the concept of an engineering project in contrast to the timeless representations of the Other in Saidian orientalism. For a brief discussion of the two endeavors and the parallels and departures, see Wael B. Hallaq, *Restating Orientalism: A Critique of Modern Knowledge* (Columbia University Press, 2018), 17; Edmund Burke III, *The Ethnographic State: France and the Invention of Moroccan Islam* (University of California Press, 2014), 6; Charles-Louis Balzac, François-Charles Cécile, and Gilbert-Joseph-Gaspard de Chabrol de Volvic, *Description de l'Egypte ou recueil des observations et des recherches qui ont été faites en Egypte pendant l'expédition de l'armée française* (Paris, 1809), http://ark.bnf.fr/ark:/12148/bpt6k53406479; Adolphe Hedwige Alphonse Delamare, *Exploration scientifique de l'Algérie pendant les années 1840, 1841, 1842, 1843, 1844 et 1845* (Paris, 1850), http://ark.bnf.fr/ark:/12148/bpt6k664958.
42. This reading is a literal one. Benjamin Claude Brower, *A Desert Named Peace: The Violence of France's Empire in the Algerian Sahara, 1844-1902* (Columbia University Press, 2011), 10, 11.
43. Said, *Orientalism*, 123–48.
44. Adolphe Hedwige Alphonse Delamare, *Exploration scientifique de l'Algérie pendant les années 1840, 1841, 1842, 1843, 1844 et 1845 : Archéologie* (Imprimerie Nationale, 1850).
45. Christopher Harrison, *France and Islam in West Africa, 1860-1960* (Cambridge University Press, 1988), 20.
46. Louis Faidherbe, quoted in William B. Cohen, *Rulers of Empire: The French Colonial Service in Africa* (Hoover Institution Press, 1971), 11.
47. Norbert Elias, *The Civilizing Process* (Blackwell, 1978).
48. Michel Foucault, *The Order of Things: An Archaeology of Human Sciences* (Knopf Doubleday, 2012), chap. 8; Said, *Orientalism*; James Turner, *Philology: The Forgotten Origins of the Modern Humanities* (Princeton University Press, 2014); Tomoko Masuzawa, *The Invention of World Religions: or, How European Universalism Was Preserved in the Language of Pluralism* (University of Chicago Press, 2005); Maurice Olender, *The Languages of Paradise: Race, Religion, and Philology in the Nineteenth Century* (Harvard University Press, 1992).
49. Roger Pasquier, "L'Influence de l'expérience algérienne sur la politique de la France au Sénégal (1842-1869)," in *Perspectives nouvelles sur le passé de l'Afrique noire et de Madagascar: Mélanges offerts à Hubert Deschamps* (Publications de la Sorbonne, 1974), 263–84.
50. For background on Faidherbe, see Barrows, "The Merchants and General Faidherbe," 236–83.
51. Amir Syed, "Al-Hājj Umar Tāl and the Realm of the Written: Mastery, Mobility and Islamic Authority in 19th Century West Africa" (PhD diss., University of Michigan, 2017), http://search.proquest.com/docview/1917831465/.
52. Paul Holle and Frédéric Carrère, *De la Sénégambie française* (Paris: Firmin-Didot frères, fils et cie, 1855), 195, 196, http://gallica.bnf.fr/ark:/12148/bpt6k57810629.
53. Claudine Gerresch, "Jugements du moniteur du Sénégal sur al-Hajj 'Umar, de 1857 à 1864," *Bulletin de l'Institut fondamental d'Afrique noire, Série B: Sciences humaines* 35, no. 3 (1973): 587.

INTRODUCTION

54. Gerresch, "Jugements du moniteur du Sénégal sur al-Hajj 'Umar."
55. This pattern was widespread throughout the colonial world. Hussin, *The Politics of Islamic Law*.
56. Mahmood Mamdani, *Good Muslim, Bad Muslim: America, the Cold War, and the Roots of Terror* (Pantheon, 2004).
57. James Philip Johnson, "The Almamate of Futa Toro, 1770–1836: A Political History" (PhD diss., University of Wisconsin, 1974); Constance Bernette Hilliard, "The Formation of the Islamic Clerisy of the Middle Valley of the Senegal River, c. 1670–c. 1770" (PhD diss., Harvard University, 1977); David Robinson, *Chiefs and Clerics: Abdul Bokar Kan and Futa Toro, 1853–1891* (Oxford University Press, 1975); Oumar Kane, "Le Fuuta-Tooro des satigi aux almaani: (1512–1807)" (Thèse de doctorat de 3è cycle, Université de Dakar, 1986); Mouhamed Moustapha Kane, "A History of Fuuta Tooro, 1890s–1920s: Senegal Under Colonial Rule; The Protectorate" (PhD diss., Michigan State University, 1987).
58. Amar Samb, *Essai sur la contribution du Sénégal à la littérature d'expression arabe* (Institut français d'Afrique noire, 1972); Vincent Monteil, *L'Islam noir: Une religion à la conquête de l'Afrique*, 3e éd. ref. (Seuil, 1980), http://hdl.handle.net/2027/mdp.39015002328121; El Hadji Ravane Mbaye, "L'Islam au Sénégal" (Thèse de doctorat de 3è cycle, Université de Dakar, 1976); Shārnū Kāh, *al-Shaykh Mūsá Kamara (1864-1945): Ḥayātuhu wa-Afkāruh*, (Īfān-Jamiʻat al-Shaykh Anta Jūb bi-Dakār, 2014).
59. Said Bousbina, "Musa Kamara, un savant 'autodidacte,'" *Islam et sociétés au sud du Sahara* 6 (1992): 75–81; Robinson, "Un historien et anthropologue sénégalais"; Anna Pondopoulo, "Une traduction 'mal partie' (1923–1945): Le 'zuhur al-basatin' de Cheikh Moussa Kamara," *Islam et sociétés au sud du Sahara*, no. 7 (1993): 95–110.
60. Kamara, *Florilège au jardin de l'histoire des Noirs*.
61. Shaykh Musa Kamara, *Zuhūr al-Basātīn fī tārīkh al-Sawādīn : Mudawwanat Shuʻūb Gharbī Ifrīqiyyā fī al-tārīkh wa-l-Ansāb wa-l-Anthrūbūlūjiyā* [Flowers from among the Gardens in the History of the Blacks: a historical, genealogical, and anthropological record of the peoples of West Africa], ed. Nacereddine Saidouni and Muawiya Saidouni (Al Babatain, 2010), http://archive.org/details/compressed_201910.
62. Shārnū Kāh, al-Shaykh Mūsá Kamara; Mbaye Lo, "Jihad as a Tradition of Peace in the Writings of Cheikh Moussa Kamara (1864–1945)," paper presented at the Islam and World Peace Conference, Columbia University, New York, September 12, 2015; Mbaye Lo, " 'The Last Scholar': Cheikh Moussa Kamara and the Condemnation of Jihad by the Sword," *Transcultural Islam Research Network* (blog), April 23, 2016, https://tirnscholars.org/2016/04/23/the-last-scholar-cheikh-moussa-kamara-andthe-condemnation-of-jihad-by-the-sword/index.html.
63. Diop, "La vie et l'oeuvre de Cheikh Moussa Kamara de Ganguel."
64. Harrison, *France and Islam in West Africa, 1860–1960*; Rüdiger Seesemann, "African Islam or Islam in Africa? Evidence from Kenya," in *The Global Worlds of the Swahili: Interfaces of Islam, Identity and Space in 19th- and 20th-Century East Africa*, ed. Roman Loimeier and Rüdiger Seesemann (Lit Verlag, 2006); Jean-Louis Triaud, "L'islam au sud du Sahara: Une saison orientaliste en Afrique occidentale: Constitution

d'un champ scientifique, héritages et transmissions," *Cahiers d'études africaines* 50, no. 198-200 (2010): 907-50; Robinson, *Paths of Accommodation*.

65. Cemil Aydin, *The Idea of the Muslim World: A Global Intellectual History* (Harvard University Press, 2017).

66. John Hunwick, "Sub-Saharan Africa and the Wider World of Islam: Historical and Contemporary Perspectives," *Journal of Religion in Africa* 26, no. 3 (1996): 230-57, https://doi.org/10.2307/1581644; Rüdiger Seesemann, *The Divine Flood: Ibrahim Niasse and the Roots of a Twentieth-Century Sufi Revival* (Oxford University Press, 2011); Ghislaine Lydon, *On Trans-Saharan Trails: Islamic Law, Trade Networks, and Cross-Cultural Exchange in Nineteenth-Century Western Africa* (Cambridge University Press, 2009); Scott Steven Reese, *Imperial Muslims: Islam, Community and Authority in the Indian Ocean, 1839-1937* (Edinburgh University Press, 2018); Roman Loimeier, *Muslim Societies in Africa: A Historical Anthropology* (Indiana University Press, 2013); Chanfi Ahmed, *West African "Ulamā" and Salafism in Mecca and Medina: Jawab al-Ifrīqī—The Response of the African* (Brill, 2015); Chanfi Ahmed, *AfroMecca in History: African Societies, Anti-Black Racism, and Teaching in al-Haram Mosque in Mecca* (Cambridge Scholars Publishing, 2019); Stefan Reichmuth, *The World of Murtada Al-Zabidi (1732-91): Life, Networks and Writings* (Gibb Memorial Trust, 2009); Zachary Valentine Wright, *Realizing Islam: The Tijāniyya in North Africa and the Eighteenth-Century Muslim World* (University of North Carolina Press, 2020), https://www.jstor.org/stable/10.5149/9781469660844_wright; Ousmane Kane, *Beyond Timbuktu: An Intellectual History of Muslim West Africa* (Harvard University Press, 2016); Cheikh Anta Babou, *The Muridiyya on the Move: Islam, Migration, and Place Making* (Ohio University Press, 2021).

67. Louis Brenner, *Controlling Knowledge: Religion, Power, and Schooling in a West African Muslim Society* (Indiana University Press, 2001); Ware, *The Walking Qur'an*; Kane, *Beyond Timbuktu*; Cheikh Anta Mbacké Babou, *Fighting the Greater Jihad: Amadu Bamba and the Founding of the Muridiyya of Senegal, 1853-1913* (Ohio University Press, 2007); Fallou Ngom, *Muslims Beyond the Arab World: The Odyssey of 'Ajamī and the Murīdiyya* (Oxford University Press, 2016).

68. P. F. de Moraes Farias, *Arabic Medieval Inscriptions from the Republic of Mali: Epigraphy, Chronicles and Songhay-Tuăreg History* (Oxford University Press, 2001).

69. Toby Green and Benedetta Rossi, eds., *Landscapes, Sources and Intellectual Projects of the West African Past: Essays in Honour of Paulo Fernando de Moraes Farias* (Brill, 2018); Mohamed Shahid Mathee, "The Kitab Al-Turjuman: A Twentieth-Century Historiographical (Re)Mapping of the Southern Sahara and Sahel," *The Journal of African History* 61, no. 3 (2020): 359-82, https://doi.org/10.1017/S0021853720000596; Mauro Nobili, *Sultan, Caliph and the Renewer of the Faith: Ahmad Lobbo, the Tārīkh al-fattāsh and the Making of an Islamic State in West Africa* (Cambridge University Press, 2020); Stephanie Zehnle, *A Geography of Jihad: Sokoto Jihadism and the Islamic Frontier in West Africa* (De Gruyter, 2020); Paul Naylor, *From Rebels to Rulers: Writing Legitimacy in the Early Sokoto State* (James Currey, 2021); Camille Lefèbvre, *Des pays au crépuscule* (Fayard, 2021).

70. Lamin Sanneh, "The Origins of Clericalism in West African Islam," *Journal of African History* 17, no. 1 (1976): 49-72; Louis Brenner, *West African Sufi: The Religious*

INTRODUCTION

Heritage and Spiritual Search of Cerno Bokar Saalif Taal (University of California Press, 1984); Babou, *Fighting the Greater Jihad*; Seesemann, *The Divine Flood*; Zachary Valentine Wright, *Living Knowledge in West African Islam: The Sufi Community of Ibrahim Niasse* (Brill, 2015); Ware, *The Walking Qur'an*; Kane, *Beyond Timbuktu*.

71. My approach is profoundly inspired by the one pioneered by Ronald A. T. Judy in *(Dis)Forming the American Canon: African-Arabic Slave Narratives and the Vernacular* (University of Minnesota Press, 1993).
72. Gayatri Chakravorty Spivak, *Death of a Discipline* (Columbia University Press, 2003).
73. David L. Szanton, "The Origin, Nature, and Challenge of Area Studies in the United States," in *The Politics of Knowledge: Area Studies and the Disciplines*, ed. David L. Szanton (University of California Press, 2004), 1–33.
74. Manan Ahmed Asif, "Technologies of Power—from Area Studies to Data Sciences," *Spheres: Journal for Digital Cultures*, no. 5 (2019): 1–13.
75. Fortunately, I somehow avoided the explicit ethical dilemmas that would have resulted from a Boren award, which requires a commitment to working in national security.
76. Cyril Lionel Robert James, *Black Studies and the Contemporary Student* (Friends of Facing Reality, 1969).
77. Stefano Harney and Fred Moten, *The Undercommons: Fugitive Planning and Black Study* (Minor Compositions, 2013).
78. Ali Al-Amin Mazrui, *The Africans: A Triple Heritage* (Little, Brown, 1986).
79. Ousmane Kane, *Intellectuels non Europhones*, Document de travail 2003, no. 1 (Codesria, 2003).
80. Spivak, *Death of a Discipline*, 9.
81. Tobias Warner, *The Tongue-Tied Imagination: Decolonizing Literary Modernity in Senegal* (Fordham University Press, 2019), https://muse.jhu.edu/book/63648/.
82. Annette Lienau, *Sacred Language, Vernacular Difference: Global Arabic and Counter-Imperial Literatures* (Princeton University Press, 2024).
83. Judy, *(Dis)Forming the American Canon*.
84. On the idea of reading as poaching, see Michel de Certeau, "Reading as Poaching," in *The Practice of Everyday Life*, trans. Steven Rendall (University of California Press, 1984), 165–76.
85. Muusa Kamara, *Tabshīr al-Khāʾif al-Ḥayrān wa Tadhkīruhu bi-Saʿa Raḥmat Allah al-Karīm al-Mannān* [The announcement of the good news to the fearful and confused and his reminder of the breadth of the mercy of God, the Generous Bestower], ed. Demba Tewe (al-Maʿhad al-Islāmī bi-Dakār, 2014); Muusa Kamara, *Akthar al-Rāghibīn fī al-Jihād baʿd al-Nabīʾīn man Yakhtāru al-Ẓuhūr wa-Malaka al-Bilād wa-lā Yubālī bi-man Halaka fī Jihādihi min al-ʿIbād* [Most of the Would-be Jihadists after the prophets are the ones who choose prevailing and dominion of the land and who do not care who perishes in his jihad from among the people] (Maʿhad al-Dirāsāt al-Ifrīqiyya, 2003); Kamara, *Sheikh Moussa Kamara's Islamic Critique of Jihadists*; Kamara, *Florilège au jardin de l'histoire des Noirs*; Kamara, *Zuhūr al-Basātīn fī Tārīkh al-Sawādīn*; Muusa Kamara, *Ashhá al-ʿUlūm wa-Aṭayab al-Khabar fī Sīrat al-Ḥājj ʿUmar* [The Most Delicious of Sciences and the Tastiest of the News in the Life of Hajj Umar], (Maʿhad al-Dirāsāt al-Ifrīqiyya, 2001).

86. Edward W. Said, *Beginnings: Intention and Method* (Basic Books, 1975).
87. James Turner, *Philology: The Forgotten Origins of the Modern Humanities* (Princeton University Press, 2015).
88. Maximillian Forte, "The Human Terrain System and Anthropology: A Review of Ongoing Public Debates," *American Anthropologist*, no. 1 (2011): 149–53.
89. Edward W. Said, "Return to Philology" in *Humanism and Democratic Criticism* (Columbia University Press, 2003), 57–84.

1. Beginnings: The Text, the World, and the Sufi

1. ʿAbd al-Wahhāb ibn Ahmad Shaʿrānī, *Laṭāʾif al-minan wa-al-akhlāq fī wujūb al-taḥadduth bi-niʿmat Allāh ʿalá al-iṭlāq* (Bayrūt: Dār al-Kutub al-ʿIlmīyah, 2015).
2. Muhammad ibn al-Mukhtar ibn Ahmad ibn Abi Bakr al-Kunti, *al-Ṭarāʾif wa-l-Talāʾid min Karāmāt al-Shaykhayn al-Wālida wa-l-Walāʾid*, http://gallica.bnf.fr/ark:/12148/btv1b10535164b; For information about this unpublished manuscript see Ariela Marcus-Sells, *Sorcery or Science? Contesting Knowledge and Practice in West African Sufi Texts* (Pennsylvania State University Press, 2022), 7, 19.
3. ʿUmar al-Fūtī Tāl, *Rimāḥ Ḥizb al-Raḥīm ʿalá Nuḥūr Ḥizb al-Rajīm* (Bayrūt: Kitāb - Nāshirūn, 2020), chap. 30.
4. Ibn ʿAṭāʾ Allāh al-Iskandari, *The Subtle Blessings in the Saintly Lives of Abu al-Abbas al-Mursi & His Master Abu al-Hasan al-Shadhili: Kitab Lataif Al-Minan fi Manaqib Abi al-Abbas al-Mursi Wa Shaykhihi Abi al-Hasan*, trans. Nancy Roberts (Fons Vitae, 2005).
5. Qurʾan 19:15, translation from Seyyed Hossein Nasr, ed., *The Study Quran: A New Translation and Commentary* (HarperOne, 2015), 768.
6. Qurʾan 19:33, translation from Nasr, *The Study Quran*, 772, 773.
7. Musa Kamara, *Tabshīr al-Khāʾif al-Ḥayrān wa Tadhkīruhu bi-Saʿa Raḥmat Allah al-Karīm al-Mannān* [The announcement of the good news to the fearful and confused and his reminder of the breadth of the mercy of God, the Generous Bestower], ed. Demba Tewe (al-Maʿhad al-Islāmī bi-Dakār), 2014), 1, 2.
8. There are two Arabic editions and one French edition of Kamara's autobiography available in Senegal. While the one published by Muhammad Saidou Bâ (2022) is of the best scholarly quality, I use the 2014 edition published by the Islamic Institute of Dakar as I only acquired the more recent text well after drafting much of this book. Kamara, *Tabshīr al-Khāʾif al-Ḥayrān* (2014); Musa Kamara, *L'Annonce de la Bonne Nouvelle à l'apeuré Désemparé et Rappel à Lui de l'amplitude de la Miséricorde de Dieu le Généreux Bienfaiteur* [The announcing of the good news to the frightened and helpless and reminder to him of the magnitude of the mercy of God the generous benefactor], trans. Demba Tewe, Cheikh Fall, Ismaila Diop, Alioune Diop, Babacar Niane, and Amadou Sokhna Ndao (Institute Islamique de Dakar, 2015); Musa Kamara, *Tabshīr al-Khāʾif al-Ḥayrān wa-Tadhkīruhu bi-Saʿa Raḥmat Allah al-Karīm al-Mannān* [The announcement of the good news to the fearful and confused and his reminder of the breadth of the mercy of God, the Generous Bestower], by Musa Kamara, ed. Muhammad Saʿīd Bāh (Manshūrāt Maktabat al-Shaykh Mūsá Aḥmad Kamara, 2022).

1. BEGINNINGS

9. Mana Kia, "Lingering with Adab Before Rushing to Literature," *History of Humanities* 9, no. 1 (2024): 65–79, https://doi.org/10.1086/729075.
10. Edward W. Said, *The World, the Text, and the Critic* (Harvard University Press, 1983), 1.
11. Terry Eagleton, *Literary Theory: An Introduction* (University of Minnesota Press, 1983); Raymond Williams, *Culture and Society* (Columbia University Press, 1958).
12. This is beginning to change with the exciting scholarly and literary interventions of Oludamini Ogunnaike and others. Oludamini Ogunnaike, *"Poetry in Praise of Prophetic Perfection: A Study of West African Arabic Madih Poetry and Its Precedents* (Islamic Texts Society, 2020).
13. Karin Barber, *The Anthropology of Texts, Persons and Publics: Oral and Written Culture in Africa and Beyond* (Cambridge University Press, 2007).
14. Walter J. Ong, *Orality and Literacy: The Technologizing of the Word* (Routledge, 2002), https://doi.org/10.4324/9780203426258; Jacques Derrida, "Signature Event Context," in *Margins of Philosophy* (University of Chicago Press, 1982), 307–30.
15. William A. Graham, "Basmala," in *Encyclopaedia of the Qur'an*, ed. Jane Dammen McAuliffe (Brill Academic, 2001), 1:207–12, https://link.gale.com/apps/doc/CX2686400077/GVRL?sid=bookmark-GVRL&xid=af21668b.
16. Edward W. Said, *Beginnings: Intention and Method* (Basic Books, 1975), 4–13.
17. J. L. Austin, *How to Do Things with Words: The William James Lectures Delivered at Harvard University in 1955*, 2nd ed., ed. J. O. Urmson and Marina Sbisà (Clarendon Press, 1975); Ruth H. Finnegan, *The Oral and Beyond: Doing Things with Words in Africa* (James Currey, 2007).
18. Waïl S. Hassan, translator's introduction to *Thou Shalt Not Speak My Language*, by Abdelfattah Kilito (Syracuse University Press, 2008), ix–xii, https://doi.org/10.2307/j.ctt1pk86bj.3; Abdelfattah Kilito, *Thou Shalt Not Speak My Language*, trans. Waïl S. Hassan (Syracuse University Press, 2008), 23–37.
19. Michael Cooperson, "Biographical Literature," in *Islamic Cultures and Societies to the End of the Eighteenth Century*, ed. Robert Irwin, vol. 4 of *The New Cambridge History of Islam* (Cambridge University Press, 2010), 458, https://doi.org/10.1017/CHOL9780521838245.020.
20. John Renard, *Tales of God's Friends: Islamic Hagiography in Translation* (University of California Press, 2009); Shahzad Bashir, *Sufi Bodies: Religion and Society in Medieval Islam* (Columbia University Press, 2011), https://doi.org/10.7312/bash14490.
21. Toni Morrison, *The Source of Self-Regard: Selected Essays, Speeches, and Meditations* (Knopf, 2019), 106.
22. Michael Winter, *Society and religion in early Ottoman Egypt: studies in the writings of 'Abd al-Wahhab al-Sharani* (Transaction Books, 1982).
23. Nile Green, *Sufism: A Global History* (Wiley-Blackwell, 2012), 8.
24. L. Gardet, "Karāma," in *Encyclopaedia of Islam*, vol. 4 (Brill, 1997), 615–16.
25. M. M. Bakhtin, *The Dialogic Imagination: Four Essays* (University of Texas Press, 2004).
26. Ronald B. Inden, *Querying the Medieval: Texts and the History of Practices in South Asia* (Oxford University Press, 2000), 13–15.

1. BEGINNINGS

27. Shahab Ahmed, *What Is Islam? The Importance of Being Islamic* (Princeton University Press, 2016), 356–62.
28. Ahmed, *What Is Islam?*, 357.
29. Eagleton, *Literary Theory*, 7.
30. Qurʾan 19:15 and 19:33, translation from Nasr, *The Study Quran*, 768, 772, and 773.
31. Kamara, *Tabshīr al-Khāʾif al-Ḥayrān wa Tadhkīruhu bi-Sāʿat Raḥmat Allāh al-Karīm al-Minān* (2014).
32. Mbaye Lo has proposed the elegant rendering of *tabshīr* as "herald." While this is a felicitous translation, I want to emphasize its status as a verbal noun, which "announcement" better reflects, as opposed to the more static noun "herald."
33. Ibrahima Thioub, *Le cheikh des deux rives: Actes du colloque international* (Presses universitaires de Dakar, 2017); David Robinson, *Paths of Accommodation: Muslim Societies and French Colonial Authorities in Senegal and Mauritania, 1880–1920* (Ohio University Press, 2000), 161–77.
34. On the theoretical fecundity that this practical problem raises, see Jacques Derrida, "Des Tours de Babel," in *Acts of Religion*, trans. Gil Anidjar (Routledge, 2001).
35. For the implications of this two-tiered relationship to language, see Lienau's great study on the global and regional implications for Arabophone literature. Annette Damayanti Lienau, *Sacred Language, Vernacular Difference: Global Arabic and Counter-Imperial Literatures* (Princeton University Press, 2024).
36. Musa Kamara, *al-Majmūʿ al-Nafīs Sirran wa-ʿalāniyya fī Dhikr Baʿḍ al-Sādāt al-Bīḍāniyya wa-l-Fulāniyya* [The precious collection of secrecy and publicity in the memory of some of the Bīḍān and Fulani nobles], ed. Nani Wuld al-Hassan (Manshūrāt al-Zaman, 2015); Constance Bernette Hilliard, "The Formation of the Islamic Clerisy of the Middle Valley of the Senegal River, c. 1670–c. 1770" (PhD diss., Harvard University, 1977).
37. Kamara, *Tabshīr al-Khāʾif al-Ḥayrān*, 3.
38. Renard, *Tales of God's Friends*, 152–55.
39. Ahmet T. Karamustafa, *Sufism: The Formative Period* (University of California Press, 2007), 1–7.
40. Shahzad Bashir, "Documenting the Living Dead," in *A New Vision for Islamic Pasts and Futures* (MIT Press, 2022), https://doi.org/10.26300/bdp.bashir.ipf.living-dead.
41. Irvin Cemil Schick, "Text," in *Key Themes for the Study of Islam* (Oneworld, 2010), 321–35, https://hdl.handle.net/2027/heb30809.0001.001.
42. Annemarie Schimmel, *As Through a Veil: Mystical Poetry in Islam* (Columbia University Press, 1982).
43. Shaykh Ibrahim Niasse, *The Removal of Confusion, Concerning the Flood of the Saintly Seal Ahmad Al-Tijani: A Translation of Kashif al-Ilbas an Fayda al-Khatm Abi' Abbas by . . . al-Hajj Ibrahim - b. 'Abd-Allah Niasse*, trans. Abdullahi El-Okene, Muhtar Holland, and Zachary Wright (Fons Vitae, 2010), xiv.
44. John William Johnson, *The Epic of Son-Jara: A West African Tradition* (Indiana University Press, 1986); Amadou Hampaté Bâ, *Kaïdara* (Three Continents Press, 1988);

Muusa Kamara, *Ashhá al-ʿUlūm wa-Aṭayab al-Khabar fī Sīrat al-Ḥājj ʿUmar* (Maʿhad al-Dirāsāt al-Ifrīqīya, 2001).

45. Tal Tamari, *Les castes de l'Afrique occidentale: Artisans et musiciens endogames* (Société d'ethnologie, 1997); Tal Tamari, "The Development of Caste Systems in West Africa," *Journal of African History* 32, no. 2 (1991): 221–50, https://doi.org/10.1017/S0021853700025718.
46. Hampâté Bâ describes a similar relationship explored by Jeppie between his guide Tierno Bokar and the traditional healer. Shamil Jeppie, "History for Timbuktu: Aḥmad Bulʿarāf, Archives, and the Place of the Past," *History in Africa* 38, no. 1 (2011): 401–16; Amadou Hampâté Bâ, *A Spirit of Tolerance: The Inspiring Life of Tierno Bokar* (World Wisdom, 2008).
47. Perhaps the best example of this is Siré Abbas Soh, discussed in chapter 4. He was a noted genealogist who produced on command two manuscripts that would later be rendered into a chronicle with the effort of a colonial intervention. Siré-Abbâs-Soh, *Chroniques du Foûta sénégalais* (Ernest Leroux, 1913).
48. Rudolph T. Ware III, *The Walking Qurʾan: Islamic Education, Embodied Knowledge, and History in West Africa* (University of North Carolina Press, 2014).
49. Nehemia Levtzion and J. F. P. Hopkins, eds., *Corpus of Early Arabic Sources for West African History*, trans. J. F. P. Hopkins (Cambridge University Press, 1981), 296.
50. Ware, *The Walking Qurʾan*.
51. Kamara, *Tabshīr al-Khāʾif al-Ḥayrān* (2014), 4.
52. Johannes Pedersen, *The Arabic Book* (Princeton University Press, 1984), 101–2.
53. Qurʾan 96:1–5, translation from Nasr, *The Study Quran*, 1537.
54. Bruce Hall and Charles C. Stewart, "The Historic 'Core Curriculum,' and the Book Market in Islamic West Africa," in *The Trans-Saharan Book Trade: Arabic Literacy, Manuscript Culture, and Intellectual History in Islamic Africa*, ed. Graziano Krätli and Ghislaine Lydon (Brill, 2011), 109–74.
55. Ḥarīrī, *Maqāmāt Abī Zayd al-Sarūjī*, ed. Michael Cooperson and Devin J. Stewart (New York University Press, 2020), and *Impostures*, trans. Michael Cooperson (New York University Press, 2020).
56. Rita Felski, *The Limits of Critique* (University of Chicago Press, 2015), chap. 1.
57. ʿUmar al-Fūtī Tāl, *Rimāḥ Ḥizb al-Raḥīm ʿalá Nuḥūr Ḥizb al-Rajīm*; Farah El-Sharif, "Kitāb al-Rimāḥ of ʿUmar Fūtī Tāl: Sealing Muhammadan Sainthood in Nineteenth Century West Africa"; John Hunwick, "An Introduction to the Tijani Path: Being an Annotated Translation of the Chapter Headings of the Kitab al-Rimah of al- Hajj 'Umar," *Islam et Sociétés Au Sud Du Sahara* 6 (1992): 17–32; John Hunwick, "An Introduction to the Tijani Path: Being an Annotated Translation of the Chapter Headings of the Kitab al-Rimah of al- Hajj 'Umar," *Islam et sociétés au sud du Sahara* 6 (1992): 17–32; M. Hiskett, "Material Relating to the State of Learning Among the Fulani Before Their Jihād," *Bulletin of the School of Oriental and African Studies, University of London* 19, no. 3 (1957): 550–78; Ronald A. T. Judy, *(Dis)Forming the American Canon: African-Arabic Slave Narratives and the Vernacular* (University of Minnesota Press, 1993).
58. Hans-Georg Gadamer, *Truth and Method* (Continuum, 2004), 268–306.
59. "Fiche de Renseignements," Archives nationales du Sénégal 13 G 6 (17), Dakar.

2. A Degree of Prophecy

1. Said Bousbina, "Musa Kamara, un savant 'autodidacte,'" *Islam et sociétés au sud du Sahara* 6 (1992): 75–81.
2. Amar Samb, *Essai sur la contribution du Sénégal à la littérature d'expression arabe* (Institut fondamental d'Afrique noire, 1972); Bousbina, "Musa Kamara, un savant 'autodidacte'"; Abdoul Malal Diop, "La vie et l'oeuvre de Cheikh Moussa Kamara de Ganguel (1864–1945)" (PhD thesis, Université de Cheikh Anta Diop, 2014); Jean Schmitz, "Introduction," in *Florilège au jardin de l'histoire des Noirs: Zuhūr al-basātīn* (CNRS Éditions, 1998), 9–79; David Robinson, "Un historien et anthropologue sénégalais: Shaikh Musa Kamara" *Cahiers d'études africaines* 28, no. 109 (1988): 89–116; Mbaye Lo, "The Scholar, His Time, and His Work: Sheikh Moussa Kamara; A Life of Scholarship," in *Sheikh Moussa Kamara's Islamic Critique of Jihadists*, by Moussa Kamara, ed. and trans. Mbaye Lo (Lexington, 2023), 3–30.
3. Shārnū Kāh, *al-Shaykh Mūsá Kamara (1864–1945): Ḥayātuhu wa-Afkāruh* (Īfān-Jamiʿat al-Shaykh Anta Jūb bi-Dakār, 2014); Muhammad Saʿīd Bāh, "Muqaddima al-Mahquq," in *Tabshīr al-Khāʾif al-Ḥayrān wa-Tadhkīruhu bi-Saʿa Raḥmat Allah al-Karīm al-Mannān* [The announcement of the good news to the fearful and confused and his reminder of the breadth of the mercy of God, the Generous Bestower], by Musa Kamara, ed. Muhammad Saʿīd Bāh (Manshūrāt Maktabat al-Shaykh Mūsá Aḥmad Kamara, 2022).
4. Two exceptions come to mind. As discussed in chapter 6, recent work by Thierno Kâ has highlighted this more religious dimension of Kamara. Also, Joseph Hill mentions Kamara's dream in passing even though Kamara is not the focus of his work. In his discussion of female Islamic leaders in a Tijani Sufi movement, Hill refers to Kamara's dream of Hajj Umar Tal, discussed in the following section as an example of dreams as a legitimate source of knowledge in the regional and broader tradition. Shārnū Kāh, *al-Shaykh Mūsá Kamara (1864–1945)*; Joseph Hill, *Wrapping Authority: Women Islamic Leaders in a Sufi Movement in Dakar, Senegal* (University of Toronto Press, 2018), 36, https://doi.org/10.3138/9781487517014.
5. Rita Felski, *The Limits of Critique* (University of Chicago Press, 2015), 14–51.
6. Katherine P. Ewing, "Dreams from a Saint: Anthropological Atheism and the Temptation to Believe," *American Anthropologist* 96, no. 3 (1994): 571–83.
7. Djibril Samb, *L'interprétation des rêves dans la région Sénégambienne suivi de la clef des songes de la Sénégambie, de l'Egypte pharaonique et de la tradition islamique* (Nouvelles éditions africaines du Sénégal, 1998), 79–168.
8. Muusa Kamara, *Ashhá al-ʿulūm wa-Aṭayab al-Khabar fī Sīrat al-Ḥājj ʿUmar* (Maʿhad al-Dirāsāt al-Ifrīqīya, 2001); Muusa Kamara, *La vie d'el-Hadji Omar*, trans. Amar Samb (Éditions Hilal, 1975).
9. Kamara, *Ashhá al-ʿulūm wa-Aṭayab al-Khabar fī Sīrat al-Ḥājj ʿUmar*, 23.
10. Elizabeth Sirriyeh, *Dreams and Visions in the World of Islam: A History of Muslim Dreaming and Foreknowing* (I. B. Tauris, 2015), 5–8, https://doi.org/10.5040/9780755623655. Sirriyeh reflects on the question of whether a dream is true in the introduction to her synthetic overview of dreams and visions in the Islamic

2. A DEGREE OF PROPHECY

tradition. She shows that this question has often framed the way modern scholars have dealt with the appearance of dreams in a diversity of historical contexts. She concludes that it is impossible to know if a dream is authentic, even as we might come up with reasons for an actual vision or its fabrication that seek to explain it, and therefore settles the matter with a simple word of caution.

11. John Renard, *Friends of God: Islamic Images of Piety, Commitment, and Servanthood* (University of California Press, 2008), 67–89, https://doi.org/10.1525/9780520940956.
12. David Robinson, *Paths of Accommodation: Muslim Societies and French Colonial Authorities in Senegal and Mauritania, 1880-1920* (Ohio University Press, 2000), 167–77; Ibrahima Thioub, ed., *Le cheikh des deux rives: Actes du Colloque international* (Presses universitaires de Dakar, 2017).
13. David Robinson, *The Holy War of Umar Tal: The Western Sudan in the Mid-Nineteenth Century* (Clarendon Press, 1985).
14. Boubacar Barry, *Senegambia and the Atlantic Slave Trade* (Cambridge University Press, 1998); Toby Green, *A Fistful of Shells: West Africa from the Rise of the Slave Trade to the Age of Revolution* (University of Chicago Press, 2021); Paul E. Lovejoy, *Jihād in West Africa During the Age of Revolutions* (Ohio University Press, 2016); James L. A. Webb, *Desert Frontier: Ecological and Economic Change Along the Western Sahel, 1600-1850* (University of Wisconsin Press, 1995).
15. Robinson, *The Holy War of Umar Tal*.
16. Mouhamed Moustapha Kane, "A History of Fuuta Tooro, 1890s–1920s: Senegal Under Colonial Rule; The Protectorate" (PhD diss., Michigan State University, 1987); John H. Hanson, *Migration, Jihad, and Muslim Authority in West Africa: The Futanke Colonies in Karta* (Indiana University Press, 1996).
17. Muusa Kamara, *Akthar al-Rāghibīn fī al-Jihād baʿd al-Nabīʾīn man Yakhtāru al-Ẓuhūr wa-Malaka al-Bilād wa-lā Yubālī bi-man Halaka fī Jihādihi min al-ʿIbād* [Most of the Would-be Jihadists after the prophets are the ones who choose prevailing and dominion of the land and who do not care who perishes in his jihad from among the people] (Maʿhad al-Dirāsāt al-Ifrīqiyya, 2003), 48–62; Mbaye Lo, "Jihad as a Tradition of Peace in the Writings of Cheikh Moussa Kamara (1864-1945)," paper presented at the Islam and World Peace Conference, Columbia University, New York, September 12, 2015); Moussa Kamara, *Sheikh Moussa Kamara's Islamic Critique of Jihadists*, trans. Mbaye Lo (Lexington, 2023).
18. Dwight F. Reynolds, ed., *Interpreting the Self: Autobiography in the Arabic Literary Tradition* (University of California Press, 2001), 88–93.
19. See the previous chapter for a discussion of textual beginnings as objects worthy of critical attention.
20. Annemarie Schimmel, *Mystical Dimensions of Islam* (University of North Carolina Press, 1975), 382.
21. My thinking about presence is affected by Haeri's reflections on presence and meaning in the study of religion. Niloofar Haeri, *Say What Your Longing Heart Desires: Women, Prayer, and Poetry in Iran* (Stanford University Press, 2021), 64–68, https://doi.org/10.1515/9781503614253.
22. I am grateful to Ariela Marcus-Sells for bringing this to my attention.

2. A DEGREE OF PROPHECY

23. Musa Kamara, *Tabshīr al-Khāʾif al-Ḥayrān wa Tadhkīruhu bi-Saʿa Raḥmat Allah al-Karīm al-Mannān* [The announcement of the good news to the fearful and confused and his reminder of the breadth of the mercy of God, the Generous Bestower], ed. Demba Tewe (al-Maʿhad al-Islāmī bi-Dakār, 2014), 9, 10.
24. We can consider this image of facing and drawing close to the Prophet to be a motif of Sufi writing. Hajj Umar writes similarly of his visit to the Prophet's tomb in Medina during the composition of one of his first poems. Claudine Gerresch-Dekais, "Tadkirat Al-Mustarsidin Wa Falâh at-Tâlibîn, Épître d'Al-Hâjj Umar Tâl: Introduction, Édition Critique Du Texte Arabe et Traduction Annotée," *Tadkirat Al-Mustarsidin Wa Falâh at-Tâlibîn, Épître d'Al-Hâjj Umar Tâl. Introduction, Édition Critique Du Texte Arabe et Traduction Annotée* 42, no. 3 (1980): 524–53; Amir Syed, "Al-Ḥājj Umar Tāl and the Realm of the Written: Mastery, Mobility and Islamic Authority in 19th Century West Africa" (PhD diss., University of Michigan, 2017), 87–110, http://search.proquest.com/docview/1917831465/; Wendell Hassan Marsh, "Compositions of Sainthood: The Biography of Ḥājj ʿUmar Tāl by Shaykh Mūsā Kamara" (PhD diss., Columbia University, 2018), 76, https://doi.org/10.7916/D81G23P4.
25. Vincent J. Cornell, *Realm of the Saint: Power and Authority in Moroccan Sufism* (University of Texas Press, 1998), xvii–xxi.
26. Muhammad Al-Bukhari, Sahih al-Bukhari, vol. 9, bk. 87, 144.
27. Sirriyeh, *Dreams and Visions in the World of Islam*, 62.
28. Al-Bukhari, Sahih al-Bukhari, vol. 9, bk. 87, 119.
29. Kamara, *Tabshīr Al-Khāʾif al-Ḥayrān*, 10.
30. Robinson, *Paths of Accommodation*, 161–77; Thioub, *Le cheikh des Deux rives*.
31. Glen Wade McLaughlin, "Sufi, Saint, Sharif: Muhammad Fadil Wuld Mamin; His Spiritual Legacy, and the Political Economy of the Sacred in Nineteenth Century Mauritania" (PhD diss., Northwestern University, 1997), ProQuest (9731303).
32. Ariela Marcus-Sells, *Sorcery or Science? Contesting Knowledge and Practice in West African Sufi Texts* (Pennsylvania State University Press, 2022).
33. As Marcus-Sells has shown, exclusivity as a key marker of the corporate identity of Sufi orders, taken for granted today, was not nearly as common in the nineteenth century. My work suggests that this might even be true well into the colonial period in which Kamara lived. Marcus-Sells, *Sorcery or Science?*, 46–53.
34. McLaughlin, "Sufi, Saint, Sharif," 189. McLaughlin cites a biography of Saʿad Buh that identified some two hundred Biḍan Sufi disciples, and some three thousand among the Blacks of the region: Muhammad Yuslih ibn al-Imana, "Hayat al-Shaykh Saʿad Buh b, Muhammad Fadel b. Mamin. 16.
35. Robinson, *Paths of Accommodation*, 175, 176.
36. Kamara, *Tabshīr al-Khāʾif al-Ḥayrān*, 2.
37. Kamara, *Tabshīr al-Khāʾif al-Ḥayrān*, 5.
38. Shahzad Bashir, *The Market in Poetry in the Persian World* (Cambridge University Press, 2021).
39. Mana Kia, "Lingering with Adab Before Rushing to Literature," *History of Humanities* 9, no. 1 (2024): 67, https://doi.org/10.1086/729075.
40. Kamara, *Tabshīr al-Khāʾif al-Ḥayrān*, 5.

41. Another factor that one of the anonymous reviewers suggested is worth mentioning. Saʿad Buh was well aware of his visibility to colonial officials and may have wanted to discourage the growth of an entourage just outside the colonial town.
42. ʿUmar ʿAbd al-Razzāq Naqar, *The Pilgrimage Tradition in West Africa: An Historical Study with Special Reference to the Nineteenth Century* (Khartoum University Press, 1972); Ousmane Oumar Kane, "The Transformation of the Pilgrimage Tradition in West Africa," in *Islamic Scholarship in Africa: New Directions and Global Contexts*, ed. Ousmane Oumar Kane (Boydell & Brewer, 2021), 90–110, https://doi.org/10.1017/9781787446076.007.
43. Robinson, *The Holy War of Umar Tal*; Syed, "Al-Ḥājj Umar Tāl and the Realm of the Written."
44. Kamara, *Tabshīr al-Khāʾif al-Ḥayrān*, 6.
45. Kamara, *Tabshīr al-Khāʾif al-Ḥayrān*, 6.
46. *Lahib ar-Rushd wa as-Saʾada wa Nayl al-Husna wa az-Ziyada fi as-Salat ʿala Ṣāḥib as-Siyada; Kitab az-Zuhd fi Damm ad-Dunya wa Mujibat al-buʿd.*
47. Kamara, *Tabshīr al-Khāʾif al-Ḥayrān*, 6.
48. Kamara, *Tabshīr al-Khāʾif al-Ḥayrān*, 27, 28.
49. Kamara, *Tabshīr al-Khāʾif al-Ḥayrān*, 45.
50. For an insightful examination of the history of talismanic writing as a social practice in the Saharan West, see Erin Pettigrew, *Invoking the Invisible in the Sahara: Islam, Spiritual Mediation, and Social Change* (Cambridge University Press, 2023), 4–11.
51. Kamara, *Tabshīr al-Khāʾif al-Ḥayrān*, 15–22.
52. *Musa Kamara, Dalil as-Salik ʿala Maʿani Alfiyyat Ibn Malik*, n.d. (Dakar: Institut Fondamental d'Afrique Noire, n.d.), Cahier 7, Fonds Kamara. On the *Alfiyya*, see Sidney Glazer, "The Alfiyya of Ibn Malik," *Muslim World* 31, no. 3 (1941): 274–79.
53. Kamara, *Tabshīr al-Khāʾif al-Ḥayrān*, 17.
54. Kamara, *Tabshīr al-Khāʾif al-Ḥayrān*, 17.
55. Diop, "La vie et l'oeuvre de Cheikh Moussa Kamara de Ganguel," 24n1. The source for this story is an oral informant, Malal Seriba Thioub (1916–1998), a former mayor of Matam. Separately, Diop informs us that Kamara stopped smoking in 1912 (47).
56. Kamara, *Tabshīr al-Khāʾif al-Ḥayrān*, 12.

3. Islam Noir: Surveillance Ethnography and the Politics of Representation

1. David Robinson, "Un historien et anthropologue sénégalais: Shaikh Musa Kamara," *Cahiers d'études africaines* 28, no. 109 (1988): 97.
2. Archives nationales de Mauritania, El-52 Gorgol, "Rapports du cercle 1913–1919" (Rapport de tournee du 17/5/1913), cited and translated in Mouhamed Moustapha Kane, "A History of Fuuta Tooro, 1890s–1920s: Senegal Under Colonial Rule; The Protectorate" (PhD diss., Michigan State University, 1987), 190.

3. ISLAM NOIR

3. I take "problem-space" from David Scott for whom it is "an ensemble of questions and answers around which a horizon of identifiable stakes (conceptual as well as ideological-political stakes) hangs. What defines this discursive context are not only the particular problems that get posed as problems as such (the problem of 'race,' say), but the particular questions that seem worth asking and the kinds of answers that seem worth having." David Scott, *Conscripts of Modernity: The Tragedy of Colonial Enlightenment* (Duke University Press, 2004), 4. I take from David Scott also the directive to engage with theories of the political as the central task of criticism *after* postcoloniality. David Scott, *Refashioning Futures: Criticism after Postcoloniality* (Princeton University Press, 1999).
4. Abdoul Malal Diop, "La vie et l'oeuvre de Cheikh Moussa Kamara de Ganguel (1864–1945)" (PhD thesis, Université de Cheikh Anta Diop, 2014), 41.
5. Nehemia Levtzion, *Ancient Ghana and Mali* (Methuen, 1973).
6. David Robinson, *Chiefs and Clerics: Abdul Bokar Kan and Futa Toro, 1853–1891* (Oxford University Press, 1975); Kane, "A History of Fuuta Tooro, 1890s–1920s," 23–28.
7. Jean Schmitz, introduction to *Florilège au jardin de l'histoire des Noirs: Zuhūr al-basātīn*, by Muusa Kamara (CNRS Éditions, 1998), 28.
8. Kane, "A History of Fuuta Tooro, 1890s–1920s," 187.
9. These reflections are greatly influenced by Timothy Mitchell, who argues that modernity is not simply a stage of historical development but also the physical staging of difference. This difference takes two forms: the difference between the West and the rest, or the modern and the traditional, on the one hand, and the difference between reality and its organization as a space of representation, on the other. Timothy Mitchell, *Colonising Egypt* (University of California Press, 1988), and *Questions of Modernity* (University of Minnesota Press, 2000).
10. Robinson, *Chiefs and Clerics*; A. S. Kanya-Forstner, *The Conquest of the Western Sudan: A Study in French Military Imperialism* (Cambridge University Press, 1969).
11. John H. Hanson, *Migration, Jihad, and Muslim Authority in West Africa: The Futanke Colonies in Karta* (Indiana University Press, 1996); John Hanson, *After the Jihad: The Reign of Ahmad Al-Kabir in the Western Sudan* (Michigan State University Press, 1991).
12. For a comparative perspective of how this worked in British Africa and a meticulous delineation of the process of making a colonial "Islamic law" see Rabiat Akande, *Entangled Domains: Empire, Law and Religion in Northern Nigeria* (Cambridge University Press, 2023).
13. Mahmood Mamdani, *Citizen and Subject* (Princeton University Press) 17, 37–67.
14. Mahmood Mamdani, *Good Muslim, Bad Muslim: America, the Cold War, and the Roots of Terror* (Pantheon, 2004).
15. Christopher Harrison, *France and Islam in West Africa, 1860–1960* (Cambridge University Press, 1988), 49–56.
16. Edmund Burke III, *The Ethnographic State: France and the Invention of Moroccan Islam* (University of California Press, 2014), 43.
17. Alice L. Conklin, *In the Museum of Man: Race, Anthropology, and Empire in France, 1850–1950* (Cornell University Press, 2013), https://doi.org/10.7591/j.ctt32b4r8.
18. Burke, *The Ethnographic State*; Jonathan Wyrtzen, *Making Morocco: Colonial Intervention and the Politics of Identity* (Cornell University Press, 2016), https://doi

.org/10.7591/j.ctt18kr50m; Baz Lecocq, "Distant Shores: A Historiographic View on Trans-Saharan Space," *Journal of African History* 56, no. 1 (2015): 23-36, https://doi.org/10.1017/S0021853714000711.
19. Wyrtzen, *Making Morocco*, 72-78.
20. Douglas W. Leonard, *Anthropology, Colonial Policy and the Decline of French Empire in Africa* (Bloomsbury Academic, 2020); Paul Marty, *Études sur l'islam au Sénégal* (Paris: Ernest Leroux, 1917).
21. Hanretta perceptively describes this competition and the ways that it shaped the fortunes of one of Kamara's contemporaries, Yacouba Sylla. Sean Hanretta, *Islam and Social Change in French West Africa: History of an Emancipatory Community* (Cambridge University Press, 2009), 121-50.
22. Kane, "A History of Fuuta Tooro," 187.
23. Diop, "La vie et l'oeuvre de Cheikh Moussa Kamara de Ganguel," 22-33.
24. Harrison, *France and Islam in West Africa*, 40.
25. Harrison, *France and Islam in West Africa*, 20-23; Octave Depont and Xavier Coppolani, *Les confréries religieuses musulmanes* (Algiers, 1897), https://gallica.bnf.fr/ark:/12148/bpt6k81468k.
26. Harrison, *France and Islam in West Africa*, 39, 40.
27. Arnaud is best known for his influence on colonial Muslim policy and as the founding author of a distinct school of French Algerian literature under the pen name of Robert Randau. Anna Pondopoulo, "Amadou Hampâté Bâ and the Writer Robert Arnaud (Randau): African Colonial Service and Literature," *Islamic Africa* 1, no. 2 (2010): 229-47, https://doi.org/10.5192/215409910794105823; Harrison, *France and Islam in West Africa*, 43-47; David Robinson, *Paths of Accommodation: Muslim Societies and French Colonial Authorities in Senegal and Mauritania, 1880-1920* (Ohio University Press, 2000), 72, 73.
28. Robert Arnaud, *Précis de politique musulmane* (Alger: A. Jourdan, 1906).
29. Arnaud, *Précis de politique musulmane*, 178.
30. Robinson, *Paths of Accommodation*, 39.
31. Robert Arnaud, *L'islam et la politique musulmane française en Afrique occidentale française* (Comité de l'Afrique française, 1912), 119-20, https://hdl.handle.net/2027/mdp.39015011952879.
32. Arnaud, *L'islam et la politique musulmane française en Afrique occidentale française*, 82.
33. Arnaud, *L'islam et la politique musulmane française en Afrique occidentale française*, 122.
34. Robinson, *Paths of Accommodation*, 172,173.
35. Paul Marty, *Études sur l'islam en Côte d'Ivorie* (Ernest Leroux, 1922); *Études sur l'islam au Sénégal*; *L'islam et les tribus dans la colonie du Niger* (P. Geuthner, 1930); *Études sur l'islam au Dahomey: Le bas Dahomey, le haut Dahomey* (Ernest Leroux, 1926); *Les tribus de la haute Mauritanie* (Comité de l'Afrique française, 1915); *Études sur l'islam maure: Cheikh Sidïa; Les Fadelia; Les Ida Ou Ali* (Ernest Leroux, 1916); *Études sur l'islam et les tribus du Soudan*, vol. 2 (Ernest Leroux, 1920), https://hdl.handle.net/2027/wu.89012185724; *L'islam en Guinée: Fouta-Diallon* (Ernest Leroux, 1921); *Études sur l'islam et les tribus maures: Les Brakna* (Ernest Leroux, 1921), https://hdl.handle.net/2027/mdp.39015027030322; and *L'émirat des Trarzas* (Ernest Leroux, 1919), http://ark.bnf.fr/ark:/12148/bpt6k6540894b.

36. Harrison, *France and Islam in West Africa*.
37. Paul Marty, *Les mourides d'Amadou Bamba*, cited in Harrison, *France and Islam in West Africa*, 116.
38. Jean-Louis Triaud, "Islam in Africa Under French Colonial Rule," in *The History of Islam in Africa*, ed. Nehemia Levtzion and Randall Lee Pouwels (Ohio University Press, 2000), 169–87. On the notion of world religion and its relationship to philology, see Tomoko Masuzawa, *The Invention of World Religions: or, How European Universalism Was Preserved in the Language of Pluralism* (University of Chicago Press, 2005).
39. Mamadou Diouf, "The French Colonial Policy of Assimilation and the Civility of the Originaires of the Four Communes (Senegal): A Nineteenth Century Globalization Project," *Development and Change* 29, no. 4 (1998): 671–96, https://doi.org/10.1111/1467-7660.00095.
40. Alfred Le Chatelier, *L'islam dans l'Afrique occidentale* (Paris : G. Steinhall, 1899), 348, cited in Triaud, "Islam in Africa," 173.
41. Harrison, *France and Islam in West Africa*, 50, 73.
42. Kathleen Davis, *Periodization and Sovereignty: How Ideas of Feudalism and Secularization Govern the Politics of Time* (Philadelphia: University of Pennsylvania Press, 2008); André Cabanis, "La métaphore féodale dans l'interprétation par le colonisateur du régime foncier traditionnel," in *Mélanges en hommage à André Cabanis* (Presses de l'Université Toulouse Capitole, 2021), 643–51, https://doi.org/10.4000/books.putc.9869.
43. E. Ann McDougall, "Discourse and Distortion: Critical Reflections on Studying the Saharan Slave Trade," *Outre-mers: Revue d'histoire* 89, no. 336-337 (2002): 195–227, https://doi.org/10.3406/outre.2002.3990.
44. Marty, *Études sur l'islam au Sénégal*, 29.
45. Rudolph T. Ware III, *The Walking Qur'an: Islamic Education, Embodied Knowledge, and History in West Africa* (University of North Carolina Press, 2014), 20.
46. For an argument about the relatively recent development of the notion of the exclusivity of Sufi orders, see Ariela Marcus-Sells, *Sorcery or Science? Contesting Knowledge and Practice in West African Sufi Texts* (Pennsylvania State University Press, 2022), 10, 11, 46–53.
47. Moustapha Ndiaye, "Rapports entre Qadirites et Tijanites au Fouta Toro aux XIXe et XXe siècles à travers Al-Haqq Al-Mubin de Cheikh Moussa Kamara," *Bulletin de l'Institut fondamental d'Afrique noire, Série B: Sciences humaines* 41, no. 1 (1979): 190–207.
48. Louis Brenner, *West African Sufi: The Religious Heritage and Spiritual Search of Cerno Bokar Saalif Taal* (University of California Press, 1984), 32–59.
49. Edward W. Said, *Orientalism* (Vintage, 1994), 20–22.
50. G. Wesley Johnson, *The Emergence of Black Politics in Senegal: The Struggle for Power in the Four Communes, 1900-1920* (Stanford University Press, 1971).
51. Mahmood Mamdani, *Citizen and Subject: Contemporary Africa and the Legacy of Late Colonialism* (Princeton University Press, 1996), 82–86.
52. Abdou Salam Kane, "Du régime des terres chez les populations du Fouta sénégalais," *Bulletin du Comité d'études historiques et scientifiques de l'Afrique occidentale française* 18 (1935): 449–61.

3. ISLAM NOIR

53. David Scott, *Refashioning Futures: Criticism After Postcoloniality* (Princeton University Press, 1999).
54. Mbaye Lo, "The Scholar, His Time, and His Work: Sheikh Moussa Kamara; A Life of Scholarship," in *Sheikh Moussa Kamara's Islamic Critique of Jihadists*, trans. Mbaye Lo (Lexington, 2023), 18.
55. Wendell Hassan Marsh, "Compositions of Sainthood: The Biography of Ḥājj ʿUmar Tāl by Shaykh Mūsā Kamara" (PhD thesis, Columbia University, 2018), https://doi.org/10.7916/D81G23P4; Muusa Kamara, *Ashhá al-ʿUlūm wa-Aṭayab al-Khabar fī Sīrat al-Ḥājj ʿUmar* [The most delicious of the sciences and the tastiest of the news in the life of Hajj Umar] (Maʿhad al-Dirāsāt al-Ifrīqiyya, 2001).
56. This close reading uses Lo's English translation of Kamara, *Sheikh Moussa Kamara's Islamic Critique of Jihadists*. See also Muusa Kamara, *Akthar Al-Rāghibīn: fī al-Jihād Baʿd al-Nabīʾīn man Yakhtāru al Ẓuhūr wa-Malaka al-Bilād wa-Lā Yubālī bi-man Halaka fī Jihādihi min al-ʿibād* [Most of the would-be jihadists after the prophets are the ones who choose prevailing and dominion of the land and who do not care who perishes in his jihad from among the people] (Maʿhad al-Dirāsāt al-Ifrīqīyah, 2003).
57. Lo, "The Scholar, His Time, and His Work," 20, 25.
58. Talal Asad, *Formations of the Secular: Christianity, Islam, Modernity* (Stanford University Press, 2003).
59. Hent de Vries and Lawrence Eugene Sullivan, *Political Theologies: Public Religions in a Post-Secular World* (Fordham University Press, 2006).
60. Wilfred Cantwell Smith, *The Meaning and End of Religion* (New American Library, 1964); Rushain Abbasi, "Did Premodern Muslims Distinguish the Religious and Secular? The Dīn-Dunyā Binary in Medieval Islamic Thought," *Journal of Islamic Studies* 31, no. 2 (2020): 185–225, https://doi.org/10.1093/jis/etz048; Rushain Abbasi, "Islam and the Invention of Religion: A Study of Medieval Muslim Discourses on Dīn," *Studia Islamica* 116, no. 1 (2021): 1–106, https://doi.org/10.1163/19585705-12341437; Hayrettin Yücesoy, *Disenchanting the Caliphate: The Secular Discipline of Power in Abbasid Political Thought* (Columbia University Press, 2023), https://public.ebookcentral.proquest.com/choice/PublicFullRecord.aspx?p=7193557.
61. Muḥammad ibn ʿAbd al-Karīm Maghīlī, *Sharīʿa in Songhay: The Replies of Al-Maghīlī to the Questions of Askia al-Ḥājj Muḥammad*, trans. John O. Hunwick (Oxford University Press, 1985); Lamin O. Sanneh, *The Jakhanke: The History of an Islamic Clerical People of the Senegambia* (International African Institute, 1979), chap. 1; Ivor Wilks, "The Transmission of Islamic Learning in the Western Sudan," in *Literacy in Traditional Societies* (Cambridge University Press, 1968), 162–97; Ivor Wilks, "The Juula and the Expansion of Islam Into the Forest," in *The History of Islam in Africa*, ed. Nehemia Levtzion and Randall Lee Pouwels (Ohio University Press, 2000), 93–115.
62. Robert Launay, *Beyond the Stream: Islam and Society in a West African Town* (University of California Press, 1992), 78–81.
63. Ousmane Kane, *Beyond Timbuktu: An Intellectual History of Muslim West Africa* (Harvard University Press, 2016), chap. 5; Marcus-Sells, *Sorcery or Science?*; Amir Syed, "Political Theology in Nineteenth-Century West Africa: Al-Ḥājj ʿUmar, the Bayān Mā Waqaʿa, and the Conquest of the Caliphate of Ḥamdallāhi," *Journal of African*

History 62, no. 3 (2021): 358–76, https://doi.org/10.1017/S0021853721000505; Stephanie Zehnle, *A Geography of Jihad: Sokoto Jihadism and the Islamic Frontier in West Africa* (De Gruyter, 2020); Marsh, "Compositions of Sainthood," chap. 2.
64. Asad, *Formations of the Secular*; Claude Lefort, "The Permanence of the Theologico-Political?," in *Political Theologies: Public Religions in a Post-Secular World*, ed. Hent de Vries and Lawrence E. Sullivan (Fordham University Press, 2006), https://doi.org/10.5422/fso/9780823226443.003.0007.
65. Kamara, *Sheikh Moussa Kamara's Islamic Critique of Jihadists*, 35.
66. Oumar Kane, *La première hégémonie peule: Le Fuuta Tooro de Koli Tenella à Almaami Abdul* (Karthala Editions, 2004).
67. Kamara, *Sheikh Moussa Kamara's Islamic Critique of Jihadists*, 36.
68. Lovejoy, following an even larger historiography, argues along similar lines about this period. Paul E. Lovejoy, *Jihād in West Africa During the Age of Revolutions* (Ohio University Press, 2016).
69. Tal Tamari, *Les castes de l' Afrique occidentale: Artisans et musiciens endogames* (Société d'ethnologie, 1997).
70. Kamara, *Sheikh Moussa Kamara's Islamic Critique of Jihadists*, 37.
71. Kamara, *Sheikh Moussa Kamara's Islamic Critique of Jihadists*, 38.
72. Robinson, *Paths of Accommodation*, 175, 176.
73. On the basis of careful codicological study, Ousmane Diaw has challenged the inclusion of the so-called ninth chapter, arguing instead that it is either its own work or a part of another. Ousmane Diaw, al-Shaykh Mūsá Kamara, al-Faṣl al-Tāsiʿa min "Akthar al-Rāghibīn" : fī Maḥaba Rūʾasāʾ Farānsa li, taḥqīq: Aḥmad al-Shukri wa Khadim Mbakke, taqdīm: Aḥmad al-Shukri, Maʿhad al-Dirāsāt al-Ifrīqīya, Jamiʿa Muḥammad al-Khamis bi-l-Rabat, silsila nuṣūṣ wa-wathāyiq (13), m. 2016, ṣ 66, Research Africa Reviews 3, no. 1 (2019) https://sites.duke.edu/researchafrica/ra-reviews/volume-3-issue-1-april-2019/.
74. Kamara, *Sheikh Moussa Kamara's Islamic Critique of Jihadists*, 87.
75. Edward W. Said, *The World, the Text, and the Critic* (Harvard University Press, 1983), 5–9; Erich Auerbach, *Mimesis: The Representation of Reality in Western Literature* (Princeton University Press, 2013), ix–xxxii, https://doi.org/10.1515/9781400847952.
76. Auerbach, *Mimesis*, 3.

4. A Monumental Text in an Orientalist Season

1. Kamara uses three titles of this work interchangeably: *Zuhūr al-Basātīn fī Tārīkh al-Sawādīn* [Flowers from among the gardens in the history of the Blacks], *Intiṣār al-Mawtūr fī Dhikr Qabāʾil Futa Toro* [Victory of the wronged in the memory of the tribes of Futa Toro], and *Iḥyāʾ mā ʿAfā wa-Andarasa min ʿUlūm Tārīkh al-Sūdān wa-Inṭamas* [Revival of what has been effaced and extinguished from the historical arts of the Blacks and obliterated]. "Zuhūr al-basātīn fī tārīkh al-sawādīn" is the most common title used in the scholarly literature. The question of when, how, and by whom the different titles were used and to what ends is worth further study.

4. A MONUMENTAL TEXT IN AN ORIENTALIST SEASON

See Shaykh Musa Kamara, *Zuhūr al-basātīn fī tārīkh al-sawādīn : Mudawwanat Shuʿūb Gharbī Ifrīqiyyā fī al-Tārīkh wa-l-Ansāb wa-l-Anthrūbūlūjiyā* [Flowers from among Gardens in the History of the Blacks: a historical, genealogical, and anthropological record of the peoples of West Africa], ed. Nacereddine Saidouni and Muawiya Saidouni (Babatain, 2010), 12, 71, http://archive.org/details/compressed_201910; Abdoul Malal Diop, "La vie et l'oeuvre de Cheikh Moussa Kamara de Ganguel (1864–1945)" (PhD thesis, Université de Cheikh Anta Diop, 2014), 191.

2. Siré-Abbâs-Soh, *Chroniques du Foûta sénégalais*, trans. Maurice Delafosse, with Henri Gaden (Ernest Leroux, 1913); Octave Victor Houdas and Maurice Delafosse, trans., *Tarikh el-fettach, ou, chronique du chercheur, pour servir à l'histoire des villes, des armées et des principaux personnages du Tekrour* (Ernest Leroux, 1913); Mauro Nobili, *Sultan, Caliph, and the Renewer of the Faith: Aḥmad Lobbo, the Tārīkh al-Fattāsh and the Making of an Islamic State in West Africa* (Cambridge University Press, 2020), 235–41.
3. Jean-Louis Triaud, "L'islam au sud du Sahara: Une saison orientaliste en Afrique occidentale: Constitution d'un champ scientifique, héritages et transmissions," *Cahiers d'études africaines* 50, no. 198–200 (2010): 907–50.
4. Alain Messaoudi and Jean Schmitz, "Octave Houdas," in *Dictionnaire des orientalistes de langue français* (École des hautes études en sciences sociales, accessed July 25, 2022, http://dictionnairedesorientalistes.ehess.fr/document.php?id=120.
5. Aberrahmane es-Sa'adi, Tarikh es-Soudan, trans, Ocatave Houdas, Ernest Leroux, 1900. I use the original Arabic here as the text is widely known by it, and because I do not want to confuse readers with Kamara's history which has a similar name. Subsequent page numbers appear parenthetically in the text
6. Jean-Louis Triaud, "Haut-Sénégal-Niger, un modèle 'positiviste'? De la coutume à l'histoire: Maurice Delafosse et l'invention de l'histoire africaine," in *Maurice Delafosse: Entre orientalisme et ethnographie; L'itinéraire d'un africaniste, 1870–1926*, ed. Jean-Loup Amselle and Emmanuelle Sibeud (Maisonneuve & Larose, 1998); Nobili, *Sultan, Caliph, and the Renewer of the Faith*. Nobili has successfully revised our understanding of the *Tarikh al-Fattash* as a virtual text and for the histories it bears.
7. H. R. Trevor-Roper, *The Rise of Christian Europe* (Thames & Hudson, 1965), 9.
8. Alice L. Conklin, *A Mission to Civilize: The Republican Idea of Empire in France and West Africa, 1895–1930* (Stanford University Press, 1997).
9. Jean Schmitz, "L'Afrique par défaut ou l'oubli de l'orientalisme," in *Maurice Delafosse: Entre orientalisme et ethnographie; L'itinéraire d'un africaniste, 1870–1926*, ed. Jean-Loup Amselle and Emmanuelle Sibeud (Maisonneuve & Larose, 1998), 157–78.
10. Maurice Delafosse, *Haut-Sénégal-Niger (Soudan français)* (Émile Larose, 1912), http://ark.bnf.fr/ark:/12148/bpt6k103554s.
11. Roy Dilley, *Nearly Native, Barely Civilized: Henri Gaden's Journey Through Colonial French West Africa (1894–1939)* (Brill, 2014), http://ebookcentral.proquest.com/lib/rutgers-ebooks/detail.action?docID=1604067.
12. N. Levtzion, "A Seventeenth-Century Chronicle by Ibn al-Mukhtār: A Critical Study of 'Ta'rīkh al-Fattāsh,'" *Bulletin of the School of Oriental and African Studies, University of London* 34, no. 3 (1971): 571–93.

4. A MONUMENTAL TEXT IN AN ORIENTALIST SEASON

13. Nobili, *Sultan, Caliph, and the Renewer of the Faith*, 44-57.
14. P. F. de Moraes Farias, *Arabic Medieval Inscriptions from the Republic of Mali: Epigraphy, Chronicles and Songhay-Tuăreg History* (Oxford University Press, 2001).
15. Siré-Abbâs-Soh, *Chroniques du Foûta sénégalais*, 3.
16. Siré-Abbâs-Soh, *Chroniques du Foûta sénégalais*, 6.
17. Dipesh Chakrabarty, *Provincializing Europe: Postcolonial Thought and Historical Difference* (Princeton University Press, 2000); Kathleen Davis, *Periodization and Sovereignty: How Ideas of Feudalism and Secularization Govern the Politics of Time* (University of Pennsylvania Press, 2008).
18. Here I refer to the version of the manuscript held at the Institut fondamental d'Afrique noir. There are at least two other versions. On these different manuscripts, see Jean Schmitz, "Introduction," in *Florilège au jardin de l'histoire des Noirs: Zuhūr al-basātīn*, by Muusa Kamara (CNRS Éditions, 1998), 69-71. For a discussion of script styles, see Mauro Nobili, "Arabic Scripts in West African Manuscripts: A Tentative Classification from the De Gironcourt Collection," *Islamic Africa* 2, no. 1 (2011): 105-33. Citations in this chapter uses the partial edition published in 2010. Shaykh Musa Kamara, *Zuhūr al-basātīn fī tārīkh al-sawādīn : Mudawwanat Shuʿūb Gharbī Ifrīqiyyā fī al-Tārīkh wa-l-ansāb wa-l-anthrūbūlūjiyā* ed. Nacereddine Saidouni and Muawiya Saidouni (Al Babatain, 2010), (Babatain, 2010).
19. For recent work that challenges the postcolonial common sense that colonial borders were completely arbitrary, see Camille Lefebvre, *Frontières de sable, frontières de papier: Histoire de territoires et de frontières, du jihad de Sokoto à la colonisation française du Niger, xixe-xxe siècles* (Éditions de la Sorbonne, 2015), https://doi.org/10.4000/books.psorbonne.36501; Stephanie Zehnle, *A Geography of Jihad: Sokoto Jihadism and the Islamic Frontier in West Africa* (De Gruyter, 2020).
20. Delafosse, *Haut-Sénégal-Niger*; Triaud, "Haut-Sénégal-Niger, un modèle 'positiviste'?"; Schmitz, "Florilège au jardin de l'histoire des Noirs," 43, 44; Sophie Dulucq, *Ecrire l'histoire de l'Afrique à l'époque coloniale: XIXe-XXe siècles* (Karthala, 2009).
21. James Pickett and Paolo Sartori, "From the Archetypical Archive to Cultures of Documentation," *Journal of the Economic and Social History of the Orient* 62, no. 5-6 (2019): 773; Chase F. Robinson, *Islamic Historiography* (Cambridge University Press, 2003), 85.
22. Anna Pondopoulo, "Une traduction 'mal partie' (1923-1945): Le 'Zuhur al-basatin' de Cheikh Moussa Kamara," *Islam et sociétés au sud du Sahara*, no. 7 (1993): 101.
23. Dilley, *Nearly Native, Barely Civilized*, 356-358.
24. Triaud, "L'islam au sud du Sahara."
25. David Robinson, "Un historien et anthropologue sénégalais: Shaikh Musa Kamara [A Senegalese historian and anthropologist: Shaikh Musa Kamara]," *Cahiers d'études africaines* 28, no. 109 (1988): 89-116.
26. Musa Kamara, *Al-Majmūʿ al-Nafīs Sirran waʿalāniyya fī Dhikr Baʿd al-Sādāt al-Bīḍāniyya wa-l-Fulāniyya* [The precious collection of secrecy and publicity in the memory of some of the Bīḍān and Fulani nobles] (Manshūrāt al-Zaman, 2015); Muusa Kamara, *Ashhá al-ʿUlūm wa-Aṭayab al-Khabar fī Sīrat al-Ḥājj ʿUmar* [The Most Delicious of Sciences and the Tastiest of the News in the Life of Hajj Umar], (Maʿhad al-Dirāsāt al-Ifrīqīyya, 2001); Muusa Kamara, *Akthar al-Rāghibīn*

4. A MONUMENTAL TEXT IN AN ORIENTALIST SEASON

fī al-Jihād baʿd al-Nabīʾīn man Yakhtāru al-Ẓuhūr wa-Malaka al-Bilād wa-lā Yubālī bi-man Halaka fī Jihādihi min al-ʿIbād [Most of the Would-be Jihadists after the prophets are the ones who choose prevailing and dominion of the land and who do not care who perishes in his jihad from among the people] (Maʿhad al-Dirāsāt al-Ifrīqiyya, 2003); Muusa Kamara, "Tanqiyat al-Afham min Shubuhat al-Awham" [The purification of thoughts from delusional doubts]," Cahier 7, Fonds Kamara, Institut fondamental d'Afrique noire, n.d.; Musa Kamara, Tabshīr al-Khāʾif al-Ḥayrān wa-Tadhkīruhu bi-Saʿa Raḥmat Allah al-Karīm al-Mannān [The announcement of the good news to the fearful and confused and his reminder of the breadth of the mercy of God, the Generous Bestower], ed. Demba Tewe (al-Maʿhad al-Islāmī bi-Dakār, 2014) ; Robinson, "Un historien et anthropologue Sénégalais," 103–6; Schmitz, "Florilège au jardin de l'histoire des Noirs," 31n37.

27. Robinson, "Un historien et anthropologue sénégalais," 99.
28. Kamara, Tabshīr al-Khāʾif al-Ḥayrān wa-Tadhkīruhu bi-Saʿa Raḥmat Allah al-Karīm al-Mannān, 23–42.
29. Robinson, "Un historien et anthropologue sénégalais," 101.
30. Robinson, Islamic Historiography, chap. 4; Dwight F. Reynolds, ed., Interpreting the Self: Autobiography in the Arabic Literary Tradition (University of California Press, 2001), 36–48; Michael Cooperson, "Biographical Literature," in The New Cambridge History of Islam, vol. 4, Islamic Cultures and Societies to the End of the Eighteenth Century, ed. Robert Irwin (Cambridge University Press, 2010), 458–73, https://doi.org/10.1017/CHOL9780521838245.020.
31. Ahmed El Shamsy, The Canonization of Islamic Law: A Social and Intellectual History (Cambridge University Press, 2013).
32. Kamara, Zuhūr al-Basātīn fī Tārīkh al-Sawādīn : Mudawwanat Shuʿūb Gharbī Ifrīqiyyā fī al-Tārīkh wa-l-ansāb wa-l-anthrūbūlūjiyā, 74, 78, 84.
33. Kamara, 124, 178; Eric Calderwood, "The Beginning (or End) of Moroccan History: Historiography, Translation, and Modernity in Ahmed B. Khalid al-Nasiri and Clemente Cerdeira," International Journal of Middle East Studies 44, no. 3 (2012): 399–420, https://doi.org/10.1017/S0020743812000396; Sahar Bazzaz, "Historiography in the Maghrib in the 19th and Early 20th Century," in Oxford Research Encyclopedia of African History, Oxford University Press, September 26, 2017, https://doi.org/10.1093/acrefore/9780190277734.013.102; Aḥmad ibn Khālid al-Nāṣirī, Kitāb al-Istiqṣā li-Akhbār Duwal al-Maghrib al-Aqṣá, 9 vols. (Manshūrāt Wizārat al-Thaqāfah wa-l-Ittiṣāl, 2001); ʿAbd Allāh Abū al-Suʿ ūd and Kitāb al-Dars al-Tāmm fī al-Tārīkh al-ʿām al-Mulakhkhaṣ min Kutub al-Tawārīkh al-ʿŪrūbīyah wa-l-ʿArabīya fī al-Sāḥah al-Khidīwīyah:li-Qaṣd Tadrīsihi ti-Ṭalabat al-ʿilm bi-Madrasa Dār al-ʿŪlūm al-Miṣrīyah (al-Qāhirah: Maṭbaʿah Wādī al-Nīl al-Miṣrīyya, 1289h), http://catalog.hathitrust.org/api/volumes/oclc/37041702.html; Evelyn Richardson, "Specters of Ancient Pasts and the Ends of History: The Arabic Discourse of Revival in the Tanzimat Era (1839–1876)" (PhD diss., University of Chicago, 2022), 107, 108, 133, 134, 168–217, https://www.proquest.com/docview/2706759922/abstract/.
34. Thomas Philipp, "Language, History, and Arab National Consciousness in the Thought of Jurjî Zaidân (1861–1914)," International Journal of Middle East Studies 4, no. 1 (1973): 3–22, https://doi.org/10.1017/S0020743800027240.

4. A MONUMENTAL TEXT IN AN ORIENTALIST SEASON

35. Kamara, *Tabshīr al-Khāʾif al-Ḥayrān wa-Tadhkīruhu bi-Saʿa Raḥmat Allah al-Karīm al-Mannān*, 21.
36. Kamara, Kamara, *Zuhūr al-basātīn fī tārīkh al-sawādīn : Mudawwanat Shuʿūb Gharbī Ifrīqiyyā fī al-Tārīkh wa-l-ansāb wa-l-anthrūbūlūjiyā*, 68–69. See also Diop, "La vie et l'oeuvre de Cheikh Moussa Kamara de Ganguel (1864–1945)," 196–98; Pondopoulo, "Une traduction 'mal partie,'" 101, 108; Kamara, *Tabshīr al-Khāʾif al-Ḥayrān wa-Tadhkīruhu bi-Saʿa Raḥmat Allah al-Karīm al-Mannān*, 21, 22; Schmitz, "Florilège au jardin de l'histoire des Noirs," 29, 30.
37. Siré-Abbâs-Soh, *Chroniques du Foûta sénégalais*, 3.
38. Khatib al-Tabrizi, *Mishkāt al-Maṣābīḥ*, Book 9, Hadith 41.
39. Kamara, *Tabshīr al-Khāʾif al-Ḥayrān wa-Tadhkīruhu bi-Saʿa Raḥmat Allah al-Karīm al-Mannān*, 21, 22.
40. Marc Michel, "Un programme réformiste en 1919: Maurice Delafosse et la 'politique indigène' en AOF," *Cahiers d'études africaines* 15, no. 58 (1975): 313–27, https://doi.org/10.3406/cea.1975.2600; Louise Delafosse, *Maurice Delafosse, le Berrichon conquis par l'Afrique* (Société française d'histoire d'outre-mer, 1976), https://bac-lac.on.worldcat.org/oclc/715221182.
41. Maurice Delafosse, *Les noirs de l'Afrique* (Payot, 1922), http://archive.org/details/lesnoirsdelafriq00delauoft.
42. Anna Pondopoulo, *Les Français et les Peuls: Histoire d'une relation privilégiée* (Indes savantes, 2008), 173; Douglas W. Leonard, *Anthropology, Colonial Policy and the Decline of French Empire in Africa* (Bloomsbury Academic, 2020), 47–77.
43. Schmitz, "Florilège au jardin de l'histoire Des Noirs," 30.
44. Sometime later the manuscript was located and sent to the Ahmed Baba Center in Timbuktu. Schmitz, "Florilège au jardin de l'histoire Des Noirs," 71.
45. See the March 28, 1929, letter in Fonds Kamara 19, Institut fondamental d'Afrique noire, Dakar.
46. Pondopoulo, "Une traduction 'mal partie,'" 102.
47. The *École spéciale des langues orientales* (Special School of Oriental Langages) became the *École nationale des langues orientales vivantes* in 1914. On Gaudfroy-Demombynes see Pondopoulo, "Une traduction 'mal partie,'" 103.
48. C. E. Bosworth, "Al-Ḳalḳashandī," in *Encyclopaedia of Islam*, 2nd ed., Brill, April 24, 2012, https://referenceworks.brillonline.com/entries/encyclopaedia-of-islam-2/al-kalkashandi-SIM_3832?s.num=0&s.f.s2_parent=s.f.cluster.Encyclopaedia+of+Islam&s.q=al-Qalqashandi&s.f.s2_parent_title=Encyclopaedia+of+Islam%2C+Second+Edition.
49. Oliver Ihl, "The Market of Honors: On the Bicentenary of the Legion of Honor," *French Politics, Culture & Society* 24, no. 1 (2006): 8–26, https://doi.org/10.3167/153763706781007144.
50. Bruno Dumons, *Les "saints de la république"—les décorés de la Légion d'honneur (1870–1940)* (Boutique de l'histoire, 2009), https://shs.hal.science/halshs-00431160.
51. Olivier Ihl, *Le mérite et la république: Essai sur la société des émules* (Gallimard, 2007), https://shs.hal.science/halshs-00349459.
52. "Founding Principles and History | La Grande Chancellerie," accessed August 17, 2023, https://www.legiondhonneur.fr/en/page/founding-principles-and-history/403.

4. A MONUMENTAL TEXT IN AN ORIENTALIST SEASON

53. Richard L. Roberts, *Conflicts of Colonialism: The Rule of Law, French Soudan, and Faama Mademba Sèye* (Cambridge University Press, 2022), 45, 46, 124, 210; "Mademba, Seye—Légion d'honneur—base de fonnées Léonore," accessed August 18, 2023, https://www.leonore.archives-nationales.culture.gouv.fr/ui/notice/240982.
54. Roberts, *Conflicts of Colonialism*, 46.
55. Roberts, *Conflicts of Colonialism*, 11–16.
56. Archives nationales du Sénégal, O169 (31), Arrêté 209; Pondopoulo, "Une traduction 'mal partie,'" 105; Céline Labrune-Badiane and Étienne Smith, *Les hussards noirs de la colonie: Instituteurs africains et petites patries en AOF (1913-1960)* (Karthala, 2018).
57. Labrune-Badiane and Smith, *Les hussards noirs de la colonie*, 234–38.
58. Marie-Ève Humery, "Fula and the Ajami Writing System in the Haalpulaar Society of Fuuta Tooro (Senegal and Mauritania): A Specific 'Restricted Literacy,'" in *The Arabic Script in Africa: Studies in the Use of a Writing System*, ed. Meikal Mumin and Kees Versteegh (Brill, 2014); Jack Goody, "Restricted Literacy in Northern Ghana," in *Literacy in Traditional Societies* (Cambridge University Press, 1968), 199–264.
59. West African Arabic Manuscript Database, accessed August 18, 2023, https://waamd.lib.berkeley.edu/home; J. O. Hunwick, *Arabic Literature of Africa: The Writings of Western Sudanic Africa* (Brill Academic, 2003), 465–70, http://site.ebrary.com/lib/columbia/docDetail.action?docID=10090514.
60. Kamara, *Tabshīr al-Khāʾif al-Ḥayrān wa-Tadhkīruhu bi-Saʿa Raḥmat Allah al-Karīm al-Mannān*, 23–39.
61. Siré-Abbâs-Soh, *Chroniques du Foûta sénégalais*.
62. Labrune-Badiane and Smith, *Les hussards noirs de la colonie*, 222–26.
63. Abdou Salam Kane, "Du régime des terres chez les populations du Fouta sénégalais," *Bulletin du Comité d'études historiques et scientifiques de l'Afrique occidentale française* 18 (1935): 449–61.
64. Abdou Salam Kane, "Coutume civile et pénale toucouleur," in *Coutumiers juridiques de l'Afrique occidentale française*, ed. Jean Ortoli and Alfred Aubert (Larose, 1939), 55–115, https://gallica.bnf.fr/ark:/12148/bpt6k82525t.
65. Anna Pondopoulo, "Une histoire aux multiples visages: La reconstruction coloniale de l'histoire du Fuuta sénégalais au début du XXe siècle," *Outre-mers: Revue d'histoire* 93, no. 352 (2006): 57–77, https://doi.org/10.3406/outre.2006.4224.
66. Pondopoulo, "Une traduction 'mal partie,'" 98; David Robinson, *Colonial Politics and Historical Texts: The Case of the Umarian Narratives* (African Studies Center, Boston University, 1991); Sylvianne Garcia, "Al-Hajj Seydou Nourou Tall 'grand marabout' Tijani: L'histoire d'une carrière (c. 1868–1980)," in *Le temps des marabouts: Itinéraires et stratégies islamiques en Afrique occidentale française, 1880-1960*, ed. David Robinson and Jean-Louis Triaud (Karthala, 1997); Rüdiger Seesemann and Benjamin F. Soares, "'Being as Good Muslims as Frenchmen': On Islam and Colonial Modernity in West Africa," *Journal of Religion in Africa* 39, no. 1 (2009): 91–120, https://doi.org/10.1163/157006609X409067; Ibrahima-Abou Sall, "Cerno Amadu Mukhtar Sakho: Qadi supérieur de Boghe (1905-1934) Futa Toro," in Robinson and Triaud, *Le temps des marabouts*, 221–45, https://doi.org/10.3917/kart.robin.1997.01.0221.

4. A MONUMENTAL TEXT IN AN ORIENTALIST SEASON

67. See the August 26, 1937, letter from the general secretary to the governor of French West Africa, Archives nationales du Sénégal, 13 G 6 (17), Dakar.
68. Rudolph T. Ware III, *The Walking Qurʾan: Islamic Education, Embodied Knowledge, and History in West Africa* (University of North Carolina Press, 2014).
69. Andrea Brigaglia, "Fī Lawḥin Maḥfūẓ: Towards a Phenomenological Analysis of the Quranic Tablet," in *The Arts and Crafts of Literacy: Islamic Manuscript Cultures in Sub-Saharan Africa*, ed. Andrea Brigaglia and Mauro Nobili (De Gruyter, 2017), 69–102, https://doi.org/10.1515/9783110541441-003.
70. Ibn Battuta, "Rihla," in *Corpus of Early Arabic Sources for West African History*, ed. Nehemia Levtzion and J. F. P. Hopkins, trans. J. F. P. Hopkins (New York: Cambridge University Press, 1981), 296.
71. Jacques-François Roger, *Kelédor: Histoire africaine; Recueillie et publiée par M. le. Baron Roger.* (Paris: A. Nepveu, 1828), xi; Sylviane A. Diouf, *Servants of Allah: African Muslims Enslaved in the Americas*, 15th anniversary ed. (New York University Press, 2013), 24, 25.
72. Ware, *The Walking Qurʾan*, 211–14.
73. See the April 8, 1938, letter from the office of Indigenous Affairs to Jules Marcel de Coppet, Archives nationales du Sénégal 13 G 6 (17), Dakar.
74. Muusa Kamara, *Kāda al-Itifāq wa-l-Iltaʾām an Yukūna bayna Dīn al-Naṣāra wa-Dīn al-Islām* [The near agreement and uniting of the religion of Christianity and the religion of Islam; translated by Samb as *L'islam et le christianisme*], Cahier 16, Fonds Kamara, Institut fondamental d'Afrique noire, n.d.; C. M. Kamara, "L'islam et le christianisme," *Bulletin de l'Institut fondamental d'Afrique noire, Série B: Sciences humaines* 35, no. 2 (1973): 269–322; "Lettre ouverte au Président Macky SALL: Cheikh Moussa CAMARA le Saint, le Savant et l'érudit de GANGUEL. (1864–1945)" May 12, 2014, https://www.pressafrik.com/Lettre-ouverte-au-President-Macky-SALL-Cheikh-Moussa-CAMARA-le-Saint-le-Savant-et-l-erudit-de-GANGUEL-1864-1945_a122079.html, accessed April 12, 2025.
75. See the April 29, 1938 unsigned report about Kamara's text, Archives nationales du Sénégal 13 G 6 (17), Dakar.
76. See the undated translation of letter from Shaykh Musa Kamara to M. Moutet by Benhamouda, Archives nationales du Sénégal 13 G 6 (17), Dakar.
77. Pondopoulo, "Une traduction 'mal partie,'" 104.
78. See May 31, 1938, document titled "Note pour Hp/2," Archives nationales du Sénégal 13 G 6 (17), Dakar; Catherine Coquery-Vidrovitch, "Nationalité et citoyenneté en Afrique occidentale français: Originaires et citoyens dans le Sénégal colonial," *Journal of African History* 42, no. 2 (2001): 285–305.
79. Kamara, *Tabshīr al-Khāʾif al-Ḥayrān wa-Tadhkīruhu bi-Saʿa Raḥmat Allah al-Karīm al-Mannān*, 23.
80. Shahzad Bashir, *Sufi Bodies: Religion and Society in Medieval Islam* (Columbia University Press, 2011), https://doi.org/10.7312/bash14490.
81. Dilley, *Nearly Native, Barely Civilized*, 356.
82. Dilley, *Nearly Native, Barely Civilized*, chap. 9; Henri Gaden, *Proverbes et maximes Peuls et Toucouleurs, traduits, expliqués et annotés* (Institut d'ethnologie, 1931), http://name.umdl.umich.edu/AHD1115.0001.001; Mohammadu Aliyu Caam, *La vie d'el Hadj Omar: Qacida en poular* (Institut d'ethnologie, 1935).

4. A MONUMENTAL TEXT IN AN ORIENTALIST SEASON

83. Pondopoulo, "Une traduction 'mal partie,'" 104. See the July 18, 1939, letter from Théodore Monod to the Office of Political Affairs, Fonds Kamara 19, Institut fondamental d'Afrique noire, Dakar, in which Monod suggests taking official action to reclaim the part of the manuscript in Benhamouda's possession.
84. Agbenyega Adedze, "In the Pursuit of Knowledge and Power: French Scientific Research in West Africa, 1938–65," *Comparative Studies of South Asia, Africa and the Middle East* 23, no. 1 (2003): 335–44; Marie-Albane De Suremain, "L'IFAN et la 'mise en musée' des cultures africaines (1936–1961)," *Outre-mers: Revue d'histoire* 94, no. 356 (2007): 151–72, https://doi.org/10.3406/outre.2007.4289; Jean-Hervé Jézéquel, "Les professionnels africains de la recherche dans l'État colonial tardif: Le personnel local de l'Institut français d'afrique noire entre 1938 et 1960," *Revue d'histoire des sciences humaines* 24, no. 1 (2011): 35–60, https://doi.org/10.3917/rhsh.024.0035; Alice Bellagamba, "Indigenous Ethnologists, National Anthropologists, Post-Colonial Intellectuals: The Trajectory of Anthropology in French-Speaking West and Equatorial Africa," in *Histories of Anthropology*, ed. Gabriella D'Agostino and Vincenzo Matera (Springer International, 2023), 271–97, https://doi.org/10.1007/978-3-031-21258-1_9.
85. See the May 4, 1939, letter from Théodore Monod to Henri Gaden, Fonds Kamara 19, Institut fondamental d'Afrique noire, Dakar.
86. See the August 4, 1939, letter from Maurice Gaudfroy-Demombynes to Théodore Monod, Fonds Kamara 19, Institut fondamental d'Afrique noire, Dakar.
87. See the March 12, 1959, letter from Théodore Monod to Bachir Ly, Fonds Kamara 19, Institut fondamental d'Afrique noire, Dakar.
88. Pondopoulo, "Une traduction 'mal partie,'" 108.
89. See the 22 Muharram 1944, letter from Shaykh Musa Kamara to Théodore Monod, Fonds Kamara 19, Institut fondamental d'Afrique noire, Dakar.
90. See the May 25 and 28, 1944, letters from Shaykh Musa Kamara to Théodore Monod, Fonds Kamara 19, Institut fondamental d'Afrique noire, Dakar.
91. Bintou Sanankoua, "Amadou Hampâté Bâ (v. 1900–1991)," in *Le temps des marabouts Itinéraires et stratégies islamiques en Afrique occidentale française v. 1880–1960*, ed. David Robinson and Jean-Louis Triaud (Karthala, 1997), 407.

5. The Pitfalls of National Literature

1. Personal communication, July 1, 2021, regarding Musa Kamara, *Al-Majmūʿ al-Nafīs Sirran Wa-ʿAlāniyya fī Dhikr baʿḍ al-Sādāt al-Bīḍāniyya wa-l-Fulāniyya* [The precious collection of secrecy and publicity in the memory of some of the Bīḍān and Fulani nobles], ed. Nani Wuld al-Ḥussaīn (Manshūrāt al-Zaman, 2015).
2. Monteil adopted the name "Mansour" later in life, after publicly embracing Islam. Jean-Louis Triaud, "Monteil, Vincent," in *Dictionnaire des orientalistes de langue française*, ed. François Pouillon (Karthala, 2008), 697–99.
3. Anna Pondopoulo, *Les Français et les Peuls: Histoire d'une relation privilégiée* (Indes savantes, 2008), 173.

5. THE PITFALLS OF NATIONAL LITERATURE

4. Vincent Monteil, *L'islam noir* (Seuil, 1964), 7.
5. Jean-Louis Triaud, "Monteil, Vincent," in *Dictionnaire des orientalistes de langue française*, ed. François Pouillon (Karthala, 2008), 698.
6. Vincent Monteil, *Aux cinq couleurs de l'islam* (Maisonneuve & Larose, 1989).
7. Monteil, *L'islam noir*, 12–13.
8. Vincent Monteil, "Les manuscrits historiques arabo-africains," *Bulletin de l'Institut français d'Afrique noire. Serie B: Sciences humaines*, 27, no. 3–4 (1965): 540; For more on Djenidi and his relationship with Monteil, see the notes in Diaw. Ousmane Diaw, "Al-Shaykh Mūsá Kamara, *Al-Fasl al-Tāsiʿa min "Akthar Al-Rāghibīn" : fī maḥaba rūʾasāʾ farānsa lī*, taḥqīq: Aḥmad al-Shukri wa-Khadim Mbakke, taqdīm: Aḥmad al-Shukri, Maʿhad al-Dirāsāt al-Ifrīqīyah, Jamiʿat Muḥammad al-Khamis bi-l-Rabat, silsilat nusus wa-wathāyiq (13), m. 2016, ṣ 66," *Research Africa Reviews* 3, no. 1 (2019) https://sites.duke.edu/researchafrica/ra-reviews/volume-3-issue-1-april-2019/.
9. Roland Barthes, *Image, Music, Text* (Noonday Press, 1988), 142–48.
10. Jack Goody, "Restricted Literacy in Northern Ghana," in *Literacy in Traditional Societies* (Cambridge University Press, 1968), 199–264.
11. On epistemic violence, see Gayatri Spivak, "Can the Subaltern Speak?," in *Marxism and the Interpretation of Culture*, ed. Cary Nelson and Lawrence Grossberg (University of Illinois Press, 1988), 280.
12. Kwame Nkrumah, *Neo-Colonialism: The Last Stage of Imperialism* (International Publishers, 1966), xi.
13. Aimé Césaire, *Discourse on Colonialism* (Monthly Review Press, 2000), 42, 43.
14. This description of Négritude, which famously belongs to Jean-Paul Sartre, appears in the preface to Léopold Sédar Senghor, *Anthologie de la nouvelle poésie nègre et malgache de langue française*, 2. éd. (Presses universitaires de France, 1969), xiv.
15. On African humanism as an appropriation with organic African development see Olúfẹ́mi Táíwò, *Against Decolonisation: Taking African Agency Seriously* (Hurst, 2022). I also read Adom Getachew's compelling analysis and narration of worldmaking after empire as a detailed account of this project of African humanism, even as Black thinkers struggled to transcend the nation-state form. Adom Getachew, *Worldmaking after empire: The rise and fall of self-determination* (Princeton University Press, 2019).
16. Frantz Fanon, *The Wretched of the Earth* (Grove Press, 2004); *Xala*, directed by Ousmane Sembene (New Yorker Films, 1974).
17. Léopold Sédar Senghor, *Liberté 1: Négritude et humanisme* (Seuil, 1964), 288.
18. Souleymane Diagne, "Négritude," in *The Stanford Encyclopedia of Philosophy*, ed. Edward N. Zalta (Stanford University: Summer 2010), http://plato.stanford.edu/archives/sum2010/entries/negritude/.
19. Léopold Sédar Senghor, "Negritude: A Humanism of the Twentieth Century," in *Colonial Discourse and Post-Colonial Theory*, ed. Patrick Williams and Laura Chrisman (Routledge, 1994), 27, 28.
20. Léopold Sédar Senghor, "Le Sénégal, le latin et les humanités classiques," *Bulletin de l'Association Guillaume Budé* 1, no. 1 (1974): 27, 60, https://doi.org/10.3406/bude.1974.3250.

5. THE PITFALLS OF NATIONAL LITERATURE

21. Senghor, "Negritude," 30.
22. Senghor, "Le Sénégal, le latin et les humanités classiques," 53–54.
23. Amadou Hampâté Bâ, *Contes initiatiques peuls: Njeddo Dewal, mère de la calamité: Kaïdara* (Stock, 1994). See also Bintou Sanankoua, "Amadou Hampâté Bâ: A Testimony," *Islamic Africa* 1, no. 2 (June 3, 2010): 143–66, https://doi.org/10.1163/21540993-90000015; Ralph A. Austen and Benjamin F. Soares, "Amadou Hampâté Bâ's Life and Work Reconsidered: Critical and Historical Perspectives," *Islamic Africa* 1, no. 2 (December 21, 2010): 133–42, https://doi.org/10.5192/215409910794105805.
24. Amadou Hampaté Bâ, *L'empire peul du Macina* (Institut français d'Afrique noire, Centre du Soudan, 1955); and "The Living Tradition," in *General History of Africa I: Methodology and African Prehistory*, ed. Joseph Ki-Zerbo (Heinemann, 1981).
25. Amadou Hampaté Bâ, *Aspects de la civilisation africaine: Personne, culture, religion* (Présence africaine, 1993).
26. Paulin J. Hountondji, *African Philosophy: Myth and Reality*, 2nd ed. (Indiana University Press, 1996); Werewere Liking, *Une vision de Kaydara d'Hamadou-Hampaté-Bâ* (Nouvelles editions africaines, 1984); Adama Kante, "L'historian Mamadou Diouf recadre l'ecrivain Amadou Hampate Ba," Seneweb.com, January 17, 2012, http://www.seneweb.com/news/Culture/l-rsquo-historien-mamadou-diouf-recadre-l-rsquo-ecrivain-amadou-hampathe-ba-laquo-la-plus-grosse-betise-qui-est-jamais-sort_n_57699.html.
27. On the racial consciousness of the Muridiyya, see Cheikh Anta Mbacké Babou, *Fighting the Greater Jihad: Amadu Bamba and the Founding of the Muridiyya of Senegal, 1853-1913* (Ohio University Press, 2007); Fallou Ngom, *Muslims Beyond the Arab World: The Odyssey of ʿAjamī and the Murīdiyya* (Oxford University Press, 2016).
28. Cheikh Anta Diop, *The African Origin of Civilization: Myth or Reality*, trans. Mercer Cook (Lawrence Hill, 1974), xiv.
29. Diop, *The African Origin of Civilization*, xiv.
30. Cheikh Anta Diop, "Quand pourra-t-on parler d'une renaissance africaine?," *Le musée vivant*, no. 36 (1948): 57–65; Cheikh Anta Diop, "When Can We Talk of an African Renaissance?," in *Towards the African Renaissance: Essays in African Culture and Development, 1946-1960*, trans. Egbuna P. Modum (Karnak House, 1996), 33–45.
31. Danielle Maurice, "Le musée vivant et le centenaire de l'abolition de l'esclavage: Pour une reconnaissance des cultures africaines," *Conserveries mémorielles: Revue transdisciplinaire*, no. 3 (2007), https://journals.openedition.org/cm/127?lang=en.
32. Brent Hayes Edwards, *The Practice of Diaspora: Literature, Translation, and the Rise of Black Internationalism* (Harvard University Press, 2003).
33. Diop, "When Can We Talk of an African Renaissance?," 34–35.
34. Diop, "When Can We Talk of an African Renaissance?," 39.
35. Ngom, *Muslims Beyond the Arab World*, 22–25.
36. Diop, "When Can We Talk of an African Renaissance?," 34.
37. Diop, *The African Origin of Civilization*, xvi. See also LeRoi Jones, "The Myth of a 'Negro Literature,'" in *Within the Circle: An Anthology of African American Literary Criticism from the Harlem Renaissance to the Present*, ed. Angelyn Mitchell (Duke University Press, 1994), 165–71, https://doi.org/10.1515/9780822399889-018.

5. THE PITFALLS OF NATIONAL LITERATURE

38. Olaudah Equiano, *The Interesting Narrative of the Life of Olaudah Equiano, or Gustavus Vassa, the African* (Norton, 2001); Henri Grégoire, *De la littérature des nègres, ou recherches sur leurs facultés intellectuelles, leurs qualités morales et leur littérature: Suivies de notices sur la vie et les ouvrages des nègres qui se sont distingués dans les sciences, les lettres et les arts* (Paris: Chez Maradon, 1808), http://ark.bnf.fr/ark:/12148/bpt6k844925; W. E. B. Du Bois, *Black Reconstruction in America*, ed. David Levering Lewis (Free Press, 1998); Maurice Delafosse, *Les Noirs de l'Afrique* (Payot, 1922), http://archive.org/details/lesnoirsdelafriq00delauoft.
39. Diop, "When Can We Talk of an African Renaissance?," 33.
40. Robert A. Orsi, "The Disciplinary Vocabulary of Modernity," *International Journal* 59, no. 4 (2004): 879–85, https://doi.org/10.2307/40203989.
41. Amar Samb, *Matraqué par le destin: Ou, la vie d'un talibé* (Nouvelles éditions africaines, 1973).
42. Cheikh Hamidou Kane, *L'aventure ambigue: Recit* (Juilliard, 1966); al-Ṭayyib Ṣāliḥ, *Mawsim al-Hijra ilá al-Shamāl* (Dar al-ʿAwda, 1969); al-Ṭayyib Ṣāliḥ, *Season of Migration to the North* (Heinemann Educational, 1970).
43. Mbye B. Cham, "Islam in Senegalese Literature and Film," *Africa: Journal of the International African Institute* 55, no. 4 (1985): 447–64, https://doi.org/10.2307/1160177.
44. Ousmane Kane, "Arabic Sources and the Search for a New Historiography in Ibadan in the 1960s," in *Africa: Journal of the International African Institute* 86, no. 2 (2016): 344–46, https://doi.org/10.1017/S0001972016000097; Kwame Nkrumah, "Speech at the Congress of Africanists December 12, 1962," in *Revolutionary Path* (Panaf, 1973).
45. Amar Samb, *Essai sur la contribution du Sénégal à la littérature d'expression arabe* (Institut fondamental d'Afrique noir, 1972).
46. Samb, *Essai sur la contribution du Sénégal*, 127.
47. Samb, *Essai sur la contribution du Sénégal*, 110.
48. Samb, *Essai sur la contribution du Sénégal*, 128.
49. Samb, *Essai sur la contribution du Sénégal*, 110.
50. Amar Samb, "L'islam et l'histoire du Sénégal," *Bulletin de l'Institut fondamental d'Afrique noire, Série B: Sciences humaines* 33, no. 3 (1971), 463.
51. Charles Pellat, "Défense et illustration de la civilisation des Noirs par un écrivain du IX siècle: Jâḥiẓ," Introduction by Amar Samb, *Notes africaines: bulletin d'information et de correspondence de l'Institut français d'Afrique noire* 153 (1977), 1.
52. Edward W. Said, *Orientalism* (Vintage, 1994), 123–48.
53. Ronald A. T. Judy, *(Dis)Forming the American Canon: African-Arabic Slave Narratives and the Vernacular* (University of Minnesota Press, 1993), 23.
54. Samb, *Essai sur la contribution du Sénégal à la littérature d'expression arabe*, 107.
55. Samb, "L'islam et l'histoire du Sénégal," 501.
56. Samb, *Essai sur la contribution du Sénégal à la littérature d'expression arabe*, 3, quoting Marius-François Guyard, *La littérature comparée* (Presses universitaires de France, 1965).
57. Guyard, *La littérature comparée*, 7.
58. For a much needed update on a comparative reading of Senegalese Arabic literature that puts it in dialogue with developments in Egypt and Indonesia, see

Annette Damayanti Lienau, *Sacred Language, Vernacular Difference: Global Arabic and Counter-Imperial Literatures* (Princeton University Press, 2024).

59. Amar Samb, "Influence de l'Islam sur la litterature 'wolof,'" *Bulletin de l'Institut fondamental d'Afrique noire, Série B: Sciences humaines* 30, no. 2 (1968): 628–41.
60. As it turns out, the politics of transcription has been no trivial matter in the history of Senegalese letters. Tobias Warner, "Senghor's Grammatology: The Political Imaginaries of Writing African Languages," in *The Tongue-Tied Imagination* (Fordham University Press, 2019), 123–51, https://doi.org/10.1515/9780823284313-006.
61. Samb, "Influence de l'islam sur la litterature 'wolof,'" 630.
62. Samb, "L'islam et l'histoire du Sénégal," 497.
63. Mamadou Youry Sall, *Mesure de l'arabophonie du Sénégal* (Presses universitaires de Dakar, Baajoordo centre de recherche, 2017).
64. Thierno Diallo, *Catalogue des manuscrits de l'I.F.A.N.: Fonds Vieillard, Gaden, Brevié, Figaret, Shaykh Mousa Kamara et Cremer en langues arabe, peule et voltaïques* (Institut fondamental d'Afrique noire, 1966).
65. Ravane Mbaye and Babacar Mbaye, "Notes et documents: Supplément au catalogue des manuscrits de l'IFAN," *Bulletin de l'Institut fondamental d'Afrique noire, Serie B: Sciences humaines* 37, no. 4 (1975): 878–95.
66. Louis Brenner and David Robinson, "Project for the Conservation of Malian Arabic Manuscripts," *History in Africa* 7 (1980): 329–32, https://doi.org/10.2307/3171669; Ismaël Diadié Haidara, "The State of Manuscripts in Mali and Efforts to Preserve Them," in *The Meanings of Timbuktu*, ed. Shamil Jeppie and Souleymane Bachir Diagne (HSRC Press, 2008), 265–69; Muhammad Ould Youbba, "The Ahmed Baba Institute of Higher Islamic Studies and Research," in Jeppie and Diagne, *The Meanings of Timbuktu*, 287–301.
67. Amar Samb, "Condamnation de la guerre sainte par Cheikh Moussa Kamara," *Bulletin de l'Institut fondamental d'Afrique noire, Serie B: Sciences Humaines*, 38 (1976): 158–99; Moustapha Ndiaye, "Rapports entre Qadirites et Tijanites au Fouta Toro aux XIXe et XXe siècles à travers al-haqq al-mubin de Cheikh Moussa Kamara," *Bulletin de l'Institut fondamental d'Afrique noire, Série B: Sciences Humaines* 41, no. 1 (1979): 190–207; Muusa Kamara, *La vie d'el-Hadji Omar*, trans. Amar Samb (Éditions Hilal, 1975); Samb, "Condamnation de la guerre sainte par Cheikh Moussa Kamara"; Cheikh Moussa Kamara, "L'islam et le christianisme," *Bulletin de l'Institut fondamental d'Afrique noire, Série B: Sciences humaines* 35, no. 2 (1973): 269–322; Cheikh Moussa Kamara, "Histoire du Boundou," *Bulletin de l'Institut fondamental d'Afrique noire, Serie B: Sciences humaines* 37, no. 4 (1975): 784–816; Cheikh Moussa Kamara, "Histoire de Ségou," *Bulletin de l'Institut fondamental d'Afrique noire, Serie B: Sciences humaines* 40, no. 3 (1978): 458–88; Cheikh Moussa Kamara, "Histoire du Maasina," *Bulletin de l'Institut fondamental d'Afrique noire, Serie B: Sciences humaines* 35, no. 2 (1970): 388–89, 399–410.
68. Muḥammad al-Muntaqá Tāl, *Al-Jawāhir wa-l-durar fī Sīrat al-Shaykh al-Hājj ʿUmar* (Dār al-Burāq, 2005)
69. David Robinson, "Un historien et anthropologue sénégalais: Shaikh Musa Kamara *Cahiers d'études africaines* 28, no. 109 (1988): 101.
70. Samb, *Essai sur la contribution du Sénégal à la littérature d'expression arabe*, 115-116. See also Kamara, *La vie d'el-Hadji Omar*, 9–10.

71. Samb, *Essai sur la contribution du Sénégal à la littérature d'expression arabe*, 116.
72. Samb, *Essai sur la contribution du Sénégal à la littérature d'expression arabe*, 128.
73. Samb, *Essai sur la contribution du Sénégal à la littérature d'expression arabe*, 117.
74. Isabella Alston, *Eugène Delacroix* (TAJ, 2014).
75. Samb, *Essai sur la contribution du Sénégal à la littérature d'expression arabe*, 118.
76. Audre Lorde, *Sister Outsider: Essays and Speeches* (Crossing Press, 1984), 106–9.
77. Samb, *Essai sur la contribution du Sénégal à la littérature d'expression arabe*, 7.
78. Georg Wilhelm Friedrich Hegel, *The Philosophy of History* (Dover, 1956), 99
79. Hegel, *The Philosophy of History*, 93.
80. Partha Chatterjee, *Nationalist Thought and the Colonial World: A Derivative Discourse* (University of Minnesota Press, 1993), 38.
81. Oumar Ba, *La pénétration française au Cayor: Du règne de Birima N'Goné Latyr à l'intronisation de Madiodo Dèguène Codou* (Dakar: En vente chez l'auteur, 1976).
82. David Robinson, "50 Years of Research on Islam and West African History," *Research Africa Reviews* 4, no. 2 (2020): 6, 8; David Robinson, *Chiefs and Clerics: Abdul Bokar Kan and Futa Toro, 1853–1891* (Oxford University Press, 1975), 181; "Muusa Kamara, *Sheikh Moussa Kamara's Islamic Critique of Jihadists*, trans. Mbaye Lo (Lexington, 2023), 129–33.
83. Jean Schmitz, "Introduction," Muusa Kamara, *Florilège au jardin de l'histoire des Noirs: Zuhūr al-basātīn* (CNRS Éditions, 1998), 69–74.
84. Schmitz, "Introduction," 69–79.
85. Abdoul Malal Diop, "La vie et l'oeuvre de Cheikh Moussa Kamara de Ganguel (1864–1945)" (PhD thesis, Université de Cheikh Anta Diop, 2014); Kamara, *Florilège au jardin de l'histoire des Noirs*, 63.
86. Ron Parker, "The Senegal-Mauritania Conflict of 1989: A Fragile Equilibrium," *Journal of Modern African Studies* 29, no. 1 (1991): 155–71, https://doi.org/10.1017/S0022278X00020784; David L. Szanton, *The Politics of Knowledge: Area Studies and the Disciplines* (University of California Press, 2004).
87. Yambo Ouologuem, *Le devoir de violence: Roman* (Seuil, 1968).
88. Wendell Hassan Marsh, "Compositions of Sainthood: The Biography of Ḥājj ʿUmar Tāl by Shaykh Mūsā Kamara" (PhD thesis, Columbia University, 2018), https://doi.org/10.7916/D81G23P4.
89. Christopher Wise, "Qur'anic Hermeneutics, Sufism, and 'Le Devoir de Violence': Yambo Ouologuem as Marabout Novelist," *Religion & Literature* 28, no. 1 (1996): 85–112.
90. Fanon, *The Wretched of the Earth*, 149.

6. The Secular-Religious Afterlife of Shaykh Musa Kamara

1. Ramadan has since been acquitted of the charges against him in Switzerland. "Tariq Ramadan a été acquitté dans une affaire de viols en Suisse, la partie plaignante fait appel," *Le monde*, May 24, 2023, https://www.lemonde.fr/societe/article/2023/05/24/tariq-ramadan-acquitte-dans-une-affaire-de-viols-en-suisse_6174621_3224.html.
2. *Clash en direct débat Israël Palestine le Dr Bakary Samb avec le traitre de Tariq Ramadan*, 2015, https://www.youtube.com/watch?v=K2ycePU_bto.

6. THE SECULAR-RELIGIOUS AFTERLIFE OF SHAYKH MUSA KAMARA

3. Bakary Sambe, "Africains musulmans et questions internationales: La partie invisible du débat avec Tariq Ramadan," *Islam, societé, diversité, universalité* (blog), accessed October 20, 2023, http://bakarysambe.unblog.fr/2014/09/01/africains-musulmans-et-questions-internationales-la-partie-invisible-du-debat-avec-tariq-ramadan/.
4. Muusa Kamara, *Sheikh Moussa Kamara's Islamic Critique of Jihadists*, trans. Mbaye Lo (Lexington, 2023).
5. Susana Molins Lliteras has described the vast manuscript heritage of Timbuktu as an "iconic archive" whose potency has attracted state intervention and whose meanings circulate among distinct publics to different ends. She provides a thorough examination of this long history and meanings of Timbuktu. Susana Molins Lliteras, "Iconic Archive: Timbuktu and Its Manuscripts in Public Discourse," in *Babel Unbound* (Wits University Press, 2020).
6. Ibn Battuta, *The Travels of Ibn Battuta, A.D. 1325-1354*, vol. 1, trans. H. A. R. Gibb (Published for the Hakluyt Society at the University Press, 1958); Johannes Leo Africanus, *The Cosmography and Geography of Africa*, ed. and trans. Anthony Ossa-Richardson and Richard J. Oosterhoff (Penguin, 2023).
7. Michael A. Gomez, *African Dominion: A New History of Empire in Early and Medieval West Africa* (Princeton University Press, 2018), 219-57.
8. Ousmane Kane, *Beyond Timbuktu: An Intellectual History of Muslim West Africa* (Harvard University Press, 2016), 10-16.
9. Carl J. Richard, *The Golden Age of the Classics in America: Greece, Rome, and the Antebellum United States* (Harvard University Press, 2009), https://doi.org/10.4159/9780674054493.
10. The project "Global Timbuktu: Meanings and Narratives of Resistance in Africa and the Americas," directed by American historian Carolyn Brown, has drawn on these symbolic connections. https://ruafrica.rutgers.edu/images/Global_Timbuktu_Booklet.pdf.
11. Henry Louis Gates, et al., *Wonders of the African World*, distributed by PBS Home Video, 2011; Henry Louis Gates Jr., Virginia Quinn, and Mark Bates, *Africa's Great Civilizations*, PBS, 2017.
12. Shamil Jeppie, "Re/Discovering Timbuktu," in *The Meanings of Timbuktu*, ed. Shamil Jeppie and Souleymane Bachir Diagne (HSRC Press, 2008), 1-16.
13. Jeppie, "Re/Discovering Timbuktu," 8.
14. Thabo Mbeki, "I Am an African," speech presented at the adoption of the Republic of South Africa Constitutional Bill 1996 by South Africa's Constitutional Assembly, May 8, 1996, https://www.youtube.com/watch?v=dCeLwTITRoQ.
15. H. D. Jocelyn, "*Homo Sum: Humani Nil a Me Alienum Puto*" (Terence, *Heauton Timorumenos* 77)." *Antichthon* 7 (1973): 14-46.
16. Thabo Mbeki, "I Am an African,"
17. Pixley Ka Isaka Seme, "The Regeneration of Africa," *African Affairs* 5, no. 20 (1906): 404-8, https://doi.org/10.1093/oxfordjournals.afraf.a094874.
18. Kwame Nkrumah, "Speech at the Congress of Africanists December 12, 1962," in *Revolutionary Path* (Panaf, 1973); Nnamdi Azikiwe, *Renascent Africa* (Negro Universities Press, 1969).
19. Cheikh Anta Diop, *Towards the African Renaissance: Essays in African Culture and Development, 1946-1960*, trans. Egbuna P. Modum (Karnak House, 1996).

6. THE SECULAR-RELIGIOUS AFTERLIFE OF SHAYKH MUSA KAMARA

20. "The African Renaissance Statement of Deputy President, Thabo Mbeki," Department of International Relations and Cooperation, Republic of South Africa, August 13, 1998, https://dirco1.azurewebsites.net/docs/speeches/1998/mbek0813.htm.
21. "The African Renaissance Statement of Deputy President, Thabo Mbeki."
22. Sabelo J. Ndlovu-Gatsheni, "Revisiting the African Renaissance," in *Oxford Research Encyclopedia of Politics*, July 29, 2019, https://oxfordre.com/politics/display/10.1093/acrefore/9780190228637.001.0001/acrefore-9780190228637-e-720.
23. Ngũgĩ wa Thiong'o, *Something Torn and New: An African Renaissance* (BasicCivitas, 2009).
24. Thiong'o, *Something Torn and New*, 70, 71.
25. Kohei Saito, *Slow down: The Degrowth Manifesto* (Astra, 2024).
26. Yogita Goyal, *Romance, Diaspora, and Black Atlantic Literature* (Cambridge University Press, 2010); David Scott, *Conscripts of Modernity: The Tragedy of Colonial Enlightenment* (Duke University Press, 2004).
27. Ngũgĩ wa Thiong'o, *Something Torn and New*.
28. "Senegal Imams Condemn Huge Statue," BBC News, December 11, 2009, http://news.bbc.co.uk/2/hi/africa/8409233.stm.
29. Mamadou Diouf, *Tolerance, Democracy, and Sufis in Senegal* (Columbia University Press, 2013).
30. Mahmood Mamdani, *Scholars in the Marketplace: The Dilemmas of Neo-Liberal Reform at Makerere University, 1989–2005* (Fountain Publishers, 2007).
31. Ousmane Kane, *Beyond Timbuktu: An Intellectual History of Muslim West Africa* (Harvard University Press, 2016), 178–99.
32. Marlise Simons, "Prison Sentence Over Smashing of Shrines in Timbuktu: 9 Years," *New York Times*, September 27, 2016, https://www.nytimes.com/2016/09/28/world/europe/ahmad-al-faqi-al-mahdi-timbuktu-mali.html; Elliott Colla, "On the Iconoclasm of Isis," March 5, 2015, http://www.elliottcolla.com/blog/2015/3/5/on-the-iconoclasm-of-isis; Elliott Colla, "Preservation and Destruction," September 9, 2015, http://www.elliottcolla.com/blog/2015/3/27/pm0t4j35d00plvir68mkffl6fyquh0; Finbarr Barry Flood, "Between Cult and Culture: Bamiyan, Islamic Iconoclasm, and the Museum," *Art Bulletin* 84, no. 4 (2002): 641–59, https://doi.org/10.1080/00043079.2002.10787045.
33. Joseph Andoni Massad, *Islam in Liberalism* (University of Chicago Press, 2015).
34. Majala al-Dirāsāt al-ʿArabiyya wa-Islāmiyya, *Waqāʾiʿ al-Multqā al-ʿIlmī Ḥawl Ḥayāt wa-ʿāmal al-Shaykh Mūsá Kamara* [Proceedings of conference on Shaykh Musa Kamara, 13 July 2013] (al-Maʿhad al-Islāmī bi-Dakār), 2014).
35. *Cheikh Moussa Kamara—Symposium 1*, 2017, https://www.youtube.com/watch?v=7MhYCFICfPM.
36. Muusa Kamara, "Aktar Ar-Rāgibīn: Fī al-Jihād Baʿda an Nabiyyina Man Yakhtāru Az-Zuhūr Wa-Mulk al Bilād Wa Lā Yubālī Bi Man Halaka Fī Jihādihi Min al-ʿibād," *Revue d'études arabes et islamiques* 1, no. 1 (2013): 139–59.
37. Majala al-Dirāsāt al-ʿArabiyya wa-Islāmiyya, *Waqāʾiʿ al-Multqā al-ʿIlmī Ḥawl Ḥayāt wa-ʿāmal al-Shaykh Mūsá Kamara* 7.
38. Musa Kamara, *Tabshīr al-Khāʾif al-Ḥayrān wa-Tadhkīruhu bi-Saʿa Raḥmat Allah al-Karīm al-Mannān* [The announcement of the good news to the fearful and

6. THE SECULAR-RELIGIOUS AFTERLIFE OF SHAYKH MUSA KAMARA

confused and his reminder of the breadth of the mercy of God, the Generous Bestower], ed. Demba Tewe (al-Maʿhad al-Islāmī bi-Dakār, 2014); Musa Kamara, *L'annonce de la bonne nouvelle à l'apeuré désemparé et rappel à lui de l'amplitude de la miséricorde de Dieu le généreux bienfaiteur*, trans. Demba Tewe Cheikh Fall, Ismaila Diop, Alioune Diop, Babacar Niane, and Amadou Sokhna Ndao (Institute Islamique de Dakar, 2015).

39. Shārnū Kāh, *al-Shaykh Mūsá Kamara (1864–1945)*: Hayātuhu wa-Afkāruh (Īfān-Jamiʿat al-Shaykh Anta Jūb bi-Dakār, 2014).
40. Shārnū Kāh, *al-Shaykh Mūsá Kamara*, 5.
41. Abdoul Malal Diop, "La vie et l'oeuvre de Cheikh Moussa Kamara de Ganguel (1864–1945)" (PhD thesis, Université de Cheikh Anta Diop, 2014).
42. Musa Kamara, *Al-Majmūʿ al-Nafīs Sirran wa-ʿalāniyya fī Dhikr Baʿḍ al-Sādāt al-Bīḍāniyya wa-l-Fulāniyya* [The precious collection of secrecy and publicity in the memory of some of the Bīḍān and Fulani nobles], ed. Nani Wuld al-Hussaīn (Manshūrāt al-Zaman, 2015).
43. Mbaye Lo, "'The Last Scholar': Cheikh Moussa Kamara and the Condemnation of Jihad by the Sword," *Transcultural Islam Research Network* (blog), April 23, 2016, https://tirnscholars.org/2016/04/23/the-last-scholar-cheikh-moussa-kamara-andthe-condemnation-of-jihad-by-the-sword/index.html; Mbaye Lo, "Jihad as a Tradition of Peace in the Writings of Cheikh Moussa Kamara (1864–1945)," paper presented at the Islam and World Peace Conference, Columbia University, New York, September 12, 2015); Kamara, *Sheikh Moussa Kamara's Islamic Critique of Jihadists*.
44. Mūsá Kamara, *Al-Faṣl al-Tāsiʿa min Akthar Al-Rāghibīn: fī Maḥaba Rūʾasāʾ Farānsa lī*, taḥqīq: Aḥmad al-Shukri wa-Khadim Mbakke, taqdīm: Aḥmad al-Shukri (Maʿhad al-Dirāsāt al-Ifrīqīyya Jamiʿat Muḥammad al-Khāmis, 2016); Mūsá Kamara, *Akthar al-Rāghibīn fī al-Jihād baʿd al-Nabīʾīn man Yakhtāru al-Ẓuhūr wa-Malaka al-Bilād wa-lā Yubālī bi-man Halaka fī Jihādihi min al-ʿIbād* (Maʿhad al-Dirāsāt al-Ifrīqiyya, 2003); Mūsá Kamara, *Ashhá al-ʿUlūm wa-Aṭayab al-Khabar fī Sīrat al-Ḥājj ʿUmar* (Maʿhad al-Dirāsāt al-Ifrīqīyya, 2001).
45. Ousmane Diaw, "Al-Shaykh Mūsá Kamara, Al-Faṣl al-Tāsiʿa min 'Akthar Al-Rāghibīn': fī maḥaba rūʾasāʾ farānsa lī, taḥqīq: Aḥmad al-Shukri wa-Khadim Mbakke, taqdīm: Aḥmad al-Shukri, Maʿhad al-Dirāsāt al-Ifrīqīyah, Jamiʿat Muḥammad al-Khamis bi-l-Rabat, silsilat nusus wa-wathāyiq (13), m. 2016, ṣ 66," *Research Africa Reviews* 3, no. 1 (2019).
46. Mūsá Kamara, *Tabshīr al-Khāʾif al-Ḥayrān wa-Tadhkīruhu bi-Saʿa Raḥmat Allah al-Karīm al-Mannān* ed. Muḥammad Saʿīd Bāh (Manshūrāt Maktabat al-Shaykh Mūsá Aḥmad Kamara, 2022).
47. Conversation with the author in Dakar, June 2018.
48. One might read Felski's turn away from critique for what she describes as the oddly religious dimensions it seems to have taken as symptomatic of a contemporary desecularization, or postsecularity, of contemporary humanities scholarship. Rita Felski, *The Limits of Critique* (University of Chicago Press, 2015).
49. Kâ, *Cheikh Moussa Kamara*, 6, 7.
50. Wendell H. Marsh, "Reading with the Colonial in the Life of Shaykh Musa Kamara, a Muslim Scholar-Saint," *Africa* 90, no. 3 (2020): 604–24.

6. THE SECULAR-RELIGIOUS AFTERLIFE OF SHAYKH MUSA KAMARA

51. Muhammad Said Bâ, "Muqaddima al-Mahquq," in *Tabshīr Al-Khāʾif al-Ḥayrān Wa Tadhkīruhu Bisāʿat Raḥmat Allah al-Karīm al-Mannān* (Manshūrāt Maktabat al-Shaykh Mūsá Aḥmad Kamara, 2022), b.
52. For a persuasive refutation of the so-called prohibition of the image as an antisemitic trope that has been projected onto Muslims, see Wendy Shaw, *What is "Islamic" art?: Between Religion and Perception* (Cambridge University Press, 2019), 40–56.
53. Allen F. Roberts, Mary Nooter Roberts, Gassia Armenian, and Ousmane Gueye, *A Saint in the City: Sufi Arts of Urban Senegal* (Fowler Museum of Cultural History, 2003).
54. Pádraig Carmody, "Transforming Globalization and Security: Africa and America Post-9/11," *Africa Today* 52, no. 1 (2005): 97–120; Benjamin F. Soares and René Otayek, eds., *Islam and Muslim Politics in Africa* (Palgrave Macmillan, 2007); Jeremy Keenan, "A New Crisis in the Sahel," Al Jazeera, January 3, 2012, http://www.aljazeera.com/indepth/opinion/2012/01/20121274447237703.html.
55. Mamadou Diouf, ed., *Tolerance, Democracy, and Sufis in Senegal* (Columbia University Press, 2013); Sarah Eltantawi, *Shari'ah on Trial: Northern Nigeria's Islamic Revolution* (University of California Press, 2017), https://doi.org/10.1525/california/9780520293779.001.0001; Brandon Kendhammer, *Muslims Talking Politics: Framing Islam, Democracy, and Law in Northern Nigeria* (University of Chicago Press, 2016), https://doi.org/10.7208/chicago/9780226369174.001.0001; Noah Salomon, *For Love of the Prophet: An Ethnography of Sudan's Islamic State* (Princeton University Press, 2016), https://doi.org/10.1515/9781400884292; Zekeria Ould Ahmed Salem, *Prêcher dans le désert: Islam politique et changement social en Mauritanie* (Éditions Karthala, 2013).
56. Arjun Appadurai, "Disjuncture and Difference in the Global Cultural Economy," *Public Culture* 2, no. 2 (1990): 1–24, https://doi.org/10.1215/08992363-2-2-1.
57. I borrow the language of potency from Lliteras, who has worked extensively and critically on the actual manuscript collections. Lliteras, "Iconic Archive."
58. Kane, *Beyond Timbuktu*, 178–99.
59. Oumar Ba, "Contested Meanings: Timbuktu and the Prosecution of Destruction of Cultural Heritage as War Crimes," *African Studies Review* 63, no. 4 (2020): 743–62, https://doi.org/10.1017/asr.2020.16.
60. Kane, *Beyond Timbuktu*, 160–77; Beth A. Buggenhagen, "Islam's New Visibility and the Secular Public in Senegal," in *Tolerance, Democracy, and Sufis in Senegal* (Columbia University Press, 2015), 51–72, https://doi.org/10.7312/diou16262-006; Diouf, *Tolerance, Democracy, and Sufis in Senegal*.
61. Li provides a compelling history of the present through ethnographic lawyering for prisoners of the war on terror. My reflections here have profoundly benefited from studying his work. Darryl Li, *The Universal Enemy: Jihad, Empire, and the Challenge of Solidarity* (Stanford University Press, 2020), https://doi.org/10.1515/9781503610880.
62. Elizabeth Kai Hinton, *From the War on Poverty to the War on Crime: The Making of Mass Incarceration in America* (Harvard University Press, 2016).
63. I credit Abdourahmane Seck for this reframing. For an alternative timeline that focuses on the racialization of the figure of the terrorist as Arab, Muslim,

and South Asian, see Deepa Kumar, "Terrorcraft: Empire and the Making of the Racialised Terrorist Threat," *Race & Class* 62, no. 2 (2020): 34–60, https://doi.org/10.1177/0306396820930523.

64. I am using "concern" here in the sense proposed in Latour's reading of Heidegger. Bruno Latour, "Why Has Critique Run Out of Steam? From Matters of Fact to Matters of Concern," *Critical Inquiry* 30, no. 2 (2004): 225–48, https://doi.org/10.1086/421123.

65. E. Ann McDougall, "Saharan Peoples and Societies," in *Oxford Research Encyclopedia of African History* (Oxford University Press, 2018–), published February 25, 2019, https://doi.org/10.1093/acrefore/9780190277734.013.285; E. Ann McDougall, "Constructing Emptiness: Islam, Violence and Terror in the Historical Making of the Sahara," *Journal of Contemporary African Studies* 25, no. 1 (2007): 17–30, https://doi.org/10.1080/02589000601157022; Brittany Meché, "Bad Things Happen in the Desert: Mapping Security Regimes in the West African Sahel and the 'Problem' of Arid Spaces," in *A Research Agenda for Military Geographies*, ed. Rachel Woodward (Edward Elgar, 2019), https://www.elgaronline.com/view/edcoll/9781786438867/9781786438867.00012.xml.

66. For a precious reflection on the impact of the Iranian revolution in Senegalese universities, see this interview with Souleymane Bachir Diagne. Suren Pillay and Carlos Fernandes, "Transmission, Obligation and Movement: An Interview with Souleymane Bachir Diagne," *Social Dynamics* 42, no. 3 (2016): 542–54, https://www.tandfonline.com/doi/abs/10.1080/02533952.2016.1264094.

67. This argument builds on and extends the argument of Seck, who proposed that Islam is an idiom for the nation. It provides the dominant mode of socialization and to great extent participation in public life. Abdourahmane Seck, *La question musulmane au Sénégal: Essai d'anthropologie d'une nouvelle modernité* (Karthala, 2010). The argument also engages with Darryl Li's thoughts on the horizon of belonging. Li, *The Universal Enemy*, 14.

68. Mamadou Diouf, *Histoire du Sénégal: Le modèle islamo-wolof et ses périphéries* (Maisonneuve & Larose, 2001).

69. "Mapping Africa's Islamic Economy," Economist Impact, November 17, 2015, https://eiuperspectives.economist.com/economic-development/mapping-africa%E2%80%99s-islamic-economy.

70. Sambe, "Africains musulmans et questions internationales."

71. I am grateful to Mamadou Diallo for pointing out this association.

72. Robert A. Orsi, "The Disciplinary Vocabulary of Modernity," *International Journal* 59, no. 4 (2004): 879–85, https://doi.org/10.2307/40203989.

73. Talal Asad, *Genealogies of Religion: Discipline and Reasons of Power in Christianity and Islam* (Johns Hopkins University Press, 2009).

74. Talal Asad, *Formations of the Secular: Christianity, Islam, Modernity* (Stanford University Press, 2003).

75. For a legal perspective on how "confining and defining" has worked out since Nigeria's colonial episode, see the meticulous and theoretically sophisticated work in Rabiat Akande, *Entangled Domains: Empire, Law and Religion in Northern Nigeria* (Cambridge University Press, 2023).

76. Kamara, *Akthar al-Rāghibīn*; and *Sheikh Moussa Kamara's Islamic Critique of Jihadists*.

77. As Mbaye Lo has pointed out, Samb's translation of this work as "Condemnation of Holy War" is incorrect from the perspective of Islamic scholarship. Condemning something indicates a much higher degree of disapproval and requires a certainty that Kamara likely avoided claiming. Instead, he "invalidated" the use of jihad, claiming not that it was unacceptable transhistorically but that for his context it was no longer valid. Amar Samb, "Condamnation de la guerre sainte par Cheikh Moussa Kamara," *Bulletin de l'Institut fondamental d'Afrique noire, Serie B: Sciences humaines* 38 (1976): 158–99; Lo, " 'The Last Scholar.' "
78. Kamara, *Sheikh Moussa Kamara's Islamic Critique of Jihadists*.
79. Cheikh Moussa Kamara, "L'islam et le christianisme," *Bulletin de l'Institut fondamental d'Afrique noire, Série B: Sciences humaines* 35, no. 2 (1973): 269–322.
80. Elsewhere this tradition has been described in the literature as the Suwarian tradition in West African Islam. Lamin O. Sanneh, *Beyond Jihad: The Pacifist Tradition in West African Islam* (Oxford University Press, 2016). However, Kamara's references suggest that his intellectual influence on this question was not Hajj Salim Suware, who lived farther south, but a Saharan tradition that followed the eleventh-century Abbasid scholar al-Mawardi; Muusa Kamara, *Florilège au jardin de l'histoire des Noirs: Zuhūr al-basātīn* (CNRS Éditions, 1998), 11n3.
81. Amar Samb, *Essai sur la contribution du Sénégal à la littérature d'expression arabe* (Institut fondamental d'Afrique noire, 1972), 128.
82. On the concept of religion making, see Markus Dressler and Arvind-pal Singh Mandair, *Secularism and Religion-Making* (Oxford University Press, 2011). This discussion is profoundly influenced by many conversations and collaborations over several years with Mamadou Diallo. I am grateful for his insights.
83. "La question laïque au Senegal [par A. Aziz Mbacke Majalis]," *Xalima.com* (blog), March 2, 2016, https://www.xalimasn.com/la-question-laique-au-senegal-par-a-aziz-mbacke-majalis/.
84. Cheikh Anta Mbacké Babou, *Fighting the Greater Jihad: Amadu Bamba and the Founding of the Murīdiyya of Senegal, 1853–1913* (Ohio University Press, 2007); Fallou Ngom, *Muslims Beyond the Arab World: The Odyssey of ʿAjamī and the Murīdiyya* (Oxford University Press, 2016).
85. Shahzad Bashir, "Documenting the Living Dead," in *A New Vision for Islamic Pasts and Futures* (MIT Press, 2022), https://doi.org/10.26300/bdp.bashir.ipf.living-dead.

Coda: Long Live Philology!
Or, Remembering the Future of the Humanities

1. Oliver Liffran, "Sénégal: Retour sur les circonstances tragiques de la mort de Fallou Sène," *Jeune Afrique*, May 17, 2018, https://www.jeuneafrique.com/560407/societe/senegal-retour-sur-les-circonstances-tragiques-de-la-mort-de-fallou-sene/; "Meurtre à l'UGB: Ce qui s'est passé dans la chambre où Seynabou Ka Diallo a été tuée," Seneweb News, March 31, 2022, https://www.seneweb.com/news/Politique/meurtre-a-l-rsquo-ugb-ce-qui-s-rsquo-est_n_375120.html; "Deces

d'un étudiant l'UGB: Une enquete en cours," *RTS Officiel* (blog), February 10, 2024, https://www.rts.sn/actualite/detail/a-la-une/ugb-deces-dun-etudiant-lors-de-manifestations; Barry Souleymane, "Décès de l'étudiant Prosper Clédor Sène, le Conseil académique de l'UGB décrète 'une semaine de deuil,'" Sene.News, February 21, 2024, https://www.senenews.com/enseignement-superieur/deces-de-letudiant-prosper-cledor-sene-le-conseil-academique-de-lugb-decrete-une-semaine-de-deuil_484799.html. I am grateful to Gaston Berger University doctoral candidate Dieynaba Sarr for these references.
2. Sonia Sanchez, "For Sweet Honey in the Rock," in *Shake Loose My Skin: New and Selected Poems* (Beacon, 1999), 148–50.
3. This analysis is profoundly influenced by conversations with the historian and theorist Mamadou Diallo. Mamadou Diallo, "Ci-gît la république des évolués du Sénégal," SenePlus, April 12, 2024, https://www.seneplus.com/opinions/ci-git-la-republique-des-evolues-du-senegal.
4. I am grateful to the political scientist Takiyah Harper-Shipman for discussions that have helped me think through the new landscape.
5. World Bank, "Senegal Economic Update 2023: Addressing the Needs of Vulnerable Groups for National Development," June 21, 2023, https://www.worldbank.org/en/country/senegal/publication/senegal-economic-update-2023-addressing-the-needs-of-vulnerable-groups-for-national-development.
6. Abdoul Malal Diop, "La vie et l'oeuvre de Cheikh Moussa Kamara de Ganguel (1864–1945)" (PhD thesis, Université de Cheikh Anta Diop, 2014), 22–33.
7. I am, of course, thinking with Wynter here. My colonial humanism is close to her Man_2. Sylvia Wynter, "Unsettling the Coloniality of Being/Power/Truth/Freedom: Towards the Human, After Man, Its Overrepresentation—an Argument," *CR: The New Centennial Review* 3, no. 3 (2003): 257–337, https://doi.org/10.1353/ncr.2004.0015.
8. Tomoko Masuzawa, *The Invention of World Religions: or, How European Universalism Was Preserved in the Language of Pluralism* (University of Chicago Press, 2005).
9. V. Y. Mudimbe, *The Invention of Africa: Gnosis, Philosophy, and the Order of Knowledge* (Indiana University Press, 1988).
10. la paperson, *A Third University Is Possible* (University of Minnesota Press, 2017), 99.
11. Helen Small, *The Value of the Humanities* (Oxford University Press, 2013).
12. On the illusory quality of social scientific concepts in African knowledge production, see Abdourahmane Seck, "Vers une théorie de la mémographie: Piste pour in-discipliner les études africaines," *Revue d'études décoloniales*, no. 8 (October 15, 2024): 66.
13. Olúfẹ́mi O. Táíwò, *Reconsidering Reparations* (Oxford University Press, 2022), 29–32, https://doi.org/10.1093/oso/9780197508893.001.0001.
14. Sabelo J. Ndlovu-Gatsheni, *Epistemic Freedom in Africa: Deprovincialization and Decolonization* (Taylor & Francis, 2018).
15. Michael Neocosmos, *Thinking Freedom in Africa: Toward a Theory of Emancipatory Politics* (Wits University Press, 2016).
16. Elleni Centime Zeleke, *Ethiopia in Theory: Revolution and Knowledge Production, 1964-2016* (Brill, 2020).

17. C. Duermeijer, M. Amir, and L. Schoombee, "Africa Generates Less Than 1 Percent of the World's Research; Data Analytics Can Change That," March 22, 2018, https://www.elsevier.com/connect/africa-generates-less-than-1-of-the-worlds-research-dataanalytics-can-change-that.
18. This formulation was developed through our inaugural study group that worked to create a localized translation of Stefano Harney and Fred Moten, *The Undercommons: Fugitive Planning and Black Study* (Minor Compositions, 2013).
19. Abdourahmane Seck, "Après le développement: Détours paradigmatiques et philosophie de l'histoire au Sénégal: Une contribution africaine au temps des communs," *Présence africaine*, no. 192 (2015): 13–32.

Acknowledgments

The principal difficulty in making an account of the debts I have accumulated over the course of this project is pinpointing when exactly it began. No matter the date I might give for it, the list is long. So instead of starting at a beginning, I will start at home. Thankfully, this accounting is not a statement of my poverty but a testimony to my great fortune. I am thankful first and foremost to my family, who has given the most to bring this book into being. To my enchanted wife, Jamilah Abu-Bakare, who could not have possibly known that she would have to think so much about a poorly known Muslim scholar from Senegal, I am grateful for all your sacrifices and expenditures of attention and care. I commit to matching the enthusiasm and support that you have shown this project for your projects to come. To Zora Mai, thank you for sharing time that was rightfully yours. I hope I have produced something that you can learn from and from which you might develop your own relationship to study. Veda Roodal Persad and Ayesha Abu-Bakare, too, have poured their support into this project with everything from punctuation to compulsory calisthenics.

I want to thank, too, the family members of Shaykh Musa Kamara, who have shown me great hospitality, warmth, and encouragement on several occasions in Dakar, Ganguel, Matam, and Nouakchott. In particular, the current head of the family, Thierno Mohammadu Bassirou Camara; the family spokesperson, Ismaïla Camara; and the Mauritanian sociologist

ACKNOWLEDGMENTS

Cheikh Saad Bouh Kamara require special mention. Thank you all for entrusting me with access to your homes and your private collections and with the story of your forefather. While I do not pretend to tell it the way you all might, I hope that he is nevertheless recognizable to you in my presentation. If I have fallen short in any way, please blame it on my head and not my heart. Shaykh Musa has left something for the world, and studying his life and works, I believe, has improved me as a person. I want to also acknowledge the generosity and guidance of the group of scholars close to the family who are working diligently to advance research in the emerging field of Kamara studies and the broader Arabo-Islamic heritage of Futa Toro. Abdoul Malal Diop, Mamadou Youry Sall, and Muhammad Saidou Ba are scholars who should be studied and engaged. I commit to supporting these efforts in securing Kamara's legacy.

The Mauritanian researchers Mariam Baba Ahmed, Baba Addou, and Ahmed Maouloud Eida El-Hilal guided me through what was very new terrain for me. While we worked together for a different project, their crash course in all things Mauritania and their social connections proved vital for this project as well. My Pulaar-language-instructor-turned-research-assistant, Muhammad Camara, deserves mention here, as he helped me navigate Senegal's rural north on several occasions. As someone who had grown accustomed to Dakar, he taught me that "Futa wona ga." Ousmane Diaw helped me at a very early, but pivotal, stage of bibliographical research in Cairo. And Moustafa Fouad's tutoring also in Cairo was essential in helping me make the leap from Arabic courses to Arabic textual research. I also want to thank the staff at the Archives Nationales du Sénégal and at the Laboratoire d'Islamologie of the Institut Fondamental d'Afrique Noire, especially Om Kalsoum and Suleymane Gueye.

So much of my thinking has been stimulated by and filtered through prolonged and ongoing conversation with a core group of fellow travelers who I am humbled to have as interlocutors and friends. Mamadou Diallo, Alden Young, Tommaso Manfredini, Abdourahmane Seck, Anand Venkatkrishnan, Basma Radwan, Ira Dworkin, Rebecca Faulkner, and Safa Khatib have all read several chapters and proposals, helped me with thinking about specific language, and reminded me to remember the purpose of all of this. Ariela Marcus-Sells—who has probably taught me more about the academic study of religion in general and of Sufism in West Africa in

ACKNOWLEDGMENTS

particular and about the culture of academia than any other single person—warrants special mention, as she meticulously combed through the entire manuscript and made it all the better. My only regret is that I was not able to more fully reflect her suggestions. And I thank her for always telling me the hard truth.

I am also grateful for the teachers and mentors from my time at Columbia University that prepared me for this undertaking. To Mamadou Diouf, I owe an inestimable debt for which there is no accounting. Though I doubt he would claim the blame, Gil Anidjar taught me, although later than ideal, how to read. That gift is priceless. Sudipta Kaviraj and Souleymane Bachir Diagne have given me precious models of rigorous thinking to which I aspire. Mana Kia paid attention when few others would. Brinkley Messick supported me early and often in ways that were foundational. Katherine Ewing gave me some remarkable opportunities when I needed them the most and showed great patience and compassion. And Manan Ahmed Asif deserves a medal for his work in helping faculty of color learn the hidden curriculum needed for academic success.

Colleagues at Rutgers University in Newark and New Brunswick have supported me terrifically. Through the Islamic Humanities cluster hire and related activities spearheaded by Sadia Abbas and supported by former Chancellor Nancy Cantor, I have benefited from being in a dynamic cohort with Alex Dikka Seggarman and Amir Moosavi. Our conversations and projects have had a definite impact on this book—fundamentally in making the need for a transformative humanities the subject of inquiry in its own right. The working group sponsored an early manuscript workshop for this project where I benefited from the interventions of R. A. Judy, Jean Allman, Shobana Shankar, Laura Lomas, and James Goodman. I am also grateful for the generous leaves and reduced teaching load from the university that gave me time to write. My dean, Jacqueline Mattis, has been especially supportive. John Keene, Belinda Edmonson, Wendell Holbrook, Salamishah Tillet, and Darién Davis have been great senior colleagues. Mayte Green-Mercado, James Jones, Catherine Clepper, Kyle Riismandel, Hyacinth Miller, and Audrey Truschke have all helped me navigate the institution in one way or another. And, of course, the inimitable Christina Strasburger deserves so much credit for keeping the whole place running. The Center for African Studies has also supported this work, especially

ACKNOWLEDGMENTS

Barbara Cooper, Ouesseina Alidou, and Genese Sodikoff. Undergraduate research assistants Chelsea Egu, Erika Jean-Baptiste, and Jaila Benson, too, contributed to this project.

I benefited greatly from a two-year postdoc at the Buffett Institute of Global Affairs at Northwestern University. The Program of African Studies, the Institute of Islamic Thought in Africa, and the Herskovits Library, among other spaces, were incredible resources and provided unparalleled community for clarifying my relationship to the study of Islam in Africa, deepening my engagement with Black studies, and exploring global studies as a field. Sean Hanretta, Rachel Riedl, Elizabeth Shakman Hurd, Robert Orsi, Adia Benton, Charles Stewart, Paul Naylor, Zekeria Ahmed Salem, Rebecca Shereikis, Robert Launay, Brannon Ingram, Esmeralda Kale, Helen Tilley, Darryl Li (whole also made great comments on chapter 6), Junaid Quadri, Diego Arispe-Bazan, and Christopher Paul Harris are among the Chicagoland scholars who helped to make this period a generative one.

I have also benefited from exchanges with and feedback from Benjamin Soares, Mbaye Lo, Hisham Aidi, Ann McDougall, John Hanson, Joseph Hill, Asad Haider, Jean Schmitz, Etienne Smith, Nathanial Mathews, Elleni Centime Zeleke, Madina Thiam, Jason Derby, Yusuf Hassan, Rhea Rahman, Rasul Miller, Amelia Herbert, Ayodeji Ogunnaike, Oludamini Ogunnaike, Takiyah Harper-Shipman, Jeremy Dell, Ezgi Güner, George Bajalia, Yitzhak Lewis, Amir Syed, Mauro Nobili, and Abdulbasit Kassim. I am especially thankful for David Robinson's reading of the manuscript. His enthusiasm for the project was especially validating in a moment of great self-doubt. Audiences for talks delivered at Barnard College's History Department, Dartmouth College's History Department, Cornell University's Comparative Muslim Societies Seminar, the Department of African American Studies at UCLA, the Center for Global Islamic Studies at the University of Florida, and the World History Center at the University of Pittsburgh have all contributed to making this a better project.

Finally, I acknowledge the masterful developmental editing and patience of Kali Handelman, who supported me in moving from a "dissertation-book" to something far more interesting. The anonymous reviewers for my article "Reading with the Colonial in the Life of Shaykh Musa Kamara, a Muslim Scholar-Saint" in the journal *Africa* greatly helped in this process by prompting some key reflections about Kamara's

ACKNOWLEDGMENTS

canonicity. The reviewers for this manuscript, too, offered very helpful feedback. I am also grateful for the conscientious stewardship of this project by former Columbia University Press editor Eric Schwartz who went above and beyond in nurturing this project and current editor Alyssa Napier who has gotten us over the finish line. Aude Tournaye suggested I consider the artwork of Arébénor Bassene who graciously agreed to have his painting grace the cover. And I thank Jonathan Adjemian, whose unique combination of skills, interests, and kindness makes him an editorial guardian angel.

Despite all these interventions, both human and divine, this book remains a debt, the responsibility for which I alone carry. May it help you accumulate your own.

Index

Abd al-Qadir, Emir, 19, 21
Abdul (Almamy), 124
Abu Hurayra, 72
accommodation, M. Kamara and, 12, 14
adab (literature), 79
Addou, Baba, 79
African idea, 188
African National Congress, 186
African Renaissance, 35, 182–92; C. A. Diop on, 154–56; European Renaissance and, 188–90; GWOT and, 141, 202–3, 211–12; humanism of, 185–87, 189–90, 192; M. Kamara and, 184–85; modernity and, 185; slavery and, 186–87
African Renaissance Institute, 187
African Renaissance Monument, 190–91
"African Renaissance Statement" (Mbeki), 187
Africanus, Leo, 183
Africa's Great Civilizations (documentary), 183
Ahmad ibn Ahmad (of Masina), 173–74
Ahmed, Mariam Baba, 79
Ambiguous Adventure (*L'aventure ambiguë*) (Kane, C.), 159
al-ʿandalīb (nightingale), 49

Announcement of the Good News to the Fearful and Confused and His Reminder of the Breadth of the Mercy of God, the Generous Bestower, The (Kamara, M.), 32, 33, 34, 228; Bâ and, 199–200; *basmala* in, 42; beginnings in, 38–60; *bishara* in, 47, 52, 53, 72; Buh in, 77–78, 82; *bushrā* in, 47; dreams of M. Kamara in, 70–75; GWOT and, 209; hagiography in, 44, 46–47, 52; *The History of the Blacks* and, 125, 138–39; literary prize and, 133; Malcolm X and, 60; memory in, 55–60; philology in, 48–49, 60; "Pre-Text, Text, and Con-Text" of Revelation in, 46; prophecy in, 61–85; Prophet Muhammad in, 42, 64; publication of, 196–97; Qurʾan memorization in, 58–59; *tabshīr* in, 47; *tarjama* in, 43–46, 49–50
antihumanism, 3, 37
apparent (*ẓāhir*), 52
Arab awakening (*Nahḍa*), 2
arabisants (speakers of Arabic), 19
Arabs Before Islam, The (Zaydan), 127
Archinard, Louis, 90
Arnaud, Robert, 96–99, 100, 246n27; colonial humanism and, 221

[277]

INDEX

Asad, Talal, 108, 109, 207
asceticism: M. Kamara on, 83; in Sufism, 51–52
Atlantic Revolutions, 6
Auerbach, Erich, 60, 113–14
Aux cinqs couleurs de l'islam (Monteil, V.), 144–45
al-ʿAynayn, Muhammad Ma, 13–14
ʿAli ibn Abi Talib, 67–68
Azawad, 202
Azikwe, Nnamdi, 186

Bâ, Amadou Hampâté, 140–41, 152, 178
Bâ, Muhammad Said, 196–97, 199–200, 237n8
Ba, Oumar, 177
Baal, Ceerno Sulaymane, 9–10, 110, 124
Baba, Ahmad, 183, 184, 212
bad dreams (*ḥulm*), 72
Bah, Kuumba, 88
Bah, Sammba Joom, 86–87, 90–94
al-Bakri, 164–65
Balla, Thierno Tafsirou, 84
Bamba, Amadou, 12, 206
baraka (spiritual blessing), 104, 170
Barrows, Leland, 15
barzakh (meditating bridge between the hidden and the manifest), 68
basmala, 42
bāṭin (hidden), 52
battle of Médine, 22–23, 25
Battle of Tondibi, 187
beginnings: in *The Announcement of the Good News to the Fearful and Confused and His Reminder of the Breadth of the Mercy of God, the Generous Bestower*, 38–60; in Qurʾan, 42; Said on, 42; of textual life, 51–55
Beginnings (Said), 32
Benhamouda, M., 140
Bergson, Henri, 150–51
Bilal, 124
bishara, 47, 52, 53, 72, 139
Black internationalism, xii
Bludgeoned by Fate (*Matraqué par le destin*) (Samb), 158–59

Blyden, Edward, x
Boisson, M., 133
Bonnel de Mézières, Albert, 120–21
Book of Lances (Tal, U.), 11, 58
Bousbina, Saïd, 177
Braahiima, Ceerno, 171
Brigaud, Félix, 164
Brown, John, 183
Budé, Guillaume, 151
Buh, Saʿad, 50, 59, 104, 244n41; in *The Announcement of the Good News to the Fearful and Confused and His Reminder of the Breadth of the Mercy of God, the Generous Bestower*, 77–78, 82; dreams and, 85; dreams of M. Kamara and, 67, 74–75, 77–78; *Islam noir* and, 99; *The Life of Hajj Umar* and, 65; *Naṣīḥa* by, 112; in Saint-Louis, 76–83
Bulletin de l'enseignement de l'Afrique occidentale française, 132
Bulletin de l'Institut fondamental d'Afrique noire, 170
Bulletin du Comité d'études historiques et scientifiques e d'Afrique occidentale française, 133–34
Bureaux Arabes, 19
Burke, Edmund, 18–19
Burkina Faso, 217
bushrā, 47

Caam, Muhammad Ali, 121
Camara, Ismaïla, 195
Camara, Moussa, 206
Camara, Thierno Mouhamadou Bassirou, 195
Carlyle, Thomas, 172
Carrère, Frédéric, 23
caste system, 6; in Futa Toro, 11; *Islam noir* and, 111–12; *L'islam et la politique musulmane française en Afrique-occidentale française* on, 97; *ṭarīqa* and, 8
Cathédrale du Souvenir Africain, 134, 209
Césaire, Aimé, 149
Chatterjee, Partha, 176

[278]

INDEX

al-Chokri, Ahmad, 196
Christianity, 5; *The Coming Together of Christianid Islam* and, 136–37, 170, 174; in Futa Toro, 9; icons of, 200; paganism in, 190; Qurʾan and, 24; scholasticism in, 189; Tal and, 11; U. Tal and, 21–22
Chronicle of the seeker (*Tarikh al-fattash*), 26–27, 120–21
Chroniques du Foûta sénégalais (Soh), 121, 129
Cissé, Coumba, 119
Citizen's Broom, The (*Le Balai Citoyen*), 215
Clear Truth in the Brotherhood of All Believers, The (Kamara, M.), 104, 170
closeness (*walāya*), 71, 79
colonial humanism, 220–21; goal of, 226
coloniality of knowledge, 222–23
Columbian Orator, The (Douglass), x
Coming Together of Christianity and Islam, The (Kamara, M.), 136–37, 174; translation of, 170
commandant de cercle (district officer), 123
commitment to read again (*relegere*), 228
comparative literature, Samb and, 166–67
Complete Lesson in General History, The, 126
"Condemnation of the Holy War" (Samb), 267n77
contextualism, 26–27
Cooperson, Michael, 44
Coppet, M. de, 138
Coppolani, Xavier, 95–96, 99, 116
counter-Enlightenment, 150
COVID-19 pandemic, 215, 216

Dadî, Kumba, 39
Dadî, Maryam, 39, 48–49
Damga, 105
dan Fodio, Uthman, xiii, 58
Deeniyankooɓe dynasty, 124
Delacroix, Eugène, 173

Delafosse, Maurice, 116, 119, 219; antiracist works of, 157; *Chroniques du Foûta sénégalais* and, 121; colonial humanism and, 221; *The History of the Blacks* and, 124, 128–30; C. Monteil and, 144; philology of, 122; *Tarikh al-Sudan* and, 120; Timbuktu Chronicles and, 128–29
Description of Egypt, 17
dhikr (devotional worship), 84–85
diaspora, 155, 194; Malcolm X on, xii
Diaw, Ousmane, 196, 249n73
digitization, 28
dīn (religion), 108–9
Diop, Abdoul Malal, 13, 27, 84, 177, 196, 197; Islam noir and, 94; Samb and, 165
Diop, Cheikh Anta, 153–57, 179; African Renaissance Monument and, 191; Mbeki and, 186
Diouf, Mamadou, 102; African Renaissance Monument and, 191
district officer (*commandant de cercle*), 123
divine gnosis (*maʿrifa*), 8
Djenidi, Abdallah, 146
Dodds, Alfred-Amédée, 90
Donation of Constantine, 36
Don Quixote (fictional character), 17
Douglass, Frederick, x
Drame, Mamadou Lamine, 82, 124
dreams: of A. al-Naʾari, 84–85; Sirriyeh on, 241n10
dreams of M. Kamara, 32–33, 61–78; in *The Announcement of the Good News to the Fearful and Confused and His Reminder of the Breadth of the Mercy of God, the Generous Bestower*, 70–75; Buh and, 67, 74–75, 77–78, 85; hermeneutics of suspicion in, 62; jihad in, 62–63; in *The Life of Hajj Umar*, 85; Prophet Ibrahim in, 70–71, 73, 81, 85; Prophet Muhammad in, 71–75, 81, 85; of Qurʾan, 70–75; U. Tal in, 33, 64–68, 85, 241n4
Du Bois, Felix, 120

INDEX

Du Bois, W. E. B., 157
dunya (world), 108

école franco-arabe, 136
Enlightenment, 18, 35; counter-Enlightenment and, 150; literary prize in, 132
Entry of the Crusaders in Constantinople, The (Delacroix), 173
Equiano, Olaudah, 157
Erasmus of Rotterdam, 163
Essai sur la contribution du Sénégal à la littérature d'expression arabe (Essay on Senegal's contribution to Literature of Arabic expression) (Samb), 160, 170–71, 175
Eurocentrism, 28
European Renaissance: African Renaissance and, 188–90; humanism of, 163, 190
exemplary acts (*manāqib*), 45
experiential knowledge, 8, 73
Exploration scientifique de l'Algerie, 19

Fadiliyya, 76
Faidherbe, Louis, 15, 19–22, 132; on U. Tal, 23–24
Fall, Baye, 200
Fanatics of Tangier (Delacroix), 173
Fanon, Frantz, 149
Farias, Paolo, 26–27, 120
fatāwā (nonbinding legal opinions), 22
Faye, Bassirou Diomaye, 215
Fees Must Fall, 215
Felski, Rita, 264n48
Fields, Julia, xii
Flowers from among the Gardens in the History of the Blacks (*Zuhūr al-Basātīn fī Tārīkh al-Sawādīn*) (Kamara, M.), 1, 115, 229n1, 249n1
Floyd, George, 215
formations of the secular, 108
French Legion of Honor, 130–32
French Revolution, 18, 130
friend of God or saint (*wali*), 70–75
friendship, M. Kamara and, 32, 55, 79, 163–64

Futa Toro, 1, 2, 4–5; caste system in, 11; Gaden and, 127–28; history of, 127–28; Islam noir in, 87, 93–94, 110–12; orientalism in, 122; Robinson on, 176–77; slaves from, 10–11; Soh and, 133; U. Tal and, 23; Tooroodo revolution and, 4

Gaden, Henri, 1, 219; *Chroniques du FoÛta sénégalais* and, 121; colonial humanism and, 221; *The History of the Blacks* and, 123–24, 127–28, 130, 132, 139–40
Gadhafi, Muammar, 204
GAEC. *See* Groupe d'Action et d'Étude Critique-Africa
galgol, 49
Gallieni, Joseph, 92
Ganguel, 181, 195; research center in, 217–18
Gates, Henry Louis, Jr., 183, 212
Gaudfroy-Demombynes, Maurice, 130, 140, 146
glad tidings (*bishārāt*), 139
globalization, 28; GWOT and, 205; modernity and, 157
Global War on Terror (GWOT), 265n61; African Renaissance and, 141, 202–3, 211–12; *The Announcement of the Good News to the Fearful and Confused and His Reminder of the Breadth of the Mercy of God, the Generous Bestower* and, 209; M. Kamara and, 201–12; modernity and, 202; Sahel in, 204–5; secular religion and, 201–12; September 11, 2001 terrorist attack and, 28, 203, 204; in Timbuktu, 201–3
gnosis (*maʿrifa*), 73
Gramsci, Antonio, 229n5
Grande Ecole of Engineering (Polytechnique at Metz), 16
Green, Nile, 45
Grégoire, Henri, 157
griots, 1, 50, 54–55
Groupe d'Action et d'Étude Critique—Africa (GAEC), 227–28
gum arabic, 15

INDEX

Guriki (slanted tree), 5
Guyard, Marius-François, 166
GWOT. *See* Global War on Terror

hadith nafsi (dreams relating personal worries or wishes), 72
ḥāfiẓ al-Qurʾan, 56
hagiography, xiii, 16; in *The Announcement of the Good News to the Fearful and Confused and His Reminder of the Breadth of the Mercy of God, the Generous Bestower*, 44, 46–47, 52; of U. Tal, 31
Hajj (Mecca pilgrimage): IID and, 195; M. Kamara on, 56, 81–82, 183; B. Seck and, 11, 21; Tal on, 5, 11, 21
hajji (person who has performed the hajj), 21
Haley, Alex, x–xi
Hallaj, Mansur, al-, 144
Hallaq, Wael, 18, 233n41
Hamallah, 104–5
Hamas, 180
Hanretta, Sean, 246n21
Hariri, 58
Harney, Stefano, 29, 269n18
Harrison, Christopher, 102
al-Hasan, ʿAbd al-Rahman, 84
Hassani Arabs, 6, 10
Haut-Senegal-Niger (Delafosse), 119
Hegel, G. W. F, ix, 175, 176
hermeneutics: M. Kamara and, 25–30; in Sufism, 52–53; of suspicion, in dreams of Kamara, M., 62
hidden (*bāṭin*), 52
el-Hilal, Ahmed Maouloud Eida, 79
Hill, Joseph, 241n4
Hilliard, Constance, 143–44
historicity, 41; GWOT and, 206; nationalism and, 176; orality of, 152; of Samb, 164, 174–76; in *Tarikh al-Sudan*, 117
History of the Blacks, The (Kamara, M.), 25–26, 31, 33–34, 116, 181, 228; commentaries in, 126; compensation for, 137–38; compilation of documents in, 125–26; Delafosse and, 124, 128–30; denial of M. Kamara as author of, 143–48, 157; Gaden and, 123–24, 127–28, 130, 132, 139–40; humanism and, 129; in IFAN, 142; Islam noir and, 114, 147; modernity and, 123–41; orientalism and, 122–41; philology and, 146, 213–14; Prophet Muhammad and, 126; Qurʾan and, 126, 128; Robinson and, 177; Timbuktu Chronicles and, 128–29; translation of, 129–41, 170, 177–78
Holle, Paul, 23
Houdas, Octave: on orientalism, 116–19; *Tarikh al-Sudan* and, 117–21; Timbuktu Chronicles and, 128–29
ḥulm (dreams motivated by bad spirits), 72
humanism, 2, 18–19; of African Renaissance, 185–87, 189–90, 192; colonial, 220–21, 226; of European Renaissance, 163, 190; *The History of the Blacks* and, 129; M. Kamara and, 213; in national literature, 147–58; orientalism and, 119, 166; philology and, 36, 59, 213–28; of Samb, 34–35, 164–66; social engineering and, 132; in Sufism, 53. *See also* Delafosse, Maurice; Gaden, Henri
al-Hussain, Nani Wuld, 196

Ibn ʿAtaʾ Allah, 38, 45
Ibn Battuta, 56, 126, 183
Ibn Khaldun, 126, 146
Ibn Mukhtar, 120
Warjabi ibn Rabis, 6, 165
Ibrahim (Almamy), 81, 83, 85
Ibrahim (Prophet), 70–71, 73, 81
IFAN. *See* Institut Fondamental d'Afrique Noire
Iḥyāʾ mā ʿafā wa andarasa min ʿulum tārikh al-sudan wa intamas (Revival of what has been effaced and extinguished from the historical arts of the Blacks and obliterated) (Kumar, M.), 229n1, 249n1
IID. *See* Islamic Institute of Dakar

INDEX

IJMES. *See* International Journal of Middle East Studies
Institute fondamental d'Afrique, 251n18
Institute of Egypt, 17
Institut Fondamental d'Afrique Noire (IFAN), 122, 133, 136; bequeathed works to, 140–41; booklet on M. Kamara by, 197–98; *Bulletin de l'Institut fondamantal d'Afrique noire* of, 170; *History of the Blacks* in, 142; M. Kamara in, 226–27; Monod of, 140; V. Monteil at, 144–45; *The Precious Collection* in, 142–43; Robinson and, 176–77; Samb and, 142, 169–70
Institut Français d'Afrique Noire, 142
International Decade for People of African Descent, 188
International Journal of Middle East Studies (IJMES), xiv
Intiṣār al-Mawtūr fī dhikr qabāʾil Futa Toro (Victory of the wronged in the memory of the tribes of Futa Toro) (Kumara, M.), 229n1, 249n1
iqraʾ, 57–58
Islamic Institute of Dakar (IID), 195–96
Islam in Senegal (Marty), 103
Islam noir, 26, 33, 86–114; Buh and, 99; caste system and, 111–12; in Futa Toro, 87, 93–94, 110–12; *The History of the Blacks* and, 147; jihad and, 90–91; orientalism and, 102, 113; partition and politics of representation in, 88–95; philology and, 106; *politique des races* and, 91–92, 102–3; representation of politics in, 106–14; rule of experts in, 95–106; in Saint-Louis, 102; *Service des Affaires Musulmanes* and, 99–100; *shariʿa* and, 90–91; slavery and, 103; Sufism and, 95–96, 98, 101; *tarjama* in, 100
islamologie, 160

James, C. L. R., 29
Jeppie, Shamil, 55, 184
jihad, xiii, 13–14; in dreams of M. Kamara, 62–63; Islam noir and, 90–91; in Pax Gallica, 66; Tal and, 5. *See also Most of the Would-Be Jihadists*
Jones, Leroi, 156
Judy, Ronald A. T., 30, 165, 236n71

Ka, Moussa, 154–55, 159
Kâ, Thierno, 27, 197–98, 241n4
al-Kabir, Ahmad, 90
Kaïdara, 152
Kamara, Musa, xiii–xiv, 1–4, 206; accommodation and, 12, 14; African Renaissance and, 184–85; on asceticism, 83; birth of, 5; career of, 83–85; colonial humanism and, 221, 226; coloniality of knowledge and, 223; controversies with, 217–19; in dream of A. al-Naʾari, 85; dreams of, 32–33, 77–78, 81; French Legion of Honor to, 130–32; friendship and, 32, 55, 79, 163–64; in Ganguel, 181; GWOT and, 201–12; on Hajj, 56, 81–82, 183; hermeneutics and, 25–30; humanism and, 213; iconization of, 192–201; in IFAN, 226–27; Islam noir and, 26, 33, 86–114; Abou Salam Kane and, 134; modernity and, 182; nationalist literature and, 142–79; native literature and, 116–22; on orientalism, 115–41; philology and, 213; on Prophet Muhammad, 83; Qurʾan and, 135–36; religious knowledge of, 217–19; in Sahel, 4–14; Samb and, 161–64, 170–74, 197; secular-religious afterlife of, 180–212; Soh and, 134; textual life and afterlives of, 30–37; wives of, 11. *See also specific topics and works*
Kamara, Tourad, 79
Kan, Abdul Kader, 5, 10–11, 14–15, 124
Kane, Abdou Salam, 89, 94, 107, 112; in *Bulletin du Comité d'études historiques et scientifiques e d'Afrique occidentale française*, 133–34; M. Kamara and, 134
Kane, Abdul Bokar, 90
Kane, Cheikh Hamidou, 159
Kane, Mamadou Mamadou, 5, 89, 94, 134
Kane, Mouhamed Moustapha, 86, 94

[282]

INDEX

Kane, Ousmane, 183
karamāt (tokens of nobility or marvels), 45
Kāshif al-Ilbās, 52–53
Ka'ti, Mahmoud, 120
khāṣṣ (spiritual elite), 45
Kia, Mana, 78
King, Martin Luther, Jr., xii
kinship (mbokk), 227–28
kultur, 176
Kunta, 76; economic authority of, 231n16; Qadiriyya Sufism and, 8; in Timbuktu, 8
al-Kunti, Sidi al-Mukhtar, 8, 9, 38, 45

Labrune-Badiane, Céline, 133
La nouvelle poésie negre et malagache, 154
L'aventure ambiguë (Ambiguous Adventure) (Kane, C.), 159
La vie d'el Hadj Omar (Caam), 121
Le Balai Citoyen (The Citizen's Broom), 215
Le Bon, Gustave, 172
Le Chatelier, Alfred, 102
Le devoir de violence (Ouologuem), 178
Lefort, Claude, 109
Légendes et coutumes sénégalaises (Soh), 121
Le moniteur, 23–24
Les Ateliers de la Pensée, 217
Les confréries religieuses musulmanes, 95
Levtzion, Nehmia, 120
Li, Darryl, 265n61
Lienau, Annette, 30
lieutenant (moqqadem), 104
Life of Hajj Umar, The (Kamara, M.), xiii, 33, 63, 66, 68, 69, 83; Buh and, 65; dreams of M. Kamara in, 65, 85; The History of the Blacks and, 125; Islam noir and, 107–8; Ouologuem and, 178; Samb on, 171, 173; translation of, 170
L'islam et la politique musulmane française en Afrique-occidentale française (Arnaud), 97–98
L'islam noir (Monteil, V.), 144, 145
literary prize, 132–34

literature (adab), 79
Lliteras, Susana Molins, 262n5
Lo, Mbaye, 27, 107, 112, 208, 239n32, 247n56, 267n77
Lobbo, Ahmad, xiii, 120
Lorde, Audre, 175
Ly, Bachir, 140

al-Maghili, Muhammad, 109
"Maintaining Security of the Territory," 96–97
Malcolm X, x–xii, 37; The Announcement of the Good News to the Fearful and Confused and His Reminder of the Breadth of the Mercy of God, the Generous Bestower and, 60; on diaspora, xii
Malick, El Hadji, 206
Mamdani, Mahmood, 90
manāqib (exemplary acts), 45
Mansur, Ahmad, 187
Maqāmāt (Hariri), 58
maraboutic system, 98–99
Marcus-Sells, Ariela, 231n17, 243n33
marriage, by Sunni Muslims, 11
Marty, Paul, 93, 99–101, 103, 116; colonial humanism and, 221
massalik, 73
Massignon, Louis, 130; al-Hallaj and, 144
Mas'udi, al-, 126
Matraqué par le destin (Bludgeoned by Fate) (Samb), 158–59
Maurel & Prom, 15
Mawsim al-Hijra ilā al-Shamāl (Season of Migration to the North) (Salih), 159
Mayram, Aali, 9
Mays, Benjamin E., xii
Mazrui, Ali, 29
ma'rifa (divine gnosis), 8, 73
Mbacké, Khadim, 177, 196
Mbakke, Amadou Bamba, 155, 200; school of Touba of, 161
Mbaye, Rawane, 142–43
Mbeki, Thabo, 184, 185–88, 192, 212
mbokk (kinship), 227–28
Mecca pilgrimage. See Hajj

INDEX

Medina: Bilal at, 124; Prophet Muhammad's tomb at, 81, 243n24
Médine, battle of, 22–23, 25
meditating bridge between the hidden and the manifest (*barzakh*), 68
médrasa, 19, 137
mémographie, 227
memoir (*tadhkira*), 47
memory/memorization: in *The Announcement of the Good News to the Fearful and Confused and His Reminder of the Breadth of the Mercy of God, the Generous Bestower*, 55–60; on Prophet Muhammad, 56; of Qurʾan, 24, 56–59, 135
messianism, 11; B. Seck and, 24–25; of U. Tal, 12, 22, 76
Mimesis (Auerbach), 113–14
Mitchell, Timothy, 232n36, 245n9
modernity, 30, 171–72; African Renaissance and, 185; disciplinary vocabulary of, 157–58; GWOT and, 202; *The History of the Blacks* and, 123–41; M. Kamara and, 182; religion and politics in, 108; Samb and, 176; U. Tal and, 22–23
Monod, Théodore, 140
Monteil, Charles, 144
Monteil, Vincent-Mansour, 140, 142, 143–48, 157; at IFAN, 144–45; orientalism of, 144, 145
Moors, 15, 26; Islam noir and, 111
moqqadem (lieutenant), 104
Morrison, Toni, 178–79
Most Delicious of the Sciences and the Tastiest of the News in the Life of Hajj Umar, The (Kamara, M.), 31, 63–64
Most of the Would-Be Jihadists (Kamara, M.), 31, 207, 212, 228; *The History of the Blacks* and, 125; Islam noir and, 107–8, 110, 112–13; translation of, 170, 208
Moten, Fred, 29, 269n18
Mourides. *See* Muridiyya Sufism
Moutet, Marius, 137–38
Movement for Black Lives, 215

Muhammad (Prophet), 6; in *The Announcement of the Good News to the Fearful and Confused and His Reminder of the Breadth of the Mercy of God, the Generous Bestower*, 42, 64; in dream of A. al-Naʾari, 85; in dreams of M. Kamara, 71–75, 81, 85; *The History of the Blacks* and, 126; M. Kamara on, 83; memory of, 56; prohibition of image of, 265n52; Qurʾan and, 57–58; Sufism and, 45, 243n24; U. Tal and, 243n24; transmitted knowledge by, 7–8
Muhammad, Askia, 109
Muhammad, Elijah, x
Muridiyya Sufism, 101, 219; Anta Diop of, 153–54
muṣḥaf, 57
Muslim Affairs Service, 93

Nahḍa (Arab awakening), 2
al-*najah* (safety), 49
Napoleon Bonaparte, 16–18, 130
Naṣīḥa (Buh), 112
al-Nasiri, Ahmad ibn Khalid, 2
al-Nasiri, Ahmad, 126
nationalism/nationalist literature, xii; contradictions in, 174–76; historicity and, 176; *The History of the Blacks* and, 143–48; humanism in, 147–58; M. Kamara and, 142–79; of Samb, 34–35, 158–74, 219. *See also* Diop, Anta; Senghor, Léopold Sédar
native literature: M. Kamara and, 116–22; orientalism and, 116–22. *See also* Delafosse, Maurice; Gaden, Henri; Houdas, Octave; al-Saʿadi, Abd al-Rahman
al-Naʾari, Ahmed Alpha Muhammad al-Futi, 84
al-Naʾari, Saʿid Alpha, 84–85
Ndar. *See* Saint-Louis
Ndiaye, Moustapha, 106, 170
Négritude, 148, 149–50, 156; African Renaissance Monument and, 191
New Partnership for Africa's Development (NEPAD), 184, 187

[284]

INDEX

Niang, Mamadou, xiv
Niasse, Ibrahim, 52–53, 200–201
nightingale (*al-ʿandalīb*), 49
Njeddo Dewel, 152
Nkrumah, Kwame, 149, 160, 186
Nobili, Mauro, 120
nonbinding legal opinions (*fatāwā*), 22

Office of Political Affairs, 138
orientalism: Burke on, 18–19; Delafosse on, 119; in Futa Toro, 122; *The History of the Blacks* and, 122–41; Houdas on, 116–19; humanism and, 119, 166; Islam noir and, 102, 113; M. Kamara on, 115–41; of V. Monteil, 144, 145; native literature and, 116–22; philology and, 122; Said on, 16–18, 36, 106, 113, 117, 173; Samb and, 173; U. Tal and, 23–24
Orientalism (Said), 36
Original and Inherited Knowledge Regarding the Marvels of the Two Shaykhs, My Mother and My Father (al-Kunti), 38
Orsi, Robert, 157–58
Ouologuem, Yambo, 178
our good grandparents (*sunu maam yu baax yi*), 206

paganism, in Christianity, 190
Parisian École Nationale des Langues Orientales Vivantes, 144
Pax Gallica, 5, 65–66
Petrarch, 163, 189–90
philology, 35; in *The Announcement of the Good News to the Fearful and Confused and His Reminder of the Breadth of the Mercy of God, the Generous Bestower*, 48–49, 60; deaths of, 1–37; of Delafosse, 122; diaspora and, xii; *The History of the Blacks* and, 146, 213–14; humanism and, 36, 59, 213–28; Islam noir and, 106; M. Kamara and, 213; as love of study, ix–xiv; orientalism and, 122; Said on, 36–37, 60
Plan of 1854, 15–16
Plato, 151

politique des races (racial policy), 91–92, 102–3
Polytechnique at Metz (Grande Ecole of Engineering), 16
Pondopoulo, Anna, 140
Ponty, William, 91–92, 102
Precious Collection, The (Kamara, M.), 50; *The History of the Blacks* and, 124, 138; in IFAN, 142–43; *mbokk* in, 227–28; publication of, 196
Précis de politique musulmane, 96–97
"Pre-Text, Text, and Con-Text" of Revelation, 46
problem-space, 87, 245n3
professeur agrégé, 156
prophecy, in *The Announcement of the Good News to the Fearful and Confused and His Reminder of the Breadth of the Mercy of God, the Generous Bestower*, 61–85
Protet, Auguste, 15–16
Proverbes Peuls et Toucouleurs (Soh), 121
Pulaar-English Dictionary, xiv
Purification of Thoughts from Delusional Doubts (Kamara, M.), 125, 138

Qadiriyya Sufism, 9, 11; jihad in, 14; Kunta Sufism and, 8; al-Shaʿrani and, 45; Tijaniyya Sufism and, 104–5. *See also* Buh, Saʿad
al-Qalqashandi, 130
Qurʾan: alternative names for, 57; Baal and, 9; beginnings in, 42; Christianity and, 24; in dream of M. Kamara, 70–75; *The History of the Blacks* and, 126, 128; IID and, 195; M. Kamara and, 135–36; memorization of, 24, 56–59, 135; Ouologuem and, 178; Prophet Muhammad and, 57–58; religious knowledge in, 7
Qurʾanic student (*talibé*), 159

racial policy (*politique des races*), 91–92, 102–3
Ramadan, Tariq, 180–81, 261n1
Ranke, Leopold von, 172
rational knowledge, 8

[285]

INDEX

"Regeneration of Africa, The" (Seme), 186
relegere (commitment to read again), 228
religion (*dīn*), 108–9
religion making, 182, 203, 209, 210, 219, 267n82
religious knowledge, 7
Renaissance. *See* African Renaissance; European Renaissance
Revival of what has been effaced and extinguished from the historical arts of the Blacks and obliterated (*Ihyā' mā ʿafā wa andarasa min ʿulum tārikh al-sudan wa inṭamas*) (Kumar, M.), 229n1, 249n1
Revue d'études arabes et islamiques, 195
Revue du monde musulman, 102
Rhodes Must Fall, 215
Robert Randau (Arnaud pen name), 246n27
Robinson, David, 171, 176–77
Romanticism, 150–51
Roper, Hugh Trevor, 118

Sacy, Silvetre de, 18–19
safety (*al-najah*), 49
Sahel: in GWOT, 204–5; M. Kamara in, 4–14
Said, Edward, 32, 229n5; on beginnings, 42; on orientalism, 16–18, 36, 106, 113, 117, 173; on philology, 36–37, 60
Saint-Louis (Ndar), 15, 20–21, 35–36, 74; Buh in, 76–83; development in, 215–16; Gaden in, 140; Islam noir in, 102
Sakho, Boghé Ahmadou Mokhtar, 134
Salafi, 180
Salih, Tayeb, 159
Sall, Macky, 195, 209; mandates of, 216
Samb, Amar, 157, 208, 267n77; comparative literature and, 166–67; historicity of, 164, 174–76; humanism of, 34–35, 164–66; IFAN and, 142, 169–70; M. Kamara and, 161–64, 170–74, 197; on *The Life of Hajj Umar*, 171, 173; modernity and, 176; nationalism of, 34–35, 158–74, 179, 219; orientalism and, 173
Samba, Golgol, 49
Sambe, Bakary, 180–81, 206
Sanko, Ousmane, 216
Saʿadi, Abd al-Rahman al-, 117, 188, 212; *Tarikh al-Sudan* by, 26–27, 117–21, 188
Schmitz, Jean, 25–26
Scholars of sciences of religion (*ʿulūm al-dīn*), 7–8
scholasticism, in Christianity, 189
school of Guéde, 161
school of Touba, 161
scientific imperialism, 92
Scott, David, 107, 245n3
Season of Migration to the North (*Mawsim al-Hijra ilā al-Shamāl*) (Salih), 159
Seck, Abdourahmane, 36, 213, 265n63, 266n67; *mémographie* of, 227
Seck, Bou el-Mogdad, 11, 21, 22; messianism and, 24–25; U. Tal and, 161
Seck, ʿAynayn, 84
secular religion, 182; GWOT and, 201–12
self-regard, 178–79
Sembene, Ousmane, 149
Seme, Pixley ka Isaka, 186
Senghor, Clédor, 215
Senghor, Léopold Sédar, 149–52, 156, 157, 179; African Renaissance Monument and, 191; Samb and, 165
September 11, 2001 terrorist attack, 28, 203, 204
Service des Affaires Musulmanes, 2, 99–100
Sèye, Mademba, 131–32
sharif (biological descendant of Prophet Muhammad), 76
shariʿa: GWOT and, 205; Islam noir and, 90–91; al-Maghili on, 109
shaykh, xii–xiii; in Sufism, 59. *See also specific individuals*
Shaykh Musa Kamara (Kâ), 196, 197–98
Shaʿrani, ʿAbd al-Wahhab al-, 38, 45
Sheikh Moussa Kamara's Islamic Critique of Jihadists (Lo), 208
Shurr Bubba, 6
Sirriyeh, Elizabeth, 241n10

INDEX

slanted tree (*Guriki*), 5
slaves/slavery, ix–x, 194, 219; African Renaissance and, 186–87; Bilal as, 124; from Futa Toro, 10–11; Islam noir and, 103
Smith, Etienne, 133
social engineering, 21; humanism and, 132; Office of Political Affairs and, 138; Qur'an and, 136; surveillance in, 92, 140–41
Soh, Siré Abbas, 115, 129, 240n47; Futa Toro and, 133; M. Kamara and, 134; native literature of, 121
Something Torn, Something New (Thiong'o), 188
Songhai Empire, 6, 27, 109, 120, 187–88
Sonko, Ousmane, 215
speakers of Arabic (*arabisants*), 19
spiritual blessing (*baraka*), 104, 170
spiritual elite (*khāṣṣ*), 45
Spivak, Gayatri, 28
Splendor of the Names and the Warmest Protection (Kamara, M.), 84
Steff (Captain), 86–87, 92, 93
Studia Humanitas, 189–90
Subtleties of Benefaction in the Marvels of My Shaykh Abi, al-Abbas al-Mursi and My Shaykh Abi al-Hassan, The (Ibn 'Ata' Allah), 38
Subtleties of the Benefactor and the Morals in the Obligations of Conversation with the Blessing of God the Absolutely Exalted, The (al-Sha'rani), 38
Sufism (*taṣawwuf*), xiii; asceticism in, 51–52; brotherhoods of, 19; colonial humanism and, 221; corporate identity of, 243n33; devotional worship in, 84–85; experiential knowledge of, 8; hermeneutics in, 52–53; humanism in, 53; ibn Abi Talib and, 67–68; Islam noir and, 95–96, 98, 101; Prophet Muhammad and, 45, 243n24; shaykh in, 59; Tal and, 5. See also *specific sects, topics, and individuals*
Sunna, 7, 24
Sunni Muslims, 11

sunu maam yu baax yi (our good grandparents), 206
Suware, Salim, 109
Sy, Malick, 12, 200
Syed, Amir, 23

al-Tabari, 126
tabshīr, 239n32; in *The Announcement of the Good News to the Fearful and Confused and His Reminder of the Breadth of the Mercy of God, the Generous Bestower*, 47
tadhkira (memoir), 47
Tal, Agibu, 81–92
Tal, Muntaga, 170
Tal, Seydou Nouru, 134
Tal, Umar, xiii–xiv, 5, 11, 12, 14; Ahmad and, 173–74; at battle of Médine, 25; Christianity and, 21–22; colonial humanism and, 221; in dreams of M. Kamara, 33, 64–68, 85, 241n4; Futa Toro and, 23; hagiography of, 31; *The History of the Blacks* and, 124; messianism of, 12, 22, 76; modernity and, 22–23; orientatalism and, 23–24; Prophet Muhammad and, 243n24; school of Guéde of, 161; B. Seck and, 161; Tijaniyya Sufism and, 45, 104; tobacco and, 13. See also *Life of Hajj Umar, The*
talibé (Qur'anic student), 159
Tarikh al-fattash (Chronicle of the seeker), 26–27, 120–21
Tarikh al-Sudan (al-Sa'adi), 26–27, 188; Houdas and, 117–21
ṭarīqa (Sufi religious order), 8–9, 73, 231n17
tarjama: in *The Announcement of the Good News to the Fearful and Confused and His Reminder of the Breadth of the Mercy of God, the Generous Bestower*, 43–46, 49–50; in Islam noir, 100
taṣawwuf. See Sufism
ṭawīl, 79
Teilhard de Chardin, Pierre, 150–51
Terrance, 151
thingification, 149

INDEX

Thiong'o, Ngũgĩ wa, 188–89
al-Tijani, Ahmed, 85
Tijaniyya Sufism, xiii, 11–12, 219; devotional worship in, 84–85; Niasse and, 52–53; Ouologuem of, 178; Qadiriyya Sufism and, 104–5; S. Tal and, 134; U. Tal and, 45, 104
Tilléré, Thierno, 111–12
Timbuktu, 35; African Renaissance and, 182–92; Arabic manuscripts in, 153; Coppolani in, 96–97; destruction in, 192–93; GWOT in, 201–3; Kunta Sufism in, 8; Lliteras on, 262n5; tomb destruction in, 181
Timbuktu Chronicles, xiv, 120; *Chroniques du FoÛta sénégalais* and, 121; Delafosse and, 128–29; The *History of the Blacks* and, 128–29; Houdas and, 128–29
tobacco, 8, 13, 84, 218
Togalla, Jajji, 39
tokens of nobility or marvels (*karamāt*), 45
Tombouctou Manuscript Project, 184
Tondibi, Battle of, 187
Tooroodo revolution, 110; Futa Toro and, 4
Tounkara, Alpha Yero, 215
Touré, Samory, 13–14, 82
transmitted knowledge, by Prophet Muhammad, 7–8
triple heritage, 29

ʿulamā (horizontal body of scholars), 103
ʿulūm al-dīn (sciences of religion), 7–8
Umar. *See* Tal, Umar

Valla, Lorenzo, 36, 163
Victory of the wronged in the memory of the tribes of Futa Toro (Intiṣār al-Mawtūr fī dhikr qabāʾil Futa Toro) (Kumara, M.), 229n1, 249n1

Wade, Abdoulaye, 191, 195
Wahabi, 180
walāya (closeness), 71, 79
wali (friend of God or saint), xiii, 70–75
Ware, Rudolph, 104
Warner, Tobias, 29–30
Washington Consensus, 194
Wayfarer's Guide to the Meaning of Ibn Malik's Alfiyya (Kamara, M.), 83–84
Wheatley, Phillis, x
"When Can We Talk of an African Renaissance?" (Diop, Anta), 154
wives, 13
Women of Algiers in Their Apartment (Delacroix), 173
Wonders of the African World (documentary), 183
world (*dunya*), 108
worries or wishes (*hadith nafsi*), 72
Wright, Zachary, 52–53

Xala (Sembene), 149

ẓāhir (apparent), 52
Zayd, Abi, 58
Zaydan, Jurji, 2, 127
Zuhūr al-Basātīn fī Tārīkh al-Sawādīn (Flowers from among the Gardens in the History of the Blacks) (Kamara, M.), 1, 115, 229n1, 249n1
Zwaya, Shurr Bubb and, 6

GPSR Authorized Representative: Easy Access System Europe, Mustamäe tee 50, 10621 Tallinn, Estonia, gpsr.requests@easproject.com